B ZHENG, C.
CLEMENTS, JONATH
COXINGA AND THE
  THE MING DYNAS
2006/11/

WITHDRAWN

D0517992

Coxinga

AND THE FALL OF THE
MING DYNASTY

JONATHAN CLEMENTS

Alameda Free Library
1550 Oak Street
Alameda, CA 94501

SUTTON PUBLISHING

For my parents

This book was first published under the title
Pirate King: Coxinga and the Fall of the Ming Dynasty

This new paperback edition first published in 2005 by
Sutton Publishing Limited · Phoenix Mill
Thrupp · Stroud · Gloucestershire · GL5 2BU

Copyright © Muramasa Industries Limited, 2004

All rights reserved. No part of this publication may be reproduced,
stored in a retrieval system, or transmitted, in any form, or by any
means, electronic, mechanical, photocopying, recording or
otherwise, without the prior permission of the publisher and
copyright holder.

Jonathan Clements has asserted the moral right to be identified as
the author of this work.

British Library Cataloguing in Publication Data
A catalogue record for this book is available from the British
Library.

ISBN 0 7509 3270 8

Typeset in 10.5/12pt Goudy.
Typesetting and origination by
Sutton Publishing Limited.
Printed and bound in Great Britain by
J.H. Haynes & Co. Ltd, Sparkford.

CONTENTS

'The lives of few men in history are richer in dramatic possibilities than was Coxinga's. It is small wonder, then, that even those who have professed to be writing biographical accounts have been led into colourful tales which have every merit save that of truth.'

Donald Keene

'For a thousand autumns, men will tell of this.'

Zhang Huang-yan

LIST OF ILLUSTRATIONS

ACKNOWLEDGEMENTS

This book first took shape in 1991, when I found Coxinga's story in Lynn Struve's *Southern Ming*. My interest was encouraged by George Hlawatsch at the Kansai University of Foreign Studies, and then endured with very little eye-rolling by Ellis Tinios, whose retirement from the University of Leeds deprived that institution of a great authority on both Chinese history and Japanese erotica. Turning my obsession into a book took many years of research, chiefly at the library of London's School of Oriental and African Studies, whose staff were ever helpful. The Hanshan Tang bookstore kept me supplied with material when even the resources of SOAS failed.

The concept was championed and sold by my agent, Chelsey Fox of Fox and Howard. Though she infamously feels neither pity nor remorse, she still bought me lunch because she feared I was not eating properly. Towards the end of this book's genesis, she also kindly dropped a Le Creuset casserole lid on her foot and broke two toes, to ensure that she had plenty of time to read the manuscript in bed. Jaqueline Mitchell of Sutton Publishing demonstrated wholly unscrupulous and piratic behaviour at the London Book Fair, kidnapping my proposal and holding it hostage to prevent my agent showing it to anyone else. Such behaviour demonstrated a faith in the book's potential that she maintained throughout its long gestation.

Others have patiently put up with my many excited calls about new discoveries, and offered much advice, encouragement or help of their own, including Donna Anstey, Polly Armstrong, Lee Brimmicombe-Wood, Rebecca Cape, Hugh David, Sue Dickinson, Erika Dowell, Jane Entrican, Rhonda Eudaly, Ian Everard, Kimberly Guerre, David Hughes, Clare Jackson, Simon Jowett, Macabe Keliher, Kathryn Kerns, Ruby Lee, Lee Shu-hui, Tom Mes, Paul Overmaat, Kate Pankhurst, Louis Savy, Wei Te-wen, and all at Sutton. Andrew Deacon not only made helpful comments on the manuscript, but also provided much-needed Chinese translation assistance. Motoko Tamamuro translated vital Japanese sources about the Nanjing campaign when time became tight. John Freeman pointed me at Stefan Landsberger's website, and Landsberger himself tracked down the propaganda print of Coxinga found in this book. I owe my thanks to all of the above, and also to my personal warrior princess, Kati Mäki-Kuutti, who was not around for the book's beginning, but was the first to hear its end.

My grateful acknowledgement goes to Brill Academic Publishers for permission to quote from Leonard Blussé's articles in Vermeer's *Decline and Development of Fukien Province in the 17th and 18th Centuries*, and *Leyden Studies in Sinology*; to Cambridge University Press for permission to quote passages from Donald Keene's *Battles of Coxinga*; and to the Regents of the University of California Press for permission to quote from Frederic Wakeman's *The Great Enterprise: The Manchu Reconstruction of Imperial Order in Seventeenth-Century China*.

PROLOGUE

1644: Brightness Falls

On 8 February 1644, the first day of the Chinese New Year, the ministers of the Emperor of Lofty Omens woke before dawn and journeyed through the streets of Beijing. At the break of day, in keeping with tradition that stretched back for centuries, they would greet their 33-year-old ruler, whom the gods had selected to reign over the entire world. Then, the assembled throng would welcome in the new year, the 4341st since China's first, legendary kings, and entreat the gods and ancestors to bring them good fortune.

The city, however, was quiet. Many of its inhabitants had succumbed to a harsh outbreak of disease the previous year, and according to one diarist, 'no babies had been born in the city for the previous six months'.[1] Not all the ministers arrived at the palace on time. Those that did found the gates jammed shut, and were only able to open them with some difficulty. Eventually they found the Emperor of Lofty Omens, in the Hall of the Central Ultimate. He was weeping.[2]

China was doomed. The Dynasty of Brightness, the Ming, which had ruled the world's largest nation for centuries, had lost its hold on power. A Confucian scholar would have been scandalised at the low attendance that morning; without a full complement of ministers, how could they perform the necessary ceremonies? But not even the Emperor himself bore a grudge against the absentees, or those who arrived late, wheezing breathless apologies. No amount of prayers and ceremony would change the inevitable, and no sacrifice, however elaborate, would attract the ancestors' attention from the afterlife.

Besides, the Emperor could not afford it. Ever since the disastrous reign of his father, the nation's budgets had spiralled wildly out of

1

control. Attempts to curtail imperial luxuries were not enough, fundamental cornerstones of civilisation had gone to ruin. The Grand Canal to the south was falling into disrepair, and the postal system had been shut down. Smallpox had wrought havoc among the farming communities, who struggled in vain to tease crops from the earth – though few realised at the time, the middle of the seventeenth century gripped the world in a mini ice age. The same weather conditions that were then freezing over the Thames in London were also bringing deadly cold to the lands north of the Great Wall.

The unit of currency in seventeenth-century China was the *tael*, an ounce of silver. It took 400,000 taels each month to maintain and supply the troops who defended the northern border. The Finance Minister already knew that the money would run out before March. After that point, there would be little incentive for the soldiers who guarded the Great Wall to stay at their posts. The ministers expected the worst.

North of the Great Wall was China's worst nightmare – the barbarian warriors of Manchuria had become increasingly bold in recent years. They had stolen former Ming territory from the Chinese, and even proclaimed that they were now the rightful rulers of China. Though they were nominally led by a child, the true power behind the throne was Prince Dorgon, a 32-year-old warrior who believed he could conquer the Celestial Empire in a matter of months. The Great Wall would hold the Manchus for a while, but once the money ran out, there was not much hope. China's greatest general, Wu Sangui, held the crucial Shanhai pass where the Great Wall met the sea . . . if he could keep his men's hearts on defending the Wall, then China might be able to hold out for a miracle.

The Emperor was fated to fall, but not at the hands of the Manchus. While the Great Wall still held, a new enemy struck from within. Starved of food and decimated by disease, a distant inland province rose up in revolt. An army of disaffected soldiers and peasants began to march on the capital city, led by the rebel Li Zicheng.

Li Zicheng, formerly one of the post-riders who delivered mail along China's once-great roads, had been obsessed with seizing control of the Empire from his youth. Not even losing an eye in battle dimmed his ardour, as one old prophecy had predicted the

Empire would fall to a man with only one eye. His previous dealings with other members of the imperial family had been less than favourable. During his campaigns, he not only killed the Emperor's uncle the Prince of Fu, but drank his blood, mixing it into his venison broth.[3] Li Zicheng was the leader of a horde of almost 100,000 soldiers, boiling across the country towards Beijing, gathering still greater numbers as peasants flocked to its banners proclaiming a tax-free future.

On New Year's Day, as the Ming Emperor sat sobbing in his palace, Li Zicheng announced his intention to found a new dynasty. The Dynasty of Brightness, he said, had fallen. Long live the *Da Shun*, the Dynasty of Great Obedience.

With the usurper Li Zicheng advancing ever closer to Beijing, the Emperor of Lofty Omens knew it was time for drastic measures. Drunk and disoriented, he ordered for the Ming Heir Apparent to be smuggled out of the city. He gathered the rest of his family about him and informed them that it was time to die. Some of his wives and concubines had already committed suicide, and were found hanged or poisoned in their chambers. Others had fled. There was no such option for the immediate family of the Emperor, who attacked his own children with a sword. The fifteen-year-old Princess Imperial held out her right arm to stay his attack, and the Emperor hacked it off. The maimed girl fled screaming through the halls, leaving a trail of blood. Her younger sisters were not so lucky, and both died where they stood, stabbed by their own father. The Emperor then went to a nearby hilltop, where he wrote a final message in his own blood, before hanging himself as Li Zicheng's army drew closer. Later writers would claim the Emperor's last words blamed his ministers and his own 'small virtue' for the collapse of the Ming Dynasty, and exhorted the rebels to spare his people from suffering. In fact, the Emperor's bleeding finger simply traced the plaintive, spidery characters 'Son of Heaven'.[4] His body lay undiscovered for three days.

On the battlements of the capital, guns boomed in the city's defence, although they had no cannonballs and their reports were empty gestures of defiance. Astrological graffiti, scrawled on the wall of the palace itself, announced that the Ming star had fallen, and it was time to follow another. Li Zicheng rode into the capital in triumph, entering through the Gate of Heaven's Grace. On a whim, he stopped beneath it and drew his bow, taking aim at the character for 'Heaven' on the gate's lintel. He let an arrow fly, claiming that if he struck the word, it would be a sign that Heaven approved of his acts. It was an easy shot.

He missed.[5]

His men laughed it off and carried on into the town. Beijing belonged to Li Zicheng, and before long he would be enthroned by the ministers who had failed his predecessor, and, according to custom, failed themselves by not taking their own lives.

North of the Great Wall, General Wu Sangui was faced with a difficult choice – should he continue to face off the Manchus to the north, march south to retake the capital, or proclaim his allegiance to the usurper? When news reached him that his favourite concubine had been raped by Li Zicheng, he chose a fourth option. Wu Sangui sent a messenger to the Manchu army and invited them in.

The thousands of miles of the Great Wall, designed to protect China's northern borders, were suddenly worth nothing. A combined army of Manchus and their new-found allies walked through the wide-open gates and marched on Beijing. Wu Sangui had betrayed his people, and north China was now a battleground between two rival rebels. The Ming Emperor lay dead, the self-proclaimed Shun Emperor was on the run at the head of his army, and now the invader Prince Dorgon ordered the enthronement of his nephew as a third contender – the new ruler of the Manchu *Qing* dynasty, the Dynasty of Clarity. The capital was lost.

Or rather Beijing, the *northern* capital was lost. Nanjing, the southern capital, lay several hundred miles away from the civil strife, home to a shadow government that had been preparing for the disaster for some time. Even as Li Zicheng fled from Beijing, and Dorgon proclaimed his nephew the new child-Emperor of China, the civil servants of Nanjing planned the Ming resistance. One emperor's violent death did not mean that his dynasty was immediately finished, and the people of Nanjing were not about to submit to foreign invaders. They hoped they would be able to hold them off, and that their example would bring others rallying to their cause.

One man was crucial to the establishment of this 'Southern Ming' resistance. His name was Zheng Zhilong, though he was known to most foreign observers by his Christian name, Nicholas Iquan. The 41-year-old Iquan was a successful merchant and soldier, a former smuggler who had become the admiral of the Chinese fleet. He was the leader of a loose confederation of pirates and privateers, a warlord who was the *de facto* ruler of south-east China, and a man of such wealth and importance that some observers mistakenly referred to him as the King of South China. He preferred the term Lord of the Straits, referring to the thin channel that separated his main domains of Amoy and Taiwan.

Iquan was the kingmaker of the Southern Ming. His personal wealth was greater than that of some contemporary nations, and only he could fund the resistance effort that was to come. The newly created southern Emperor promised Iquan his eternal gratitude, and Iquan, sensing the opportunity for even greater power, offered his eternal service.

Within two years, Iquan would betray him and the Emperor would be dead. The Manchus would have a new ally, but the troubled Ming dynasty would gain one last hero – Iquan's son Coxinga. The Zheng family, who began as pirates and privateers, would eventually become the kings of their own island domain. Their most famous son would become a god – twice.

It was the Manchus and the Dutch who called Coxinga a pirate, the English and the Spanish who called him a king. His Chinese countrymen called him both, depending on their mood. But he saw himself as neither; instead, he wanted to be known as a scholar and a patriot, unexpectedly plucked from a privileged upbringing and thrust into the forefront of a terrible war. A child prodigy from a wealthy trading family in seventeenth-century China, Coxinga became a nobleman at twenty-one, a resistance leader at twenty-two, and was a prince at thirty. The last loyal defender of the defeated Ming dynasty, he was the invincible sea lord who raided the coasts for ten years, before leading a massive army to strike at the heart of China itself. Still plotting to restore a pretender he had never seen, he was dead at thirty-nine, only to be canonised by his former enemies as a paragon of loyalty.

In a China that shunned contact with the outside world, Coxinga was a surprisingly cosmopolitan individual. His mother was Japanese, his bodyguards African and Indian, his chief envoy an Italian missionary. Among his 'Chinese' loyalist troops were German and French defectors. His enemies were similarly international, including Chinese relatives and rivals, the Dutch against whom he nursed a lifelong hatred, and the Manchus who invaded his country. Betrayed and deserted by many of his own friends and family, Coxinga's stubborn character was most similar to that of his most famous foe – the Swedish commander whom he defeated in his last battle.

Famous for his pathological insistence on justice and correctness, Coxinga was ever troubled by his shadowy origins. His father was an admiral and the richest man in China, but also a crook who had cheated, murdered and bribed his way to the top of south China's largest criminal organisation. Though Coxinga grew up in a palace, his family had clawed their way to their fortune, and had made many enemies in the process.

This, then, is the man that was known to European writers as that 'heathen idolater and devil-worshipper', the mutilator of his enemies and a heartless brute who could execute a Dutch priest and ravish the man's bereaved daughter on the same day. But Coxinga is also the loyalist lauded by the Chinese as the last son of a departed dynasty, who steadfastly refused to surrender to foreign invaders when millions of his countrymen submitted willingly. He was demonised in Europe, deified in China, and remains a contentious figure to this day.

This is his story. It is also the story of his father, Nicholas Iquan, and of his deals and double-crosses with the Europeans he despised. To the superstitious, it is also the story of the goddess of the sea, and how she granted fortune on the waters to one family for forty long years. Though it ends with saints and gods, it begins with smugglers and pirates.

1

THE PIRATES OF FUJIAN

Cut off from the rest of China by a semicircle of high mountains, the south-eastern province of Fujian was almost a separate nation. The slopes that pointed towards the sea were carved into terraces, where the locals grew native produce like lychees and *longans* ('dragon's eyes'), tea and sugar-cane. Cash crops were the order of the day, and not merely for sale as exotic foodstuffs. The Fujianese grew flax for the manufacture of cloth, and mulberry trees for feeding silkworms. They were particularly renowned for their dyed silks, and locally grown indigo plants formed the basis for Fujian blue, while safflowers were harvested to make a multitude of reds. With textiles and a growing porcelain industry, the Fujianese were bound to seek trading opportunities, and the province's walled-off existence afforded a unique possibility. The populace huddled in bays and estuaries, from which the easiest mode of transportation was by ship. The Fujianese became accomplished fishermen, and inevitably found other uses for their boats.

By command of the Emperor, China had no need for foreign trade. China was the centre of the world, and it was heresy to suggest that any of the barbarian nations had anything of value to offer the Celestial Empire. Occasional parties of foreigners were admitted to bear 'tribute', arriving in China with fleets of goods, which would be graciously exchanged between government agents for treasures of equivalent value, but it was a cumbersome way of doing business, and, by its very nature, excluded private entrepreneurs.

Two hundred years earlier, in the heyday of the Ming dynasty, the mariner Zheng He had sailed across the Indian Ocean in a fleet of massive vessels, returning from distant lands with bizarre beasts and stories. He also bore 'tribute', assuring the Emperor that barbarians

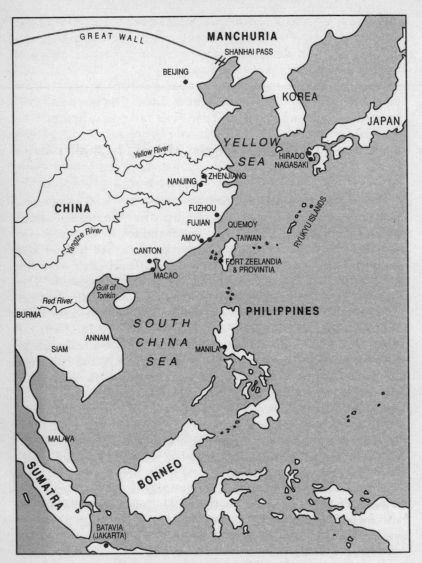

East Asia in the seventeenth century.

as far away as Africa had acknowledged him as the ruler of the world. However, after Zheng's famous voyages, the Ming dynasty retreated into self-absorption once more, confident that there was little in the wider world worth seeing.

Iquan, the future Lord of the Straits, was born in 1603 in the small Fujianese village of Nan-an, near Amoy. The place had only two relatively minor claims to fame. The first was a strange rock formation at a nearby river-mouth, said by the locals to represent five horses – four galloping out to sea, while a fifth shied away, back towards land. Later writers would interpret this as referring to Iquan, his son Coxinga, his grandson Jing and two of his great-grandchildren, Kecang and Keshuang.

The second famous place in Nan-an was a rock, shaped like a crane, which bore an inscription by a philosopher of a bygone age who had been posted to the region as a civil servant. He had announced, to the locals' great surprise, that the area would one day be the birthplace of 'the Master of the Seas'. The same site was visited centuries later by the founder of the Ming dynasty, who was aghast at the powerful *feng shui*. He announced that the region risked becoming the birthplace of an Emperor, and ordered that the stone inscription should be altered. This act, it was later said, is what kept Iquan's family from becoming the true rulers of all China.[1]

Iquan shared his surname, Zheng ('Serious'), with the famous mariner of times gone by, but this was merely a coincidence. The historical Admiral Zheng was a eunuch and a Muslim from China's interior, whereas Iquan hailed from a clan that had lived in coastal Fujian for generations. His father was Zheng Shaozu, a minor official in local government, while his mother was a lady of the Huang trading family.[2] Shaozu seemed determined to bring respectability to his family, and encouraged his children in China's most acceptable way of advancement. He was wealthy enough to afford a good education for his sons, and hoped that they would find success in the civil service examinations: the only way of achieving office in the Chinese government. Shaozu's ambitions for his family were not uncommon, and Fujian province was a hotbed of academic endeavour – it sent more graduates into the civil service than any other province in China. However, Shaozu's sons were to bring him an endless series of disappointments, and he did not live to see the incredible achievements of their later life. In the case of his eldest son Iquan,[3] it was undeniable that the meek, conservative genes of the Zheng strain had lost out to the wild-card heritage of the Lady Huang, whose family, it was later discovered, were a group of reprobates involved in questionable maritime enterprises.

Iquan had many names in the course of his life, but was known at home simply as 'Eldest Son'. As is common with some Chinese families even today, he and his brothers also concocted a series of semi-official nicknames. In the case of the Zheng boys, they named each other after imagined animal attributes. As the eldest, Iquan seized Dragon for himself – the noblest of Chinese beasts and the symbol of imperial authority. The next eldest brothers grabbed the next-best names – Bao the Panther, Feng the Phoenix and Hu the Tiger. An avian theme among the younger brothers implied they were the sons of a different mother, with names including Peng the Roc, Hú the Swan and Guan the Stork.

The chief source for the youth of Iquan is the *Taiwan Waizhi* or *Historical Novel of Taiwan*, a late seventeenth-century account of the pirate kings that mixes verifiable historical facts with fantastically unlikely tales of their deeds and accomplishments. As seems traditional for all Chinese books on figures who would later find fame, it begins by describing Iquan in familiarly glorious terms that would please any Confucian scrutineer. According to the *Historical Novel*, he was able to read and write by age seven, a not inconsiderable feat, and displayed a great aptitude for dancing and other forms of the arts. Before long, however, the *Historical Novel* slips from empty platitudes of child prodigy, and into accounts of events more in keeping with Iquan's later life.

His most distinctive characteristic, evident even in his childhood, was his rakish charm, which often allowed him to get away with mischief. The first story of Iquan's remarkable life takes place somewhere around 1610, when the boy was playing with his younger brother Bao the Panther in the street near the house of the local mayor Cai Shanzhi. Close within the walls of Cai's gardens, the boys could see a lychee tree – the luscious fruits were native to Fujian, and highly prized. They tried to knock some of the ripe lychees down by throwing sticks into the branches, and, when the local supply of sticks was exhausted, tried using stones instead. Unfortunately for Iquan, one of his well-aimed rocks sailed past the tree and into the garden, where the unsuspecting mayor was sunning himself. It hit him on the head, causing him to fly into a rage and summon both Iquan and his father for disciplinary action.

However, the story goes that Cai's anger immediately abated 'when he saw the lovely child', and instead of venting his anger he allowed the boy to go without punishment, announcing to the world that the future had great things in store for him.[4]

It is unlikely that Iquan's father would have agreed, since he saw the boy as a nuisance. Iquan's mother was not Shaozu's principal wife, but merely a concubine, making Iquan little more than another troublesome mouth to feed. With at least six brothers and half-brothers, it is highly likely that Iquan had a similar number of female siblings, though these remain unrecorded in chronicles about his life. Father and son fell out when Iquan's mother's looks began to fade, and her patron tired of her, but their chief causes for argument were mainly Iquan's doing. In such a precarious family position, it would have been smart to avoid drawing unwelcome attention to oneself, and yet the teenage Iquan seemed to covet danger. As his boyhood high spirits gave way to surly adolescence, Iquan made a show of disobeying his father's advice, and neglected his obvious academic potential. He was also caught in bed with his own stepmother, which was the final straw. Strictly speaking, Iquan had committed a capital offence and hastily left his home town for Macao, where, his father imagined, he was bound to come to a bad end.[5]

To most Chinese, Macao might as well have been a whole world away, several hundred miles down the Chinese coast, at the very edge of civilisation. South of Macao, there was nothing but the sweeping curve of what is now Vietnam, a land of questionable provenance in the eyes of the snobbish Chinese. Beyond that lay Malaya and the Indonesian Spice Islands – lands of opportunity, but also of savagery and danger. Conveniently positioned for trade at the mouth of the Pearl river estuary, Macao was originally founded as a trading post by merchants from Iquan's native Fujian.

It was named after A-Ma-Gong, or Matsu, the sea goddess worshipped by all local sailors. Matsu had once been a mortal, a Fujianese virgin who had been able to leave her sleeping body in phantom form to rescue troubled sailors. After her death, sightings of her ghost were often reported in coastal communities, and sailors continued to make sacrifices to her in the hope of safe journeys.[6] Reputedly, some of these offerings were even *human* sacrifices.

Macao's new occupants, the Catholic Portuguese, were deeply suspicious of such foreign cults and renamed the city in praise of a more acceptable divine virgin, calling it the 'City of the Mother of God'. The town was a vital point on the unofficial trade routes in and out of China, only a few miles from the Pearl river delta and the great city of Canton. This location made Macao a place of vital strategic importance, and it would remain so for two more centuries until the nearby village of Hong Kong fell into the hands of the British and superseded it.

The Portuguese had gained a toehold in Macao by clearing the Pearl river estuary of pirates, but their presence at the edge of the Celestial Empire was barely tolerated. They were still not permitted entry into China proper, but the city was home to many traders and missionaries who hoped the strict laws would be lifted. While they waited, they did their best to interest the local Chinese in their cargoes and their religion.

Accompanied by his brothers Bao the Panther and Hu the Tiger, who were probably as much of a handful as he was, the teenage Iquan arrived in Macao at the house of his grandfather Huang Cheng, who was a merchant in the city. The *Historical Novel* describes 'a youth eighteen years of age, lazy by nature with no taste for learning; strong-armed, fond of boxing and martial arts. He secretly went to [Macao] in Canton, and visited Huang Cheng, his mother's father.'[7] Considering the recent upheavals back home in Fujian, it is possible that the boys arrived in the company of Lady Huang herself, returning to her family home after her fall from favour.

Life in Macao would have been a great surprise to Iquan, particularly after the stuffy environment of his father's house. The Huangs were just as keen on advancement and success, but rated material wealth over academic accolades – they were merchants and traders, and Iquan found his natural talents were far better suited to business than study. Business was good for the Huangs, but that did not mean that business was always legal.

Iquan was destined to discover south China's not-so-secret vice – communication with the outside world. The later emperors preferred to cower behind the natural and man-made barriers that kept the barbarians at bay, but their influence was not all-encompassing, even within their own borders. A government report of the time noted that Fujian was a place where 'cunning bullies can carry out their crafty schemes'. Thanks to the many inlets and secluded harbours along the coast, private traders could flourish, out of the sight of the tax inspector.[8]

Chinese sailors were permitted to leave port to fish or move goods along the coast to the next local port, but their seaward ventures were supposed to stop there. Supposedly, no Chinese vessel carried more than two days' fresh water for its crew[9] – a rule which should have confined all shipping to the coastline, within reach of resupply. However, the fishermen of Fujian knew what was beyond the horizon. They were, after all, the descendants of the voyagers who had sailed distant oceans in the company of the eunuch mariner Zheng He, and the local city of Quanzhou was still the designated port for receiving embassies from the tributary nation of the Ryukyu Islands. Unlike their landlocked brethren of the hinterland, they saw the sea on a daily basis, and did not fear it.

Chinese vessels could hug a coastline, but were hardly suitable for ocean-going travel. However, as one of the few points on the Chinese coast with a tradition of dealing with foreign places, Fujianese shipwrights knew how to build vessels that could sail to other lands. But these ships were expensive, over ten times the cost of mundane vessels – less wealthy local entrepreneurs found other ways to rig their ships for longer voyages. Within sight of the coast, the Fujianese vessels were flat-bottomed affairs that sat low in the water – only a madman would take one out into the open sea. But as soon as the sailors cleared the watchful eyes of the local law enforcement, they would transform their vessels, bolting fences of split bamboo around the bulwarks to stay waves from washing over the deck, and lowering a giant knife-like wooden blade into the water that served as an auxiliary keel to keep the ships stable.[10]

Putting out to sea from a Fujian village, a local boat could pretend to make along the coast, before running for the east the moment it was out of sight of land. As the shallow coastal shelf fell away, most Chinese sailors recoiled in fear at the sight of the darkening waters below their vessels, telling horror stories about the 'Black Ditch' that lay just off the coast. Dangerous currents and savage sea monsters lurked in the fearsome depths, and stories about them were enough to keep many Chinese sailors reliably close to shore.[11] But for the sailors of Fujian, there was something beyond the Black Ditch.

From the ports of Fujian, it was less than two days' sail to the lawless island of Taiwan. The mandatory two-day supplies were sufficient to sustain the crew for a one-way trip out of Chinese waters and into a whole new world. After restocking in Taiwan, it was possible to hop along the Ryukyu island chain, all the way to the Japanese ports of Hirado and Nagasaki. Other merchants preferred to make the seaward leap out towards the Spanish-occupied Philippines, or smaller hops along the coast of Annam (now known as Vietnam), down towards Java, where the Dutch East India Company had made its base.

The people of Fujian had settled in some of these destinations. Chinese merchants and their families (or, in many cases, their *local* wives and children) formed distinct Chinatown communities in Manila and Nagasaki. Few of them expected to be permanent immigrants, but as it became economical for organisations to keep representatives in foreign ports, the practice of taking on a temporary foreign posting became known as *yadong*, or 'hibernation'. Surely no true Chinese could stay for too long away from the Celestial Empire, but there seemed little harm in a short foreign stay, especially if there was profit to be made.

Officially, China had *no* foreign trade, but decades of illegal commerce had brought many new items, some of which had exerted a great influence on the culture of the time. The chilli, a vital ingredient in Chinese cookery, particularly in spicy Sichuan cuisine and the hot-sour soup of Beijing, was not native to China at all. This exotic plant was brought to the Philippines from South America by the Spanish, and traded there with Chinese merchants – there were no modern chillies in China before the sixteenth century, and yet today it is impossible to imagine Chinese food without them.

Another import from the New World was tobacco, which followed a similar route to China through Spanish hands. During the 1600s, rumours spread through China that the Fujianese had invented a miraculous breathable smoke that made the inhaler drunk. After early popularity with the sailors, the 'Dry Alcohol' plant was soon cultivated in the soil of Fujian itself, and merchants began to process it and sell it as a local product. Hundreds of factories sprang up in Fujian and neighbouring Canton, and the vice took off all over the country – it was particularly popular with soldiers, and one authority reported that by 1650, 'everyone in the armies had started smoking'.[12]

But these were relatively minor fads compared with the immense impact of yet another import. In a period of great climactic uncertainty, plagued with floods and famines, the Fujianese merchant Chen Zhenlong was greatly impressed by the high-yield, fast-growing sweet potatoes he saw cultivated in the Philippines. He bought some of the exotic American plants and brought them home, growing them experimentally on a plot of private land. When Fujian was struck by a crippling famine in 1594, the canny Chen approached the governor with his new discovery, and persuaded him to introduce it that season. The venture was rewarded with a crop that saved the lives of thousands of Fujianese. The governor gained the nickname 'Golden Potato', and the incident led to the composition of He Qiaoyuan's 'Ode to the Sweet Potato', part of which went:

> Sweet potato, found in Luzon
> Grows all over, trouble-free
> Foreign devils love to eat it
> Propagates so easily.
>
> We just made a single cutting
> Boxed it up and brought it home
> Ten years later, Fujian's saviour
> If it dies, just make a clone.
>
> Take your cutting, then re-plant it
> Wait a week and see it grow
> This is how we cultivate it
> In our homeland, reap and sow.
>
> In a famine we first grew it
> In a Fujian starved and rude
> But we gained a bumper harvest
> People for a year had food.[13]

The trade was by no means one-way, and rich rewards awaited those who were prepared to take the risks. A length of Chinese silk could sell in Japan for ten times its domestic price. Iron pots and pans could also fetch a high return if anyone was prepared to run the gauntlet up to the Japanese harbours. Owing to a convenient accident of international diplomacy, the Ryukyu Islands were officially a tributary state to both the emperors of Japan and China. Though both nations supposedly frowned on international private trade, it was difficult to prove that a group of Chinese sailors arriving in Nagasaki weren't actually Ryukyu Islanders, and therefore locals. Equally, when the same sailors were heading for home, they were Ryukyu Islanders until they reached the coast of China, at which point they miraculously transformed into Fujianese fisherman once more, albeit Fujianese whose hold would often turn out to have suspiciously large amounts of Japanese silver in it.

Inspections, however, were rare. In outlawing almost all foreign trade, the Chinese government had effectively criminalised every Fujianese sailor with an interest in making money. This only forced innocent men into the company of rogues, and led many to set their sights on the richer pickings of still greater criminal activities. Bribery and corruption became rife in Fujianese ports, as local harbour masters were encouraged to look the other way when 'fishing fleets' put out to sea with no nets but holds full of silk. The more damaging long-term implications came when more hard-core criminal elements realised they had little to lose. Since trade itself was illegal, some reasoned that it was a more economic use of manpower and facilities to equip a fleet, not of merchantmen, but of warships. Lying in wait just off the coast of Fujian, a canny sailor could observe the approach of his rivals' trading fleets and seize control of their cargoes.

Such an attitude led the merchants to seek their own protection. Fleets of traders began to arm themselves with swords and cannon, and before long the traders of Fujian were in control of vast fleets of warships. This in turn led to them enjoying considerably more attention and respect from the new European arrivals in the region. Realising that these locals would be less of a pushover than those in Africa and the South Sea islands, the Dutch, English and Portuguese at least tried to deal with them civilly, if not with respect, then with acknowledgement of the military might at their disposal.

Amid this time of black-market commerce, the Zheng boys were put to work at Huang's trading company. Garbled accounts from later Dutch and Chinese sources describe Iquan as a 'tailor', so it is likely that much of his early profits rested on Chinese silks. His face also became well known in the alien quarter, where he associated with the Portuguese and their allies, and somehow gained himself a Portuguese 'godfather', who left him a substantial sum of money.[14] He befriended local missionaries, who taught him Portuguese and baptised him as a Catholic, with the Christian name of Nicholas Gaspard Iquan – Nicholas being the name of his wealthy patron.

It is unlikely that Iquan's Catholic faith was particularly devout. He adopted it partly out of a desire to learn more about his foreign acquaintances, and partly in gratitude for the success of a missionary doctor in curing his mother of an illness. Later accounts of his faith point to someone who merely treated it as another superstition, rather than a way of life. As one observer noted:

> The Portuguese . . . observed that Iquan had a very curious oratory, in which they remarked among other things, the statues of our Saviour and the Virgin Mary, and of diverse other Saints, but it must not be imagined that these were any marks of Christian piety . . . It is very credible that though Iquan had been baptised, yet he was ignorant of the Principles of the Christian faith, for the Portuguese could never observe that he rendered more honour to Jesus than he did to his Idols, neither did they perceive him to do the least action of a Christian . . . [nor did he] ever so much as speak of the Gospels, Sacraments or Commandments either of God or his Church, and as for the manner of his life, that was less Christian, either this uninformed man was so impious, or so ignorant that he equally burnt incense to Jesus Christ and his Idols.[15]

The foreigners Iquan met through his 'conversion' were also sources of information about the outside world – a valuable asset to a would-be traveller. The Portuguese complexion and hair-colour were relatively unthreatening to the tanned, dark-haired southern Chinese, but their settlement contained many examples of more exotic and fearsome foreignness. Many Chinese were petrified of the black slaves the Portuguese had brought from Africa – tall men with skin the colour of demons, who were given a wide berth by superstitious locals. The settlement also had a few residents from northern Europe, described by the Chinese as having 'the noses of eagles and the eyes of cats'.

One of the most striking alien residents was Adam Schall, a towering, fair-haired German missionary in his late twenties. A

Jesuit, Schall had volunteered for a China posting several years earlier. He had endured an eighteen-month sea voyage to Macao, with the disease and deprivation of shipboard life made even more unpleasant by compulsory Chinese lessons. Unlike other religious orders, the Jesuits recognised the importance of fitting in and learning the ways of the cultures they encountered – a policy that was to cause problems for the order in years to come. The Jesuits were also scientists, and insisted that their missionaries had transferrable skills beyond a faith in God. Some of the first Western doctors and engineers in China were Jesuits, but Adam Schall specialised in other matters. He was a trained astronomer and mathematician. He was also something of an expert on artillery – an area of knowledge that was to make him highly popular with the Chinese. But though Schall's path crossed with Iquan's in Macao, the two men were from very different worlds. Their separate destinies would eventually find them neighbours again two decades later, a thousand miles away in Beijing, the capital of the Celestial Empire.

Iquan's charm and linguistic ability (which, by all accounts, was less a gift for languages than a case of being the least-worst at communicating with foreigners), soon took him away from his grandfather, and into the company of more associates of his family. The *Historical Novel* records Iquan's big break, when his grandfather wanted to send a cargo of 'white sugar, calambak wood and musk'[16] to Japan. He found a trader prepared to take it on the lucratively illegal run up the Ryukyu Islands, and put Iquan on board to watch over the cargo. Iquan left on the ship as an employee of his grandfather, but would be absent for a long while. The journey convinced him that he had found his true vocation, and he joined the trading organisation of the ship's owner.

Iquan's new employer was Li Dan, a Fujianese merchant in his seventies who had long dwelt outside his native land. Once the head of the 'hibernating' Chinese community in the Philippines, local legend had it that Li had been enslaved aboard a Spanish galley for nine years, before escaping and establishing himself once more as the lord of the south China smugglers. In his later years, he spent increasingly more time in Japan, where he had several wives and a large mansion. There he was a pillar of the local Chinese community, friend of the Japanese authorities, and also the English merchants, who referred to him as Captain China. His associates (often referred to as 'brothers' in contemporary sources) ran much of his operation for him, from headquarters in Manila and Macao. Captain China's ships followed a forked trade route from Japan, down the Ryukyus to Taiwan, and then either south to the Philippines or west to Fujian, then down the south China coast to Annam and the Gulf of Tonkin. Iquan joined this operation in some capacity at Macao, and accompanied the Captain on voyages south to the Philippines and Annam, and north to Japan. When the Captain decided to remain for an extended stay at his holdings in the Japanese port of Hirado, Iquan stayed with him.

Even Iquan's travels across Asia could not have prepared him for Japan. The nation stood at the eastern edge of China's world, whence came its well-known name, the Land of the Rising Sun. It was thought by many to be the mythical island settled by Chinese nobles in the distant past, but also regarded by some emperors as a danger on their doorstep. The Japanese had a fearsome reputation across Asia – they were the nation that had held out against the Mongol conquest several centuries earlier, defying Khublai Khan by calling on the elements themselves to protect them. After conquering all of China, the Mongols had set their sights on Japan, sending a massive fleet across the strait that separated Japan from Korea. Off the coast of Japan, the entire fleet had been wiped out by a terrible storm, which Japanese priests claimed had been sent down by Japan's guardian deities, a Divine Wind or *Kamikaze*.

Since the time of the failed Mongol invasion, the Japanese had not presented such a united front. The country had been torn by a century of civil war, which only came to an end in 1603, with the appointment of the barbarian-quelling General (*Shôgun*) Tokugawa Ieyasu. A Japan at peace, however, could often be bad news for the rest of Asia, as itinerant peasants who normally earned a living as soldiers suddenly found themselves out of work and looking for a new occupation. When there was no war to fight in Japan, the coastlines of the China Sea were regularly plagued by outbreaks of piracy, and many Chinese records spoke of attacks by the Dwarf Barbarians of Japan.[17] Now the shogun was master of Japan, the nation was fated to slowly settle into a period of self-imposed seclusion – the years that followed Iquan's arrival in Japan saw the nation take successive steps to close its doors, in an attempt to shut out the outside world.[18] The nation's last foreign exploit had been an ill-fated invasion of Korea at the close of the sixteenth century, which had at least kept the military classes occupied for a few years. One of the families that benefited most from the Korean operation was the Matsuura of the Nagasaki region, who had gone from disreputable seafarers to landed gentry in the space of a generation. The continued presence of foreign traders in the Nagasaki area owed at least some of its existence to the former contacts and interests of the Matsuura from their seagoing days.[19]

To prevent them from interfering in local politics, foreigners had been gradually herded into special areas. Hirado and Nagasaki, the ports open to Chinese merchants such as Iquan, were also two of the last places in Japan where the exotic foreigners of distant Europe were still tolerated. The Portuguese, whose Catholic preaching had already caused local troubles for the Japanese, were no longer welcome, but the Protestant Dutch had convinced the shogun that they were more trustworthy. The English, through the influence of their agent Will Adams,[20] had similarly capitalised on their non-Catholic status. Dutch, English and Chinese lived together in the enclaves of Hirado and Nagasaki, bringing Iquan into contact with yet more foreigners who were to shape his fate.

Captain China was a person of considerable wealth and influence, described by his English business rivals as 'now chosen captain chief commander of all the Chinas in Japan, both at Nagasaki, Hirado and elsewhere'.[21] He appears in the diaries of the English merchants on several occasions, often encountered at functions hosted by the local lord Matsuura Takanobu, or seen in conference with the governor of Nagasaki. He also appears on the surface to have offered considerable support and encouragement to the English in Nagasaki.

Such *bonhomie* conceals much of his true nature. His friendliness to the newly arrived English was certainly of no surprise to the Dutch, who were heard to comment that the captain was sly and untrustworthy. The Dutch had been in Hirado for considerably longer, and had already been burnt in several deals with the captain. The English and the Dutch had enjoyed an uneasy truce for some years, but both nations were aware that their mutual rivalry was soon bound to ignite into open hostility once more. The captain glad-handed the English, sent them gifts, invited them to parties, and even asked their leader to be a godfather to his youngest daughter, Elizabeth.[22]

At the time that Iquan began his association with the captain, the boom trade was in Chinese silk. The captain and his associates had gained a licence from the Shogun to trade in Tonkin, but rarely made it further than the Pescadores Islands off the coast of Taiwan. There, they were welcomed as locals and permitted to anchor and trade with their kinsmen (such as Iquan's grandfather Huang), who would haul as much silk across from Fujian as they could cram in their boats. Returning to Hirado armed with a few tales about the weather in Tonkin, the brothers would unload their cargo, which had cost them considerably less than similar items obtainable in Annam or Malaya.

Iquan was ideal for this sort of work. The volatile conditions and underworld connections in such deals often required less management than they did riot control. The captain's business partners were smugglers, criminals and, in the case of some Taiwanese associates, cannibals. Someone with Iquan's charisma was a distinct asset, particularly with the ability to speak both Chinese and Portuguese, which last was then the international language of trade. Iquan had another attribute which may have endeared him to the aging captain – they were very much alike.

As might be expected after a lifetime of wheeling and dealing, the captain was a supreme conman. His own son, Augustin, was a disappointment to him, having fallen for the preaching of the Portuguese missionaries and converted to the discredited Catholic faith (in fact, as anti-Christian sentiment grew, his grandson was destined to become one of Japan's martyrs some fifteen years later). Iquan, however, was the Captain's kind of scoundrel. The boy who could hit a local dignitary with a rock and get away with it, or seduce his own stepmother and somehow escape intact, hit it off very well with the aging sea dog.

Iquan and Captain China certainly shared a sense of humour. At the time Iquan joined his organisation, the captain was several years into an outrageous swindle, involving the hapless representative of the English East India Company in Japan, Richard Cocks.

The English attempt to run a successful Japanese trading post was troubled from the start, when they were forced to dwell in Hirado alongside their Dutch rivals. The English had the opportunity to press for another town, and Will Adams had urged them to try for a port nearer to the centre of the Japanese government, where they would be both closer to the shogun, but also further removed from their detested Dutch enemies. For some reason, the company men ignored Adams's sound advice, and meekly agreed to base their representatives in Hirado.

The English trade mission at the time was under the leadership of Cocks, a kindly old man whose chief interests were gardening and goldfish. Described euphemistically as 'honest Mr Cocks' by his former boss, he was already something of a laughing stock in the town, where he was often seen dragging his wayward underlings out of local brothels, much to the annoyance of local pimps. Cocks's business was also plagued with numerous warehouse fires and accidents, which he blamed on the Dutch, probably with good reason. Worst of all for the future of English trade, East India Company representatives had arrived in Japan ready to offload vast quantities of cheap fustian cloth, only to discover that the Japanese preferred their own local silks and cottons. Before long, the English shamefacedly admitted that *they* preferred the Japanese clothes too, which left them with very little worth trading. Consequently, Cocks and his men had pinned all their hopes on the successful opening of the Chinese market, and their desperate longing for a change in their fortunes left them with a misplaced faith in some of the elements they encountered in Hirado.

Captain China was one of the first 'friends' the English made in Japan, a coup he achieved by becoming their landlord. The surviving notes on the rental of premises implies that it was in some disrepair, but that the captain somehow convinced the grateful English that he would get round to fixing the problems. He also graciously agreed to fully furnish the house 'according to the fashion of the country',[23] which, the English later discovered, meant 'with mats'.

Despite this questionable early encounter, the English had nothing but praise for Captain China, perhaps occasioned by tales of his success in the mainland trade. Cocks was particularly taken with the captain's profits from his new route to Taiwan, and scandalised to hear that there was so much silk on offer during a recent trip that the captain could only buy half of it. Such tales of riches, true or otherwise, were a great solace to Cocks, who was persuaded to invest 600 taels of silver on Captain China's next run to the south. Strangely, however, the captain and Iquan never seemed to get quite as good a deal when they were using someone else's money. Captain China's trade continued, and he began to direct increasing numbers of his ships east of the Pescadores, to Taiwan itself.

With little clue about the real situation in China or Taiwan, Cocks was forced to believe whatever the captain told him. The Taiwan trade was good most of the time, but not always, particularly when Cocks's money was involved. The trade into China was even better, but sadly for Cocks he was ethnically unsuited to pass as a local trader. Cocks continued to wine and dine the captain, and though he was reciprocated with matching Chinese hospitality, his chances of ever securing better trade for the East India Company were extremely remote. He did, however, get a number of very nice goldfish out of their friendship – his diary mentions several occasions when his god-daughter Elizabeth would arrive at his house bearing new additions for his ponds. The captain seems to have realised early on that Cocks doted on the girl, and that a visit from her would distract the English trader from asking too many questions about the progress of the China negotiations.

Cocks came to believe that the captain was powerful enough to influence the government of China itself. All the foreign merchants were intensely jealous of the captain's route into the heart of the world's largest market when it was still closed to non-Chinese traders. Cocks hopefully wrote to his masters in England that his friends might be able to secure the English a toehold in China proper, as the Dutch had unsuccessfully tried to gain in Canton, and the Portuguese in Macao. Whatever the captain had told him, it was as likely as the English securing a trade agreement with Martians. Cocks's letters home revealed a man with touching faith in his 'friends':

> But if it please God we get trade into China, as I hope we shall . . . three or four of my Chinese friends are labouring to get us trade in their country, and do not doubt it will take effect. The place they think fittest is an island and near the city of [Nanjing], to which place we may go from hence, if the wind be good, in three or four days. Our demand is for three ships to come and go . . . If we can but procure this, I doubt not but in short time we may get into the mainland itself.[24]

As if the English did not have enough trouble, the captain strung them along with more outrageous claims. After relieving Cocks of several thousand taels, the captain told him that the bribe was sufficient to sway local Fujianese officials to listen to his 'demands', and that the provision of a similar sum in the future, say, when the current Emperor died, would probably secure the trading agreement he required. When the Emperor remained inconveniently alive for a number of years, the captain instead claimed that the Son of Heaven was planning on resigning, and that strategically placed bribes would secure a sympathetic ear from his successor. When nothing came of that, the captain convinced Cocks that a letter from the King of England, accompanied by suitably valuable 'gifts', might be enough to sway the Emperor's mind. And since, of course, the English could not take their tribute themselves, the captain kindly offered to ferry all their hopeful offerings across to China. Unsurprisingly, however, none of the captain's entreaties on behalf of the English ever seemed to gain a response from the Chinese government.

Though Cocks was taken in, not all of his countrymen were as gullible. Several English captains commented that Cocks seemed a little too hopeful, though none seem to have made the obvious observation – that the captain was highly unlikely to help foreigners gain legal footholds into the China trade, when it was their exclusion that allowed him to earn his living.

By the time Iquan arrived in Hirado, the captain had fleeced Cocks of 6,250 taels, ostensibly for use in securing the opening of a Chinese treaty port. Cocks had invested an additional four-figure sum in the captain's own trading missions, not to mention incalculable amounts squandered on gifts and entertainment.

Despite the captain's bad treatment of Cocks, and the seething enmity with which the Dutch greeted the English arrivals, the residents of Hirado were forced to get along, and were often entertained *en masse* by the governor. Cocks and the Dutch remained ever at odds, but Captain China's new assistant was a palpable hit. Nicholas Iquan was particularly popular with the Dutch East India Company representative Jacques Specx – a career company man who was coming to the end of his tour of duty in Japan. Despite Iquan's association with Captain China, he became firm friends with the Dutchman. Part of this amity can be ascribed to Iquan's legendary charm, but some of Iquan's popularity may have stemmed from wily ambitions of Specx's own. After serving his time in Hirado, Specx was due to return to his Dutch homeland, but he spent barely twelve months of his working life back in the Netherlands. He would soon return to the headquarters of the Dutch East India Company in Java. He would one day be the Governor General of the whole of the Dutch East Indies, and would end his days as one of the seventeen supreme bosses of the Dutch East India Company back in Holland. But Specx's rise to power was still a long way off. At the time he met Nicholas Iquan, he was still a humble trader in his early thirties, the father of a three-year-old half-Japanese daughter by the name of Sara.

Specx, like his Dutch masters, also coveted a direct route into China, and believed that Captain China and his associates would be best suited to arrange it at some future point. He saw two possible ways of trading with the Chinese – either by stealing Macao from its Portuguese masters, or perhaps planting a base just off the shore of Fujian, on the Pescadores or Taiwan itself. Specx foresaw that the time would come for the Dutch to make their move, and he suspected he would need the help of Captain China's organisation. But the captain was not a young man, and one day he would have to step down in favour of one of his lieutenants. The natural choice, Augustin, was still part of the organisation, but his focus seemed almost exclusively concentrated on Japan itself – unlike his sea-roving father, Augustin had grown too attached to one place. Iquan, on the other hand, seemed to have the respect of the men in Captain China's service – Specx cultivated a friendship with someone he saw as the heir apparent. And if Iquan became too powerful and caused too much trouble for the Chinese, of course, the Dutch could always offer to 'deal with the pirate problem' in exchange for a treaty port somewhere on the China coast. This was, the Dutch believed, how the Portuguese first secured Macao, and the Dutch were prepared to try a similar tactic themselves.[25]

Future business partners were not the only contacts Iquan made in Japan. By all accounts, he also fell in love. At one of the local soirées, Lord Matsuura was attended upon by a number of samurai girls, one of whom caught Iquan's eye. That may have been part of the plan – since she shared a surname with a prominent family in the region, her parents may have been playing Cupid.

Miss Tagawa[26] is a figure of some dispute among writers on the history of the Zheng family. Her origins are unclear, and commentators have manipulated the available information to fit their own agendas. Enemies of the Zheng have described her as a courtesan, a common harbour prostitute, or a mere bar-girl whom Iquan encountered on his travels. This is doubtful, as Lord Matsuura would have been unlikely to have had such girls in his public entourage. Other authorities, particularly allies and admirers of the Zheng, have been keen to claim that Tagawa was nothing less than a princess, but this is also unlikely. She may have been the daughter of Tagawa Yazayemon, a samurai in the service of Lord Matsuura – but the word 'samurai' has assumed a semi-mythic quality outside Japan. At the time, it was a term applied to every military class from the noblest of knights to the common foot soldier. Miss Tagawa's lineage fell somewhere between those two categories, but the fact that she was Japanese, and that she was a samurai girl, were two important elements. Her descendants, who still live in Japan to this day, possess a genealogy that traces their lineage seventeen generations before Yazayemon to Taira no Shigemori, a famous medieval warrior, whose father briefly ruled Japan in the name of the emperor. In the unlikely event that the Tagawa genealogy is genuine, it would mean that Miss Tagawa's nineteenth-generation ancestor was Kammu Tenno, the fiftieth Emperor of Japan. This might at least explain the contradictory tales of her origins – she may have been descended from a living god, but separated from true divinity by over eight hundred years of interbreeding with mere humans.

Meanwhile, Chinese sources, particularly those in a Taiwan keen to gloss over the island's links to Japan, make other claims for her. Some are eager to speculate that while she grew up in Japan, her ancestors were themselves probably Chinese. Confusion over her names led one source to claim she was herself of mixed Chinese and Japanese blood, and met Iquan through her father or stepfather, a Chinese swordsmith by the name of Weng Yihuang.

The seventeenth-century writer Liu Xianting offered an apocryphal account of the pair's courtship, which emphasised Iquan's relatively lowly status at the time:

When [Iquan] was young he fled to Japan. There he did sewing for people in order to earn a living. He had sewn his savings of three coppers into the collar of his clothes, but they fell out. He wandered along a road looking for them. When he could not find his money he burst into tears. There was a Japanese woman, newly widowed, who was standing inside her gate. She saw him searching and asked what the matter was. [Iquan] told her. The woman said: 'With your talents, it should be easy for you to earn three million coppers as it would be to pick up a blade of grass. How could you come to such a state for three coppers?' She gave herself to [Iquan] and spent the night with him. When [Iquan] achieved success, he married her.[27]

Liu was not the only contemporary writer to suggest that Iquan may have been employed as a tailor in Japan, but his tale does seem doubtful. Iquan is unlikely to have been scrabbling over copper coins in the service of Captain China, and 'when he achieved success', events conspired to keep him and Tagawa apart for much of the time. Other elements of Liu's description ring true, however. Miss Tagawa was a year older than Iquan, which would put her in her early twenties. This would have been rather advanced in years for an unmarried woman of her time – perhaps she really was a widow, whom Matsuura retainers hoped to marry off to the charming foreign merchant with prospects.

Whatever the truth behind Tagawa's background and her first meeting with Iquan, the pair were soon seeing more of each other in a relationship close enough to qualify as common-law marriage in the eyes of commentators of the time. The couple's later behaviour would suggest that there was a genuine love between them, but their relationship was troubled in the early stages, not just by Iquan's regular duties abroad, but by political goings-on elswhere. While Miss Tagawa seemed to have been Iquan's first love, his associates had a more 'suitable' spouse in mind.

Captain China's thoughts on the matter are unrecorded. Whether he or Iquan was the more eager is unclear, but someone in the captain's organisation wanted Iquan to marry someone else. Iquan was offered the hand of Lady Yan, a Fujianese girl who was probably a daughter of Yan Sixi, another of Captain China's lieutenants. Considering the organisation's intermeshing ties of adoption and marriage, Lady Yan may have also been the captain's granddaughter or niece.[28]

It was the perfect opportunity for Iquan to cement his alliances. He was being offered the chance to marry into Captain China's clan; to literally become one of the family. It might not have pleased his prospective relative Augustin, but it would give Iquan an extra lever if he wanted to take control of operations after Captain China died. From the captain's point of view, such a marriage would also encourage Augustin, Yan Sixi and Iquan to work together for mutual benefit – reducing the chances of a power struggle within the captain's fleets. As a dynastic alliance it made perfect sense, but there were personal issues involved. If Iquan agreed to a wedding with Lady Yan, it would forever destroy Miss Tagawa's chances of becoming his principal wife.

However, before Iquan could give the captain his answer, both men were caught up in someone else's war, much to their personal and financial benefit. The Dutch were just about to attack Macao.

2

THE DEAL WITH THE DEVILS

Ships from the Netherlands could sail all the way around the world to the Dutch East India Company at Batavia, the site of modern-day Jakarta. But from there, it was still a long haul to Hirado in Japan – a trading post the Dutch did not gain until 1611. What the Dutch really wanted was a base close to China itself, a port on the outskirts like the Portuguese foothold in Macao. For two decades, the Dutch considered taking Macao itself by force from its Catholic owners. Two vessels made an abortive attempt in 1601, and a flotilla of five junks had been humiliatingly repelled by the Portuguese later that same year. Many of the crew were captured and seventeen of them were hanged, although a couple of younger sailors were spared.

The Dutch, however, were not put off. Far from regarding the Portuguese presence on Macao as unassailable, they merely waited for another chance to oust them. Once a year, the Portuguese would send a galleon heavy with treasure and luxuries to Nagasaki, to return loaded with even more valuable Japanese goods, ready to be routed back to Europe. On 6 June 1604, the Dutch had targeted the galleon instead of its owners, sending Admiral Wybrand van Warwick in the ships *Erasmus* and *Nassau* right into Macao harbour. The unprepared Portuguese were forced to stand back and watch as the Dutch stole vast quantities of silk from the galleon as she prepared to leave port.

In 1607, the Dutch tried a different tactic. The *Erasmus* returned, accompanied by the *Orange*, the *Mauritius* and an unnamed yacht, all under the command of Admiral van Maatelief. Instead of attacking the Portuguese, they demanded audience with the Chinese and began negotations for establishing trade relations of

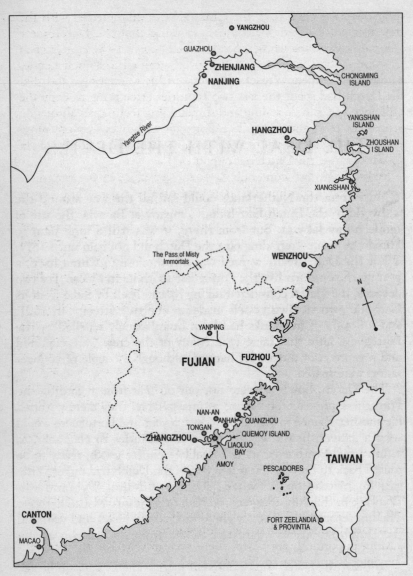

Maritime South China.

their own. For their part, the Chinese were unimpressed with the ingenuity of these new arrivals, assuming that the Dutch were ignorant barbarians whose ancestors had been visited by the great Chinese sailor Zheng He. The Chinese surmised that their famous admiral had somehow reached Europe in his wanderings, and that the Dutch had spent the last two centuries attempting to copy the brilliance of Chinese sailing and shipbuilding techniques through a process of trial and error. The Portuguese, however, were more frightened by the arrival of their enemies, and sent a flotilla of six vessels to chase the Dutch out of port.

In 1609, the two contending powers signed a twelve-year truce, but resentment continued to boil beneath the surface. The Dutch gained their foothold in Hirado, but still saw the Portuguese doing better in their trade with the Japanese. In 1619, two years before the truce was due to end, the Dutch and the English signed a short-lived pact in which they promised to aid each other against the Spanish and the Portuguese. With the English no longer a threat, the new Dutch Governor General, Jan Pieterszoon Coen, decided that the capture of Macao would solve all the Dutch traders' problems. It would give them direct access to Chinese silk from Canton, and reduce their overheads in obtaining material to trade with both the Japanese and their clients back in Europe. It would also effectively cut the Portuguese off from East Asia, and force them to fall back on their distant bases in India. And as an added bonus, it would give the Dutch a port from which they could sail out to intercept the Chinese silk ships sailing to the Spanish-held Philippines.

The Dutch–Portuguese treaty officially lapsed in 1621, but many assumed it was renegotiable. Such an extension, however, might take several months to arrange, and it could be another year before news of the deal reached the Far East. It gave the Dutch an appropriate loophole to pursue their rivalry with the Portuguese, and the opportunity to plead ignorance if their masters were to arrive later and tell them to call off hostilities.

More importantly for Coen, there was no time like the present. The Spice Islands were finally subjugated, Batavia was uncontested in Dutch hands without local resistance, and he had intercepted a letter in early 1622 that advised of the woeful inadequacy of Macao's defences. He swiftly wrote to the company directors advising them a force of maybe a thousand men could easily take Macao and hold it 'against the world'. He also noted that unless the Dutch struck swiftly, the Portuguese would soon be able to bribe the Chinese authorities in order to allow more defensive cannon into the city.[1]

Coen wanted to impress upon his bosses that this might be the last chance for the Dutch in the Far East to seize the town. As he saw it, it was only a matter of time before the Portuguese constructed fortifications that the limited local manpower of the Dutch would be unable to overrun. But until they did so, Macao was open to assault.

The Portuguese were well aware of the lack of their own defences, but the Chinese were deaf to their requests – clearly working on the assumption that if the Portuguese were sufficiently entrenched in Macao to resist a Dutch attack, they would be equally unassailable to the Chinese themselves. The Portuguese had resorted to fortification by bribery, sneaking money into the hands of corruptible Chinese officials in order to complete limited defences while their landlords looked the other way. The Chinese, of course, had problems of their own north of the border, about which the Europeans knew very little. All that they had witnessed was that the Chinese were behaving increasingly erratically in their dealings with the Europeans, and that former bravado was being replaced by a more desperate willingness to accept any kind of help. As even Coen noticed:

> In October 1621, by order of the King of China, an order was sent by the mandarins of [Beijing] to the people of Macao to ask them for the assistance of 100 men and some cannon against the Tartars [i.e. Manchus]. The Jesuits that these Mandarins had previously driven from [Beijing] are now again received there in order to teach the Chinese the use of cannon from books. [2]

In other words, whatever the defensive capabilities of Macao, the majority of its Portuguese garrison was currently out of town in the north of China, on an ill-fated expedition to bring European military technology to the aid of the Chinese in their ongoing skirmishes with the Manchus. As far as Coen's spies could judge, Macao now had barely fifty musketeers, and another hundred *moradores* – veterans who would be expected to take up arms in a time of trouble.

Coen could wait no longer, and dispatched a fleet to attack Macao. Captain Cornelis Reijersen was given command of a fleet of eight vessels: the *Zierikzee*; the *Groeningen*; the *Oudt Delft*; the *Enchuyzen*; the *De Gallias*; the captured English warship *The Bear*; and the yachts *St Nicholas* and *Palicatta*, crewed with Dutchmen, a few English, Bandanese from the Dutch Spice Islands, Gujarat sailors from India and some African slaves. As he sailed up the coast of Indochina, he gained several more vessels – six weeks out of Batavia, he joined forces with the *Haan* (*Cockerel*), *Tiger*, *Victoria* and *Santa Cruz*, all Japan-bound yachts under a Captain van Nijenroode. As he neared Macao, he also gained two more recruits – the Dutch ships *Tronew* and *Hoop* (*Hope*) laying in wait on the sea approaches. Two English vessels had trailed sulkily behind the main fleet, providing only superficial support, ever since the supremely confident Dutch had told their allies-of-the-moment that they would be unwilling to split any of the forthcoming booty with them. The fleet was remarkably multi-racial already, but soon gained an East Asian contingent when it encountered a warship of the king of Siam, crewed in part by twenty Japanese sailors who had fled Portuguese service and wanted to join the Dutch. They were duly permitted to do so – considering the supposed ban on Japanese sailors abroad in this period, it is highly likely that they were associates of the pirates of Fujian, if not of Captain China, then of one of his immediate rivals.

With 600 Europeans, and another 200 crewmen of other races, the ships reached Macao on 22 June 1622. Reijersen immediately sent three men in a boat to the Chinese quarter, hoping to bully the local population into supporting their Dutch 'liberators'. The Chinese, however, had wisely locked themselves out of harm's way, and the boat returned with no answer from a native representative.

Aware of the Dutch presence, the Portuguese firmly believed that their enemies would storm the coastal citadel of San Francisco. Reijersen let them continue to think that, and sent the *Groeningen*, *De Gallias* and *Bear* into a prominent position nearby, with instructions to shell the fortress on the evening of the 23rd. The Portuguese diligently returned fire, and the ships sailed back into the darkness, but their mission was successful – the Portuguese now believed that the fort of San Francisco was the main target of the Dutch.

The *Groeningen* and *De Gallias* were back at dawn, bombarding the fortress with rapid salvos. The Portuguese swivelled their cannons into place and returned fire, and the bay was soon thick with smoke. For the artillerymen in the fortress, it appeared that fate was on their side, as while the two ships did little appreciable damage to the fortress, the Portuguese scored a direct hit on the *De Gallias*. The ship was badly damaged, and the Dutch bombardment lessened in intensity.

But the damage to the *De Gallias*, while unfortunate, was an acceptable part of Reijersen's plan, as he had no intention of going anywhere near the fort. For the previous two days, he had instead been planning to land the bulk of his forces further up the coast on the sandy beach of Cacilhas. Amid the debris in the bay was a barrel of damp gunpowder fitted with a slow-burning fuse, which Reijersen had deliberately floated into the middle of the fray. It drifted towards the shore emitting a cloud of thick black smoke, which, courtesy of the confusion caused by the fight between the decoy ships and the fortress, mingled with the pall of other fires hanging over the morning sea. Hidden behind the smokescreen came the rest of Reijersen's forces, edging ever closer to the shoreline in thirty-two small boats.

However, not all the Portuguese were manning the guns in the fortress. One Antonio Rodrigues Cavalinho stood on the beach at Cacilhas, accompanied by sixty Portuguese musketeers, and another ninety *moradores*. Spotting Reijersen's sneak attack, the troops began firing volley after volley at the approaching boats. Reijersen's men were spaced widely enough to be able to aim and fire their own weapons, leading to a second, small-calibre exchange between the landing forces and the defenders of the beach, joining the thunderous guns of the ships and forts.

Once again, the Portuguese had the upper hand. Standing on firm ground, and in partial cover behind sandbanks, they were able to take careful aim, while the attacking Dutch were obliged to fire from rocking boats. Not a single Portuguese soldier was injured on the beach, but the defenders of Macao were able to wound a number of high-profile attackers – a Captain Cook was wounded in the arm, and Reijersen himself was shot in the stomach, and forced to retire from the assault.

With the Dutch ships now close to the shoreline, Hans Ruffijn assumed command. He was not a sailor like Reijersen, but an accomplished soldier who even gained approving remarks in extant

Portuguese accounts of the battle. Ruffijn was a veteran of wars in Flanders and India, and the leader of the troops who sailed with the Dutch flotilla. Knowing that the Portuguese were not so foolhardy as to resist an attacking force that outnumbered them six-to-one, Ruffijn was determined to get his men out of their boats and onto the beach. He urged his men closer to the shore until the waters were shallow enough to wade, and then leapt from his boat, leading the Dutch in a charge onto the sands of Cacilhas. The Portuguese soon fled, leaving the beach to the elated Dutch. One Dutch witness's account of the battle mocked the cowardice of the beach's defenders, but any soldier could see that they were merely making the best of a bad situation. Portuguese accounts of the same incident state quite clearly that Cavalinho's defence of the beach was planned as a mere holding action, and that the Portuguese had every intention of retreating as soon as their position was untenable.

This difference in views of the battle was to provide one of the factors in the Dutchmen's downfall. Ruffijn understood the motives of his foes all too well, and urged his masters to allow him to press on after them as swiftly as possible before they could retrench. However, news can fast become garbled in a crew from different backgrounds and disciplines, and the taking of the beach had already assumed legendary proportions among the other Dutch captains. Tellingly, the Dutch account that ridiculed the Portuguese was written by one Bontekoe, the captain of the *Groeningen*, who would have been far out in the bay bombarding the fortress at the time of the assault. His attitude reflects that of many of his countrymen, who celebrated the apparent disarray of the Portuguese, and assumed that their apparent cowardice was a sign of an easy victory to come. With Reijersen out of action, and the sensible Ruffijn outvoted by his seafaring superiors, the early success of the Dutch forces was squandered in a two-hour delay. The remaining shipboard Dutchmen, perhaps keen to get involved in what now appeared to be a pushover, insisted on holding up the forces on the beach while they landed the remainder of their men and the flotilla's three artillery pieces. Leaving a garrison of 200 on the shores of Cacilhas, the force then began a leisurely approach down the beach towards the city of Macao itself.

The delay would cost them dearly. Not only had the Portuguese been given ample time to prepare their own resistance, but the people of Macao had long enough to panic. A bell-ringer at the

Collegiate Church of São Paulo began tolling the alarm – an important rallying cry for the citizenry, who fled for sanctuary to São Paulo and the half-complete fortress Monte.

Among them were the Jesuits whom Nicholas Iquan had befriended in the foreign quarter, well aware of the dangers implicit in a Dutch victory. If the attackers were successful, not only would the Portuguese traders lose their toehold in China, but so too would the missionaries. With Catholicism out of favour in Japan, the advance of the Jesuit order would be halted back in India at the Portuguese stronghold of Goa. There would be no chance of bringing God's word to China and Japan, and East Asia would instead be in the hands of feckless Protestants like the English and Dutch. Desperate times called for desperate measures, and as their flock streamed in through the gates of their citadel, the Jesuits remembered that the incomplete Monte fortress came with four large guns already installed.

Meanwhile, Ruffijn's men were in trouble. Their advance had been halted once more by Cavalinho, who had installed his troops a little further down the coast from the beach. In a series of skirmishes, the Dutch pressed ever closer to the Portuguese, who staged a fighting withdrawal towards the foot of the rocky hill known as Guia. Just as the Dutchmen neared their goal, and prepared to encircle their foes by running along sheltered ground to their right, the ground erupted with a series of massive explosions. The Jesuits on the Monte battlements had just found a practical use for their advanced skills in mathematics, and had trained the citadel's large guns on the advancing Dutch. The Jesuits had found gunpowder and a small quantity of cannonballs that would not last long, but with the cold precision for which their order was justly famous, they ensured that every shot counted.

There was no time for Ruffijn's men to consider the proposition that they were now taking fire from a group of priests. For all they knew, Macao now possessed an entirely unexpected extra fort, crewed by artillerymen who had lain cunningly in wait, and now intended to bombard them into oblivion. Mystified by the numbers of soldiers they believed themselves to be encountering, they were now under fire from both their front and right, and had no option but to run to the left, seeking sanctuary in the stone hermitage of Our Lady of Guia. There, however, they were pushed back by yet another group of musketeers, who had already occupied the top of the Guia hill. In the confusion, it is unlikely that Ruffijn realised just how insignificant the opposing force was. The hilltop forces constituted just eight Europeans, accompanied by some twenty locals and a group of African slaves who had been armed by their masters.

Crouching down out of harm's way, the Dutch angrily debated their next move. Ruffijn once more took the lead, determined to lead his men to high ground above the Cacilhas beach, there to await reinforcement and artillery support from his allies. However, by this point, still more defenders in two other positions realised how desperate the Dutch situation had become, and sent reinforcements of their own to take the same area.

Ruffijn got to his feet, ready to lead his men out of danger, only to face an onrushing charge of Portuguese, Chinese, Africans and sword-waving Jesuits – among them the blond giant Adam Schall. As the Dutch stared in disbelief, two bullets sealed their fate. The first mortally injured Ruffijn, causing him to fall in sight of his men. The second struck a powder keg which promptly exploded, showering the confused Dutchmen with shards of wood and iron, and taking much of their ammunition with it. Had Ruffijn been alive, the chance remains that the Dutch could have mounted a successful stand, but low on gunpowder and without a strong leader to buttress their resolve, the Dutch soldiers threw down their muskets, flags and drums, and sprinted back towards the beach in panic.

Down at the Cacilhas beach, the 200 soldiers of the rearguard were unprepared for what they saw. Less than an hour earlier, they had watched grudgingly as their colleagues marched off to an easy victory, while they were left behind guarding scattered boats from nothing more threatening than crabs and seagulls. Now, they looked up from their boredom to see their countrymen dashing towards them at full speed, all thought of conquest gone, pursued by an irate multiracial mob. In disbelief, the rearguard soldiers got to their feet and prepared to repulse the attackers, confident that their fleeing countrymen were merely mounting a strategic withdrawal, and planned to stand beside them at the beach. The fleeing soldiers, however, ran straight past their comrades and into the water, desperately grabbing at the boats and dragging them away from shore. The rearguard faltered, and as the oncoming defenders grew ever closer, they too broke and ran for the boats.

Many of the Dutch attackers were shot as they ran for the water, or trampled by their own countrymen in their dash for the vessels. Still others made it to the escape craft, only to drown when weight of numbers overturned their boats. When the ragged Dutch force was finally able to count heads and dress wounds, the extent of the rout became apparent. Captain Reijersen wrote in his journal that the battle for Macao had left him with 136 men dead, and another 126 badly wounded, and that was only counting the European members of his flotilla – he avoided mentioning the dozen or so Japanese and perhaps another 100 Indians who also fell under this command. It was the biggest disaster encountered by the Dutch East India Company in the Far East, and Reijersen's fleet sailed away from Macao in shame.

On the shore, the victorious people of Macao were ecstatic. Coen's spies had not been wrong – there genuinely had been only a handful of soldiers and veterans in the town. The rest of the city's defenders had been Chinese, merchants and travellers from other parts of Asia, and the group of African slaves who were freed that day in recognition of their bravery. Adam Schall, whose mathematical training had proved so useful in the bombardment of the attackers, was one of the celebrating defenders – in the mêlée at the beach, the young Jesuit had even taken a Dutch captain prisoner.

The embarrassment of the Dutch continued over the next couple of days, when they sent messengers back into Macao in an attempt to ransom seven prisoners. The Portuguese would have none of it. By this time, the damage to the *De Gallias* had taken its toll, and the ship was beginning to sink. Reijersen transferred the remainder of his men onto the other vessels, and the defeated flotilla limped out to sea.

But the Dutch East India Company were serious about establishing a base close to China, and Reijersen was equipped with a back-up plan. In the event that he failed to secure Macao, he had orders to sail to the Pescadores and build a base there. As far as the Portuguese were concerned, this was someone else's problem. To the inhabitants of the Pescadores and Taiwan, this was clearly Captain China's problem.

Reijersen sent the ships of his fleet to their new tasks. He had lost contact with the two English vessels with whom he had refused to discuss splitting the spoils of war. Having seen enough, they turned for Japan and left the Dutch to their fate. Meanwhile the *Bear* and

Santa Cruz went briefly off along the coast of China, while the *St Nicholas*, *Hope* and *Palicatta* went in search of Portuguese shipping to attack. The remnants of Reijersen's force reached the 'deserted' Pescadores, where they were surprised to find twenty armed war-junks on one side of the large natural harbour. The Chinese associates of Captain China left the Dutch to their own devices, and Reijersen's men went on a brief excursion around the islands.

They discovered that the Pescadores possessed a beautiful, deep harbour ideal for anchoring ocean-going vessels, but that the islands were otherwise a poor choice for a permanent base. There were few trees growing on the weathered basalt of the volcanic islands, and fresh water was in short supply – the islands did possess a couple of wells, but the water in them was of low quality during the summer season. The Dutch began to realise how the Pescadores got their name – the Fishermen's Isles. They were a handy stopping-off point for 'fishing boats' plying the route between China and Taiwan, but all supplies had to be shipped in from elsewhere.

The Dutch sent an expedition east, sailing thirty miles away from the Pescadores to Taiwan itself. There, in the south of the island, they found a bay protected by a long sandbank, and also even more Chinese. While the Dutch tried to survey the inlets of Taiwan's west coast, they were followed by a group of Chinese, who offered them gifts and attempted to engage them in conversation and trade, although the Dutch journals of the expedition ruefully announced 'our men suspected them to be pirates'.[3] The Dutch continued in their attempts to act like conquering European heroes, only to be tailed by the Chinese sailors at all times – 'The pirates also followed us, and handed over some supplies which proved to be of very little use. Our men afterwards found it necessary to get rid of these questionable characters as it was noticed that they were carrying out their piracies under the protection of our own flag.'

This cryptic statement shows that relations between the Dutch and the Chinese were already souring. For the present, they gave up on the idea of Taiwan, and returned to the Pescadores where they began to construct a fort. It was now two months since the disaster in Macao, but the Dutch were still licking their wounds. Unable to inflict any damage on the Portuguese, they took to looking for trouble further up the Chinese coasts, engaging in several skirmishes with Chinese sailors. These 'victories' were scored not against the heavily armed vessels of Captain China's organisation, but against a succession of vulnerable fishing boats.

The only powerful group with whom the Dutch had any dealings were the crews of the war-junks, who soon involved the Dutch in negotiations with Captain China's own representatives, who falsely claimed that they were empowered to act on behalf of the government of China itself. As the months wore on, the Dutch indulged in a series of schizophrenic and contradictory encounters with the Chinese. Some ships preyed upon local vessels in a manner little different from the pirates the Dutch so reviled. Others befriended Chinese locals, only to ruin any new alliances. When one of Reijersen's ships was wrecked in a battle near the coast of China, the stranded survivors sought shelter with a Chinese family, who offered them food and shelter, and entertained them with indulgent hospitality through the evening. The next day, however, the Dutchmen found the rotting corpses of several Chinese on the beach nearby, and left the area in haste before their new-found friends could discover what other Dutchmen had done.

Reijersen's attitude was no saner than that of his men. In a lawless land which was nominally part of China, but clearly under the control of a nebulous organisation of seaborne traders and pirates, Reijersen had nobody with whom he could negotiate. Representatives of Captain China did not see the dwindling Dutch numbers as much of a threat, and indeed seemed to welcome the prospect of a European outpost with which they could trade so close to the coast. The Chinese government, however, was deeply concerned at the proximity of the Dutch, and determined to shoo them away from the Pescadores.

Reijersen was prepared to try literally anything. He blockaded Amoy for a while, demanding an answer from the Chinese about his 'requests' for trade privileges. When that failed to work, he found himself a fortune-telling Chinese hermit convinced that the Dutch would bring the downfall of the Chinese, and shipped the man over for a meeting with local dignitaries, where he paid him to trot out some of his more European-friendly prophecies.

One reason for the confusion was Captain China's reluctance to admit the truth – that hell would freeze over before the government he falsely claimed to represent would allow the Dutch any trade privileges. Actually telling the Dutch this would be counterproductive, and Reijersen was spun around in a series of false hopes, dead ends and futile negotiations. As is traditional in such dealings, he did not blame the captain, but the captain's interpreter, Nicholas Iquan, whom the captain had brought over from Hirado, presumably on account of his earlier friendship with Jacques Specx. Reijersen, however, was distinctly unimpressed with Iquan, writing in his journal, 'We have received a Chinese interpreter from Japan, who is little use to us at present.'[4]

His initial suspicions had been true, and the men he encountered off the coast of Taiwan were indeed pirates from the captain's trading organisation. However, so too were the occupants of the large warships patrolling the area around the Pescadores. Reijersen began what he believed to be negotiations with representatives of the Chinese government, only to find that he was dealing with Captain China, who had no official power in the government of China proper. By that time Reijersen had already been taken in by the same confidence trick that Iquan and the captain had been running on the English in Japan. The Dutch were encouraged to part with gifts and money for the captain 'as he has been so very helpful to us in everything, and in order to increase his partiality for us'.[5] Concrete results, however, were long in coming; the captain had business elsewhere, and every time he sailed off for Manila, Taiwan or Hirado, his carefully balanced deception would falter and fall apart.

The deadlock between the Dutch and Captain China's organisation stretched on for over a year, until news reached the captain that the game would shortly be up. Although he and Iquan had been repeatedly assuring the Dutch that the Chinese government was seriously considering their surly requests for trade, over on the mainland the government was stirred into a different kind of action. Far from preparing a welcoming committee, the Chinese were assembling a maritime force of 10,000 men in Fujian, with which they intended to wipe the Dutch off the face of the earth. This was also bad news for the captain, as the last thing he needed was for the provincial government to create a battalion devoted to policing southern waters – after the Dutch were chased from Chinese jurisdiction, the temptation would be too easy to turn on the smugglers who had been flouting the law for so long.

The Dutch had their first taste of the new hard-line policy on 18

November 1623, when a Commander Franszoon met with armed resistance off the coast of Amoy. For his part, he had been in 'peaceful negotiations' with a representative of the Chinese government, who had been bullied into talks after the Dutch had blockaded Amoy. The journals of the traders record Franszoon's polite but petulant attitude:

> We replied that our intentions had always been good and upright; and that although he thought we came to rob the Chinese and had brought neither money nor merchandise with us, this was entirely false, as our intention, now as ever, was simply to engage in peaceful trade – a request we first made twenty-three years ago.[6]

The Chinese appeared to finally agree to Franszoon's demands, and offered him some local beer in celebration. But as the Dutch spat out a brew that they rightly suspected to be poisoned, a flotilla of Chinese ships sneaked up on Franszoon's ships. The *Erasmus* fled for Taiwan after fighting off three fireships, but its sister ship the *Muyden* was less lucky. The ship erupted in a fireball from which no living creature could escape – the Dutch reported that it was 'blown up with man and mouse.'[7]

The Dutch could see that the Chinese were serious. The new military governor of Fujian, Nan Juyi, was keen to get rid of them once and for all, and informed the prefectural government that he was raising troops and buying warships. He arrived in the Pescadores on 28 May with a considerable army, and soon had the Dutch boxed inside one of their forts, surrounded by the sea on three sides. The Dutch physically dug away the landward side to create a moat, trusting to their ships to keep the channel defended and keep them supplied with fresh water.

Panic was setting in. Inside the fort there were a number of Chinese guests and hostages, and the Dutch began to fear an internal uprising. They eventually sent most of the Chinese occupants away, though Iquan seems to have remained with them, as he is likely to have been the interpreter who accompanied the Dutch to negotiate a surrender on 2 July.[8] However, the Chinese were not open to negotiations, and pressed on in their attacks on the fortress.

After a succession of failures in his dealings with the Chinese, and still smarting from the embarrassment of the attack on Macao, Reijersen was relieved by Martin Sonk, who arrived from Batavia on the *Zeelandia* on 1 August 1624, in the middle of a Chinese assault on the fort. The Dutch had only 873 fighting men, and another 118 non-combatant boys, while the Chinese forces comprised 10,000 men and 200 ships.

Sonk was aghast, but was ready to blame his own countrymen, not Captain China, for the parlous state of affairs. Sonk was arriving from Batavia, where letters and personal recommendations from the newly returned Jacques Specx had already endeared Captain China to him. Even as the Dutch began a new regime with a new leader in the area, Captain China already had another unrealistically hopeful supporter, and Sonk immediately dispatched a message to the Chinese, suggesting that they call a truce until the captain could arrive from Taiwan.[9] Negotiations always seemed to go better when the captain was around, chiefly because he told both sides whatever they wanted to hear.

By this time, the Dutch had been clinging on to the Pescadores for almost two years. They had discovered that the soil was very poor, and that the islands were dry and waterless for most of the year, until the summer months, when 35 inches of rain would pour from the sky in just a few weeks.

Arriving as promised on 17 August, Captain China reiterated his suggestion that the Dutch relocate to Taiwan. To many fearful government officials in China, the extra thirty miles made a world of difference. Taiwan was beyond the horizon, technically 'out of reach' of everyday shipping, and out of sight was out of mind. The Dutch departed in the company of Iquan, while the captain returned to China with the leader of the Chinese forces, there to report a resounding victory scored against the invading barbarians. Chinese history is crowded with commanders who report a tactical withdrawal as a full victory, only to discover that the respite from trouble has been merely temporary. To this day, the temple of the sea goddess Matsu on the islands commemorates the Chinese 'victory'.[10]

Despite the departing Reijersen's obvious dissatisfaction with him as an interpreter, Nicholas Iquan somehow managed to stay with the Dutch, charming his way into Sonk's inner circle, and becoming the prime adviser for the Dutch migration. He already knew Taiwan well from his numerous visits there with Captain China's organisation, which had recently extended beyond simple trading missions to ventures of a more wide-ranging nature.

Unknown to the Dutch, the Chinese mainland was spiralling ever further into anarchy, as the Emperor's grip on power was undermined by financial crises, internal rebellions and the continued presence of the Manchus in the north. The Emperor of Heavenly Enlightenment, who had come to the throne in 1621 aged only fifteen, was an illiterate wastrel who preferred to lose himself in carpentry. He left the country in the hands of a eunuch associate of his mother, who instituted a reign of terror that led many Chinese to believe the Ming dynasty had already lost the mandate of heaven. As conditions began to worsen, many Chinese in the south sought to flee ahead of the approaching storm. In Fujian and other coastal regions, the most obvious course of action involved somehow quitting China entirely, and booking passage across the unknown sea. Captain China's fleet had for some time been offering such would-be refugees the escape route they desired, in numbers that the Dutch were to find surprisingly large.

So it was that when the small Dutch fleet returned to the little bay they had previously scouted in south Taiwan, they found that the local population had swelled massively. Instead of a few scattered huts, populated by suspicious natives, the area now boasted a population of over 25,000 men, accompanied by lesser numbers of women and children. In addition to trade and low-level manufacturing, Captain China's impromptu colonists had tamed the land, and were now farming surplus quantities of rice and sugar that formed a separate export industry in their own right.

The Dutch could not believe their luck. After years of surly and unproductive dealings with the Chinese, they met with an enthusiastic welcome from thousands of eager traders and customers. China proper might be 100 miles to the west, but in Taiwan there was silk and trade aplenty. There was more good news to come – shortly after Reijersen left for Batavia, Martin Sonk received a communiqué from an Amoy official, announcing that Captain China had been successful in his negotiations:

The captain in China has repeatedly represented that the fort in [the Pescadores] has been forsaken, and the place properly restored, from which we observe that you have been acting truthfully. We therefore assure ourselves of your friendship. The viceroy understands that the Dutch people, coming from distant lands, wish to trade with us . . . We have, accordingly, decided . . . to place ourselves in a relation of friendship to you.[11]

Considering the hostility and mistrust on both sides, and the history of double-dealings, the news seemed too good to be true. The Dutch were able to report to Batavia that they had secured some form of trade with China. In fact, this was misleading. Captain China had merely handed them a vague proclamation of interest from an official in Amoy, which was highly unlikely to be ratified by the authorities in Fujian because he had neglected to tell them about it. Far from receiving trading permissions from the Chinese government, the Dutch were now smugglers little different from the captain himself. Although Captain China had sailed from the Pescadores with the Chinese military, this seems to have been engineered merely to persuade the Dutch that he had the ear of the government. Far from consenting to the Dutch demands, the authorities on the mainland remained deeply distrustful of them and their ally. One official wrote of the captain:

At present he is in Amoy under a pretext of settling his private debts and performing religious rites for his ancestors. But the real aim of his coming is nothing of the sort. I believe he intends to purchase raw silk and goods in which our government prohibits us to trade, and to sell them to the Dutch, and moreover to assess the situation on the Dutch behalf. I am of the opinion that the government should take hold of him as a hostage and make him dispatch a letter to the Dutch, telling them not to disturb our coast.[12]

Military governor Nan Juyi not only saw through the captain's schemes, but placed no trust in the Dutch, and even suspected that the foreigners planned to ally with the Japanese in an invasion of China:

In my view, enemy movements are always treacherous . . . There is no use in exchanging official messages . . . Their intention of invading China by tempting the Japanese betrays itself in their constant preparation for sailing on the pretext of voyaging for Japan. Moreover, Li Dan chief of the pirates [i.e. Captain China], with Japanese men secretly taken in his ship, is acting as agent for their invasion into mainland China. It is so long since these cunning foreigners have established themselves along the coast. Their treacherous movements are repeated frequently and their rude acts continue. If left alone, their behaviour will certainly turn more and more atrocious. For this reason, it is advisable to order the officials of each district to investigate all the smugglers who had hitherto escaped punishment, and to control the evil-doers more strictly . . . to multiply defence power until our military forces are improved to a considerable extent, and then, as the opportunity offers itself, to strike and annihilate the Dutch.[13]

Nan Juyi's words mark him out as one of the most sensible men of his day, and a wise strategist who could see all angles. His fear of a Dutch–Japanese alliance was mere speculation, but not impossible considering the times and his enemies' past behaviour. Essentially, he was right – the Dutch *would* return to attack China, the problem would not go away until someone dealt with it, and Captain China's organisation was a local problem that the Chinese really ought to be addressing. He had every reason to fear a Japanese attack like the invasion of Korea a generation earlier, but had no way of knowing that Japan would not present a problem to China for decades. However, Nan Juyi's wise words were lost in the Chinese excitement.

It was a triumph of diplomacy for Captain China and Nicholas Iquan, chiefly because they were the true beneficiaries. Captain China's organisation now had strong and grateful foreign allies in the shape of the Dutch, and the undying gratitude of the mainland government, which was readily taking the credit for the Dutch departure. Meanwhile, the captain's Taiwan colony now had live-in foreign merchants who were happy to buy as much silk as the Chinese could supply. Captain China was able to increase the number of local sailings between Fujian and Taiwan, and leave the Dutch to make the more difficult and dangerous long-distance voyages from Taiwan to Batavia. But even Captain China had cause to be slightly uneasy with the situation. After all, the Dutch were traders, and no strangers to profits and balance sheets. After the initial elation wore off, they were sure to notice that the captain was still the gatekeeper to China itself. However cheaply the Dutch thought they were buying their commodities in Taiwan, the captain was still reaping a profitable percentage on the short hop from the mainland. It would only take a rival offer to undercut him, or a renewal of the Dutch desire to deal directly with the mainland, and the captain's carefully constructed scheme could so easily fall apart.

With renewed vigour and the consummate approval of Iquan, the Dutch began the construction of a fort just off the coast of Taiwan, naming it Zeelandia. The siting of the fort seems to have been greatly influenced by the Dutchmen's belief that they were finally out of trouble, as it demonstrates a supreme confidence that little in the region could threaten the Europeans.

A small archipelago of islets and sandbanks sheltered Tai Bay from the sea, and was accessible by a single, deeper channel that the Dutch called *Lakjemuyse*, or the Deer's Ear. The harbour was not quite as good as the one the Dutch had left behind on the Pescadores, and larger heavily laden vessels or warships would have to wait for a high tide before they could get in or out of the sheltered area.

The southernmost of the islets was a mile-long bank called Tayouan, so close to the shore at its southern tip that it was possible to wade across at low tide. At its northern end, where it was separated from the Taiwanese mainland by a gap of half a mile, the Dutch built their fortress. It seemed like a good idea at the time.

Though the Dutch had often been duped by the wily ways of Iquan and Captain China, the fatal decisions they took when building Fort Zeelandia were all their own. The key decision, that would cause them great difficulties in the event of an attack, was to site Zeelandia not in the best defensible position, but in the best location for loading and unloading cargoes of goods. Believing themselves safe from any attack from the mainland, their chief concern was the construction of a citadel which could shield them in the event of a native uprising – they fully intended to start taxing the local population, and would not be surprised by an occasional riot. Consequently, Zeelandia was originally built to resist nothing so threatening as a few people throwing rocks. It would not even stand up to a prolonged siege, as the water supply from its wells proved so brackish and inconsequential that fresh water had to be

Fort Zeelandia as seen from the north. The township is to the left (east) of the fort, while the redoubt of Utrecht can be discerned on a small hillock to the right. The spit of land that trails into the distance connects the islet to the Taiwanese mainland about a mile to the south, and forms the lagoon behind the fort. *(Courtesy of SMC Publishing Inc., Taipei)*

shipped in from Taiwan itself. It initially lacked an outer wall, such that a hypothetical attacking force could have literally waded across the base of Tayouan Island and walked up to it. If they had done so, the guns on the walls were mounted so high that they would have been unable to fire upon them. Eventually, the Dutch did build a wall across the island for extra defence, but did so out of the effective range of the guns in the fort itself. In order to provide additional cover, the Dutch were obliged to build a small round tower on nearby high ground. The Dutch named the little building Utrecht, after the town in Holland whose fort had once been successfully stormed by a group of women. Utrecht's guns had commanding coverage of the surrounding area, including the interior of Fort Zeelandia itself. If anyone wanted to take the castle, their best

48

option would be to take Utrecht and turn its guns on the main fort, since although Utrecht could fire on Zeelandia, Zeelandia could not fire on Utrecht. It was an unfortunate situation, but one that would be obvious only to those who dwelt within the walls of Zeelandia itself. The Dutch hoped nobody else would notice.

Still, none of this was Iquan's problem, and he continued in his dealings with the Dutch. Captain China's operation was flourishing under the Dutch umbrella, and the Taiwan trade was having a noticeable effect on other ports in Asia. Japanese records show that fully half of the captain's ships in Hirado were either leaving for Taiwan, or returning from there, leading to their appellation of 'the greatest smugglers in Formosa',[14] while agents of the captain were found delivering letters to Chinese communities as far afield as Batavia itself.

It was a time of great expansion for Captain China's smuggling empire, and Iquan's position in the organisation became ever stronger. Captain China leaned increasingly on Iquan and Yan Sixi, his man in Fujian. Some accounts claim that Yan and the captain were one and the same, but they rest much of their reasoning on the garbled over-use of the term 'China Captain' in European sources – the term was often applied to any headman in a given community of overseas Chinese, from Manila to Nagasaki. Matters are not helped by the family-oriented structure of the captain's organisation, which often led to reports of brothers, uncles and other relations whose ties were merely ceremonial. Like other organisations in other days, from religious cults to crime syndicates, the captain's organisation was run as a family, and many of the relatives discussed in contemporary accounts were figurative or adoptive. As Iquan became more successful, he gathered a set of lieutenants around him, including actual members of his family. The younger boys of the Zheng family were now adults too, and keen to leave their home town and enjoy the international success of their eldest sibling. Bao the Panther, Hu the Tiger and other members of Iquan's family began to gravitate towards Captain China's organisation.

Iquan also gained a few ceremonial relatives of his own. It was a common practice among traders-made-good to adopt the children of impoverished peasants, and raise them as future crew members. Many senior traders preferred to send their foster children on the more dangerous voyages, rather than risk their own flesh and blood.

Such men were treated as glorified slaves until they had proved themselves through long service; only then would they receive the true benefits of an adopted family member. One such adoptee was Zheng Tai, a surly, uncooperative foster-son of Iquan's who never gained the respect of the true relatives, and was once even listed in family records as 'that unthankful bastard'. Tai, however, would eventually rise to a position of prominence in the Zheng family and outlive many of his detractors.[15]

For now, the tension between the Dutch and Chinese had been defused, and the Taiwan trade was flourishing. However, the captain's 'organisation' was still a loose confederacy of lawless sailors. There was still some fence-mending to be done, most notably between Iquan and the senior lieutenant Yan Sixi. Yan was still the captain's chief man in Fujian, now forced to accept the sudden arrival of this new Taiwan operation close to his home base. Something would have to be done to ensure that the rival smugglers recognised each other as allies, and discussion turned once more to the matter of the Lady Yan, the nubile relative of the captain who was still in search of a worthy husband.

The Lady Yan was formally presented to Iquan as a prospective bride, and this time, Iquan agreed. The two were married in a lavish ceremony on the mainland that transformed Iquan from a newcomer to a cherished member of the captain's inner circle.

Iquan, however, had a secret. When he left Japan for the Pescadores in 1623 to become the interpreter, negotiator and agent for Captain China among the Europeans, he had left his lover Miss Tagawa behind in Hirado. She was pregnant with his child, and by the time of his marriage to the Lady Yan, Iquan was already a father.

3

THE MASTER OF THE SEAS

Tales of Nicholas Iquan recount a wily scoundrel, a pirate and sometime smuggler, a linguist of doubtful ability and a trader prepared to take risks. There are many stories about him, and they seem mostly plausible. They paint a picture of a lucky and charming man of relatively humble birth, who rose swiftly in a troubled society to a position of great power.

Tales of Iquan's eldest son are very different. As a reflection of Coxinga's later fame and achievements, they come accompanied by legends, prophecies and portents. The *Historical Novel* records a terrible storm that blew up in the days before his birth in August 1624: 'The dawning sky was black, the rain slashed like savage swords, the wind threw sand and stones. Waves fell upon the shore with the sound of drums, such that brave men feared the shaking of the ground.'[1]

Watchers on the shore supposedly saw a giant sea-creature rise from the ocean to dance atop the waves, its eyes glowing in the darkness – for the rest of his life, Coxinga would regard the whale as his guardian spirit, and recorded sightings of the giants as good omens.[2] In a fitful sleep, the pregnant Miss Tagawa dreamt that such a creature leapt from the sea and into her breast. She awoke and, the story goes, walked along the beach at Senrigahama, staring out to sea as the storm finally began to calm. Seized suddenly with birth pangs, she was unable to return to shelter and brought her son into the world alone on the shore, at a spot marked by a stone memorial to this day.[3]

As the child took its first breath, sailors from Captain China's organisation reported golden lights in the sky over Hirado, and the sound of celebrant drums in the air. They eagerly dispatched a message to Iquan, informing him that he was a father, and the proud parent's 'happiness was unsurpassed', not only at the birth, but also at the omens of future greatness that surrounded it.

In infancy, Coxinga was known as Fukumatsu, literally Lucky Pine, though the name is loaded with other meanings. To a Chinese reader, the two characters of the name combine the *Fu* of Fujian with the *Matsu* of Matsuura, the feudal family that ruled the Hirado area. Matsu could even have been a pun on the name of the goddess of the seas so revered by Iquan and his fellow sailors, divine patron of Fujian and Macao. In later centuries, legends linked Coxinga directly with her, claiming that while Miss Tagawa gave him life, his true mother was the goddess herself, who appeared in the spirit of the storm and the great whale on the morning of his birth, and who watched over his ships throughout his life.

The pine was also a symbol of longevity, and of loneliness, since a different kind of *matsu* was also the Japanese verb 'to wait'. If a pun was intended, then perhaps we can guess at which of the many possible readings of Miss Tagawa's first name is correct – *Fukumatsu* also means 'Fuku Waits', and wait she did.

Miss Tagawa and her son remained in Hirado, where their means of support are unknown – presumably either through occasional stipends from Iquan, or on the mercy of her stepfather. Though contemporary sources record that Iquan visited his former lover on occasion, he was occupied with the Taiwanese operation, and now had a prominent wife in Fujian who demanded more of his attention. In modern parlance, he was an absentee father.

Iquan's family was struck by bereavement in 1624, when news came of the death of his own father Shaozu. Although he had left home in disgrace years before, Iquan's filial obligations made him the new head of the household. Now a man of growing wealth and power in Captain China's organisation, he welcomed his relatives and siblings to his new quarters in Amoy, and soon put many of his brothers to work. A handful of his eldest siblings, Bao the Panther, Hu the Tiger and perhaps Peng the Roc, were already serving the captain along with Iquan. Contemporary records show a number of other relatives given probationary commands or shadowing established captains. Before long, Iquan had as many as seventeen 'brothers' scattered among the trading fleet. A list of ship's captains mentions fifteen animal nicknames among twenty-two commanders:

Hu the Tiger and *Yan the Swallow* in the first vanguard ship, *E the Osprey* and *Zhi the Leopard* in the second; *Biao the Tiger Cub* and Zhang Hong providing cover in the third; *Xie the Chimera* and Li Ming providing cover in the fourth; with *Jiao the Dragonet* and *E the Osprey* [the name is repeated] as support in the fifth; Tian Sheng and Gao Qing leading from the centre in the sixth, alternating with *Bao the Panther* and *Mao the Bear*; *Peng the Roc* and *Mang the Python* as escort in the seventh; *He the Crane* and Chen Zhongji as escort in the eighth; *Lin the Unicorn* and Chen Xun as mobile auxiliary in the ninth; *Qi the Giraffe* and Wu Huapeng supervising in the tenth.[4]

Also present as the leaders of marines were Feng the Phoenix and Luan the Mythical Bird. Since Iquan's father had at least three wives, it is not impossible that his siblings climbed into double figures, but more likely that many were cousins and adoptees rather than true brothers. With his marriage to Lady Yan, Iquan may have entered a frenzy of adoptions in order to keep his growing fleet crewed with loyal 'relatives'. As Iquan was the eldest son of Shaozu, and no older than twenty-three in 1626 when this battle formation took place, his true brothers would have been in their late teens or early twenties. Perhaps this explains why most seem to share their command with an older more experienced brother or sailor. Diminutive names like 'Tiger Cub' and 'Dragonet' imply that some may have been very young indeed.

Though there is no record of Iquan's sisters, it is likely that they existed in similar numbers, and found convenient matches made for them with a number of prominent captains. Iquan thereby secured a different kind of sway with many of the captain's lieutenants; his new-found allies in the organisation would help him hang on to his power as troubled times approached.

As the key liaison between the Dutch and Captain China, Iquan was party to decisions taken by both sides. He was also likely to have been one of the first to have spotted growing dissent among the Dutch. Although things had started well with the captain, the Dutch had soon tired of their self-appointed and deliberately unproductive liaison. Their base now secure, a number of the Dutch began to question Captain China's motives and trustworthiness. The traders of the Dutch East India Company were also under pressure to start turning a profit at last. Governor Coen sent stern missives from Batavia reminding them of the costliness of their venture. The attack on Macao, the skirmishes in the China Seas, and (most annoying for Coen) the construction, demolition and eventual abandonment of several forts in the Pescadores, had all eaten up funds. Now Sonk had relocated to Taiwan and built not one but two further forts, and Coen wanted to see some returns.[5]

Sonk's second-in-command, Gerrit de Witt, took the initiative and found himself a new supplier. He struck a deal with Xu Xinsu, a disenchanted former associate of the captain, who was prepared to offer cheaper prices on shipping silks and other commodities from the mainland. From garbled contemporary accounts, Xinsu's exact relationship to the captain is unclear, but they seem to have been close enough for the captain to bail Xinsu out of trouble in the past. This is certainly the impression given in a surviving letter from Iquan to his old friend Jacques Specx, which also alludes to growing debts in Captain China's organisation.[6] Was Xinsu a wayward son of the captain, either by birth or by clan adoption? Whatever his relationship, his dealings with the Dutch could not have come at a worse time.

The English had finally given up on the Japan trade, and shut down their factory. The Dutch were initially elated at the removal of their rivals, but unwisely tried to hurry their departure by agreeing to pay any outstanding debts. Cocks and his men were all to happy to agree, leaving the Dutch to discover that the English had run up debts of more than 70,000 taels. Among the monies owed to Japanese creditors like Lord Matsuura, there were numerous contracts with Captain China. A type of inflation was taking place among the smugglers of the China Seas, where promises to the English had been used as IOUs with the Chinese, who had agreed to hand them over to the Dutch.

The Dutch thus found themselves obliged to pay out, not only on their own unreliable agreements with the captain, but also on those that had been signed with him by their rivals. In theory, the captain was coining it in from all sides in the region. In practice, many of the people who owed him money had decided not to pay.

The captain's years of swindles were finally catching up with him. He had put all his resources behind the cash-cow of the Taiwan–Fujian trade, only to be undercut by his former associate Xu

Xinsu. Xinsu and the Dutch were ruining the captain's finances, and the captain could not bail himself out until the Dutch paid up the money they owed him. For their part, the Dutch no longer regarded the captain as a cherished ally, but a local nuisance.

Many of the captain's crews had only turned to smuggling because they had no other way to earn money for food, and the captain was responsible for literally hundreds of vessels. He was obliged to keep them all supplied, and now found himself borrowing and stealing money wherever he could.

The captain sensed that the Dutch were growing restless, and absconded from Taiwan with all the silks he could steal, several substantial bribes intended for the mainland, and a number of monetary 'gifts' from mainland officials, that he had neglected to hand over to the Dutch.

On 12 August 1625, the captain died in Hirado. Dutch accounts make no mention of foul play – it seems possible that the captain's long and adventurous life had reached a natural end. But the captain's organisation was already showing signs of strain, Xinsu was operating independently out of Fujian, Iquan was stuck with the increasingly unhappy Dutch, and the captain's son Augustin was trying to run a business of his own out of Hirado. The strongest candidate for holding the trading empire together was probably Yan Sixi, the Fujian-based trader who may have been Iquan's father-in-law, but Yan himself died barely a month after the captain.[7] We do not have the principal characters' own records of the events, merely those of third parties, who appear to watch with growing befuddlement and fear as the captain's underground collective turned on itself.

According to one account, Iquan was lucky enough to be in possession of two ships containing a valuable cargo at the time of the captain's death. Whereas other members of the organisation had little more than mounting debts and nervous crews, Iquan had the opportunity to convert goods into funds, and put them to use:

> as he was busy unloading and disposing of his merchandise, news was brought to him that his master and . . . the greatest part of those by whom he was employed were dead of the plague, which that year raged terribly in Japan, and followed after a famine, which had much afflicted and desolated the whole country . . .

Iquan therefore now forges a will for his master and the other merchants . . . and therein he declares himself sole heir for all the lading of those two vessels.[8]

After years of illegal but relatively peaceful operations, the captain's organisation was finished. A dozen of his former lieutenants were styling themselves the new leader, and it was a case of every man for himself. The perils of trading in local waters had reached new heights, with competing flotillas of increasingly daring and hungry pirates preying upon each other and passing shipping. Iquan decided to make the best of his recent contacts and experience, and used his stolen money to buy up more ships and crews of his own. He then offered his services to the Dutch, no longer as an interpreter and trade emissary, but as a privateer. Flying the Dutch flag, he went in search of Chinese ships bound for the Spanish colony in Manila, relieving them of their cargoes and treasures, and splitting his spoils with the Dutch on Taiwan. Iquan not only had the support of the Dutch, but the immeasurable benefit of European crewmembers and European technology. His time as a privateer in Dutch service gave him invaluable experience of the operations of a modern warship, 'and now he had made himself Commander-in-Chief of such a Squadron might make the Mandarins of China have no great mind to come and call him to accompt'.[9] By October 1625, Iquan had risen greatly in the estimations of the Dutch. Gerrit de Witt, now governor of Taiwan after the death of Sonk, wrote: 'Here we are from day to day expecting the man named Iquan, who once served Commander Reijersen as interpreter, to arrive leading twenty or thirty junks, which are reported to pillage the tribute ships or transports the Chinese send up to the north.'[10]

Piracy was proving to be good business for Iquan. In 1626, he presented the Dutch with nine ships carrying porcelain and produce worth 28,000 taels, and in 1627 he seized his chance to grab the profitable Fujian–Taiwan route. For a couple of years, it had lain in the hands of his former associate Xinsu, with whom Iquan had struck an uneasy deal. The rival sea captains had agreed to stay out of each other's way, whereas the Chinese government would have much preferred that they annihilated each other in a dispute over territory. To their crews, they were honest traders and privateers, striving to eke a living from the coastal waters of a troubled country. To the Chinese government, they were no better than pirates and smugglers, a stigma that both Iquan and Xinsu would prefer to shake off. Iquan's chance came in 1627, when he was approached by an agent of the Chinese government, bearing a secret letter whose seal bore the authority of the Emperor of Lofty Omens himself. The agent was Cai Shanzhi, the same official who Iquan had hit with a rock in his childhood. The letter offered him a deal, explaining that:

> being informed of his valour, the [Emperor] was desirous to make use of his services in an affair of high importance to the good and welfare of his state, and therefore offered Iquan a general pardon and indemnity for all that was past . . . And that he would not only receive him into grace, but make him High Admiral or Captain General of all the sea coasts, give him the office of Great Mandarin, and abundantly shower upon him favours and rewards.[11]

The services required of Iquan were very simple – he was commanded 'with all speed to attack the other pirate, who disputed his sovereignty over the seas'. Of course, Xinsu had received an almost identical letter, merely with the names changed, and the Chinese government sat back excitedly to watch the coming war unfold, hoping that the two fleets would destroy each other, or at least cause each other so much damage that the weaker government forces would be able to mop up. In fact, it is even possible that the two pirates received *each other's* letters by mistake, as one Japanese source reports that: 'The Ming authorities gravely issued orders to Tei Shiryu [i.e. Iquan] to capture the notorious pirate Tei Ikkwan [i.e. Iquan], to which he as gravely replied that he would endeavour to comply!'[12] Iquan had no intention of capturing himself and handing himself over to the authorities, but he appreciated the spirit, if not the letter of his orders.

Iquan did not immediately sail against Xinsu, owing to a dispute with his brother, Hu the Tiger.[13] Hu and Iquan seem to represent rival factions within their family – Iquan was keen to attain recognition and respect with the Chinese, while Hu preferred to stay friendly with the Dutch, perhaps already realising that Iquan's official appointment as a naval chief would inevitably lead to a day when he was ordered to wage war on the unwelcome foreigners. The brothers quarrelled incessantly, but Iquan gained a grudging assent from Hu after several months.

He sailed with his fleet for the port of Amoy, in numbers impressive enough to make the garrison commander Yu Zigao, former liberator of the Pescadores, flee the town. But Iquan stayed away from Amoy itself, and merely attacked Xinsu, while a number of Dutch ships looked on and waited to congratulate the victor, whoever he might be.

The battle that followed led to the death of Xinsu. The chronicler Father Palafox, never one to resist a good story, writes that Iquan himself saved the day: 'the courage and conduct of Iquan quickly gained him the victory; which he secured by leaping into his enemy's ship and with his own hand killing him, and cutting off his head'.[14]

Xinsu's death caused the survivors among his fleet to proclaim their allegiance to Iquan, increasing the size of his command still further, and putting the Chinese in the embarrassing position of having to honour their former promise. While local officials prevaricated and tried to attach appendices to the original deal, Iquan's men grew increasingly restless. He had upheld his part of the bargain, and now expected to be pardoned, and given an official title. The authorities, however, began to suspect they had created a monster – there was now literally nobody in the region who could oppose Iquan. As Palafox observed, ignorant of local folklore: 'Thus he became master of all the seas upon the coast of China.'[15]

One local official (in fact, the composer of the infamous 'Ode to the Potato') wrote to Iquan in an attempt to persuade him to disband some of his forces:

All your feelings are well known . . . You do repent of your behaviour; you do not want to murder and plunder the people of the countryside. All people know this. But of [your] more than ten thousand followers, why don't they understand your feelings? Some of them just want to fill their mouths and warm their bodies, others are fortune seekers . . . Now that you have so many followers like this, all of them being poor or bad people, runaway soldiers or criminals, they behave obsequiously towards you and become your followers, and make you 'The Great King of the Sea.' You also enjoy having this reputation, and like to live up to it.[16]

After weeks of filibustering, others intervened, including the local official Huang Menglong – he was in the advantageous position of being both a respected graduate and Iquan's maternal uncle. Iquan ceremonially surrendered to the Amoy authorities, and 'promised that his men would no longer cause clamor, and would be progressively dispersed'.[17] Accordingly, the governor of Fujian appointed Iquan as a probationary officer, charged with suppressing the region's pirate problem. In other words, he had the government seal of approval to wage war on the surviving renegades who had yet to acknowledge him as the true successor to Captain China. By the beginning of 1628, he was granted the imperial rank of patrolling admiral.[18]

Iquan's appointment, while it had a certain cachet, was also a sign of increasing desperation on the part of the Ming government. The new Emperor of Lofty Omens, younger brother to the incompetent Emperor of Heavenly Enlightenment, had inherited a land in chaos, scattered with peasant uprisings and troops in revolt. Many were bought off with pardons and government commissions, as a means of wiping the slate clean for a new reign. Others were suppressed with the appointment of anti-rebel leaders. It would seem that Iquan's appointment was a little of both.

But the new Emperor's troubles were only beginning. Shortly after Iquan accepted his new title, all of China was struck by a terrible drought, which in turn destroyed the crops and created a famine so great that reports even reached the cities of people in the countryside turning to cannibalism.[19] Though Iquan was a wealthy man in a powerful position, he attained government office at a time when many others were turning to crime out of desperation. Though he continued to ship people by the thousand out of the dying lands and across the straits to a new life in Taiwan, the less fortunate struggled to find food to eat. There would soon be more criminals, and more pirates.

Meanwhile, there had been another change of governor over on Taiwan. Sonk's former lieutenant, de Witt, who had struck the original deal with Xinsu, was recalled and replaced by Pieter Nuijts, a young and arrogant man whose tenure would prove to be an unmitigated disaster. One Dutch source calls him a *present-kaasje*,[20] or 'unwelcome gift of cheese', a euphemism for that particular breed of young men of good family, whose swift departure from their home country was somehow deemed advisable, with a foreign posting obtained through string-pulling by their well-connected relatives. With no experience and little diplomatic tact, Nuijts was mystifyingly given the dual role of Taiwan governor and ambassador to Japan. A married man who sailed with his young son, he was scandalised to find a number of Dutch merchants living in sin with local women. Frustrated in his communications with the Japanese and Chinese, he wrote bitter epistles back to Batavia about the lack of decent interpreters, prefacing some reports with disclaimers that he could only guess at the true meaning of some of the meetings he had.

Nuijts also arrived in the midst of increasing troubles in Taiwan between the Dutch and the Japanese. When the Dutch fleet first arrived on the island, Cornelis Reijersen had promised the Japanese that they would not be subject to any levies on their trade or docking, a promise that Sonk had revoked under pressure from Batavia to turn a profit. As one observer put it:

> The Japanese, however, had the impudence to ignore our Governor as lord of the land, stating that they were in no wise subject to him, and had nothing to do with him. Accordingly, when Mr Sonk sent notice of this to Batavia, he was distinctly ordered by Their Excellencies to claim and exercise supreme power . . . without fearing anyone or apologising; and to inform the Japanese that, if they were inclined to trade there, they must pay the same taxes and duties as others.[21]

The Japanese were particularly angered by the levy because they had no choice but to go to Taiwan. Following acts of piracy and theft on the mainland, they were forbidden from going to China in much the same way as the Europeans. If they wanted Chinese silk, they had to get it in Taiwan or the Pescadores, or rely on the Dutch and Chinese to transport it for them.

Nuijts first had a taste of the extent of the problem when he arrived in Japan in 1627, fully expecting an audience with the shogun, in which he intended to demand official Japanese acknowledgement of the Dutch rights to the island of Taiwan. Instead, he was kept waiting for five weeks, and then told to leave without ever getting his meeting. Meanwhile, the new chief trading official of Nagasaki, a Christian apostate by the name of Suetsugu Heizo,[22] was also annoyed at the behaviour of the Dutch on Taiwan, and ordered Hamada Yahei, one of his sea captains, to do something about it. Hamada sailed to Taiwan and rounded up seventeen mystified local tribesmen, bringing them to Nagasaki, from whence they were transported all the way to the shogun's court in Edo. There, though they spoke no Japanese and appeared to have little clue what was being said on their behalf, they were presented to the shogun as an official delegation from Taiwan, seeking Japanese protection from the predations of the Dutch. Meanwhile, Suetsugu began telling local merchants that the Dutch were shortly to be exiled from Japan, causing a number of their Japanese creditors to freeze much needed loans. Nuijts was apoplectic with rage, and called the Japanese 'uncouth, insolent and arrogant'.[23] Understandably, this outburst achieved little, and although the shogun appears not to have been taken in by Suetsugu's deception, Nuijts was still forced to sign an agreement in which he promised never to interfere with the Japanese in Taiwan again.

Nuijts also did a thoroughly good job of alienating van Nijenroode, the senior Dutch merchant in Hirado, making snide comments about his family arrangements (he had two Japanese lovers) and a series of unhelpful suggestions about how he might improve his business. At the time, Nuijts had been in the Far East for barely four months, as compared to the chief merchant's eight years.

Having successfully made nothing but enemies in Japan, Nuijts sailed for Taiwan, where he arrived in the midst of Chinese panic over Nicholas Iquan's new found power. Perhaps hoping that things could only get better, anonymous Chinese officials tried the same swindle on the Dutch as they had with Iquan, suggesting they 'put down the pirate Iquan; in return for which . . . the Dutch should certainly obtain permission to trade'.[24]

The departing governor, Gerrit de Witt, former supporter of Xinsu and presumed enemy of Iquan, told Nuijts he intended to deal with Iquan on his way back to Batavia, leaving with a small fleet of five ships. This is rather a bold statement for de Witt to make, particularly since his immediate boss in Batavia assessed Iquan's fleet at 'almost 400 junks and 60,000 to 70,000 men'. It is difficult to see what made de Witt think five ships would be enough to take on such a foe. Perhaps he was planning on targeting Iquan himself, and running for cover to leave Nuijts to deal with the aftermath.[25]

Whatever his master plan, he sailed safely until he reached the coast of China, whereupon he attacked one of Iquan's vessels. Facing open hostility from his former allies, Iquan's retaliation was swift and crushing. De Witt's forces fled the area in panic, and Iquan ordered his ships to avenge themselves on the Dutch. Damaged vessels occasionally limped into the Dutch base on Taiwan, conveying tales of the carnage to an embittered Nuijts, who now found himself with a tiny garrison and heavy losses. For a few brief days, he found himself in command of a fort with absolutely no naval support at all, and was forced to watch nervously from the battlements, praying that Iquan would not think to take the fight across the straits to Taiwan itself. As Nuijts pointedly wrote to van Nijenroode in Hirado: 'God be praised that the enemy did not put in an appearance at that time, or verily they would have captured this place without resistance'.[26] It would seem that the Dutch had rather underestimated the size of Iquan's forces. De Witt's flotilla of five stood little chance against the Master of the Seas – 'having over a thousand junks with him, he injured us in every possible way'.[27]

Just when Nuijts thought things could not get any worse, several unwelcome vessels arrived at Fort Zeelandia – a Japanese flotilla returning the 'delegation' of Taiwanese natives from their trip to Japan. The new arrivals comprised 470 Japanese men, effectively outnumbering the Dutch at the settlement. Worse still, they were commanded by Hamada Yahei, the man who had so embarrassed Nuijts in Japan.

The Dutch decided to tough it out, but even as Hamada came into port, his behaviour was notably hostile. Nuijts noted that he called out 'proposals of a most insulting kind, and also acted in a very suspicious way'.[28] Hoping that the Japanese would not notice the low strength of the Zeelandia garrison, Nuijts ordered his men to search the Japanese ships. They were grudgingly permitted onboard, where they found the merchantmen armed with six large cannon, and nine more concealed below decks with the ballast. Several Chinese passengers, who had arrived with Hamada's flotilla, hinted to the Dutch that the Japanese were up to something, and the Dutch continued their search, uncovering 'quantities of swords, guns, pikes, soap-knives, arrows, bows and other articles'.[29]

Eventually, the irate Hamada came ashore to complain about the treatment he was receiving, but Nuijts was ready for a replay of their previous meeting in Japan:

> after listening to his harangue about the examination of the junks, I answered that although such a thing had never happened before, nor had been practised under commander de Witt – who governed according to his own ideas – the governorship of that honoured gentleman had expired, but now I was here and my orders must be obeyed . . . and that he need not be astonished at this, as his own outrageous proposals had given double cause for it.[30]

Nuijts confronted Hamada with an inventory of all the weapons his men had found on the Japanese boats, and, after some embarrassment, Hamada claimed that the concealed cannon and other articles were for self-defence on the voyage.

There was nothing Nuijts liked better than scoring points: 'I replied that the danger was past now, and then when he departed everything would be restored to him.'[31] Hamada lost his temper and taunted Nuijts with his recollections of the ill-fated embassy to the shogun, stating outright that it was thanks to him that the Dutch had been made to look such fools. Hamada went on with the insults for some time, but Nuijts does not repeat them all in his letters, preferring to draw a veil over the proceedings: 'Many other blasphemous and contradictory proposals did he make, too devilish for me to attempt to send to Your Honour.'[32]

Hamada's ships stayed at Zeelandia for two or three weeks, where Nuijts refused them permission to leave, restock, or head out to the mainland in search of silk. Hamada's deception and attitude had stung Nuijts's considerable pride, and the situation in the China seas with Iquan had only made him even more irascible than usual. In fact, the Japanese were no friends of Iquan, having lost several cargoes to his privateers, but it seems that the two groups had little time to bond over their mutual hatred of the Master of the Seas. They were too busy insulting each other.

Hamada and Nuijts were well-matched antagonists, and each persisted in taunting his rival. Hamada spent several days outlining ways he could make life difficult for the Europeans in Japan, while Nuijts made a show of going through Hamada's Japanese sailing licence, pointing out the ways in which Hamada had already contravened its limits. Eventually, however, Hamada mellowed, and asked to be allowed to sail for the Pescadores. When Nuijts laughed off that obviously misleading request, Hamada simply begged to be allowed to return to Japan. This request was also refused; engineering such a return would presumably require an escort, and Nuijts was unable to admit that he did not have the ships to spare after his altercation with Iquan.

The impasse, the misunderstanding and Nuijts's obvious jumpiness were to lead to an unexpected reaction. Hamada's men began to fear for their lives – if a Japanese host had behaved in such a manner, his guests would suspect the worst. 'These people had a firm belief that they would never be allowed to depart, but be given over to perish here of hunger and distress.'[33]

On 29 June 1628, Hamada took matters into his own hands. With a number of his men, he went to Nuijts's residence and announced that he intended to leave, and that he was coming to say farewell. Nuijts again refused to allow them to sail, and an anonymous report of the incident pointedly records that he did so 'politely'.[34] The Japanese 'boldly' repeated their request. When Nuijts repeated his refusal, 'they flew upon him like roaring lions, took him by the head, bound his hands, feet, and waist with a long cloth band, and threatened to cut off his head if he called out'.

Guards outside heard the sounds of the struggle, but found themselves set upon by a different group of Hamada's sailors, who had been loitering nearby. In the scuffle that followed, several men on both sides were killed and wounded, and one of Nuijts's lieutenants ordered his men to take what shots they could at Nuijts's captors if they appeared in the windows of their barricaded room. Nuijts, however, called on his men to cease fire, announcing that he was a hostage of the Japanese, and that they had threatened to kill him if the gunmen did not withdraw.

An uneasy silence settled over Fort Zeelandia, with its commander held captive in his own rooms, and his men surrounding the quarters but unable to act. Meanwhile, more of Hamada's men gathered outside the fort, leading the Europeans to suspect that they were planning on organising a revolt among the Chinese and native Formosans.

During the negotiations that followed, the Dutch threatened to storm Nuijts's quarters, and Nuijts publicly urged them to wait, to prevent any harm coming to him or to his son Lourents, who was another hostage. However, Nuijts also smuggled a second covert message out, instructing his men to attack the following day if they saw him make a successful escape by jumping from his window. No mention is made of how he expected to transport his son.

As time wore on, Nuijts realised that such a daring escape was never going to work, and he was forced to listen to the demands of his captors. Surrounded by men armed with guns in the middle of an enemy fort, the Japanese had realised that whether they killed their hostages or not, they would have considerable difficulty fighting their way out. Accordingly, they demanded safe passage, with five hostages to accompany them all the way to Japan. As security, they offered five hostages of their own, including Hamada's own son, who would accompany the departing Japanese vessels to Nagasaki, where both sets of hostages would be freed.[33] Since they still had the upper hand, and Nuijts was clearly feeling cooperative, they also demanded that the Dutch disable their remaining ships by taking the rudders ashore, in order to give the departing Japanese a head start.

While they were at it, they demanded a large quantity (15 *piculs*) of silk, claiming that the late Governor Sonk had confiscated a similar quantity from Japanese vessels some time before. And since the Dutch were feeling so generous, the Japanese also took a further 200 piculs, claiming that they had sent money to China to purchase that amount, but that the shipment had mysteriously disappeared. Both Dutch and Japanese sides agreed that the money had probably been appropriated by their mutual rival Iquan, but the Japanese were in a position to make demands, and were determined to lift whatever they could.

By luck or calculation, the Japanese had demanded quantities that cleared out the Dutch warehouses of silk, and Nuijts's associates were forced to make up the rest of the amount with money and cheques. Dutch accountants estimated the overall loss as 13,540 taels; Captain China had taken several years to purloin a similar amount, but the Japanese had managed it in just five days. On their way out, they even pocketed the cutlery. In his sheepish report to Batavia, Nuijts complained that the departing Japanese had ransacked his office, and taken for themselves a gold chain, a silver oil can, a salt cellar, three plates, and two sets of knives and forks.

The Japanese ships left Taiwan in triumph, tailed by the aging Dutch vessel *Erasmus*, a veteran of numerous battles in the China seas. When the bizarre flotilla reached Nagasaki, the crew of the *Erasmus* immediately released their Japanese captives as agreed, but the Dutch hostages were not so lucky. Not only were they thrown in jail, but the ship that brought them was also impounded and its crew imprisoned. The *Erasmus* was stripped of anything that was not nailed down, her mast was dismantled and she was beached in a 'dry dock' that was little more than a ditch. There, she was left to rot, eventually to be sold for scrap.[36] Over the following months, other Dutch ships arriving in Japan from Siam and Taiwan were also impounded, and the after-effects of the incident would be felt for several years.

The experience may have been intensely embarrassing for Nuijts, but it was also an inspiration. He did his best to make light of the disaster in letters to acquaintances in Japan, Batavia and the Netherlands, and hoped in vain that there would be no repercussions or enquiries. Having seen how much pressure a hostage situation could bring to bear on diplomatic wrangles, he decided to give the method a try himself, and found help from an entirely unexpected source.

Turning his attentions to his stand-off with Nicholas Iquan, Nuijts flattered the former smuggler with a series of flowery letters and embassies, and promised him that his governorship would have a more friendly character than that of the hostile de Witt. When ships from both Iquan's and Nuijts's fleet found themselves sharing a port in Amoy, Iquan was invited over for a courtesy call, at which point Nuijts seized him and held him prisoner. Iquan was not permitted to leave until he agreed to a three-year treaty, in which he essentially undertook to duplicate the arrangement that the departed Xinsu had with the Dutch. This restored the trading situation in the straits to the conditions around the time of the death of Captain China – with the Dutch ships permitted to sail in the waters without fear of attack from Iquan, and Iquan's agreement to be the Europeans' point of contact with the mainland. Iquan later wrote to his old friend Jacques Specx in Batavia, complaining about the behaviour of Specx's underlings, and noting that 'the Governor moreover . . . took my brother hostage'.[37]

However, there is more to this event than meets the eye. As

previous events had amply demonstrated, Iquan was not a stupid man. What on earth could have possessed him, after open hostilities on the China seas, to simply walk aboard a Dutch ship and agree to such a deal? His hard won legitimacy in the eyes of the mainland was now under threat, as he was effectively a double agent, trading with the very Europeans whom he might be called upon to fight. Now his own brother was a hostage in Taiwan, held prisoner by Nuijts at Fort Zeelandia, as insurance against any attempt to go back on the deal. Or at least, that was Iquan's view of the situation. Nuijts, on the other hand, seemed to be a most generous jailer, with a remarkably hospitable attitude towards Hu the Tiger. Hu was a prisoner in name only, as it would appear that the brief capture of Iquan was, if not Hu's idea, then a plan in which he was readily cooperating.

A surviving letter Nuijts sent to his bosses in the Netherlands reveals an unexpected mastermind behind the scenes: 'A certain lady whom I have never met (she had been married to Iquan's father) asked me in several letters to adopt her youngest son . . . as is very customary among the Chinese'.[38] If Nuijts is to be believed (and there is no reason why he would lie in a letter the Chinese would never see) Iquan's own mother, loyal to her Huang family trading roots, had initiated the deception to keep the profitable Dutch trade flowing into the family's warehouses in Amoy. Now her son Hu was safely ensconced with the Dutch on Taiwan, and indeed the adopted son of the governor, while the wayward Iquan was forced by family obligations to stay friendly with the Dutch, at least until 1631. The motivations may not merely have been financial – Iquan had caused her much grief in his youth, and she would not be the last Zheng family wife to hold a grudge. Hu the Tiger was clearly a popular and charismatic figure with the crews of the ships, and she may have been grooming her favourite to take over the family business.

However, within a few weeks, Iquan's family was forced to pull together to deal with a new threat. Iquan was ashore in his new capacity as a government official, meeting with the governor of Fujian to discuss his latest achievements in dealing with the region's 'pirate problem'. A number of Captain China's former lieutenants had been brought to heel, but Iquan's own standing with his fleet had suffered considerably after the hostage incident. A captain called Li Kuiqi, one of Iquan's highest ranking commanders, suspected that Iquan was planning on handing him over to the authorities as the latest pirate arrest, and absconded with much of Iquan's fleet. Iquan was left in his home region of Anhai with almost nothing, and rounded up a pitiful fleet of fifty ships, crewed by the fishermen who had lent them to him, with a few hundred more fishermen handed weapons and told to act like soldiers.[39] With this tiny force, Iquan put to sea and faced a well-armed enemy fleet three times the size.

Much to the surprise of outside observers, Li Kuiqi ordered his ships away from the approaching fishing boats. Iquan could be so bold because he was relying on his many relatives; Li Kuiqi may have assumed command, but Iquan had dozens of brothers, cousins, in-laws and allies scattered throughout Li Kuiqi's fleet. Iquan knew he could count on them to support him at the crucial moment, and Li Kuiqi knew it too.

For Li Kuiqi, there was only one answer. He picked out every one of Iquan's relatives and associates in the fleet, and executed them in a massacre off the coast of Tongshan. It was a desperate measure, but to many it was a sure sign that the power of Iquan's family was finished.

Iquan's imperial masters on the mainland did not officially disown him, but waited to see the outcome. There was no love lost between them, and it is highly likely that they planned on offering Li Kuiqi the same admiral's commission they had given Iquan. In fact, some Dutch accounts of the period already assumed they had. But the government forces were wise to hedge their bets, because Iquan was eventually able to fight back. Although he was forced initially to retreat from Amoy, he maintained his force of fishermen, and strengthened his fleet by levying a massive tax on incoming and outgoing shipping. Dissent began to grow among Li Kuiqi's officers over the months that followed until one of them broke ranks.

Iquan knew that he had found a new secret ally in Li Kuiqi's fleet, a disenchanted Cantonese captain who was prepared to switch sides at the right moment. He also called in a favour with an old friend. Jacques Specx, who Iquan had first met a decade earlier in Japan, had done very well for himself. In September 1629, Specx had become the Governor General at Batavia, responsible for all Dutch activity in the Far East. Dutch activities were now under the supervision of Iquan's old drinking companion, and a man who would have taken great pleasure in reversing the decisions of his predecessor.[40]

Specx's brief tenure in Batavia saw a number of scores settled. Coen's orders had already gone out, ordering the incompetent Pieter Nuijts home, and replacing him with a more trusty leader on Taiwan. Specx's reign also oversaw yet another reversal in Dutch policy towards Iquan. The open antagonism of previous years was briefly replaced by friendship once more, and a number of Dutch ships were sent to assist Iquan in his struggle against Li Kuiqi.[41]

It took a long year of deals, espionage and desperation, but Iquan was finally ready in February 1630. The patrolling admiral drew up his fleet of fishing-boats alongside the heavy guns of his Dutch allies, and was joined by an entire wing of Li Kuiqi's fleet, led by his turncoat Cantonese ally. The combined force was enough to destroy Li Kuiqi, and Iquan was Master of the Seas once more.

The Chinese on shore were quick to thank their admiral, assuring him that they never doubted him for a moment. They congratulated him on finally dealing with the pirates, and proudly announced that he was to be promoted. Initial elation soon soured when Iquan's family realised what had happened. The patrolling admiral was being sent inland, away from his power base, to deal with an uprising in the mountains.[42]

Iquan had high hopes that his sojourn in the hinterland would be short-lived. He reluctantly left his marine operations under control of his mother and eldest brothers, and sent a relative to Batavia with a letter for Jacques Specx. In it, Iquan urged his old friend to remain on good terms with his family, and expressed his sincere wish that his family would not act in such a way as to damage the new found alliance of the Dutch and Chinese.[43] However, Specx's tenure lasted just long enough to help Iquan deal with Li Kuiqi. By the time Iquan's letter arrived in Batavia, Specx was already making preparations to return home, and his successor would not be so friendly.

4

THE HEIR OF ANHAI

Though few of the Chinese knew or cared, there was further trouble brewing in Japan. The Shogun Iemitsu, who had officially held power since 1623, was finally beginning to exert his own authority as his 'retired' father Hidetada succumbed to old age. Christianity in Japan was under increasing pressure, and reports of martyrdoms and *putschs* were on the rise. Every time there was an uprising or a peasant protest, the presence of Christians among the plaintiffs led to further debates on the risks of dealing with the outside world. Japan was slowly closing itself off; sailing licences were harder to obtain, and foreigners were regarded with increasing suspicion. For the Dutch in Hirado, times were particularly hard, as their vessels and property were still impounded in the aftermath of the Pieter Nuijts affair of 1628. The good ship *Erasmus* was now a rotting hulk, while others stood at anchor in the bay, dismasted and uncrewed. The hostages handed over to Hamada Yahei were still locked away. Some, including Nuijts's son Lourents, had already died of dysentery and neglect. The Dutch chief of trade, Cornelis van Nijenroode, was a broken man. In his youth, he had been a dashing, confident captain, who had accompanied the hapless Reijersen on his ill-fated assault on Macao – 'he preferred to follow his own ideas, and took no pleasure in prayers'.[1] Now, he was a sickly, housebound alcoholic, gambling, like many of the other Dutch in Hirado, on a massive windfall in backdated pay when the Japanese restrictions were finally lifted – a diplomatic coup eventually achieved by agents of Jacques Specx.

One of the most critical decisions of Specx's short governorship was to give the Japanese what they wanted – Pieter Nuijts. The hapless former governor was dispatched to Japan to await the judgment of the shogun. The Japanese, perhaps realising what would *really* annoy Nuijts, simply kept him waiting for several years, and sent him back again without ever deigning to put him on trial. But the arrival of Nuijts led to a thaw in relations, and the Dutch were able to trade in Japan once more, although increasing restrictions dogged them throughout the 1630s.

The droughts and famines that had rocked China were also impacting on the Japanese. Times were increasingly hard in Hirado, and doubly so for a single mother like Miss Tagawa. Iquan's former lover seems to have finally given up waiting; in 1629, she gave birth to a second son, Shichizaemon.[2] Although many sources bend over backwards in attempts to prove that Iquan was the father, it is highly unlikely. All the evidence suggests that Miss Tagawa had found a new man closer to home.

With impeccably bad timing, Iquan's brother Yan the Swallow arrived in Japan on a Zheng trading vessel, bearing a letter.[3] Miss Tagawa, who was still nursing her new son, received him courteously. In the letter, Iquan informed her of his many successes, his imperial appointment and the great wealth amassed by his family. It was widely believed, and not without justification, that Iquan was the richest man in China. His wealth now surpassed that of a small kingdom, and some commentators even assumed he was the king of the Fujian region. The Chinese continued to refer to him as the Lord of the Straits, and, of course, the Master of the Seas. As further proof of his success, Iquan included a portrait of his new home, a great palace in Anhai, close to Amoy. The waiting was finally over; Iquan wanted Miss Tagawa to leave Japan and come to China.[4]

Miss Tagawa had new responsibilities, to her newborn son and possibly to his father, so she politely declined. She may also have been understandably unwilling to travel to a distant land only to occupy a subordinate position to Lady Yan, who remained as Iquan's principal wife.

A second letter soon arrived, borne by Iquan's brother E the Osprey. It somehow persuaded her that, while there was no place for her at Anhai, the opportunity was too great for her eldest son to ignore. The next time one of Iquan's ships left Hirado, Miss Tagawa put the seven-year-old Coxinga on it, and sent him to live with his father.

The separation and ten-day voyage was traumatic for Coxinga, who genuinely adored his half-brother, and wrote loving letters to him for the rest of his life. The separation from Miss Tagawa was also a great wrench for the boy. As the *Historical Novel* records, 'Every night he would face east and look to his mother, hiding his tears.'[5]

It was the last time he would be known by his original Japanese name of Lucky Pine. On landing in China, he was embraced by his father and addressed with a name he never knew he had – *Sen*, or Forest. His father exclaimed what a Big Tree his little son had become, and the nickname stuck.[6] He was also presented to a number of younger half-brothers of whose existence he was equally unaware; Iquan already had several children by his Chinese wife. Most impressive of all to the homesick seven-year-old was the sight of Anhai itself, a luxurious castle behind an outer wall that stretched in circumference for three miles. Within this enclosure, inner battlements encircled a beautiful garden, complete with fountains and fishponds, dotted with pavilions and tea-houses, themselves stocked with calligraphy, jade and golden artefacts. The gardens also included a small zoo, where Iquan and his family could admire exotic creatures; a likely reason for some of the more far-fetched animal nicknames found among Iquan's younger brothers. Coxinga had left a modest house in a Japanese port, but he had arrived in a palace.

He had a new home, new brothers, and was also given a new mother – he was assigned to a female relative of Iquan's Chinese wife. He was to stay at Anhai until he was fifteen, a formative period that saw his father's family fighting a succession of battles. Shortly after Coxinga arrived, Iquan received his new commission in the hinterland, and went into the mountains to suppress a rebel uprising in the emperor's name. Coxinga's father was absent again, but the boy found himself surrounded by the surviving uncles, swapping stories of great skirmishes at sea, and assuring the new arrival that his father was absent on important imperial business.

Coxinga never knew his father as a smuggler or pirate. He knew him as an admiral loyal to the Ming dynasty, ruler of an extensive domain, and diligent general against the enemies of the Dragon Throne. He was also a shrewd businessman. Iquan levied a 40 per cent tax on cargoes, and extorted protection money from all ships in the region. The only way to avoid attack by pirates was to fly the Zheng family flag, an article available for sale from Iquan's agents for a mere 3,000 pieces of gold. Before long, Iquan's coffers swelled even more, and every ship in south China appeared to be part of Iquan's fleet, with the character *Zheng* ('Serious') flying from the top of every mast.[7] Business was seriously good, leading one European observer to comment: 'The difference between his former being at sea, and his present, is only this, that now he robs with the King's flag.'[8]

Coxinga's family could also point to the Dutch ships permanently stationed off Anhai, and tell him of his father's troubled but productive relationship with the red-haired barbarians from distant lands. At the time that the impressionable Coxinga first arrived in Anhai, he would have been told that the Dutch were great allies of his family. The Dutch had promised to support Iquan, and promises mean a great deal to a seven-year-old.

Coxinga grew up with tales of his father's loyalty to the Emperor of Lofty Omens, and of the value of a good education and breeding. As the eldest son of the richest man in China, he was prepared for greatness. Iquan was not yet in his thirties, but had already lived a lifetime. At last, Iquan understood why his own long-suffering father Shaozu had been so intent on bettering his family status. Iquan tried to rectify his long neglect of his father's wishes, buying academic qualifications and high offices for some of his brothers – Hu the Tiger, in particular, enjoyed a remarkably meteoric rise. But money could not buy class, and that was what Iquan expected of his eldest son.

Meanwhile, the Dutch soon hatched a new scheme to seize control of the region. The new governor of Taiwan, Hans Putmans, had inherited an island of surly, fractious natives, and a tenuous alliance with Iquan's family. He was surprised to find himself dealing not with Iquan, who was inland quelling the bandits, but with Iquan's mother and eldest brothers.

Unlike Pieter Nuijts, Putmans learned a little about the history of the region before he waded in. From his later activities, it is clear that he placed no faith at all in Iquan's continued friendship; after all, Iquan was merely the latest in a line of opportunists extending back to the legendary Captain China. But Putmans was also greatly impressed with Iquan's career path – from henchman, to pirate, to privateer, to admiral. Trawling through the books and records of the previous few years, Putmans hit on a new plan.

It was common knowledge that the Dutch had long coveted a port of their own on the coast of China. Veterans still remembered the disastrous 1622 attack on Portuguese Macao that had indirectly led to the Dutch presence on Taiwan. But it had been some time since anyone in the Dutch East India Company had given much thought to how the Portuguese had first achieved their foothold in China. They had been granted the land by the Chinese, Putmans believed, *because they had cleared the Pearl river delta of pirates*. The answer to their problem, as far as Putmans could see it, was not to wage war on the Chinese, but to wait until the pirate problem in Fujian was impossible for the Chinese to deal with, and then offer to step in and clean things up – on the condition that the Dutch could have their own little port like Macao.

Jacques Specx, who had heard it all before, diplomatically tried to talk Putmans out of the idea, since it had several critical flaws. One, which Putmans never seems to have acknowledged, was that there was a considerable difference between the relatively small area of a river delta, and the thousand miles of Fujianese coastline Putmans was proposing to patrol. More importantly, Putmans was offering to clean up a pirate infestation that was not actually there – Iquan had already pacified the region.

But Putmans had already thought of a way around this. If there wasn't a pirate problem off the coast of Fujian, then the Dutch could make one. Putmans had worked out how much the average Fujianese pirate earned in a year of plundering, and proposed that the East India Company hire a number of them, both to wreak havoc offshore, and then to sail in to the rescue under the Dutch flag. Although it sounded a trifle silly on paper, was this not essentially what Iquan had done himself? Had the Chinese not ended their recent pirate problems by picking the toughest bandit and making him an admiral?

If Specx had stayed in the Far East, things might have been different, but Putmans concocted his plan during the changeover in Batavian governors. By the time Specx's successor Hendrick Brouwer had taken office, Putmans was already blockading Amoy. The delicate peace was broken, and much-needed food failed to reach the city, causing more locals to slip once more into starvation and piracy. Meanwhile, Putmans sailed to Batavia itself to present his case to Brouwer, who was more easily persuaded than Specx.

It may appear that the Dutch demonstrated a spectacular inability to learn from their mistakes during the period, but for every old hand like Specx, there were many more officials who were either fresh off the boat from the Netherlands, or apprenticed in the Spice Islands. The Dutch policy of forcing trade deals had worked to their advantage in numerous small south-east Asian kingdoms, and each change in management often saw a new leadership who refused to believe that China could not be treated in the same way.

As the coast of Fujian descended once more into chaos, Putmans found his ideal ally. His name was Liu Xiang, and he was a former associate of Iquan, who was happy to accept Dutch aid in his raids along the coast. Putmans waited expectantly for a letter from the Chinese government, asking him to step in and save the day.

His scheme backfired when, instead of begging the Europeans for help, the Chinese recalled their admiral. With all the troubles in China, and a dangerously strong power base on the coast, Iquan might never have seen the sea again if it were not for the ruinous activities of the Dutch and their new pirate allies. Instead of advancing ever higher in the ranks of land-based officials, Iquan was ordered back to his fleet.

He arrived to find the Dutch openly fighting the Chinese. On 13 July 1633, a heavily armed fleet of twelve Dutch ships sailed into Amoy bay and attacked a squadron of Chinese vessels, some of which had been beached to be cleaned of barnacles. Putmans himself was in charge, and gleefully reported that he had wiped out Iquan's ships. Iquan responded with a letter taunting the Dutch for their cowardice, suggesting that there was little victory or honour in sneaking up on an unprepared foe.

Putmans waved away Iquan's complaints, and sent a series of letters to Chinese authorities and military officials, outlining his generous offer. He would deal with the rest of the pirates in the same manner as he had dealt with the so-called Master of the Seas, if the Chinese would only agree to his demands.[9] As a bonus, he would also offer cannons, guns and soldiers to help the Ming dynasty defend itself from the Manchus who were threatening its borders in the north. Much to Putmans's delight, a series of replies soon came back, remarking on the impressive naval capabilities of the Dutch, and announcing a willingness to enter negotiations. Seeing his chance, Putmans outlined his plans for dealing with the pirates of the region once and for all, and included the remainder of the discredited Iquan's forces in his list of foes. All he asked for in return was a port on the coast where the Dutch could engage in peaceful trade with their Chinese friends.

As August stretched into September, Putmans's plan seemed to be working. The coast of China was rocked by powerful typhoons that weakened his fleet, but reports drifted in that Iquan's own ships had been similarly troubled. More letters arrived from prominent Chinese government officials, grudgingly acknowledging that Putmans was the best choice for cleaning up the region, and asking for further clarification of his plans.

With the arrival of autumn, Putmans realised he'd been had. He had spent the entire summer in frenzied correspondence with Iquan himself, who had been dictating letter after letter from bogus officials, applying fake seals, and reading with great interest as Putmans spilled his plans, ideas and strategies. Not a single one of Putmans's letters had ever reached a real member of the Chinese authorities; or if they had, they had simply been handed over to Iquan by associates who preferred the incumbent admiral to a group of blackmailing foreigners.

To the young Coxinga, witnessing the ruse unfold in the palaces and gardens of Anhai, it must have been an interesting experience. Betrayed by the foreign barbarians, his father had avoided any actual retaliation for over two months, preferring instead to remain with his family in Anhai and humiliate his enemies by mail, until nature itself took its course. The Dutch ships blockading Amoy had ridden at anchor throughout the height of summer, their crews decimated by disease. On 6 October, the ships temporarily put to sea to evade a typhoon, after early swells had caused two vessels to slip their moorings and dash themselves on nearby rocks. Of the original twelve ships, there were now only eight.

Now that summer had passed, and the autumn seas were growing rough, Iquan wrote another letter to Putmans, and this time signed it with his own name. Never one to kick a man when he was up, Iquan mocked Putmans's presumption, asking 'how a dog can be suffered to lay his head on the Emperor's pillow?' He also finally threw down the gauntlet, issuing a challenge directly to Putmans for a duel between their fleets at Amoy. Iquan was keen to have the battle close to shore, not only so his family could watch the fun from the battlements of their fortress at Anhai, but also to demonstrate to the land-bound officials just who was the true Master of the Seas. As Iquan put it, Putmans should come close to shore 'so that the battle may be fought in sight of the high officials. Because, if the battle were fought in open sea, the officials would not be present, with the consequence that the full credit [for the victory] might not be received.'[10] In other words, if Putmans thought he had what it took, he was welcome to bring it on.

That night in his diary, Putmans railed against the Chinese as a 'perfidious and sodomitic nation', and begged God to give him victory over them once and for all. He knew that his men had superior firepower and made better use of their cannons. If Iquan came to meet him at sea, he was still confident he could teach him a lesson. Putmans needed all the help he could get, but had already unknowingly spurned a potential ally. Ironically, one of the letters that had reached him in September had been genuine. It came from Japan, and had been written by Augustin, the disinherited son of Captain China. With progressively tougher crackdowns on Christians and foreigners in Japan, the God-fearing Augustin was preparing to leave his adopted home and return to China. He also regarded it as an ideal time to seek his birthright, and wrote to Putmans, bitterly but belatedly, about the way in which Iquan had usurped control of Captain China's organisation:

> When His Excellency, the late Martin Sonk was Governor, my father took great pains in assisting the Dutch to move their fortress from the Pescadores to Taiwan, and inviting the Chinese to come over for trade. . . . Iquan, who served as an interpreter for the Company, knew this, and, cunningly and against my father's will, collected money from all the traders who came there . . . and degraded himself as a thief . . . Whenever I think of this, my feeling becomes so melancholy that in order to challenge the same Iquan, to burn up his ships and kill him, I collected a number of ships and provided men for them.[11]

Augustin's complaint was genuine, as was his desire to have Iquan killed. He begged Putmans for help, but Putmans sent a non-committal and uncooperative reply. The chances are that by this time, Putmans regarded Augustin's letter as another of Iquan's practical jokes. If Putmans had taken the chance to join forces with him, it might have presented a new and more dangerous threat to Iquan. As it was, Putmans went out to face Iquan with less support than he could have had.

Almost three full months after Putmans initiated hostilities, Iquan finally met him in battle, in Liao-luo Bay on the south side of the island of Quemoy. The bored crews on the eight Dutch ships looked up to see 150 Chinese vessels approaching, many of them crewless and already ablaze. The bay was awash with flames, as Iquan's fireships drifted ever closer to the Dutch. In shallow waters and ponderous to manoeuvre, the Dutch tried frantically to evade the hazards, but there were simply too many of them. First one, and then a second Dutch vessel caught fire. As the Dutch ships fled back towards Taiwan, a third ship was lost somewhere *en route*. Probably, it was already taking water from earlier damage, and foundered in the Taiwan Strait when the luckless Dutch were struck by another fierce typhoon. Iquan returned to Anhai, and told his adoring son that the goddess of the sea herself fought on the side of his family.

After the excitement of the battle with the Dutch, life returned to normal in Anhai. Iquan, however, did not return to the hinterland, but stayed to supervise the suppression of his remaining enemies: Liu Xiang was still at large, and Captain China's son Augustin had finally arrived, without the Dutch support he craved. At first, Iquan attempted to negotiate with Liu Xiang, sending several of his brothers to arrange a treaty with him. Liu Xiang initially feigned interest in talks, but ordered his men to open fire as their ships approached. In the ensuing battle, both Hu the Tiger and Hú the Swan were killed.[12] Bao the Panther and Biao the Tiger Cub lost their ships but escaped with their lives.

For Iquan's son, the young Coxinga, it was the first time he had witnessed his family facing a tragic reversal of fortune. At the fortress in Anhai, an angry Iquan swore vengeance, and ordered his entire fleet to assemble. The ships numbered in their hundreds, and bore down upon Liu Xiang's stronghold near Canton. The warriors of Iquan's family killed every follower of Liu Xiang and every member of their families. Liu Xiang himself committed suicide on his ship, rather than face Iquan's wrath. Before long, Captain China's son Augustin was also brought to heel. The region was pacified once more, and Coxinga had seen a side of his father he had never known before.

Amid the gardens of Anhai, Coxinga resumed his studies, which included the Confucian classics, ancient histories such as the *Spring and Autumn Annals*, and more practical lessons for the son of an admiral. Coxinga's favourite uncle seems to have been Feng the Phoenix, who was assigned to him as a tutor in the martial arts. Not only Feng, but other sparring partners reported that the boy excelled at swordsmanship, and was exceptionally brave. It was what any proud military father wanted to hear, of course, but there may have been an element of truth. Coxinga already had some experience, as his mother had already been taking him to martial arts lessons in Japan. It is difficult to imagine what experience a five- or six-year-old may have gained, but it was not unknown for Japanese children to study martial arts at such an early age. Coxinga's Japanese tutor had supposedly remarked that the boy was a swift learner, and a regular 'little warrior'.[13]

Swordsmanship was a vital component in the young Coxinga's education, not purely as a skill that a gentleman warranted, but also as a means of self-defence. Iquan had many enemies, among the Dutch, Chinese and Japanese, and China was still reeling from the after-effects of drought and famine. As the son and heir of China's richest man, Coxinga was a valuable prize for kidnappers, and he was assigned minders hand-picked from Iquan's own personal battalion, the Black Guard. When the boy asked his father where he had found such fearsome warriors, Iquan simply replied that they had come from 'beyond the sea'.[14]

Experience had taught Iquan that he could trust nobody; though he may never have known, his own mother had even conspired against him with Pieter Nuijts, so his paranoia was wholly justified. His Chinese associates were former pirates whose allegiance was unsure, his family were often out to get whatever they could, and he had long since learned never to trust the barbarians of Europe. Consequently, Iquan recruited the Black Guard from a place that had no relationship to any other country or associate: Africa.

The Black Guard, approximately 500-strong,[15] had once been Negro slaves in the service of the Portuguese, but were now all freed men. Iquan had somehow acquired them in Macao, and had turned them into his own imposing private army. Perhaps some of them were among the slaves who fought so bravely to defend Macao from the Dutch in 1622, freed in the aftermath only to find themselves thousands of miles from home, with no hope of getting back. Others may have defected from the service of the Dutch, though Chinese sources imply that Iquan bought them in Macao and freed them himself. With many of its members unable to speak any language but Portuguese, the Black Guard was Iquan's most trusted unit, and he 'confided more in them than in the Chinese, and always kept them near his person'.[16] Their mere appearance struck fear into his enemies, and rumours spread that even devils had joined Iquan's forces at Anhai: black-skinned giants with strangely curly hair, whose imposing forms were bulked out still further by hefty armour under gaudy silks. Fortunately, the Black Guard did not get to hear of such tales, as they were all devout Catholics, whose war-cry was a blood-curdling scream of *Santiago*, in praise of their patron St James.[17]

Coxinga studied and trained in the gardens of Anhai, watched over by the Black Guard, while his father resumed his role as Master of the Seas. Iquan wrote to the humiliated Putmans on Taiwan, and informed him that trade with the mainland could resume, under terms which Iquan himself would dictate. Chastened but relieved, Putmans told the remnants of his forces to stand down, and was forced to watch as Iquan's trading vessels filled the port before Fort Zeelandia. In the months that followed, Zeelandia became a hive of activity, crammed with Chinese vessels bound for Fujian and Japan, restoring an uneasy trade from which the Dutch undoubtedly profited, but not as much as they would have liked.

For a while, the Dutch gave up on China, and concentrated on deals elsewhere. As part of the conditions he had forced on them, Iquan continued to ship vast numbers of Chinese migrants out of Fujian. He always had ready volunteers, who desired to flee the droughts, famines and revolts on the mainland. Many also knew of the worsening situation in the north, where the Emperor of Lofty Omens was troubled by a financial crisis and rebel armies of successively greater sizes. And, of course, there were the Manchus on the other side of the Great Wall, a constant threat to the northern Chinese colonies unprotected by the long battlements. In 1636, a Manchu army invaded Korea and subjugated the Yi dynasty that had once resisted the Japanese. Many suspected that Ming China would be next, and willingly paid Iquan to ship them to Taiwan as human cargo, ready to start anew.

Now ready to believe Iquan was capable of anything, Putmans suspected a new plan was unfolding – although Iquan may never have heard an official declaration, the Dutch initiated a war of ideology and belief. The Dutch community at Fort Zeelandia had always regarded its immediate domain as relatively trouble-free, populated by semi-naked spear-throwing natives in feather headdresses, who, they truly thought, could be bought off with a few beads. The natives, however, were growing more restless. Witness to the wealth enjoyed by many of the Chinese traders, some native Taiwanese could not resist the temptation to attack the survivors of ships wrecked on the coast, and purloin their cargoes. Others lamented the coming of the foreigners, as a smallpox epidemic raged through the native settlements.[10] For, from being regarded as benevolent visitors bringing Christ and clothes, the Dutch had become a force of fear on the island. One local village headman was heard to threaten his people: 'Ye evil-doers, cease your wickedness; for if not we shall have to seize you, to bind you, and to deliver you over to the Dutch.'[19] The Chinese were also often regarded as unwelcome foreigners, and the Dutch were obliged to come to their aid in disputes with hostile villagers, particularly in the Taiwanese hinterland, where the Chinese were convinced there was gold to be found.

As the balance of Chinese to native tribespeople began to slip, Putmans developed a new found interest in promoting Christianity and loyalty to the Dutch among the local inhabitants. The force sent to quell the disturbances was accompanied by Reverend Robertus Junius, who did his best to establish the Europeans as kindly men bringing a beneficial religion. With the natives, he drew up a treaty, although few ever knew its entire contents. Its first article granted sovereignty of the entire island to the Dutch, but this was often omitted from public readings, for fear it 'might later be explained by some malevolent Chinese in such a way as to cause widespread irritation against us'.[20]

From the Chinese, he received assurances that they would not antagonise the natives, nor support them in any projects against Fort Zeelandia or its occupants. From the natives, he obtained promises that they would refrain from cutting the heads off any shipwrecked sailors they encountered, and also return all stolen goods. It was a start, at least, and missionaries got to work converting the islanders, and convincing them of the benefits of Christianity.

Putmans's most fervent soldier of Christ was George Candidius, a minister whose religious zeal was so great that he had even been chastised by Batavia for it. Candidius was a colourful character, who had drifted to the Far East after leaving an earlier posting under a cloud. His opposition to Dutch company men living with native concubines in the Moluccas had not proved popular, but his adherence to the letter of religious law earned him grudging respect elsewhere.

In fact, Candidius believed in all laws and contracts, almost to the point of obsession. As a Calvinist, he would have been insulted by the term 'Jesuitical', but Dutch records contain a number of arguments in which Candidius pursued arbitration and deals with impressive intensity. He was particularly annoyed about an incident during the governorship of Pieter Nuijts, in which Nuijts had somehow persuaded him to loan a large sum of money on his behalf to some islanders, and then neglected to pay him back. Nuijts seems to have taken particular pleasure in irritating Candidius in return, and even implied in a letter that he expected to soon be reinstated as governor of Taiwan, leading the irate Candidius to threaten to resign if Nuijts were allowed back.[21]

Jacques Specx himself could not resist the temptation to make a wry comment about the intense negotiations surrounding the renewal of Candidius's contract as a Taiwan missionary. Informed that Candidius was holding out for a rise, Specx wrote: 'His Reverence should not forget that his calling as a clergyman has great spiritual profit and gain, and show by his warm Christian zeal that he is not swayed by mere worldly and temporal interests.'[22] When he was governor, Specx had also vetoed a request by Candidius to marry a native Taiwanese woman, in the interests of fostering better relations between the two cultures; Specx refused on the grounds that it would be bad for 'his own person and the general welfare'.

Whether he was interested in fostering better relations or not, Candidius remained extremely keen to find a wife; lonely on an island surrounded by bare-breasted native girls, he was clearly a priest in torment. On a trip to Batavia, he finally found a girl who would marry him: Jacques Specx's own wayward daughter Sara, who had been left behind by her father when he sailed from Batavia for the last time.

No doubt swelled with pride that he had simultaneously rescued a fallen woman and married the boss's daughter, Candidius set up house with his new wife in Taiwan, where he was elated to discover that Pieter Nuijts would never be coming back. The disgraced Nuijts was finally permitted to leave Japan in 1636, and was shipped back to Batavia, where he was promptly stripped of his rank and sent back to the Netherlands.

Meanwhile, in Japan, the Dutch in Hirado resumed trading under increasingly restrictive conditions. This was not actually Nuijts's fault, but the product of eighty years of Christian missionaries, suspected of sowing dissension among the native populace and encouraging allegiance to a higher power than shogun or emperor. The Japanese government had already severed all ties with the Catholic nations of Spain, Mexico and the Philippines in 1624, and the days of the Portuguese were similarly numbered. The English had long since given up and gone home, but the Dutch pleaded with the Japanese that they were not seditious Catholics, but trusty Protestants. They reasoned that their nation was new, wrested from Catholic oppressors by bold and good-hearted people who, just like the Japanese, opposed the strange sorceries of Rome. For a while, this seemed to placate the Japanese, but paranoia about unwelcome foreign influences persisted.

In 1636, not only the Dutch, but also the Chinese found it increasingly difficult to obtain travel licences in Japan. The shogunate also issued an official declaration of isolationism: *Sakoku*, or the Closure of the Nation.[23] Henceforth, Japanese were forbidden from leaving for foreign countries, and Japanese living abroad were forbidden from returning, on pain of death. The Sakoku Edict was similarly brutal in its definition of 'Japanese'. Children of unions between Europeans and Japanese were to be deported, and couples who had adopted half-breeds were to hand over their foster children over to the Dutch for deportation, also on pain of death.[24]

All over East Asia, Japanese expatriates faced a difficult decision. Many could see that there was a war brewing between the Manchus and the Ming Chinese, and that relocation to an island kingdom would afford some protection from invasion. Those who preferred life in Japan to a freer but more dangerous existence abroad, returned to their home country in droves, hoping to slip in before the Edict was enforced. Some of the final returnees arrived in 1635, on the last licensed Japanese ship out of Siam. Its captain was Joseph Adams, son of the famous English pilot Will Adams. He brought four Japanese citizens prepared to plead that they had returned the moment they heard of the promulgation of the Edict. Of their later fate, or indeed that of the half-English Joseph, nothing more is known.[25]

The increasingly desperate situation between foreigners, Christians and Japanese led to a strange aside in the life of Coxinga. Though not mentioned in Chinese chronicles, the crackdown in Japan led to an additional tale about the Zheng family in the writings of the Europeans and Japanese, the origins of which remain a historical mystery.

Persecutions against Christians in Japan persisted, until matters came to a head in 1637. The area around Nagasaki and Hirado, where Coxinga had spent his early childhood, had become a hotbed of Christianity, thanks chiefly to the proximity of so many foreigners. Many had converted to the alien religion, only to swear they had rejected Christ when the political climate changed. Some refused to do so, and joined the ranks of Japan's Christian martyrs, while others continued to practise their religion in secret. The same period saw drastic increases in taxation, leading the local lord's son Shigeharu to combine his persecution of Christians with his extortion of rice and money from his vassals. He had even invented a torture of which he was particularly proud. Troublemakers were put in straw raincoats with their hands tied behind their backs and set on fire. Shigeharu liked to call his little spectacle the Mino dance.

Oppression in the region was severe, and there were those who hoped that someone would overthrow the local lords. In a time which saw droughts and strange weather all over the world, the end of 1637 was particularly dry. Dawn and dusk found the sky resplendent in crimsons and golds, and the exceptional conditions led the local cherry trees to blossom out of season, in the autumn. Disaffected samurai, some of them former Christians, spread a rumour that in 1614, a departing Jesuit had left a book of prophecy, called *The Mirror of the Future*. It began with the chilling words:

When five by five years have passed
Japan will see a remarkable youth
All-knowing without study
The skies shall glow red in the East and West
Dead trees shall bring forth flowers
Men shall wear the Cross on their heads
And white flags shall flutter on the sea
On rivers, mountains, and plains
To usher in the return of Christ.[26]

The secular-minded saw it as a hopeful wish that foreign missionaries would return. The more literal regarded the prophecy as an indication that they were living in the End Times, and that the Messiah was due to walk among them. With impressive happenstance, a likely candidate presented himself in the form of a local boy. Tokisada Shiro, later known as Amakusa Shiro, was a child prodigy, barely a year older than Coxinga. He was the fourth son of an impoverished samurai, whose elder brothers all died before reaching manhood. Consequently, he was treasured and cosseted by his parents and two elder sisters, and cherished as the family's sole male heir. At the age of nine, he had impressed his teachers by being able to recite the essential tenets of Confucianism from memory, and had been sent away to work as a page to a local samurai. Aged twelve, he had returned to Nagasaki, where he found employment with a Chinese apothecary among the foreign traders. The boy reputedly impressed his new employer with his remarkable memory and eerie charisma.

The people of the region were looking for someone to save them from deprivation, and stories told of Shiro breathlessly recount miracles and portentous signs. He is said to have approached the villagers of Amakusa, near Nagasaki, bearing a branch on which a sparrow perched. The bird seemed unable to fly away – Shiro had transfixed it with his mesmeric stare. When two local officials accused him of sorcery, his powers were alleged to have struck one dumb, and trapped the other in a seated position.

Another tale reports that Shiro approached a group of Christians, and prayed before them until a pigeon flew down and laid an egg on his hand. The egg was opened to reveal a portrait of Jesus and a tiny scroll of scripture, at which point the bird is said to have tweeted 'Zuiso!' ('Good Omen') three times, and flown away.

Whether they were mere conjuring tricks or the later embroideries of impressionable peasants, these miracles turned Shiro into the very leader for which the locals were searching. When the local peasantry ran out of patience and rose up in opposition to their lord, they invited the teenage boy to bring his divine wisdom to their aid. No older than fifteen, Shiro became the nominal leader of a rebel army that grew in size until it numbered in the tens of thousands.

Local lords went out to fight the rebels, who had sequestered themselves in Hara Castle: a formidable fortress at the tip of the Shimabara peninsula. It was surrounded on three sides by the sea, which crashed against sheer cliffs affording no beach or other landing point. The samurai sent to suppress the Christian revolt found themselves facing an army of fanatics led by a supposed saint, whose white banners fluttered on the battlements of an impregnable castle. They needed something special to break the resolve of the rebels, and soon they swallowed their pride and went to the Dutch.

A number of Dutch ships were preparing to sail for Taiwan, and had armed themselves heavily in case they ran into any of Iquan's privateers on the long journey. During several rounds of negotiations, including several tense banquets at which the Dutch hoped against hope they would not be asked to help, the local Japanese informed their guests that the bad old days of Pieter Nuijts were long gone, and that now the Japanese and Dutch were true allies. After several days, came the moment the Dutch had been dreading. They were 'asked' if they would send their ships to shell the fortress at Shimabara. The Dutch tried to wriggle out of the request, but were admonished sternly by the Lord of Hirado, who said accusingly: 'Your first care is your private trade, and only after that, as a secondary consideration, come matters of courtesy.'[27]

The rebels at Shimabara were Christians, supposedly the spiritual brothers of the Dutch, albeit of a different denomination and nationality. In some ways, the Shimabara rebels were the last hope for a strong Christian presence in Japan – less diplomatic foreign leaders might have even been tempted to intervene on their behalf, and establish a Christian enclave on Japanese shores. The Dutch meekly protested, but dutifully sent their ships to Shimabara, and trained their guns on the Christian rebels.

They must have been considerably relieved when their ships

reached Shimabara, and discovered that Hara Castle's cliff-top siting made it almost impossible to hit with shipboard guns. As it was, their only chance of hitting rebel forces came if they shot across the headland, over the heads of the besieging samurai. When a Dutch cannonball accidentally landed in the besiegers' camp, a polite request was sent to them, suggesting they aim at the castle, and not at their allies. Over several days, the Dutch glumly pounded the cliffs with their artillery; the castle remained untouched, but it is likely that considerable damage was done to the unprotected encampment behind the fortifications, where the women and children of the rebels had set their tents.

After many days of bombardment, the Japanese finally started to believe the complaints of the Dutch, that the high setting of Hara Castle required mortars, not cannon. The Dutch were thanked for their assistance, and permitted to leave, but asked to leave their cannons behind. At this, there was considerable protest, as they were effectively being waved off into hostile waters, stripped of the only weapons that could keep Iquan's privateers from raiding them. They were eventually permitted to take a mere four cannon with them, on what proved, to their great relief, to be an uneventful journey with no sighting of Iquan's raiders.

The Japanese were convinced they could do better, although they were hindered by two problems. Chiefly, the Dutch had not been lying, and no matter who was firing the cannons, they were simply unsuitable for the attack at hand. The Japanese were also hampered by their own limited skills in gunnery, since most of their knowledge of vectors and targeting had been imparted to them by one Pieter Nuijts during his involuntary sojourn several years earlier. Though it would be completely in character for Nuijts to have claimed expert knowledge of a subject about which he knew nothing, he may have even realised the danger of saying too much, and been deliberately misleading in some of the lessons in artillery he was called upon to give from his prison.[28]

In a change of plan, the samurai decided to starve the rebels out, and the castle eventually fell in the spring of 1638. Its weakened, emaciated defenders fell before a rain of fire-arrows and advancing swordsmen, and were butchered until the fortress was piled high with the dead and dying. Afterwards, Christianity in Japan was forced underground for over two centuries.

A peasant revolt with Christian accoutrements was of little interest to Chinese writers of the period, who had other problems in their own country. The fortunes of Christianity, a religion also regarded with suspicion by most Chinese, was not an issue that could be expected to trouble the inhabitants of the Celestial Empire, nor would it be expected to attract the attention of Nicholas Iquan. However, from his palace at Anhai, Iquan supposedly developed a deep interest in Japan's suppression of the Christians – his 'daughter' was among them.

Iquan had not spent long in Japan in his youth, but some doubtful sources believe that he found the time to sire a second child, by a woman who was not Miss Tagawa. This child had somehow reached her early teens without ever attracting the notice of any Chinese or Japanese chroniclers, and somehow fallen in with the Christians of Japan. Palafox's *History of the Conquest of China* devotes a whole page to her, claiming that she had fled Japan in the midst of the final persecutions, and somehow made it to Macao, possibly in the company of Portuguese Jesuits.

Discovering that she was safe in Macao, Iquan wrote to her guardians demanding her return, but although the Portuguese acknowledged him as her father 'yet they did not think fit to restore him his daughter, because she was a Christian, and as for him, though he had been baptised in, and made profession of the Christian faith, yet he lived like an infidel'.[29]

It was, perhaps, the wrong way to address a man with his own navy. Iquan was used to getting his own way, and issued dire threats agains the inhabitants of Macao, reminding them of the power he wielded:

> [Iquan] menaced them most terribly, that he would come and besiege Macao with a navy of five hundred or a thousand ships, that he would fetch away his daughter by force, ruin and extirpate all those who had retained her from him, and that from that very instant, he would begin to reduce them to the extremity of indigency and necessity, by putting a stop to their receipt of any provisions or commodities from China.[30]

But instead of attacking Macao, Iquan did nothing. Little more was said about the impasse for some time, until a Portuguese ship bound for

Nagasaki was forced ashore on the Chinese coast near Anhai. The travellers reported that Iquan was an outstandingly gracious host, supplying them with everything they required, and handing over passes to get through blockades further north, without once even bringing up the subject of hostages or payment, or indeed his absent daughter.

The incident, or rather lack of incident, led to a considerable thaw in relations between Iquan and the Portuguese, and his ships were soon a regular sight in Macao. As for the alleged daughter, she eventually married one Antonio Rodrigues, and the couple came to live at Anhai with the rest of the family.[31]

The playwright Chikamatsu, in his *Battles of Coxinga*, is also convinced that Iquan had a Japanese daughter, whom he names Kinshojo. But other aspects of the play are so far-fetched and fantastical that her presence in it cannot be offered as proof. Palafox, writing only a few years after the actual events, often garbled names and places and may also have been confused in this instance. Though it is not inconceiveable that Coxinga had a Japanese half-sister, it seems more likely that the girl, if she existed at all, had some other connection to Iquan's family. A more likely candidate can be found in Elizabeth, the daughter of Captain China who was baptised in Hirado in the presence of the English traders. She would have been the right age by the time these events are reported, and has more recognisable connections to Christianity. Perhaps Iquan was fulfilling his last obligation to Captain China by ensuring that he made provision for a girl better described as his niece or sister-in-law.

Whatever the truth of the matter, there must have been something that happened at the close of the 1630s that caused the inhabitants of Anhai to become much more accommodating towards Christians. Iquan's wife and mother were struck by an unknown disease, which so troubled the Master of the Seas that he felt compelled to summon a Dutch surgeon from Taiwan.[32] The doctor stayed at Anhai for three months until both patients were fully recovered, and returned to Taiwan baffled at what he had seen. The doctor reported that the Catholic Mass was said every day at Anhai, though he could think of no reason why. Whether it was the devotions of the Black Guard, Iquan's religious insurance policy in case the Catholic God could cure his mother and wife, or an indulgence to a prodigal Christian daughter, we will probably never know.

THE TREASON OF WU SANGUI

In 1639, the fifteen-year-old Coxinga left Anhai for Nanjing, the southern capital. The boy was enrolled for his higher education, where he was set to study under the renowned scholar and poet Qian Qianyi. He was sent away from Anhai with due ceremony and excitement, and someone in the family saw fit to commission a soothsayer to examine his omens before he left. The fortune teller said: 'This is a wonderful boy; his features are not ordinary; he will become the great man of his generation, no mere high official, no mere common man.'[1] The fortune teller probably trotted out the same flatteries to every rich student on his way to university, but on this occasion he was more right than he could have known. Coxinga was also given a strange warning: that his life would come to an end at a 'city of bricks'. As is traditional with fortunes, the Zheng family paid heed to the parts they liked, and discarded anything that sounded bad.[2]

Iquan was determined that his bright son should have the education he himself had spurned, as that was the only way the family would attain true legitimacy. A government career in China required a degree, and the Confucian classics were the only subject approved by the government. Full of practical wisdom on statecraft and diplomacy, the works of Confucius also emphasised the importance of gentlemanly conduct in one's dealings with others. Confucius often spoke of the need to remain loyal in relationships – sons must remain obedient to their fathers, and friends to friends. Since Confucius only achieved genuine prominence after his death, there is also an undercurrent in the canon and its commentaries about the need for purity of thought and deed, and to resist the temptations of corruption.

Coxinga's teacher, Qian Qianyi, was a man of great intellect, who had once headed the Imperial Board of Ceremonies in Beijing itself, but his life was also haunted by scandal. In the early 1620s, he had been dismissed from a government position for his membership of a group opposed to the current authorities. Some years later, when Qian became a provincial examiner, those same corrupt authorities had tried to steer a prominent government position into the hands of one of their cronies, a case of political nepotism that the fair-minded Qian had boldly opposed. His outspoken adherence to the law led to his dismissal, and he retired into private study. He was not even safe there, as jealous enemies in Beijing persuaded a local to issue a series of accusations against him, resulting in his imprisonment. Qian was eventually cleared of all charges and his accuser executed; he was released from custody to discover that the famous Nicholas Iquan was searching for someone of impeccable wisdom and character to teach his son how to be a gentleman.[3] When Iquan asked Qian to become Coxinga's mentor, the scholar soon agreed.

Qian's resolution in the face of corrupt and venal officials demonstrated how seriously he took the values of Confucius. As he had publicly shown on several occasions, he would rather live in obscurity than be part of a government that was not true to its word. Unlike many other officials of the late Ming dynasty, he had internalised the wisdom of the Confucian *Analects*. When he and his new pupil discussed passages such as this, both regarded the words as more than idle theory:

> Never let your faith falter. Love learning. If attacked, be ready to die for truth. Do not enter a place of danger, nor a state in revolt. When justice prevails under Heaven, then show yourself. When it does not, then hide your face. When government is good, be ashamed of poverty and deprivation. When government is bad, be ashamed of riches and honour.[4]

Qian reported that Coxinga was a devoted and diligent pupil. Confucius called for a gentleman to make close study of history and poetry, but whereas others were satisfied with the theory, Coxinga followed the recommendations to the letter. He studied the songs of the distant past, and chronicles of distant battles and heroes. In his spare time, he continued to practise his horsemanship and the martial arts. Like Iquan, Qian Qianyi called him Big Tree, but whereas Coxinga's father was probably commenting merely on children's unerring habit of growing fast, Qian intended another meaning. He regarded Coxinga as a commanding presence, a figure that deserved respect and attention, like a handsome pine standing tall.[5]

The teenage boy donned the robes of a Confucian scholar, and impressed his classmates with his understanding of the classics. In 1640, Qian moved his classes to the Semi-Rural Hall on the city outskirts, where he intended to set up a small academy of the very best scholars. Coxinga studied there with him, but was unable to accept his teacher's offer of a permanent career in academia. His father had other plans, and may have even come to regret selecting a mentor of such integrity.

Iquan wanted his son to have a *touch* of class, and to know enough about the Confucian classics to gain a degree and attain a government position in the correct manner. But for Iquan, public offices, qualifications and appointments were only masks and adornments. He had not paid for his son to have an expensive education only to squander it on learning for its own sake. Coxinga was to memorise what he needed from the Semi-Rural Hall, then enter Nanjing University and pass the arduous public examinations. Such success, combined with his father's high rank and great wealth, would doubtless secure him a government position close to the Emperor himself, and smooth the path of any future family endeavours. Coxinga continued with his studies, and was expected to graduate in the late 1640s.

In 1641, aged seventeen and still a student, Coxinga was presented with his first wife. Perhaps hoping the experience would focus his son's mind on the real world, Iquan arranged a marriage between Coxinga and Cuiying, a lady from the wealthy Deng family.

Iquan was keen on the marriage, but his son was non-committal, only agreeing to the wedding to please his father. The couple do not seem to have got along, and since Cuiying was a year older than her husband, it is possible that her family had found it difficult to find her a suitable spouse. Conceivably, other families were intimidated by their wealth and status. More probably, nobody wanted to be saddled with a woman who was used to getting her own way.

Cuiying was a spoiled rich girl with a fearsome temper, obsessed with fashion and fineries, and Coxinga's polar opposite.[6]

The loyal Confucian scholar tried to make the best of it, and reportedly said to his bride: 'For the two of us, love must come later.'[7] It is unlikely that this impressed her much, but despite initial frosty relations, the couple dutifully produced an heir. Iquan was not yet forty, and already a proud grandfather; the baby was named Jing, but his grandfather called him *Jin-She*: – 'Bright Prospect for the House'.

However, Iquan and his family had enjoyed such a meteoric rise in part because the power of the Ming dynasty was fading. By the 1640s, its decline was impossible to ignore. When Iquan was made an admiral, he had been bought off by an administration that had other things on its mind. His imperial commission was granted to him by the new Emperor of Lofty Omens, then the seventeen-year-old inheritor of a throne whose power had been considerably undermined through years of misrule. In the years that Coxinga grew to manhood and began his education in Nanjing, China faced a continual barrage of droughts, themselves causing famines, leading to outbreaks of disease – particularly smallpox, which ravaged the empire. Heaven was clearly angry about something, and the court tried to stave off imminent financial crisis. Where possible, troublesome rebels were bribed into submission, and Iquan was not the only local warlord who found himself granted an imperial post to bolster the Emperor's failing powers.

The Emperor of Lofty Omens was prepared to try anything to wrest his country out of chaos, and believed his abilities were seriously hampered by his court astronomers. It was vital that the ruler knew in advance what portents would be appearing in the sky, but his own people were continually miscalculating the timings of eclipses. Rumours already spread throughout the nation that Heaven had revoked its Mandate, and that the Ming dynasty was finished; it was imperative that the correct rites were performed at the correct time, to hold off further famines, droughts and plagues.

The Chinese calendar was supremely confusing, counting in sixty-year cycles of twelve yearly animal signs, combined with imperial reigns of varying lengths. It had a long pedigree (AD 1630, by Chinese reckoning, was actually the year 4327), but it had reached the point where the calculations of local astronomers were often out by hours, or even days. While the court debated the failures and inaccuracies of its astronomers, someone circulated a copy of a dissertation on solar and lunar eclipses by a European. It had been written by Adam Schall, the unlikely Jesuit hero of the battle of Macao some years earlier, now a missionary on the banks of the Yellow river. As a Jesuit, Schall had supreme knowledge of the latest developments in science and technology; far from Rome and the prying eyes of the Pope, he even made a serious study of the forbidden writings of Galileo.

The Emperor was impressed by Schall's conclusions and accuracy, and ordered the Board of Rites to call for European help: 'We know well that the founder of our dynasty had the desire to correct the calendar . . . War prevented the execution, or at least achievement of His purpose. Let the Board do everything that is required, and see that We are informed of all that takes place.'[8]

Adam Schall and his fellow Jesuits came to Beijing, where they were permitted to set up an observatory. They introduced the Chinese to the telescope, and even came into the Forbidden City where the Emperor dwelt, to be offered dishes from his table – it was a great honour for anyone, all the more for the agents of the Christian religion.

Though he never met the Emperor of Lofty Omens, Schall went to the palace on many occasions. He befriended some of the ladies, concubines and eunuchs with access to the Emperor, and convinced many of them of the virtues of Christianity. Rumour had it in Beijing that Christianity was a lucky charm in the palace household, and that those concubines who accepted Schall's alien God had enjoyed greater success in the imperial bedchamber. It was not exactly what the Pope had in mind when he sent missionaries to the Far East, but the Jesuits were a pragmatic order, and would try anything to get their message across, even if the message lost a little in translation. Schall numbered his converts by the thousand, each choosing an exotic Christian name to mark their new affiliation. Among the Chinese Marys and Madeleines, Agathas and Isabellas, Judiths and Susannas, were many princesses and consorts.[9]

Their rivals, however, were less pleased. The Jesuits endured constant backbiting and intrigues from the astronomers they had replaced, with adherents of Chinese and Arabic science eternally claiming that their calculations were incorrect, or that they were the secret agents of a cult that desired to consign Confucius himself to hell. But they persevered, and conscientiously oversaw the translating of numerous foreign manuals. In its way, their arrival constituted a mini-renaissance, but the Chinese court was growing increasingly nervous.

In 1642, the fifty-year-old Schall received an unexpected visitor from the Forbidden City. The minister of war wished to discuss some areas of applied mathematics, particularly levels of elevation and trajectories for shells. The conversation, which began as small talk and pleasantries, turned increasingly technical, until the minister revealed his true colours. He announced that Schall seemed to be eminently qualified in the manufacture and use of artillery, and that he was hence commanded by imperial order to do so.[10]

Schall protested that he was a man of God, and had no practical knowledge of warfare – excepting, of course, his valorous conduct in the defence of Macao. But his complaints fell on deaf ears, and he was duly seconded to the ministry of war. Given twenty servants, the reluctant Schall constructed a foundry in the capital. On the first day of operations, his blacksmiths immediately began preparing to make offerings to the God of Fire, leading their scandalised new boss to install a Christian altar, complete with picture of Jesus. Each day, he insisted that his workers join him in prayer for success, and then they would commence work making guns.[11]

The initial production of the Jesuit arms factory comprised 20 prototype cannon, which were taken many miles outside the city for their first test. Schall followed the cannons to the testing ground with an excitable party of eunuchs and ministry officials, and stood at a safe distance while luckless servants gingerly lit the fuses. Much to Schall's surprise, but to the great elation of the government officials, the guns worked perfectly. The Emperor duly placed an order for 500 copies, specifying that they should be light field-pieces of 60lb, all the better to be portable on the men's shoulders in the event of a retreat. Schall did as he was told, but wryly noted in private that Chinese soldiers 'were not so stupid as to burden themselves with cannon when fleeing from the battlefield'.[12]

The Jesuit was also consulted on Beijing's new fortifications and ordered to submit a plan for defence. He spent several days on a wooden model of the city, proposing modern, European-style triangular bastions to give wide fields of fire for defenders. The Emperor approved the plan, but as construction began on Schall's defences, interfering eunuchs in the Forbidden City vouched for a rival plan by a Chinese official. Even though it called for square turrets, with blind spots and structural weaknesses, the plan was somehow put ahead of Schall's. The Jesuit watched the construction of the new fortifications in dismay, and observed that the Chinese were actually making life *easier* for potential attackers.[13]

The official reason for all this activity was the growing strength of the Manchu armies north of the Great Wall. Far from being disorganised barbarians, the Manchus claimed a noble pedigree, and thought themselves the descendants of an ancient dynasty that once ruled China in the Middle Ages.

Over several generations, the Manchus had endured a love–hate relationship with Chinese colonists sent north of the Great Wall to settle on the Liaodong peninsula, the strip of land that stretched up to the north-east, and eventually connected with the border of Korea at the Yalu river.[14] The Chinese clustered along a thin coastal strip, and further inland in a couple of river valleys, but nevertheless came into contact with the Manchu locals.

The Chinese were quite obviously on someone else's territory. They were, after all, north of the Great Wall. As a half-hearted attempt to delineate the northern colony, earlier Ming dynasties constructed an earthern rampart, sometimes with a ditch or low wooden stockade, stretching up from the Shanhai Pass and around to the Yalu river. The Chinese were so keen on the region for the same reason that the Manchus wanted to hold onto it – it was the best place to find the magical *ginseng* root, which was literally worth its weight in silver. The Chinese, intent on setting up fixed farming communities, contrasted greatly with the mobile, nomadic Manchus. Relations varied between friendly trade and hostile conflict, but over time the Manchus asserted greater power. They had wealth and prowess in battle, whereas the Chinese colonists with whom they competed had limited support from the waning Ming dynasty. For anyone spending any length of time in the liminal region between the two cultures, the Manchu way of life often began to take on a certain allure.

The soldiers of the Ming Emperor often began as loyal to their imperial master, but grew disenchanted with life on the frontier. It was difficult enough fighting the highly trained Manchu legions, toughened by years of campaigning among the distant Mongols, but worse still to endure the deprivations of their corrupt superiors. Beijing sent money for supplies and recruitment, but much of it seemed to go astray *en route* to the frontier.

For military men fighting a losing battle on the frontier, the Manchus made very tempting offers. They were formidable foes in battle, but also masters at assimilating their enemies. Their successes in the north increased, at least in part, because many of their military officers were turncoats. As several Chinese generals were to discover, surrender to the Manchus was not the beginning of imprisonment, torture and death.

A traditionally minded Chinese general might prefer to commit suicide upon his defeat, but those who remained alive found out that the Manchus could be extremely gracious hosts. All they required was an oath of allegiance, accompanied by the adoption of the traditional Manchu hairstyle. The male supplicant's head was shaved forward of the ears, and the remainder gathered into a long braid at the back. Some might call it a ponytail, and Chinese detractors scoffed that the Manchus made their subjects impersonate the rear end of a horse. The drastic hairstyle did put many off, but many more regarded it as a small price to pay.

Manchu subjects were also incorporated into a thoroughly military society. Everyone belonged to a 'Banner', a social unit formed around a fighting legion. Their new recruits would be placed within one of the Banner organisations, often given a rank higher than the one they had enjoyed under the Ming, and presented with rewards and gifts. One of the earliest generals to switch sides even received the hand in marriage of a Manchu princess. For those institutionalised by a life in the military, the Manchu system was particularly welcoming – everybody knew exactly where they stood in a Banner. The legion, however, was not merely for show; its ultimate aim was the conquest (or, as the Manchus claimed, the *reconquest*) of China itself.

By 1644, the Manchus were ready to make their move. Liaodong belonged to them, as did vast stretches of Mongolia. They had conquered their enemies to the north and west, and now coveted the heartland of the Celestial Empire. They were supposedly ruled by a child-emperor, but the real power lay with the boy's uncle, Prince Dorgon.

Dorgon's Chinese nemesis was Wu Sangui, the guardian of the Shanhai pass. The two generals were very like each other, both having grown up fighting over the tiny scrap of land north of the Great Wall. Wu's family had been immigrants to the Liaodong colonial region, where his father had been a frontier general, charged with guarding the borders from the Manchus. Wu's own uncle and cousins had defected to the Manchus, but his father had remained resolutely pro-Chinese, despite deprivation, hardship and even a brief demotion.

The long years of famine and drought, of smallpox and plague, of lights in the sky and storms of red rain, and of the proliferation of brigands and pirates, had all done their work. Many of the Chinese were ready to believe that the Ming dynasty had lost the Mandate of Heaven, and that the increasing troubles they faced were further signs that its time was over. Just as the peasants of the hinterland were ready to embrace the bandit Li Zicheng as their new ruler, many people of the northern frontier welcomed the Manchus and their self-proclaimed Qing dynasty. Manchu documents already spoke of the Ming as the 'southern dynasty', implying that they were a spent force awaiting annihilation.

Wu Sangui had sought a military career, like his father. His father, attempting to win new favour with his superiors after his demotion, volunteered to lead a campaign against a Chinese general who had turned bandit in Shandong province. Wu Sangui served as a major in his father's forces, and was a witness to the hollow victory of the Chinese forces. Although the Chinese campaign successfully suppressed the bandits, their leader escaped, and offered his services to the Manchus, who gratefully incorporated him into one of their Banners. It must have been particularly galling for the Chinese, since this particular turncoat was a descendant of Confucius, the paragon of civic duty.[15]

The irony was lost on the Ming dynasty, which thanked Wu's father for his loyal service, and reinstated many of his honours. The elder Wu was nearing retirement age, and took a prestigious military adviser post at the Beijing court, while his son continued to rise through the ranks. At twenty-five, Wu Sangui was in command of 1,600 men; at twenty-seven he was an acting brigade-general, running a training camp for reservists. At twenty-eight, he was a full brigade-general, leading forces in the increasingly desperate defence of Liaodong. Now thirty-two, he was in command of 40,000 soldiers on the Great Wall at the Shanhai pass. His men were hungry and agitating for back pay that would never come. The only thing that kept the guards on the walls was Wu Sangui himself. Despite a twenty-year career that had seen most of his colleagues and relatives switch sides and swear loyalty to the Manchus, Wu Sangui remained resolutely loyal to the emperor. But in May 1644, it was up to him to decide who the emperor was.

Wu Sangui had received a panicked missive from the Emperor of Lofty Omens, ordering him to rush back with his forces and defend the city from the approach of the bandit Li Zicheng. But Wu was unable to quit the Great Wall, since Prince Dorgon's army would seize the opportunity to charge through the Shanhai pass.

From the north side of the Great Wall, Wu Sangui received friendly missives from his traitorous cousins, announcing that the true emperor was the five-year-old Fulin, and inviting him to pledge his allegiance to the new ruler of the Celestial Empire. Were he to do so, he would be promoted from earl to duke as part of the new aristocracy.

Two more letters arrived from within China, one written in his father's name, both informing him that the Emperor of Lofty Omens was now dead by his own hand, and advising Wu to officially offer his service to Li Zicheng, who planned to crown himself the new Emperor of Great Obedience. Were he to do so, he would be promoted from Earl to Count, and his impoverished soldiers would be paid.

Wu Sangui hid the messengers, hoping to keep current events secret from his men while he made the most important decision of his life. There were other factors to consider, such as the likelihood that his father was being held hostage by Li Zicheng's men, and that his life would be forfeit unless Wu answered swiftly.

Wu's final consideration was to be the crucial one. He was worried about his lover in Beijing, and how she was faring at the hands of the bandits.[16]

Of the many stories of the fall of the Ming, it was the women whose tales were the most remarkable. Li Zicheng had promised his generals thirty women each from the palace harem and servants, and the troops entered the palace carrying a list of the 200 most attractive. Perfection was a prerequisite for many palace occupations, and the concubines in particular were the grand prizes. Each concubine reached the palace after being found to be the most attractive woman among a thousand contenders in her home province, through a series of rigorous tests of deportment and attitude. Without a doubt, the soldiers carried a list of some of the most beautiful girls in the world.

The concubines were also fiercely competitive. Forced to sublimate their rivalry in rituals and games, the long boredom of life in the palace had created a number of feuds among them. For some in the palace, it was the chance to settle old scores. The Lady Ren, 'of bad character but pleasing appearance', was a much-disliked consort of the previous Emperor of Heavenly Enlightenment, who had feuded for a decade with the virtuous Former Empress. Even as the Former Empress committed suicide in a hidden chamber, the Lady Ren dressed in her favourite clothes, donned her best jewels, and went out to meet the invaders. She announced that *she* was the Former Empress, and invited them to plunder the palace, before absconding with a new found lover and a case of palace jewels.[17]

Others were not so willing to betray the Ming dynasty, even in defeat. Dozens duplicated the example of an imperial consort who stood at the banks of the Imperial Canal and proclaimed: 'All who are not cowards will follow me', before leaping into the water to her death.[18] That was the Confucian way of facing defeat. Others preferred to follow biblical examples, learned from Adam Schall.

One fifteen-year-old girl was dragged from a well by a group of soldiers intent on raping her, but she stood her ground and haughtily berated them with the words: 'I am the Princess Imperial.'[19] Realising that they might be assaulting one of the future wives of their commander, the soldiers relented and brought her to their leader. Surviving palace eunuchs identified her as an imposter, since the real Princess Imperial was elsewhere, nursing the amputated stump of her arm. This imposter was the Lady Fei, a relatively lowly concubine, who was handed over to a captain.

Lady Fei, however, made it very clear who was in charge, telling her new master: 'Really and truly, I am of imperial lineage, and too high in rank to enter into an illegal or temporary union with you. Your excellency must take me as his lawful wife.'[20]

The captain, clearly smitten, agreed and brought wine, and the two celebrated their new-found relationship. Lady Fei flirted with her captain until he was drunk, and then stabbed him in the neck with a concealed dagger. As he lay drowning in his own blood, she yelled at the surprised guards: 'A mere woman has slain a rebel leader. Now I am content!' With that, she slit her own throat.

But such stories were of no interest to Wu Sangui. He wanted to know of the fate of one woman in particular, a former singer called Chen Yuanyuan. A beauty so famous that she was already the subject of poetry and song, she had been brought to Beijing as the bedmate of a member of the imperial family, but had somehow escaped from his clutches, and become the lover of Wu Sangui. By all accounts, and there are *many* accounts, Wu Sangui and Chen Yuanyuan were helplessly in love.

Exactly what happened next remains a mystery, not because of the lack of information, but because of the many differing reports of it. Official documents contradict one another, and an entire subgenre of romantic and apocryphal tales have grown up around the incident. One suggests that Li Zicheng sent a messenger to the Shanhai pass, bearing a note flushed with the arrogance of the victor. To Wu Sangui, it said:

> You have been indeed favoured by fortune in rising to so high a position, since you have never rendered any pre-eminent service to your Sovereign . . . At present you have a large army under you, but it has only a spectacular value. If my troops sweep down upon you, you have neither the will to repel their onslaught, nor the available force to defeat them. This is your last opportunity to join me. Your Emperor is dead, and may soon be followed to the grave by your own sire . . . [S]urrender to me and gain the honours I promise you . . . [Otherwise] your army is not strong enough for victory, and will be destroyed in a single morning. Your innocent father will be decapitated, and you will have lost both Sovereign and father.[21]

Some sources say nothing of Li Zicheng's letter, claiming instead that Wu Sangui's father, now a hostage, urged his son to surrender, arguing that filial duty should come before his loyalty to a dead regime. Some have Wu Sangui turning on his father, asking how he could be expected to remain a filial son, after his father had betrayed his cause. Others have him demanding the handover of the Ming Heir Apparent, who had failed to escape Beijing and was now in Li Zicheng's clutches. Wu supposedly promised to submit to Li Zicheng, if only the rebel leader would leave the Heir Apparent and Chen Yuanyuan in his custody.

However unlikely it may sound, there remains a chance that Li Zicheng might have agreed to such a reversal – after a decade of fighting, the rebel leader finally had everything he had hoped for, and still found it wanting. His troops ran riot in the city, and Li Zicheng seemed unable to control them. He had seized control of a nation in ruins, and his predecessor was laughing at him from beyond the grave. Though the Emperor of Lofty Omen's last words were often misreported, one of the most popular tales of the day was that his suicide note, written in his own blood, had simply been: 'To the new Emperor, Li. Do not oppress my people. Do not employ my minsters.'[22] Li Zicheng was now the proud owner of an empty treasury, a palace full of corpses, and a staff of ministers and eunuchs who had failed their former master and yet promised to do better in his service. There remained a chance that Wu Sangui would advance on him from the Shanhai Pass, with or without Manchu assistance. Part of Li Zicheng must have realised: he had prepared his whole life for the sacking of Beijing, but had no clue what to do next.

Li Zicheng's rhetoric after the fall of Beijing took on a new and contradictory tone. The new ruler remained troubled by his failure to hit the character for 'Heaven' with an arrow as he entered the city gates. Turncoats continued to petition him to officially accept the Mandate of Heaven and ascend the throne, but he now suspected that Heaven disapproved of his actions. In one telling incident, upon the discovery of the decomposing body of the deceased Emperor, Li Zicheng was heard to say: 'I came to enjoy the rivers and the mountains together with you. How could you have committed suicide?'[23] Such words, if they are true, are the mark of a madman. Li Zicheng had made no secret of his desire to become the emperor, not the emperor's friend.

Li Zicheng still made merry in the palace, and left his troops to carry out atrocities all over the city, but also seemed timid about crowning himself as emperor. He sought allies wherever he could, even, in one strange incident, the help of the alien god of the Christians, of whom he had heard much talk among the vanquished Ming. Adam Schall, his church now a makeshift hospital for wounded townfolk, was summoned to the palace, where Li Zicheng rose to his feet to greet the Jesuit priest, pushing away the ladies who were entertaining him. Schall accepted the rebel leader's offer of tea, but refused food, pleading that more pressing matters awaited him. The rebel assured Schall that the Christians would be safe, and Schall wisely made no comment.[24] Even as they spoke, astronomers Schall had trained were setting out the calendar for the following year, looking for an auspicious day on which Li Zicheng could be crowned emperor.

Two hundred miles to the north, Wu Sangui broke the news to his chief officers. Beijing had fallen, the Ming Emperor was dead, and many of their fellow generals had already surrendered. His men replied that they would follow his decision, and it would appear that Wu's initial decision was to accept Li Zicheng's offer, at least for now. Leaving most of his men at the Shanhai pass, he set off with a small detachment of soldiers to pay homage to Li Zicheng.

A chance meeting on the road, however, was to change the course of Chinese history. A trusted servant of Wu's father, accompanied by one of his father's concubines, met the party on the road with news from Beijing. They were the last survivors of the Wu family, having fled a massacre. Tired of waiting for an answer from Wu Sangui, Li Zicheng had ordered the execution of the entire household. Thirty-eight people were put to the sword, including Wu Xiang himself. The head of Wu Sangui's father now hung ignominiously from the city wall. As for Chen Yuanyuan, she had been spared, in a manner of speaking. The messengers reported that Wu Sangui's lover had been violated by Li Zicheng himself.

It was the final straw. Wu turned his men back towards the Shanhai pass, but even then did not contact the Manchus. Instead, he hoped to hold the pass against a northern attack, while resisting the armies he knew would be advancing from Beijing.

They were not long in coming. On 5 May 1644, Wu Sangui's army was forced to repel a force advancing north, led by a former colleague of his. Swelled with reinforcements, the attackers returned on 10 May, and were again defeated. Wu Sangui dispatched a messenger to Li Zicheng, offering a truce. Li Zicheng, however, was having none of it. He amassed his main army, and marched out to the Shanhai Pass himself. Wu Sangui knew he would finally be facing an army that could defeat him.

On 20 May, the same day that he learned of the death of the last Ming Emperor, a letter reached the Manchu Prince Dorgon from Wu Sangui. It read:

Unexpectedly the wandering bandits assaulted the capital . . . and unfortunately our Emperor died . . . I want to lead an army to punish the bandits for their crimes . . . I appeal to you for help with tears of blood . . . Therefore, please lend your ears to the loyal and righteous appeal of a lonely official whose country has just been destroyed, and dispatch your elite units as soon as you can . . . to the capital with my army, which I will lead personally, so that we can exterminate the wandering bandits at the palace, thereby showing your great righteousness in China. Then, our court will reward the northern court, not only with wealth, but also with territory. This promise I shall not break.[25]

Wu clearly still regarded his actions as that of a loyal servant of the Ming, merely seeking foreign assistance in ousting Li Zicheng from Beijing. It was not an unrealistic request, considering the history of the Manchus. There were many at the court of the Manchu child-emperor who did not want to conquer China, but preferred to regard it as a lucrative place for occasional raids. They thought of themselves as the old guard, true to nomad tradition, but Prince Dorgon's faction adhered to a different idea of what constituted Manchu heritage. Dorgon, or rather the child-Emperor for whom Dorgon was a co-regent, now possessed the seal of the Mongol Khan. He regarded himself as the inheritor of a great tradition, and the leader of a society whose ancestors had, on several occasions, been the rulers of the Celestial Empire itself.

When Wu Sangui's letter arrived, Manchu advance parties were already slipping over the Great Wall at isolated spots. The bulk of Dorgon's force was already heading south towards the Shanhai pass. The Manchus were invading, and Dorgon had every intention of staying. He sent his former enemy a reply in which he made it very clear that he would help Wu Sangui *avenge* the Ming, but not restore it:

[If Wu Sangui] were to lead his army and surrender to us, we would by all means enfeoff him with his former territory, and bestow a princedom upon him. Your state will have revenge on its enemy, and you and your family will be protected. Generation after generation of your sons and grandsons will perpetually enjoy wealth and nobility, for as long as the mountains and rivers last.[26]

His heart heavy, Wu Sangui rode out to meet the approaching forces. There, he surrendered to Dorgon, and submitted to have the front of his head shaved in the Manchu style. After a decade fighting the turncoats, Wu Sangui had become one of them.

On 27 May 1644, Li Zicheng stood on a hilltop, accompanied by the two captured sons of the dead Emperor of Lofty Omens. He saw Wu Sangui's force marching out to meet him, but behind it were tens of thousands of unexpected soldiers. Dorgon, and his brothers Ajige and Dodo had brought a massive force through the Shanhai pass, of Manchus, Mongol and Chinese turncoats from the lands north of the wall.

They clashed on the banks of the Sha river, where Li Zicheng's forces inflicted heavy casualties on Wu Sangui's. During the day-long battle, the mystery rearguard forces simply waited, as the former guardians of the Shanhai pass hurled themselves in repeated assaults on the rebels. As the day drew to a close, and Li Zicheng's men seemed to be victorious, a sandstorm blew down from the western hills, obscuring the entire scene.

Li Zicheng's men pressed through the blinding sand, believing that Wu Sangui's men were on the verge of fleeing the battlefield. Then, suddenly, an unexpected cavalry charge swept out of the storm and into their flanks. Panicked cries rose up from Li Zicheng's soldiers as they saw the distinctive shaved heads of their new attackers. The rebel line buckled and disintegrated as those who saw the Manchus fled in panic. They were no longer fighting the last defenders of the Ming, they now faced the conquering invaders of the Qing.

When the sandstorm finally dispersed, the rebels were nowhere to be seen. Wu Sangui and his foreign allies had won the day, and Li Zicheng was running back to Beijing.

As May drew to a close, Li's forces limped back into the city, fully aware that the Manchus were right behind them. The news spread among the populace, that the great general Wu Sangui had somehow defeated the rebels, and was approaching to liberate the town. The embittered survivors of the battle of Sha river looted what they could and ran from the city. But Li Zicheng could not leave the city without accomplishing his life's ambition.

On 3 June, as his men prepared to retreat from the capital, Li Zicheng was enthroned as the First Emperor of the Dynasty of Great Obedience, in a hamfisted parody of imperial protocol. Not all the correct ministers were present, since a number had been murdered or had taken their own lives, and the new ruler had not appointed replacements. The great dynastic seal, with which the Emperor was supposed to sign the document of his enthronement, was not yet ready. There was no coinage available bearing his crest. But the one-eyed general had finally achieved his dream: Li Zicheng enjoyed a single night in the capital as the supposed ruler of the world, before he was obliged to flee ahead of his pursuers. As a final gesture of spite, he set fire to the imperial palace, and left Beijing in flames.

The capital was plunged once more into chaos, as the people turned on each other. Thousands died in street fighting, as citizens attacked those who were suspected of collaborating with the former occupying forces. Followers of Li Zicheng who had not yet left town were set upon by angry mobs. Other citizens simply took a leaf from the book of their former invaders and began looting.

It was a time for settling scores with collaborators, rivals, and anyone who was conspicuously different. Two men with a grudge against the Jesuits led a mob of several dozen looters to the Christian compound in the north of the city. They were faced at the gate by a lone swordsman who dared them to approach. It was Adam Schall, a Jesuit fated to live in interesting times, who later wrote:

> Admittedly, I knew that the Chinese are of cowardly disposition, but at that moment I could not guess how far their rage would take them, nor what could be the cause of such unaccustomed excitement, so I seized a Japanese sabre and stood in front of the hall by the inner door, ready to sustain and repel any attack.[27]

His gamble paid off, and the would-be criminals retreated, calling out to him that they were looking for *looters*, not loot. It was not the last time that Schall would be in danger. There were several arson attempts on the Christian buildings, including one on the room where Schall kept all his scientific equipment. Members of his flock arrived in search of medical attention, one crippled by a cannonball, and another with an arrow in his neck. Schall also inspected a nearby house that was untouched by fire, deserted but for seven bodies hanging from the rafters. Realising that two were still alive, he cut the ropes that held them and took them back to his infirmary, where he nursed them back to health.

Schall's newest patients were attempted suicides. Like many other residents of Beijing, they had finally been broken by the years of plague, drought and famine, followed by the pillaging of Li Zicheng's forces. With the Ming Emperor dead and another army advancing on the city, they had decided to end their lives.

Others thought that their troubles were over and rejoiced. Rumours grew that the loyal Wu Sangui had routed the bandit forces, and that the beloved general was even now advancing on the city, bringing with him the son of the Ming Emperor. Scouts saw a great army approaching from the east, and the surviving people of Beijing prepared to welcome it.

On 4 June 1644, the officials who had so willingly welcomed Li Zicheng selected their finest garments with which to welcome back the Ming. Citizens bearing flowers and incense waited outside the city gates, and residents lined the streets, weeping with joy. Beijing's eastern gatekeeper waited with an imperial chariot, ready to drive the returning victors through the streets in triumph. But as a detachment of soldiers arrived, few seemed to be wearing the armour or insignia of the Chinese. Their leader dismounted and approached the waiting officials, climbing up into the imperial chariot. The soldier took off his helmet.

It was Dorgon, who told them: 'I am the Prince Regent. The Ming heir apparent will reach all of you in due course. He has assented to my being your ruler.'[28]

This was not what the officials were expecting. The crowds in the streets fell to the ground in homage as the chariot and its escorts passed, though some were confused by the strange hairstyle of the new arrival. Some told each other that this strange man was a descendant of a Ming emperor from the distant past, who had been kidnapped by the Mongols. Others dared to consider that Wu Sangui had somehow failed to hold the Shanhai pass, and that the army that grew ever nearer belonged to the Manchus.

Prince Dorgon reached the imperial residences, most of which were now smouldering ruins. One palace seemed relatively untouched, and Dorgon slowly climbed the steps, accompanied by former bodyguards of the Ming Emperor.

Stopping outside the main doors, Dorgon addressed the bewildered crowd from the top of the steps. He told them to mourn their departed Emperor for three days. And he officially informed them that the Ming dynasty was gone:

> We took revenge upon the enemy of your ruler-father in place of your dynasty. We burned our bridges behind us, and we have pledged not to return until every bandit is destroyed. In the countries, districts and locales that we pass through, all those who are able to shave their heads and surrender, opening their gates to welcome us, will be given rank and reward, retaining their wealth and nobility for generations. But if there are those who resist us disobediently, then when our Grand Army arrives, the stones themselves will be set ablaze, and everyone will be massacred.[29]

Beijing had fallen, but the Manchus still had to subdue the rest of China.

6

THE IMPERIAL NAMEKEEPER

The news of the fall of the north capital soon reached Nanjing, the south capital. Rumours contradicted each other about Wu Sangui's involvement, as some assumed he was still in the service of the Ming. In fact, the Manchus wisely sent him and the remnants of his forces in pursuit of Li Zicheng's fleeing bandits. Wu Sangui would hound the fleeing rebels for months, until the once-great army that sacked Beijing was broken into a series of squabbling bandit groups. Some of Li's men surrendered to the Manchus and served in the turncoat Banners, while others joined the Ming rebels. Li himself went missing, presumed dead and forgotten on one of numerous battlefields.[1] Accompanied by a large Manchu auxiliary, Wu Sangui headed ever further to the south-west, away from the Manchu's own planned route into the heart of south China.

With reports limping towards the south and often arriving out of chronological order, confusion reigned supreme. Li Zicheng had taken the capital, it was said, the Ming Emperor was dead, but now there was a new emperor. Was this Li Zicheng, or the Ming Heir Apparent, or Wu Sangui himself? Whose side was Wu Sangui on? Who were his strange new allies? Who was this Prince Dorgon, who was issuing proclamations in the name of a child-emperor?

As time passed, the ministers of Nanjing pieced together the news. Realising that a force of Manchus would soon be heading south, they put the city on a military footing. Coxinga's studies were abruptly curtailed. Nanjing had always maintained a shadow bureaucracy in case of trouble in the north, and the city's antiquated machineries of government sprang into action. As one of the most learned men in Nanjing, Coxinga's tutor Qian Qianyi was one of

Progress of the Manchu Invasion.

the first called to service. One of the first duties of the new government was to appoint a new emperor.

Finding another member of the Ming imperial family was not difficult. There were 80,000 minor nobles scattered throughout the country, and as refugees fled the chaos in the north, a number of them came through Nanjing. In fact, the ministers of the Southern Ming were spoilt for choice. There were several respected princes in the area, any of whom would have made an ideal candidate. However, the ministers could not afford arguments or gossip about a candidate decided by vote or patronage. They had to find the closest living relative of the departed Ming Emperor. Believing the

Heir Apparent to be dead, they had no choice but to appoint a new ruler by the strict rules of the dynasty.

The selection process reawakened an old feud that had threatened the Empire two generations earlier. The Emperor of Ten Thousand Experiences, fourteenth ruler of the Ming dynasty, had an eldest son who was passed over in the succession when his mother fell out of favour. That son was the same Prince of Fu whose blood Li Zicheng had drunk. By all accounts, he was an alcoholic, dissolute wastrel whose loss was hardly noticed by the preoccupied Ming dynasty, but the Prince of Fu had a son of his own. By the strict rules of succession, his forty-year-old heir was believed to be the next in line for the imperial throne. Setting aside their differences, the factions in Nanjing brought him to the town on 4 June, and there proclaimed him with the reign title of *Hongguang:*[2] *the Emperor of Grand Radiance*. They waited two weeks to do so, perhaps hoping that someone better would come along.

It was not to be. The Emperor of Grand Radiance was, if anything, worse than his father. As a member of the imperial family, he was forbidden from working, and with nothing else to do on his estate, had grown used to food, wine and women. He was devoted to his foster-mother, a lady only a few years older than he was, who used to encourage him in his excesses. Soon after they arrived in Nanjing, she suggested to him that he should take a wife, and the new ruler decided that only a girl from Hangzhou would do. Even as the Manchus pressed southwards from Beijing, agents were sent to Hangzhou, downstream from Nanjing and slightly to the south, where the fabled beauties of the city were rounded up and brought to the Emperor of Grand Radiance for approval. Once deflowered, none of them met his demanding standards, and scouts were forced to travel further afield, to other cities, and local brothels. Whatever it was he liked to do with the virgins he was supplied, not all of them made it out of his bedchamber alive. He managed to kill two in just a single night.[3]

The Emperor of Grand Radiance also appointed a number of new nobles and generals. With finances in such desperately short supply, the administration was also prepared to sell such positions. The Southern Ming court issued over sixty proclamations of ennoblement, essentially sending mailshots to local millionaires in the hope that they would reply with an oath of fealty. One such beneficiary was Nicholas Iquan, who was made an earl by the new regime, and ordered to help defend the south capital.

Iquan duly sent a body of men under the command of his brother, Feng the Phoenix, who were garrisoned at a crucial town on the River Yangtze. To the north were four Ming loyalist armies, though their allegiance to the Emperor of Grand Radiance was compromised by their own internal feuds. One army was led by a true loyalist, Shi Kefa, a veteran of many bandit suppression campaigns. Another chiefly comprised former bandits from Li Zicheng's army, and was led by Gao Jie, a leader who had been forced to flee Li Zicheng's forces after stealing the one-eyed general's wife, Xing. With the death of Gao Jie in battle, the army fell under the control of Lady Xing herself, making her one of the few female generals in Chinese history.

There was no love lost between the Ming and their former enemies. North of Nanjing, the Ming defensive armies squabbled over jurisdiction and supplies, and even over which towns they should occupy. While the generals quarrelled, the Manchus advanced ever closer, beating them back in a series of skirmishes. Not all Manchu conquests were violent – worse for the Ming loyalists were those victories where the Manchus not only gained ground, but also new soldiers, as turncoats were incorporated within their own armies. Soon the news arrived that the Manchus were not only attacking from the north. Prince Dorgon's brother Dodo, who had accompanied Wu Sangui in his pursuit of the fleeing Li Zicheng, was now advancing with another force from the west. In Nanjing, Qian Qianyi diplomatically brought up the topic of abandoning the city and heading south to a better stronghold. Nicholas Iquan's native Fujian was regarded as the best location, since it was a natural fortress, surrounded on three sides by high mountains, and on the fourth by the sea itself. However, moving the Emperor to Fujian would essentially place him under the control of Fujian's *de facto* ruler, and Nicholas Iquan had many enemies, jealous and fearful of his meteoric rise to power. For now, the Emperor of Grand Radiance refused to listen to his advisers. He had other, more immediate problems. His hold on the populace of Nanjing, already feeble owing to lack of funds and resources, was dealt a further blow by the arrival of a pretender to his crown – a youth who claimed to be the son of the dead Emperor, who had somehow escaped from the fall of Beijing.

The fate of Prince Cilang, the true Ming Heir Apparent, had become a subject of much debate. Conflicting reports claimed that he had been at the side of Li Zicheng in the battle of the Sha river, or that he travelled in the custody of Wu Sangui. During the winter of 1644, Qian Qianyi's ministers heard further reports that someone fitting the prince's description was in the custody of loyalists, fleeing with the other refugees. Stories reached Nanjing of a youth travelling in a most unconvincing incognito, making unrealistic demands on his companions, drinking and whoring while those around him fought over food, and addressing those he encountered in an arrogantly imperious manner. As the mystery celebrity continued south, Qian Qianyi's government ordered their agents in the north to squirrel the Heir Apparent into hiding.[4]

When the mystery youth was brought to Nanjing, he claimed to be Cilang himself, and to have shaken off his captors in Beijing during the chaos. Fleeing the city, he said, he had hidden in a ditch for the first night, before walking south for seven days, avoiding any other travellers or refugees. It was only as starvation overtook him that he sought the help and company of others, and eventually fell in with loyalists. In Nanjing, as the boy was clothed for his audience, he even recognised one of the palace eunuchs who had escaped Beijing, and addressed him by name.

The Nanjing populace were ecstatic, believing that they had custody of the eldest son of the Emperor of Lofty Omens, and that the future of the Ming dynasty was secure. If the youth really were Prince Cilang, it placed the newly proclaimed Emperor of Grand Radiance in an embarrassing position, and ministers talked over the possibilities. The Celestial Empire could not suffer a further retraction, abdication or change in government, and dissatisfied factions would undoubtedly use another change in power as an excuse to question the validity of one or both claimants. If the claimant were genuine, it would probably be best for the Emperor of Grand Radiance to adopt him as his own son.

However, the Emperor of Grand Radiance was having none of it, and berated his followers for their gullibility. During a detailed but respectful interrogation, the mystery youth was able to answer many general questions about the life of a prince in Beijing, but was much vaguer concerning specifics of the real Cilang's studies. Eunuchs who had escaped from Beijing were prepared to say that, *as far as they could recall*, his facial features did not match those of a prince they had only seen from a distance. An imperial consort, who presumably had intimate knowledge of the real Cilang, announced that while the trauma of the northern war and southern flight might have understandably altered the prince's countenance and demeanour, it also appeared to have removed several distinguishing birthmarks, and a mole she recalled seeing on the real Cilang's leg.

Although nobody wished to put their life on the line by denouncing the mystery youth outright as an imposter, some of Qian Qianyi's most trusted generals and ministers privately voiced their own suspicions. They believed that his 'escape' had begun much closer to Nanjing, and that the alleged week-long solo journey was merely a convenient way of avoiding witnesses. But the most damning evidence against the False Heir, as he came to be known, came from an unexpected source. Back in Beijing, the Manchu conquerors had sent a coded message to Ming loyalists announcing that they themselves had already killed the original.

The real Cilang had indeed fled when Beijing fell, but was recaptured by soldiers of Li Zicheng's fleeing army, who failed to recognise him. He served them for two months as a horseboy, before finally making his escape, returning to the Beijing mansion of his maternal grandfather. There he was immediately recognised, by the one-armed Huaizong, the former Princess Imperial, who burst into tears at the sight of her emaciated brother.

However, when Cilang was brought into Manchu custody, Prince Dorgon proclaimed that the boy was an imposter, and that he had been identified as such by the former Honoured Consort of the dead Emperor. The proclamation made sure to mention the boy's tearful reunion with his one-armed sister, but also identified his denouncer by name. For those few eunuchs and ministers who had been present during the last days of the Ming Emperor, the message was clear. The Honoured Consort had been dead for almost a year – she had been standing next to the Princess Imperial when her father hacked off the girl's arm, and had committed suicide later that night. If the Princess Imperial recognised the boy when she saw him, it was because he was the real Prince Cilang. And if Dorgon refuted the claim with fabricated testimony from a dead woman, it was because he needed an excuse to execute the real Cilang before the boy became a rallying point for rebels. Dorgon had the boy killed for daring to impersonate Cilang, but made sure that his proclamations reached the loyalists of the Southern Ming – the 'imposter' in Beijing had been the real Cilang, and the Manchus had killed him.

This, of course, was also bad news for the False Heir, who was imprisoned and later put on trial in April 1645. He confessed that he was really Wang Zhiming, a member of the Imperial Bodyguard, talked into running a scam by several conspiring eunuchs and fraudsters. But even the False Heir's confession failed to sway the people of Nanjing, who saw the revelation of the False Heir's 'real name' as a poor attempt by the Emperor of Grand Radiance at lying to them. It wasn't long before someone pointed out that Wang Zhiming was an anagram of *Ming zhi Wang*, or Prince of Brightness. The people of Nanjing remained convinced that the False Heir was the real Cilang, and that the Emperor of Grand Radiance was only victimising him in an attempt to hold on to power. If anything, the trial only increased the common people's conviction that the Emperor of Grand-Radiance was an evil man intent on crushing his predecessor's family, and unrest grew in the capital. Even though the False Heir had signed a confession of his crime, the Emperor of Grand Radiance could not risk falling further from public favour by executing him. Instead, the boy was installed under opulent house arrest, while Qian Qianyi's government tried to prepare for the coming attack by the Manchus.

The invaders swept through the countryside from Beijing, encountering little resistance. When they did, the Banner armies were cushioned from immediate danger by legions of turncoats in their front lines, using new recruits in the same way they had used Wu Sangui's forces at the Sha river. Chinese fought Chinese on battlefields across the north, and many simply surrendered. By turning their back on the memory of the Ming dynasty, such traitors were richly rewarded. A general at the city of Huai'an was faced with the prospect of death or promotion to the rank of viscount. He chose to become a noble in the Manchu army, and his men became members of the 'invading' force.

The next city on the Manchu list was Yangzhou, which sat north of Nanjing, where the Grand Canal from Beijing met a tributary of the Yangtze river. The two critical marching routes to Yangzhou had already fallen, their generals submitting to the Manchus and shaving the front of their heads to show their new allegiance. However, unlike the other cities before it, Yangzhou would not surrender.

Yangzhou was occupied by Shi Kefa, a 44-year-old general with fanatical loyalty to the Ming dynasty. The Manchus tried to win Shi Kefa over in a number of ways, sending numerous letters in the name of Dorgon, but actually drafted by turncoats. Shi Kefa had famously berated the Emperor of Grand Radiance on military matters, using language that would have led to the reprimand or imprisonment of a less valuable soldier. Dorgon's messages capitalised on this, reminding Shi Kefa that, loyal to the Ming or not, he was currently serving a depraved master. While the Manchus fought the Ming loyalists, wrote Dorgon's scribes, both sides lost out on the opportunity to unite and pursue the true enemy: the remnants of the forces of Li Zicheng. Dorgon urged Shi Kefa at all costs to avoid a situation in which there were 'two suns in the firmament'. But it was too late; already there were two people claiming to be the emperor of China – three, if one was prepared to count the fugitive Li Zicheng.

The army of Prince Dodo, Dorgon's brother, reached Yangzhou, where the Manchus gave the loyalist one more chance to surrender. Li Yuchun, a turncoat general, rode up to the city walls bearing the banner of Prince Dodo himself, and yelled:

The fame of your excellency's loyal and eminent services is spread throughout China, yet the Ming Emperor does not give you his confidence. Why, then, not gain a name and a reward by joining the Manchus?[5]

An arrow shot from Shi Kefa's bow just barely missed Yuchun, who scurried back to report an answer in the negative.

Dodo sent several more letters and entreaties over the days that followed, including a return visit from Yuchun, whose admittedly fair comments on the slippery nature of the Emperor of Grand Radiance earned him another arrow. This time Shi Kefa hit his mark.

Coquettish reluctance is not unknown in the Far East. It is, for example, considered seemly to refuse the offer of high appointment three times, in order to demonstrate one's humility. Consequently, it took several days for the Manchus to realise that Shi Kefa's resistance was not a theatrical show of good manners, but genuine loyalty to the Ming. In that time, Shi Kefa had his men building wooden platforms along the Yangzhou city ramparts, where he installed his secret weapon: artillery.

As an experienced soldier, Shi Kefa knew what guns could do. During his days in Beijing, he had been one of the staunchest supporters of the foundry programme that had recruited Adam Schall to cast guns for the Emperor of Lofty Omens. The Chinese had always had guns, and prided themselves on the giant 'Divine Instrument' super-cannon, that took half a day to move from the armoury to the practice field. Shi Kefa, however, was a fan of Schall's smaller, more portable field-pieces, particularly a triple-barrelled variant. Many of Schall's prototypes were scattered across numerous battlefields in the north, or already stolen by the invading Manchus, but Schall's students had become accomplished cannoneers in their own right. One such pupil of the Jesuit artilleryman had cast new guns for Shi Kefa, and these weapons now festooned the walls of Yangzhou.

When the Manchu army finally began the assault of Yangzhou, Shi Kefa's guns killed them in their thousands. The bodies piled up so high, that after a time, there was no need for siege ladders, and fresh Manchu troops climbed a mountain of corpses to reach the battlements.

The defenders of the city began fleeing the walls by jumping onto the houses immediately below, tearing off their helmets and throwing down their spears, creating an unearthly clatter as their feet smashed tiles on the rooftops. The noise brought townsfolk out of their houses in time to see the defenders running away, and soon the streets were full of refugees. But there was nowhere to run. Someone opened the south gate, and the last possible escape route was cut off by more Manchu soldiers.

In the aftermath Shi Kefa ordered his men to kill him, but his lieutenant could not bring himself to strike the death blow. With the town now in Manchu hands, Shi Kefa was brought to Dodo. The prince advised him that his loyalty had impressed his Manchu enemies.

'You have made a gallant defence,' he said. 'Now that you have done all that duty could dictate, I would be glad to give you a high post.'

Shi Kefa, however, refused to abandon his beloved Dynasty of Brightness.

'I ask of you no favour except death,' he replied.[6]

Over several days, the Manchus made repeated attempts to persuade Shi Kefa to join them, but he was adamant that the only thing he wanted was to die with his dynasty. On the third day, an exasperated Prince Dodo granted Shi Kefa his wish, and beheaded him personally.

Despite his pleas to Shi Kefa, Dodo was intensely irritated at the human cost of taking Yangzhou. He told his troops to do whatever they wanted with the city for five days, and the ensuing atrocities reached such heights that it was a further five days before Dodo regained control of his men. The surviving Manchus avenged their fallen comrades on the population of the town, slaughtering the menfolk and raping the women. The clemency shown to turncoat towns further in the north was nowhere in evidence here, as Manchus and Chinese traitors looted what they could, and murdered all the witnesses they could find. Fires broke out in numerous quarters of the city, but were largely put out by heavy rain.

A survivor reported that the corpses filled the canals, gutters and ponds, their blood drowning the water itself, creating rivulets of a deep greenish-red throughout the city. Babies were killed or trampled underfoot, and the young women were chained together ready to be shipped to the far north. Many years later, travellers in Manchuria and Mongolia would still report sightings of aging, scarred female slaves with Yangzhou accents, clad in animal skins.[7]

With Yangzhou gone, the Manchus had unimpeded passage along the Grand Canal to the Yangtze river itself. Qian Qianyi suggested to the Emperor of Grand Radiance that the time had come to evacuate Nanjing and head further south, but his words went unheeded.

The next fallback position for the Southern Ming forces was the city of Zhenjiang, a heavily fortified position on the south bank of the Yangtze, slightly to the east of Nanjing. The waterway from Yangzhou met the immense Yangtze river on the opposite side, making Zhenjiang the logical next target for the nearing Manchus. Zhenjiang was occupied by a considerable force of Ming soldiers, under the command of Coxinga's uncle and former martial arts tutor Feng the Phoenix, now made a Marquess by the Emperor of Grand

Radiance. With him was Zheng Cai, a nephew of Nicholas Iquan – possibly Feng's own or adopted son. The soldiers had occupied the nearby Golden Island, and dug in with a large number of firearms, obtained with the aid of European allies.

Feng's first problem was the retreating army of Gao Jie, which had mutinied against Lady Xing. Now reverting to the lawless state that all had feared, the army turned on its former allies. Feng the Phoenix's men were forced to sally out and fight fellow Chinese, slaughtering up to ten thousand of their attackers before they beat them back. It was another hollow victory, as the survivors were driven into the arms of the Manchus, where they surrendered and became new soldiers for the invaders. The 'Manchu' army, led by Prince Dodo and heavily swelled with Chinese turncoats, reached the north bank of the Yangtze. A mile or so to the south, across waters up to 100ft deep, waited Feng the Phoenix.

Three days passed with no action by either side. On the fourth night, 1 June 1645, the river was obscured by a dense fog, and the Manchus went into action. They floated a navy of small rafts into the water, each bearing at least one flaming torch. Seeing the lights nearing across the vast expanse of water, Feng the Phoenix assumed they were enemy landing craft, and ordered his men to open fire. The defenders began a continuous salvo of musketry and cannon that lasted for hours, expending most of their precious ammunition, shooting into the dark at the empty vessels.[8]

Meanwhile, further upstream, the vanguard of the Manchu army slipped silently across in the darkness, without a single torch to light their way. As dawn broke, Feng the Phoenix saw a Manchu force on his side of the river, advancing towards his fortifications. Realising he had been duped, Feng ordered his men to flee, abandoning Zhenjiang to the Manchus. As one contemporay account put it: 'the Chinese ran all away, as Sheep use to do when they see the Wolf, leaving the whole shore unfenced to their landing'.[9] There were those at the Nanjing court who whispered that Feng had never intended to stay for long. An experienced warrior and famously brave, he was no coward. His later actions show that he remained loyal to the Ming, and was not in league with the invaders. But the likelihood remains that his swift departure from Zhenjiang was engineered by Nicholas Iquan. Though no Manchus were killed in the taking of Zhenjiang, none of Iquan's men were injured either.

The wily Master of the Seas may have been planning all along to lure the Emperor back to his native Fujian, which had natural defences, not least of all the sea itself. It is likely that Feng the Phoenix was the only major member of Nicholas Iquan's family left in the Yangtze area. The rest, Coxinga included, had retreated to the Fujian region in the far south, to await the outcome of the Manchu arrival in Nanjing. The departure of Feng the Phoenix's men removed the Zheng family from any involvement in the defence of Nanjing.

The Emperor of Grand Radiance fled the city and south of the Yangtze, without informing any of his generals or ministers. On hearing that the Emperor had left, Qian Qianyi was forced to face facts – Nanjing was going to fall to the Manchus in a matter of days. Qian's lover, a singer turned poetess by the name of Liu Shi,[10] met with him in floods of tears, assuming that as a man of honour and Confucian virtue, he would now feel obliged to commit suicide. Qian, however, announced that he would be taking his chances with the Manchus. If the Ming were truly finished, the Manchus seemed to be behaving honourably to those who submitted to them.

Liu Shi changed her tune, instead telling Qian Qianyi that he had to kill himself, but something had already persuaded the strict Confucian scholar that submission to the Manchus would be the correct course of action. The most likely blame lay with the Emperor of Grand Radiance himself. In his debauched behaviour, and his spiteful treatment of the False Heir, the Emperor of Grand Radiance had not acted like the idealised Confucian leader he was supposed to be. It is possible that Qian saw in the fleeing emperor a sign of the true loss of the Mandate of Heaven. The evidence was certainly compelling, and many decades later, when the Manchus themselves wrote the history of their conquest, they would deliberately end the history of the Ming with the perverse and cowardly Emperor of Grand Radiance in Nanjing, instead of his nobler predecessor in Beijing.

Qian Qianyi called his closest ministers to him, and the group began making plans for the safe and peaceful handover of the city to the invaders. As the ministers agreed to welcome the arriving Manchus, and thereby save their city from the fate of Yangzhou, the populace took it upon themselves to free the False Heir from imprisonment and proclaim him as the new Ming emperor. Dressing him in an emperor's costume purloined from a theatrical store, they paid him homage and begged him to intercede with the gods. After several days of overcast skies, the sun came out briefly, leading some to assume that Nanjing would be safe. In a way, it was.

The approaching army of Dodo reached the gates of Nanjing in the middle of a heavy storm, where they were greeted by Qian Qianyi's rain-soaked ministers. Since Dodo had been mopping up Li Zicheng's forces in the hinterland for some weeks, he was unaware that Dorgon had already killed the Heir Apparent, and treated the False Heir with guarded reverence. 'We cannot distinguish true from false at the moment,' he told a turncoat minister. 'All will become clear upon our return to the north.'[11]

A section of Nanjing was set aside as the Manchu quarter, and the local families were cast out, and forced to move to a different part of town. The separation of conquerors and conquered helped avoid many of the atrocities that had accompanied the loss of Yangzhou, and Nanjing passed into Manchu hands with relative peace. Qian Qianyi had saved thousands of lives, but he had also turned his back on the Ming dynasty.

Meanwhile, the Emperor of Grand Radiance fled in search of allies south of Nanjing. He reached the camp of Huang Degong, a loyalist commander who was not at all pleased to see him. The general, who was one of those who still believed that the False Heir might have been the real Cilang, had been rather hoping that the Emperor of Grand Radiance would have died nobly in the fall of Nanjing, inspiring his followers to resist further south with the False Heir as their new leader. Instead, the Emperor of Grand Radiance had fled. Not only had he refused to die at the appropriate time, but he was now a magnet for trouble – Degong believed, rightly, that his soldiers would now attract undue attention from the approaching Manchu armies.

The Emperor of Grand Radiance, embittered and angry after days of deprivation, was heard to utter that Degong had never been a minister he could trust, and the embarrassed general pledged his allegiance.

However, it was not to last. On 15 June, a detachment of soldiers arrived, led by Chinese turncoats. They demanded that Degong hand over his imperial guest, but Degong refused. Without waiting for argument, one of the Chinese turncoats raised his bow and shot Degong in the throat. His lieutenants watched uneasily as he died, knowing that they would be next in line. When the Manchus asked a second time, they handed over the Emperor of Grand Radiance and pledged their own allegiance to their new masters.

The former Emperor of Grand Radiance was taken back to Nanjing, along roads lined with crowds who spat at him and threw stones. He was taken immediately to Dodo, who happened to be at a banquet that was also attended by the False Heir.[12] The former Emperor of Grand Radiance was seated at a position below that of the False Heir, and Dodo could not resist tormenting him. Why was it, Dodo asked, that he had not stepped down from his new imperial role the moment that the son of the Emperor of Lofty Omens appeared in the city? If, Dodo added, the Emperor of Grand Radiance were the true ruler of China as he claimed, why had it been left to the Manchus to pursue the fleeing remnants of Li Zicheng's army? The former Emperor of Grand Radiance simply sat in silence, paralysed with fear, his clothes soaked in nervous sweat. But Dodo was not finished. He was curious, he said, as to events surrounding the Emperor of Grand Radiance's cowardly flight from Nanjing as the Manchu army approached. Surely, Dodo asked, if the Emperor of Grand Radiance possessed the Mandate of Heaven, he had nothing to fear? After calling the former Emperor a usurper, an incompetent and a coward, Dodo finished with a final flourish. He informed the assembled diners that the Manchus had never intended to come so far south, but had been spurred on in their conquest by the lack of organised resistance, and by the numbers of Chinese willing to change sides.[13] Was the former Emperor of Grand Radiance aware, for example, that it would have taken but a single Ming army north of the Yellow river to wipe out the Manchu advance before it could have been swelled to invulnerable numbers with Chinese turncoats?

Bored with attacking a man who could not fight back, Dodo ordered the former Emperor of Grand Radiance to be taken away. The deposed ruler lived in seclusion near Nanjing for some time, while his Manchu captors pumped him for information about prominent surviving loyalists. Once he was of no use to his jailers, he was quietly executed. Dodo sent the False Heir to Beijing, where he survived in captivity until the following year, when he and a number of other troublesome 'Ming princes', false and otherwise, were executed *en masse* by Dorgon.

Although Qian Qianyi had submitted to the Manchus and Nanjing had changed hands, the Manchus had still only conquered half of China. As their armies pressed ever southwards, they were entering the very regions that had proved so unruly in the past, whoever the nominal ruler. They were also approaching Fujian, the centre of Nicholas Iquan's organisation.

The Ming loyalists needed a new emperor, and found a princely candidate just to the north of Fujian. He was not of the bloodline of recent emperors, but was a descendant of one of the sons of the Ming dynasty's founder. On 10 July 1645, he agreed to become a regent until such time as the fate of the Emperor of Grand Radiance was better understood. Guarded by the divisions of Feng the Phoenix, who were still heading south after their disastrous defence of Zhenjiang, the regent was hustled through one of the hazardous mountain passes into Fujian. At many towns along the route, the new regent addressed the population with speeches and decrees, proclaiming that the Dynasty of Brightness was not yet done shining, and that the time was approaching when the people of China would strike back at the invaders. He also made a point of acknowledging the loyal nobleman who was going to make all of this possible: Fujian's very own Nicholas Iquan.[14]

By 26 July, the regent had safely reached Fuzhou, the provincial capital of Fujian, which he proclaimed a temporary capital. This was no drunken debauchee like the Emperor of Grand Radiance – the regent encouraged austerity among his followers by eschewing fine clothes, and wasted no time in appointing new ministers, and ordering plans to be drawn up for a counter-offensive. On 18 August, with the fate of his predecessor now known, he was officially enthroned, with the ominous reign title of *Longwu*: Emperor of Intense Warring.[15]

The new ruler had no intention of staying long in Fuzhou. He was determined to personally lead an army back north to take China back from the Manchus. The Emperor of Intense Warring was extremely grateful to Nicholas Iquan, and expected the wealthy southerner to become the centre of the war effort. Iquan was made a Marquess, and given control of the three ministries that related most directly to martial matters. Other Zheng clan members fared similarly well. Feng the Phoenix, who had fled Zhenjiang but successfully transported the Emperor to Fuzhou, became the Count of Decisive Attack. Iquan's nephew Zheng Cai became the Count of Perpetual Victory, and Bao the Panther became Captain of the Brocade Guard, the Emperor's personal praetorians.[16]

Another beneficiary of the honours bestowed at Fuzhou was Coxinga himself, who was said to have greatly impressed the bookish Emperor of Intense Warring. Still only a youth of twenty-one, the former Confucian scholar was made assistant controller of the Imperial Clan Court. The childless Emperor also commented that he was disappointed not to have a daughter he could offer to Coxinga in marriage, and bestowed him with a new name. Once Lucky Pine, then Big Tree, the boy was now given the appellation *Chenggong*, thereby making his new given name Zheng Chenggong translate literally as 'Serious Achievement'. In a moment of supreme pride for his family, the boy was also conferred with the right to use the surname of the Ming ruling family itself. It amounted to a symbolic adoption, and he was often referred to as *Guoxingye*, the Imperial Namekeeper. Pronounced *Koksenya* in the staccato dialect of Fujian, and later transcribed by foreign observers, the title eventually transformed into the 'Coxinga' by which he is known to history.[17]

Not all at the court were happy about the attention lavished on Nicholas Iquan and his associates. Some were heard to complain, with good reason, that it was only the desperation of the hour that led the Emperor of Intense Warring to place such trust in a group of people who had been criminals only a few years before. For Iquan, however, his ennoblement to Marquess, and soon Duke, of National Pacification was a source of great pride. It may have also been a contributing factor in the arrival of a new face at Iquan's Anhai fortress.

Perhaps she had always intended to leave Japan after her second son reached manhood. Perhaps she was swayed by the news that her former lover was now a duke, or that her eldest son was the new emperor's favourite. Whatever her reasons, Miss Tagawa chose to leave Japan for good in 1645, and sail for Fujian, where she was reunited with Coxinga after over a decade of separation. There is no record of what Nicholas Iquan's principal wife had to say about the arrival of her husband's old flame, but Miss Tagawa was permitted to stay at Anhai. It is likely that she soon had cause to regret her arrival, as while Iquan's ennoblement looked good on paper, he was a noble in a China that was half overrun by enemy invaders.

There was some confusion among the Zheng family about how seriously they were taking their new Emperor. Fujian's encircling mountains had three major passes, and perhaps a hundred other minor routes that needed to be guarded against Manchu raiders. Merely keeping garrisons on these entry points was an expense that threatened to bankrupt the loyalist regime, and yet the Emperor of Intense Warring was determined to raise an army and march back through the passes to fight the Manchus in open battle. He initially announced his intention to begin marching in September 1645, but was persuaded by Nicholas Iquan to wait.

Iquan had a plan of sorts. He advised the Emperor of Intense Warring that the funds in the Fujian coffers would not be enough to fund a military campaign for long. In fact, they would not be enough to keep men guarding the entrances to Fujian for that long, either. Iquan instead suggested that the Emperor capitalise on Fujian's greatest strength, and invest critical imperial funds in mercantile operations. With millions of Chinese people starving, Iquan seriously suggested that his Emperor 'open up the sea lanes, stimulate trade in each port, in order to satisfy his material needs'.[18] Only then, when foreign trade had enriched Fujian further, should the Emperor reinvest the money in a war effort.

True enough, the person who stood to benefit most from such a policy was Iquan himself, whose men, ships and contacts would be needed to carry it out. Those who remembered the swindles of Captain China would be forgiven for thinking that this was a similar enterprise, but in spite of the great personal gain Iquan would make, his intentions may still have been honourable. Iquan himself was living proof of the money that could be made through foreign trade. Had not Fujian been saved in the past from disaster by the importation of potatoes? Were not the soldiers all around them inhaling the intoxicating smoke from the 'dry alcohol' plant, which was bringing profit to Fujianese farmers, even while their fellows beyond the passes struggled to find food after the Manchu occupation? Were there not potential allies just beyond the horizon, the Dutch in Taiwan and the Portuguese in Macao, who might be persuaded to lend military aid in exchange for trade privileges with a restored Ming government? As Duke of National Pacification, the core of Iquan's policy was to appropriate government silver, and use it to fund more of the trading missions he would have been doing anyway.

The proposed start date for the counter-offensive was moved to October 1645, and then January 1646, causing the Emperor of Intense Warring to become increasingly frustrated with Iquan. He began to see that his non-Zheng advisers had been right, and that while Nicholas Iquan wielded great authority in the Fujian area, he had little incentive to leave his natural fortress and risk his life outside it. Such a realisation cannot have been pleasant for the Emperor of Intense Warring, because if taken to its logical conclusion, it spelled danger. As the Manchus had demonstrated in their march southward, they slaughtered those who opposed them, and conferred great honour on those who did not. Since Nicholas Iquan had made him the Emperor of Intense Warring, the withdrawal of Iquan's support could also break him.

Whether through his own initiative or the careful steering of anti-Zheng associates, the Emperor left Fuzhou and established an imperial camp at Yanping in the Fujian hinterland. One of his most loyal ministers, an aging civilian in his sixties, attempted to lead a campaign through the passes and march on Nanjing, but the inexperienced man had no support from Iquan. The loyalist army marched through driving rain into a series of defeats at the hands of vastly superior Manchu forces. Its leader did eventually see Nanjing in February 1646, but only as a captive on his way to his execution.

As the Emperor of Intense Warring idled in his camp and waited for Iquan to supply the men he so desperately needed, Coxinga continued to display a loyalty and sense of duty that was lacking in his father. In spring 1646 he presented the Emperor with a plan for strengthening his position. Genuinely impressed, the Emperor conferred Coxinga with the title Count of Loyalty, and made him Field Marshall of the Punitive Expedition. Eager to serve his lord, Coxinga was soon nominally in charge of a detachment of several hundred soldiers, guarding one of the strategic passes. However, an actual counter-offensive would require Nicholas Iquan, the Duke of National Pacification, to provide the men and supplies for the punitive expedition of which his son was the putative leader, and Iquan was in no hurry.

The early excitement of the new court had begun to sour. Though Feng the Phoenix and Coxinga both exhibited continued loyalty to the Emperor of Intense Warring, courtiers had come to regard Nicholas Iquan and some of the other Zhengs with increasing suspicion. There was some elation at the news that the Empress was pregnant, which turned to disappointment when her newborn son was found to be disabled. Letters were sent to the shogun of Japan, asking for military assistance, although the closed country was unlikely to commit itself to a war on the mainland. Whispers spread abroad that the Mandate of Heaven was still not restored to the Dynasty of Brightness.

As the spring rains abated and the summer drew near, the Manchus prepared to march on the Fujian passes. Their message, as in the rest of China, was that surrender would be met with peace and great rewards, but that resistance would be met with death. For the Ming loyalists, there were decisions to be made, and the Emperor of Intense Warring knew that his men were already receiving secret communications from his enemies, exhorting them to switch sides.

It is reported that Coxinga found the Emperor mourning his fate, and said to him: 'Why does your Majesty look so disconsolate? Is it because you think my father's heart is changed towards you? I will be faithful to you even unto death.'[19]

THE ALLURE OF TREACHERY

On 13 April 1646, Prince Dorgon's nephew Bolo was appointed as the leader of the Southward Campaign, a military project designed to bring the remainder of China under Manchu control. As with the unsuccessful Yangtze defence, the Ming loyalists hoped that rivers would prove to be natural defences, but the summer was hot, and the river south of Hangzhou was shallow enough for the Manchus to wade through. Instead of being delayed for days or weeks while they placed men and horses on boats, the Manchu made it across in hours, causing yet another garrison of Chinese defenders to flee in panic.[1]

In his 'advance camp' at Yanping, where he had been earnestly trying to organise the counter-offensive for almost a year, the Emperor of Intense Warring staged a publicity stunt to appeal to his men's loyalty. His agents had intercepted over two hundred letters to the Manchus, all from prominent officials of his government, all secretly offering to defect. Facing a room full of ministers, most of whom he knew had already been prepared to betray him, the Emperor of Intense Warring set the pile of letters on fire, without reading out a single one.

Perhaps some of the Emperor's ministers and servants were shamed by his willingness to wipe the slate clean. Others, however, had already given up on him, including his paramount minister, Duke Nicholas Iquan, who was already in correspondence with Prince Bolo, the leader of the invading armies.

Bolo had offered Iquan the opportunity to cease fighting. If he would agree to shave the front of his head in the Manchu manner and swear allegiance to his new masters, he would be rewarded with the post of viceroy of Fujian and Canton. To all intents and purposes, Iquan would become the king of south-east China, obligated only to provide occasional tribute to the Manchu conquerors in the north.

Of course, if Iquan agreed to such a decision, he would have to turn his back on the Emperor of Intense Warring, but it is unlikely that Iquan was too bothered about that. In fact, although few dared mention it before, Iquan had opposed the very idea of appointing a new emperor in Fuzhou, and had been outvoted by other Zheng family members. For several months now, Iquan had been operating under the impression that the Ming were well and truly finished. It is likely that many of the honours heaped upon him and other family members had simply been attempts to hang on to their support long after the former pirates would have preferred to have taken to their ships and deserted the loyalist forces.

Iquan greeted Bolo's offer with delight. He had heard of many other turncoats further to the north, and knew that the Manchus would keep their word. With Fujian under Manchu control, the tide of invasion had now swept over Iquan's own home. There would be a sustained Ming resistance further to the south, but that, too, was fated to fall. Despite being a thorn in the Manchus' side for over a year, Iquan now had an offer he could not refuse. Iquan, they promised, would retain his dukedom and gain the official seal of approval to his paramount status in south-east China. To the wily former pirate, it seemed ideal.

At the time, the *Historical Novel* reports that Coxinga was with a small force of soldiers guarding Xianxia, the Pass of Misty Immortals, that led into Fujian. It was a highly likely target for the brunt of the Manchu advance, and required a substantially better defence than a 22-year-old youth in scholar's robes and a few hundred men. Coxinga waited expectantly for a message from his father, giving details of reinforcements. Instead, a message eventually arrived that shocked Coxinga to the core. Iquan wrote to his son, the Count of Loyalty:

While in Fuzhou, I have been informed that the troops of General Bolo are waiting for reinforcements, in order to invade Fujian and eliminate the loyalist resistance. Unfortunately, I now believe that there is no hope for the Emperor to restore the Ming to the Dragon Throne. I lack the courage to draw up my armies, as there seems little point in a vain resistance to the Manchus. I prefer to negotiate with Bolo in order to obtain favourable treatment for all members of the Zheng family. Therefore, I invite you to lay down your arms, with the hope that you will benefit from this action.[2]

Coxinga sent scouts out beyond the pass, who soon returned with reports that the Manchus were advancing with insurmountable forces. It was clear from his father's letter that Coxinga could expect no further help from Nicholas Iquan. It would be suicide to stand and fight, and Coxinga bitterly ordered the men to retreat from the pass and head for the Fujian coast.

Other members of Iquan's family shared Coxinga's shock. As Coxinga headed for the sea, the leaders of the Zheng clan entered into an intense argument, conducted chiefly by letter. Post-riders reached Coxinga as he marched, bearing news of the intense negotiations.

Iquan's brothers, particularly Feng the Phoenix, preferred to put to sea and organise continued Ming resistance, advising Iquan that 'Fish should not be taken out of the water.' Coxinga himself, reared his whole life on tales of Iquan's faithful service to the Dynasty of Brightness, wept at the news, and is said to have begged his father to reconsider, saying: 'How is it that my father, who has always taught me the virtue of loyalty, can contemplate such an ignominious surrender? How can my father expect his son to be called a traitor?'[3]

Iquan was angry at his relatives' refusal to face facts. 'When the country is in a state of chaos,' he said, 'one cannot act as one would in normal times.' Iquan had none of Coxinga's schooling in the ideals of Confucian behaviour, and none of his youthful idealism. He knew it was too late to save the Ming – in fact, the chances are that he had come to realise it not long after the fall of the south capital. With so many Chinese defecting to the Manchu side, Iquan was only following the herd. 'Besides,' Iquan added pointedly, 'what can a boy like you know of politics?'[4]

Somebody blew up the Zheng family arsenal in Fuzhou. Sources are unclear as to whether it was retreating Zheng ships keeping their supplies out of enemy hands, or agents of Nicholas Iquan attempting to cripple his family's ability to fight. Either way, the Zheng fleet was putting out to sea. Coxinga was not with them, having decided to head south to regroup with the Emperor of Intense Warring.

Iquan waited for Prince Bolo in Fuzhou, a city now aflame as the fires spread from the destroyed arsenal. The Manchu soldiers found the burning city almost deserted, but for a party of Zheng retainers waiting to meet them. However, Bolo was disappointed to discover that Iquan, the Master of the Seas, was accompanied only by some of the African warriors of the Black Guard. Bolo had assumed that a yes from Iquan would have meant the submission of his entire family, and was annoyed that Iquan had come without them. Iquan alone was a propaganda coup, but still left the fleet in enemy hands. Without the other influential members of the Zheng family – Feng the Phoenix, Zheng Cai, and Coxinga himself – Iquan's defection was considerably devalued. Even Miss Tagawa had refused to accompany him, remaining at a Zheng family stronghold in Anping.

Iquan and Bolo entertained themselves for a few days with drinking and archery competitions, waiting all the while for more members of the Zheng family to arrive. A few stragglers turned up – Iquan's aged mother, Iquan's principal wife and a couple of her children – but none of the major players. As the time passed Bolo began to mistrust his new guest, suspecting that Iquan was merely a very high-class form of distraction, sent to keep him busy while the rest of the Zheng family slipped away. Fuzhou was safely under Manchu occupation, but the rest of Fujian remained unconquered. Since Iquan had not brought the allegiances of his armies and navies with him when he defected, the Zheng family were still enemies of the Manchu. Tiring of the charade, Bolo ordered Iquan to be taken to Beijing 'for his own protection'. It was not unusual for turncoats to be taken north for an official debriefing and reassignment, but Iquan had clearly been expecting to be simply sent back to Fuzhou with a new haircut and a new master. Instead, Bolo's decision led to a scuffle in which several members of the Black Guard died defending their lord. Iquan was eventually manhandled into a palanquin and dispatched to the north, a 'guest' of the Manchu, but a prisoner in all but name.

As the Emperor of Intense Warring fled before him, Bolo's army pressed ever southwards through Fujian. Though some members of the Black Guard remained with the loyalist members of the Zheng family, 300 of the African soldiers had defected with their lord, and now fought alongside the Manchus in their own unique unit.[5] Bolo's forces looted and burned all in their path until they finally caught up with the Emperor of Intense Warring near Fujian's southern border.

One detachment broke away and headed for the Zheng stronghold at Anping, causing Coxinga's southward advance to suddenly become a race against his enemies. The castle at Anping was the last known location of Coxinga's mother, and he was determined to reach her before the Manchus.

He arrived to find the castle overwhelmed, with Manchu soldiers on the walls and the defenders fighting to the last. Coxinga's small force beat back the Manchu soldiers, but it was too late. Miss Tagawa was found dead in the ruins, although the exact nature of her demise remains a matter of some debate.

Though other sources report a simple suicide, the *Historical Novel* contains a different story of Miss Tagawa's last moments. Miss Tagawa, Coxinga was told, was a woman from a samurai family, and unlikely to go quietly. She was sighted on the battlements of the castle, fighting alongside the soldiers to repel the Manchu assault. As the attackers gained control of the walls, Miss Tagawa was last seen silhouetted against the flames that surrounded the highest tower, plunging her dagger into her throat and tumbling into the moat below.

Manchu soldiers observing Miss Tagawa's last moments are said to have remarked that if she were a typical Japanese woman, they would prefer not to fight against the men – it is often said in her home country that Miss Tagawa's fighting end was the reason why the Manchus, conquerors of all China, Mongolia and Tibet, never dared invade Japan itself.[6]

Coxinga did not take the news well, covering his eyes with both hands and weeping, his sobs turning into howls as he tore at his clothes. Taking his sword in his hand, he swung at anything and everything in the room, swearing revenge on the barbarians that had killed his mother. Family servants withdrew and left him to his grief, and nothing was seen of the brooding count for several days.

The same period saw the arrival of messengers from the south, reporting that time had caught up with the Emperor of Intense Warring. Close to Fujian's southern border, a detachment of Chinese turncoats had finally surrounded the forces of the Emperor, the pathetic remnants of what all had hoped would be the vanguard of the counter-offensive. The Empress drowned herself to evade capture, clutching the crippled infant Heir Apparent to her as she did so. The Emperor of Intense Warring was captured alive, but soon executed – the Ming had lost another ruler, and another province.

The mourning Coxinga led the stragglers of the Zheng family towards the coast at Anhai, where the family stronghold remained in friendly hands. It was only a matter of time before the vanguard of the Manchu invasion turned back towards the area to mop up any last resistance. The Zheng family could always retreat to the sea, or even across the straits to Taiwan, but Coxinga had other plans.

His impromptu procession reached a Confucian temple in his father's home village, where he called his followers to witness a bizarre ritual. As his people watched in confusion, Coxinga brought out the scholar's robes he had worn for so long, during his Confucian studies in the south capital, and as a courtier of the Emperor of Intense Warring. He threw them onto a fire, and watched as they began to smoulder.

'In the past,' he said, 'I was guided by my relatives, but now I am alone.' Nobody dared remind him that his father was still alive. By joining the invaders that had killed Coxinga's mother, Nicholas Iquan was already dead in his son's eyes.[7]

'In every man's life, there comes a time to make a stand,' said Coxinga. This was it. He called for servants to bring him armour, saying that he was a scholar no more, but an instrument of Ming vengeance. He also wrote a poem, which remains extant in the *Historical Novel*:

> The year has brought great joy and profound sorrow
> Yet if a man works hard for fortune or fame,
> Death will not spare him.
> As with idle sports, in the end all is vain
> Though men's hearts may be blind
> The Way of Heaven rewards the true of heart
> If my life must be a game of chess
> I am not afraid of the final move
> Let the people say what they will
> It is not easy to be an honest man
> In a distressed and wicked time.[8]

Curiously, his words could almost be those of his father, with his talk of the need for pragmatism, and speculation on the demands placed on ordinary people in extraordinary circumstances. But where Iquan used the situation as an excuse to switch sides once more, Coxinga clung to the dynasty that had first honoured him. And with the deaths of his mother and of the kindly Emperor who had conferred upon him the imperial surname, Coxinga would never swear allegiance to the Manchus. His plan was to use the resources of the Zheng clan for the noblest of purposes: the explusion of the Manchus from China.

His first priorities would require the support of the other clan members, and the continuation of the Zheng clan's trade – he was going to declare war on the Manchus, and wars cost money. Although Coxinga had genuinely been the favourite of the Emperor of Intense Warring, and remained the son and heir to Nicholas Iquan, there were older and more experienced members of the Zheng clan who might be expected to take over operations, or indeed oppose his patriotic ire. His clan-cousins Zheng Cai and Zheng Lian continued to occupy the offshore islands at Quemoy and Amoy, and Coxinga joined them there. Coxinga was highly disapproving of Zheng Lian, who he regarded as unreliable and untrustworthy, more interested in sex and gambling than the affairs of either the Zheng family or the Ming dynasty.[9] However, the Zheng family continued to do what they did best, and ran boatloads of fresh silk up the Ryukyu Islands to Japan in order to raise funds.

Since one of the trading vessels was known as *Coxinga's Ship*, it would seem that the Count of Loyalty took an active part in this venture.[10] However, Coxinga genuinely intended to put the money to use in the service of the Ming, and also wrote to numerous Japanese feudal lords, asking for military aid. He had even had a banner made that announced his intentions without much chance for misinterpretation. It read: 'Kill Your Father, Restore Your Country.'

Coxinga was not the only loyalist. Unaware or uncaring of his actions in Fujian, other Ming supporters far to the south attempted to keep the imperial succession going. In distant Canton, the younger brother of the Emperor of Intense Warring was enthroned as *Shaowu*: the Emperor of Bringing Belligerence.[11] The name turned out to be ironically apposite, as one of his first acts was to declare war on fellow loyalists. Only a few days later, and a few miles from the new emperor's enthronement, a second Ming emperor was proclaimed. The 22-year-old pretender was the last surviving grandson of the Emperor of Ten Thousand Experiences, and took the reign title *Yongli*: Emperor of Eternal Experiences. It was difficult for Ming supporters to know who had the better claim. True, the Emperor of Eternal Experiences was the closest blood relative to the last Ming ruler to die in Beijing. But if the Emperor of Intense Warring had legitimately been the ruler of the Ming dynasty, however briefly, then surely his younger brother was a fitting successor? Nobody seriously considered Coxinga as an alternative – his symbolic adoption of the Ming imperial surname had lost much of its credence with the death of the Emperor of Intense Warring, and the ignominious defection of Iquan.

Reports from occupied territory suggested that the Manchu armies would be waiting out the winter. Instead of cooperating on the defence of China's far south, the rival Ming courts used the time to fight each other. The Emperor of Bringing Belligerence possessed a military force that chiefly comprised criminals and river pirates, who had been offered official commissions and pardons in much the same way as a younger Iquan had been brought into imperial service. The Emperor of Eternal Experiences controlled an army that comprised veteran soldiers, although he was outnumbered by his rival's men.

The two opposing Ming claimants met in two battles on 7 January 1647, and the superior numbers of the Emperor of Bringing Belligerence carried the day. The Emperor of Eternal Experiences retreated to the west to recuperate, but it seemed for a while that his surrender was imminent.

However, as the Emperor of Bringing Belligerence celebrated his 'victory' in Canton on 20 January 1647, the city was surprised by the sudden arrival of a detachment of several hundred strange-looking horsemen. For a while, locals assumed they were outlaws from Huashan, a group of powerful bandits who had recently agreed to support the Canton regime. It was only when they were admitted into the city and started attacking bewildered guardsmen that their true nature was understood. The new arrivals were Manchus, who proclaimed to the townsfolk: 'that they should not stir, for the whole body of the Tartars were at their gates, but that they need fear nothing if they were quiet and peaceable'.[12]

For weeks, the Southern Ming had squabbled over the succession, confident that the Manchus were not advancing. In fact, the invaders had never once stopped their push southwards, but had captured a series of lookout posts and imperial seals. The loyalists in Canton realised that they had been trusting in faked reports for days, delivered by Manchu sympathisers bearing stolen credentials. As a series of local commanders surrendered or committed suicide, Canton fell to a tiny squadron of Manchu soldiers.

The people fled in panic, while the horsemen rode through in search of opposing forces they could actually engage in combat. But the local guardsmen had no interest in dying in the defence of a city that was already taken, and instead threw away their weapons and went into hiding. A small group of Chinese took up arms and managed to capture four Manchus, whom they immediately took to the Emperor of Bringing Belligerence. The proudly titled ruler was almost alone in his palace, with only a few eunuchs and concubines for company. The Emperor of Bringing Belligerence ordered that the captured invaders should be executed before him. Those four deaths were to be the only Manchu casualties in the taking of Canton.

As sunset approached, the rest of the Manchu army reached the city gates, and were surprised to find them open. They simply walked into the town and chose houses to occupy, in one of the most peaceful victories of the entire campaign.

The Emperor of Bringing Belligerence knew that the end was coming, and made his last decree in imperial style: 'The Tartars are possessed of my city, and my subjects have abandoned me; what can I now expect but death? But I will die like a King.'[13]

The Emperor of Bringing Belligerence remained seated on his throne while his favourite wives and concubines commited suicide in front of him. When a group of Manchus and Chinese turncoats eventually entered the palace in search of him, they found him slumped on his throne, dead, surrounded by the corpses of his family.

A few dozen miles to the west, the defeated Emperor of Eternal Experiences heard the news, and at first assumed it was a ruse by his rival to lure him into a final battle. But as reports drifted in of the fall of Canton, he realised that the Manchus had solved the rivalry for him. He was now the sole Ming claimant by default, and his first act as the uncontested Emperor of Eternal Experiences was to run further west ahead of the advancing enemies. Each step he took away from the sea took him further away from any help that the Zheng family might be able to provide.

The Zheng family fought on at the coast, in two distinct groups. On the northern coast of Fujian, Zheng Cai continued to harry at coastal towns that had fallen to the Manchus. A faction led by Coxinga and his uncle Feng the Phoenix stayed further to the south, mainly preying on harbours, but also mounting expeditions inland. Zheng Cai had yet another imperial prince in his entourage, and hoped to use him as a new puppet, as Nicholas Iquan had previously done with the Emperor of Intense Warring. However, Coxinga refused to recognise the new claimant, whose title did not rise above that of regent. Instead, Coxinga professed his loyalty to the receding court of the Emperor of Eternal Experiences, though communication between them was now patchy and hazardous.

For more than a year, Zheng forces made only sporadic attacks on the Manchu invaders. The Emperor of Eternal Experiences continued to head inland, fighting off pursuing Manchu and turncoat forces with varying degrees of success, while the Zheng family raided along the coast in his name. Neither the nomadic Manchu nor their landbound Chinese allies possessed the skills or resources to mount a campaign against the corsair fleet, which often counted on the assistance of land-based Chinese who had recognised the authority of the Manchu in name only. The coastal region had long made its living from the grey legal area of foreign trade, and now Coxinga controlled the means of transporting and communicating by sea. Those who wished to continue to trade by sea still had to recognise the Zheng family, or risk attacks by Zheng warships as they travelled. True Manchu sympathisers were bullied and harrassed by Zheng family agents collecting 'tribute' for the Ming Emperor, while those who aided the Zhengs risked incrimination as collaborators with the Ming. For many, the stress was too much to bear – instead they booked passage on Zheng vessels to take them away from China for good, as settlers in south-east Asia, the Philippines or Taiwan.[14]

Despite constantly annoying the Manchu occupiers of south China, Coxinga was still in a precarious position. His followers required supplies from the land, and lacked the resources to make a counter-offensive of any lasting effect. Zheng forces preyed on shipping and carried out raids inland, but rarely occupied the towns they took. It was easier to conserve their manpower by taking what they needed and leaving the Manchus and collaborators to pick up the pieces.

Coxinga, however, always planned to mount a more lasting attack on occupied towns. His first real success came in 1648 at Tongan, a port close to his stronghold at Amoy. Expecting an assault from Coxinga's forces, the Manchu garrison had heavily fortified the town against the sea. However, four platoons of Zheng family spies had infiltrated the town several days before any ships neared the town. Disguised as itinerant monks, they gained access to Tongan and bided their time. When the Zheng navy eventually arrived and launched a series of incendiary boats at the ships in the harbour, the spies in the town killed the sentries and opened the gates for a land-borne assault of footsoldiers. Although the Manchus successfully overpowered the spies at some gates,[15] the other missions were successful, and the vengeful Zheng attackers massacred every Manchu they could find.[16]

Coxinga chose the victorious aftermath of the capture of Tongan in which to send an official ambassador inland to the court of the Emperor of Eternal Experiences, establishing once and for all that he regarded the pretender as his rightful ruler. News drifted back that the fleeing monarch was heartened at the news of his general's successes on the coast, and that Coxinga was henceforth a Marquess. The re-establishment of occasional contact with the Emperor also obligated Coxinga to cease acting as a free agent and follow occasional orders from his sovereign. Some of these, he obeyed, others he conveniently forgot to acknowledge.

In 1649, at least in part due to the months of warring, Fujian suffered from a major famine. The offshore islands occupied in the north by Zheng family forces received food-aid from Japan,[17] possibly secured by Coxinga's half-brother Shichizaemon, who was in charge of the family's reserve funds. Further to the south, Coxinga headed for the Canton region, hoping to set up new bases in the area, and obtain food to ship up to the offshore islands at Matsu, Quemoy and Amoy, where the bulk of the Zheng fleet was located. As per his instructions from the Emperor of Eternal Experiences, he also hoped to link up with surviving loyalists in the area. If Coxinga could gain control of China's far south, he might be able to extend his beach-head far enough to create a corridor to the landlocked Emperor of Eternal Experiences. It would afford a means of supplying reinforcements to an extended campaign northwards, or possibly an escape route to allow the beleagured Emperor to make his way back to the coast and the protection of the Zheng family.

As the 1640s became the 1650s, Coxinga developed a reputation for stern discipline. Many of his followers were traders at heart, and gave little thought to the cause of the Ming dynasty. Like the distant Japanese government, who were prepared to sell arms and armour, but not get directly involved in resisting the Manchu conquest, it is likely that many of Coxinga's men fervently wished for some form of treaty with the Manchus, so that life could return to normality.

One such man was Shi Lang, a prominent commander in Coxinga's navy.[18] Shi Lang was an experienced sea captain, and widely believed to be the most brilliant naval strategist of his day. Shi Lang was roughly the same age as Coxinga, the child of a distinguished Fujian family, who had demonstrated early aptitude for seamanship. He had fought in many of the battles of the loyalist resistance, and had risen to become the commander of the left vanguard of ships in Nicholas Iquan's battle formations. He was also reputedly a genius at designing naval weaponry and shipboard machinery. Some called him *Zheng Hou*, or 'Zheng-in-Waiting', and his popularity with the crews of the family ships risked creating a new split in the family. Coxinga could not afford a squabble among his fleet like the one that had nearly cost his father's life two decades earlier, when the fearsome Li Kuiqi had massacred so many of his relatives. Nor, it seems, could he abide Shi Lang, who made it as plain as politely possible that he missed the good old days when Nicholas Iquan was in charge. The two men had a grudging respect for each other, but as the war with the Manchus dragged on, they began to see their purposes differently. Their first major clash was over one of Shi Lang's men, who fled Shi Lang's fleet and sought sanctuary with Coxinga after he was accused of an unnamed crime. Shi Lang sent his soldiers to Coxinga's camp, where they recaptured and summarily executed the accused, without any regard for protocol or acknowledgement of Coxinga's authority.

Shi Lang was insubordinate, regarding himself as a true pupil of Nicholas Iquan's military cunning, but also a gentleman of good breeding such as Coxinga only aspired to be. Though he never stated it in as many words, Shi Lang might be seen as the son that Iquan never had. Shi Lang's opinion of himself was not entirely unjustified, but he was still a human being prone to mistakes, one of which was openly advertising his dissatisfaction with Coxinga's leadership. His carping grew louder after Coxinga promoted Shi Lang's lieutenant, Wanli, ahead of him to be commander of the vanguard.

Around 1650, Shi Lang was taking a cargo of silver up the Ryukyu Islands to Japan, to purchase much-needed military supplies for the war effort. *En route*, his convoy ran into a terrible storm, and the valuable silver cargo was lost. Coxinga was furious, and berated the captain for his mistake. In the middle of their argument, Coxinga pushed too far. Shi Lang took offence, gathered up his long hair in his hand, and cut off his topknot, the traditional symbol of resignation. Presenting his leader with the hair, Shi Lang demanded to be permitted to leave the Zheng family organisation.[19]

It was exactly what Coxinga did not want. If he allowed a single captain to secede it would risk the complete collapse of the loyalist forces into a number of rival splinter groups little better than the pirate societies from which the force was originally formed. In the short term it would also seriously compromise Coxinga's ability to impose military discipline on his forces. If anyone disliked his command, they would simply be able to walk away.

Somehow the two men patched things up, but the following year it was Shi Lang who pushed too far. Coxinga had announced that he intended to lead a strike force into China, targeting two occupied castle towns on the coast. Coxinga wanted to take the towns by surprise, plunder them of all the money in their treasuries, and then abandon them. It was a quick way of securing more funds for the military campaign, but Shi Lang voiced his opposition. In his opinion, it made Coxinga 'little better than a thief', an accusation that managed to insult Coxinga's ancestors, family, father, and sense of duty all at once.

When Coxinga blew his top, Shi Lang made himself conveniently absent, causing Coxinga to place Shi Lang's father under house arrest. The order went out that Shi Lang was to be confined to his ship in the harbour while Coxinga decided on an appropriate course of action. Shi Lang, however, had had enough, and slipped away by night. He sought refuge at the Zheng fort of Anping, which was occupied by Coxinga's uncle Bao the Panther. Bao had presumably expressed guarded agreement with some of Shi Lang's comments in the past, but knew better than to openly challenge Coxinga's authority. He refused to grant Shi Lang sanctuary, and the admiral found himself with little choice. Accompanied by the loyal captains of his personal squadron, Shi Lang sailed into an occupied port and offered his services to the Manchus. A furious Coxinga ordered the execution of Shi Lang's father, younger brother and nephew. He also ordered a commando raid into Fujian itself,[20] with the sole purpose of assassinating Shi Lang before the defector could offer naval advice to the Manchus. However, events further to the south were to keep Coxinga occupied, and allowed Shi Lang to get away with his life, and his naval knowledge intact.

The defection of Shi Lang marks the end of a series of reorganisations and purges among the forces of the Southern Ming as the executions, retirements or defection of many of Nicholas Iquan's old guard brought a new character to the organisation. Keen to emphasise why these thousands of men were clustered on a series of tiny offshore islands while invaders roamed the mainland, Coxinga reminded them that they were not there as pirates, but as loyalists to a cause: the restoration of the Dynasty of Brightness. He even renamed Amoy, proclaiming that it should henceforth be known as *Siming*: Think Ming. It was referred to by that name in all subsequent Zheng family documents.

While Coxinga was preoccupied with his campaign in the Canton region, the Manchu attacked Amoy. The assault at the heart of his power was a great shock to Coxinga, and years later he was still able to recite the losses, defenders killed, women raped and the removal of jewels and bullion worth over a million taels.[21] Guan the Stork, the senior Zheng family representative at Amoy, ordered the evacuation of the town, and shipped all its inhabitants to a Zheng family stronghold on nearby Quemoy island, leaving the treasures of the town as ripe plunder for the occupying forces. To add insult to injury, Feng the Phoenix appears to have successfully mounted a counter-assault that pinned the Manchu attackers down. The surrounded invaders then reminded Feng that his brother Nicholas Iquan was still a 'guest' of their ruler in Beijing, and that it would be unfortunate if he were to come to any harm. Faced with such a threat, Feng the Phoenix permitted the attackers to escape unharmed.[22]

Feng's act of loyalty to his brother hid other troubles behind the scenes. Feng, like Coxinga, took issues of duty and loyalty seriously, but other family members were more like their big brother, Nicholas Iquan. Feng the Phoenix was not even supposed to be in charge of the defence of Amoy; that reponsibility actually lay with Guan the Stork, who not only singularly failed to keep Amoy safe from the Manchus, but also neglected to send vital reinforcements to help Coxinga's campaign in Canton.

Forced to pull out of Canton, with considerable loss of life among his men, and great loss of face to his Emperor, an irate Coxinga returned to Amoy determined that a head was going to roll. The head in question was Guan the Stork's, executed on Coxinga's orders. Feng the Phoenix went unpunished for protecting his brother Iquan, but was dishonoured nonetheless. The former general and marquess, who had taught the young Coxinga how to use a sword, went into quiet retirement.

The fight for Amoy also led to an unexpected thaw in relations between Coxinga and his wife Cuiying. Though not 'estranged' in a modern sense, the couple do not seem to have been on friendly terms in the first decade of their marriage. By the time of the fall of Amoy, Coxinga had acquired eight concubines, many of whom seem to have shared his loyalist zeal. Cuiying played the role of chief wife well, running Coxinga's household and overseeing the activities of the concubines. Women of a Chinese household might be expected to busy themselves with sewing and weaving – Coxinga's spouses instead made armour and military uniforms for his men.

Despite their unwillingness to cooperate with Coxinga's ill-fated campaign in the south, the Zheng family knew better than to court danger directly. When the Manchus attacked Amoy, representatives of the Zheng family were swiftly sent to Coxinga's mansion, where his wives and children were rounded up for evacuation. Cuiying, however, turned back.

Despite the protests of their bodyguards, Cuiying waved the other wives and retainers on, and dashed back to the mansion. Risking death by fire and capture by the Manchu raiders, she ran to the family shrine and snatched up a carved wooden block propped up in front of the altar. It was the ancestral tablet of Coxinga's mother, Miss

Tagawa, a symbolic representation of her soul, and of the protection she offered her descendants in the afterlife. Though it was of only sentimental value, Coxinga probably regarded it as his most valuable possession.

Cuiying, Coxinga's surly and unfriendly spouse, had demonstrated more loyalty to the Zheng family than many of his blood relatives. It was not a fact that Coxinga ever forgot, and from that day on, he consulted closely with her on Zheng family matters. Cuiying became her husband's closest confidante, and played a vital part in several key military and political decisions made by the Zheng family.[23]

In the south of Fujian, Coxinga sent his forces on another landward campaign, leaving their base on the island of Quemoy and laying siege to the coastal town of Changzhou. Coxinga's troops stayed outside the city walls for six whole months, while the inhabitants were reduced to cannibalism by the lack of food. Seeming to tire of the wait, Coxinga moved his forces to the nearby town of Haicheng, which swiftly capitulated. Once again, there appear to have been disagreements between Coxinga and some of his other men, and his lieutenant Huang Wu was fined for dereliction of duty. The general was fined 500 suits of armour.[24]

Huang Wu was lucky compared to some of Coxinga's other followers. The Count of Loyalty had very strict definitions of honour and duty, and was quite prepared to make dissenters pay the ultimate price. During a campaign near Tongan, the slave of a Manchu general is said to have cut off his master's head and defected to Coxinga's camp, expecting a handsome reward. Coxinga thanked him effusively and did indeed confer great wealth upon him, but the former slave did not have long to enjoy his new-found riches. Coxinga ordered him to be beheaded, so that he might attend upon his master in the afterlife.[25]

Coxinga's actions, and especially his defeats, were becoming a matter of increasing concern to the Dutch, who feared for their own trading position. For some years, they had been content to stay in Taiwan, using Chinese traders as middlemen in China and Japan, and paying taxes and levies to the Zheng organisation. A letter from Batavia summarised the situation:

We cannot yet free ourselves from great anxiety concerning this Mandarin Coxinga . . . who has been several times defeated by the Tartars. No doubt he will ultimately be forced to leave Amoy, and remove with his followers to safer quarters, probably to the island of Formosa, as its fertility and other good properties are as well known to him as us . . . Coxinga is not much liked by his men, who continually desert him owing to his strict ruling and lack of the necessary means for supporting him. Hence, we hope that, when compelled to flee the country, he will only have a few followers.[26]

The Manchus back in Beijing, however, did not share the fatalistic predictions of the Dutch. The only organisation with the benefit of reports from the whole country, the Manchu court was clearly rattled by Coxinga's continued presence in the south. The worry remained that the people of south China, who had so willingly capitulated to the Manchu invaders, might switch sides a second time with equal ease if Coxinga were to enjoy many more victories. Life would be considerably easier for all concerned if Coxinga would simply stop supporting a hopeless cause, and sign a treaty with the Manchus. The governor of Fujian was asked to approach Coxinga, and to broach the subject of entering negotiations for an 'honourable armistice'.

In essence, the offer was little different from the deal struck between Nicholas Iquan and the Emperor of Lofty Omens some twenty years before. The court would agree to recognise Coxinga as the *de facto* ruler of the region, confer a new noble title on him, and the armies could stand down. Coxinga, however, remained fiercely loyal to the Ming, and would never forgive the Manchus for the death of his mother. His reply was curt and to the point, all the more shocking for its refusal to adhere to the flowery prose and obsequious compliments of traditional Chinese letter-writing. It simply said: 'I cannot trust in the words of barbarians. I will not deal with a collaborator.'[27]

The governor of Fujian was removed from his post, and the Manchus looked for another way of leaning on Coxinga. In 1653, they decided to use their secret weapon: Nicholas Iquan.

THE BOILING RIVER DRAGON

Nicholas Iquan lived like a prince, although his palace in Beijing was merely a very luxurious jail. Until such time as Coxinga would agree to surrender, Iquan was of little use to the Manchus. Most defectors were swiftly repatriated to new areas and permitted to get on with new lives, but the Manchus did not trust Iquan not to switch sides again. There was also the matter of Miss Tagawa. Iquan cannot have expected his defection to result in the death of anyone close to him; in fact, his act was likely to have been motivated by a desire for self-preservation. But now, instead of a smooth transition, Iquan was alienated from his family, and had to live with the knowledge that Miss Tagawa had died in battle against his new masters.

Seeking new allies, Iquan became a friend and benefactor to the Christians, befriending several Jesuit priests, and helping to fund the construction of a new church in Beijing. Jesuits, of course, were able to walk between the worlds of Manchu and Chinese, and records of the time imply that Iquan involved himself in a number of schemes. Even in seclusion, he traded and dealt, but while his Jesuit associates had greater powers with the Manchus, they were unable to improve his conditions.

The most powerful Jesuit Iquan met in Beijing was Adam Schall, who enjoyed even greater privileges with the Manchus than those he had with the Dynasty of Brightness.[1] For that, he had to thank his mathematical ability, stubbornness, diplomacy and a series of lucky coincidences. When the Manchus originally came to power, the new dynasty still had the same concerns as the one it had replaced. There remained a need for a trustworthy calendar, outlining the movements of the planets and the opportunity to prepare for unwelcome phenomena such as eclipses and meteor showers. Now the venal officials who had once tried so hard to discredit Adam Schall tried to win him over and gain his help in calculating calendars for their new masters. He refused, preferring to prepare a calendar of his own, which not only predicted events with far greater accuracy than those of his Chinese and Muslim rivals, but also added some extra flourishes. Schall's version noted, for example, that 1 September 1644 would see a solar eclipse, but instead of giving details for the imperial observatory in Beijing, he provided its time and length in a number of different cities all over the Celestial Empire.[2] When his predictions were found to be correct, Schall was not only praised for the superiority of his European and, he was swift to remind the Manchus, *Christian* science. He was also unexpectedly made director of the Institute of Astronomy by imperial decree. He refused several times, only to have emissaries of the child-emperor repeat their requests. At first, they merely assumed that the aging foreigner was exhibiting traditional meekness in the face of high office, but in fact Schall was genuinely unwilling to take the position. After some time, however, he was talked into it by his fellow Jesuits, and found himself, at the age of sixty, becoming the chief vizier of China's heathen religion.

Prince Dorgon's nephew, Fulin, had been enthroned at the age of five as *Shunzhi*: the Emperor of Unbroken Rule. But it was widely understood that the true power rested with Dorgon, the prince regent. As the child-emperor grew older, he came to place greater trust in the alien science of the strange Jesuit, whom so many of the other courtiers seemed to hate and fear. The powers that Schall enjoyed were considerable, as the Emperor himself was expected to abide by his astrological advice. Schall continued to make a number of enemies among the Chinese and Manchu courtiers, but earned the undying love and respect of the child-emperor himself.

Schall's greatest political triumph came as the child-Emperor neared adulthood, and Dorgon began to grasp at greater authority, issuing proclamations in his own name, and arranging for new titles for himself such as the Father of the Emperor, and the Father of the Country. Some whispered that Dorgon planned to proclaim himself Emperor before young Fulin deposed his own regent, but only Schall was prepared to stand up to him.

Schall had been approached about a memorial project, in which

Fulin's supporters planned to honour Dorgon by erecting two great marble columns at the entrance to the imperial palace in Beijing. Dorgon himself also planned to build a new capital, as if Beijing itself were not enough. Schall dutifully provided advice on a pulley system that would make the building works easier, but took the opportunity to advise against the project for 'astrological reasons'. In a long note to the regent, Schall advised that the signs in the stars all warned against such a folly. Dorgon was initially angry with the foreign priest, but reluctantly acknowledged the words of the director of the Institute of Astronomy.

Dorgon died in a hunting accident in 1650, further impressing the child-Emperor Fulin with Schall's powers. Since the boy was still only twelve, a new group of wards came to power. In order to discredit their predecessor, they soon announced that they had found 'proof' that Dorgon had been conspiring against his ruler, and Fulin came to believe that Adam Schall had predicted that Dorgon would die unless he followed the directions of the stars. Schall had said nothing of the sort, but as a result, when the Emperor's mother Borjigid fell ill in 1651, it was Adam Schall who was called to attend to her. Borjigid herself was impressed with Schall, and, in what could have been a hybrid of Chinese gratitude and Christian forms of address, began referring to him as her 'foster-father'. The child-Emperor, convinced that Schall could see the future and heal the sick, began addressing the foreign missionary as 'grandfather'.[3]

Even while their armies still fought for mastery on the periphery of China, against the self-proclaimed Emperor of Eternal Experiences in the far south-west, and Coxinga, the Imperial Namekeeper in the south-east, the Manchus fought among themselves. The war in the court of Beijing was much quieter and subtler, and played out with favours and whispers, as various factions contended for the support of the child-Emperor when he reached majority.[4] As he entered his teens, a faction of eunuchs gained rising powers at court by introducing him to the pleasures of women. The young Emperor was a willing initiate, and soon became obsessed. Though his fondness for Adam Schall remained strong, his interest in Christianity began to waver – there was no way of rationalising Christian monogamy with the sexual opportunities available to an emperor. Before long, the Emperor's concubines were not enough. He even tired of his principal wife. The woman he desired more than anything in the world was a beauty called Xiao Xian[5], and she was forbidden to him because she was the wife of his brother Bombogor.[6]

He sought the advice of his 'grandfather' Adam Schall at least once a month, and slowly piled subtle honours on the unsuspecting priest. Schall was told that it was silly for him to perform the obeisances of a servant every time he saw Fulin, and was henceforth permitted to save his aching joints by not kneeling or bowing when he saw the Emperor. He was also told that he need not ask for permission to see Fulin, but could simply present himself whenever he wished. Although such concessions seem minor, they were actually rare privileges granted only to the innermost members of the imperial family. Prince Dorgon himself had been made to bow before the Emperor of Unbroken Rule until 1648.

Some at court were scandalised by the informal relationship enjoyed by the teenage Emperor and his 'grandfather'. Fulin would visit Schall at his humble dwelling and sit on common furniture, sharing the humble wines and foods Schall had prepared himself. In court banquets, Schall was offered tea from Fulin's own cup, while there are stories of the Emperor giving Schall his cloak when the priest looked cold, and offering him two hares that he himself had shot while hunting.[7] The priest was even seen to tell jokes with the Emperor at state occasions. By 1653, Adam Schall was known as the Master Who Comprehends the Celestial Mysteries, once again by imperial decree.

The Manchus, meanwhile, were trying every conceivable option to outwit Coxinga's stronghold in Fujian. Sending the Manchu general Jidu to organise a counter-offensive was an unusual form of sympathetic magic. Jidu was the 22-year-old son of the regent Jirgalang, but his choice as leader seems born out of superstition. Wishing to keep their alien origins as far from official documentation and public notice as humanly possible, the Manchus had started using Chinese names, and Jirgalang was known as Zheng, 'the Serious Prince'. In sending his young son against Coxinga, Jirgalang was essentially sending a Zheng heir to defeat a Zheng heir.

The Manchus were even willing to lean on Coxinga's reputation as a Confucian. The loyalist may have burned his scholar's robes, but his strict discipline and rectitude were legendary. And according to Confucius, the paramount duties of obligation lay between a father and his son. It was time to see if Nicholas Iquan could talk some sense into his wayward offspring.

Finally giving Iquan the somewhat low rank of marquess, the Manchus promised to deliver further honours if he would help them. It was strongly implied that Iquan's state of captivity could be suspended if the remainder of the Zheng family came over to the Manchu side. Those who knew the Manchus well knew that there was a steely menace beneath the surface. Iquan had been kept at the Manchus' pleasure for a considerable time, and if this latest ruse failed, someone was bound to ask why they bothered keeping him alive.

Iquan dutifully drafted a letter to Coxinga, claiming that the Manchus requested his attendance at peace talks. Coxinga sent one of his customarily curt replies, advising his father that his recent actions in the south had merely been in response to Manchu aggression.

A few months later, Iquan wrote a second letter, making the Manchu offer much clearer: 'The Manchu court offers territory in exchange for peace. They wish to send two noblemen to present you with the title and deeds of the Dukedom of Haicheng, allowing your followers to abide in the region.'[8]

The deal was cunningly calculated. Coxinga had recently been offered the title of Prince of Yanping by the distant Ming claimant, the Emperor of Eternal Experiences. He had turned it down with traditional modesty, but would no doubt be offered a similar title again. Meanwhile, the Manchus were offering him a duke's rank, higher than the earldom he had received from the Emperor of Intense Warring, but lower than the princedom he had recently declined. The message was clear: if Coxinga accepted the title, he would also be repudiating the honours conferred upon him by the Southern Ming claimants. As he had recently conquered Haicheng, the lands he was being 'granted' were his already. The Manchus, however, would not send a force to take the lands back, if only Coxinga would submit.

To almost anyone else, it would have seemed like a good deal. The fighting would be over, Nicholas Iquan would be freed, the Zheng family would be reunited and life could return to normal, with Coxinga a duke.

However, Coxinga did not even consider the offer, since Iquan had unwisely presumed to call on his son's sense of filial piety.

Coxinga was not called the Count of Loyalty for nothing, and let rip with a damning series of recriminations:

> For eight years now . . . my father has not regarded me as his son. I returned the sentiment. Communications have ceased, and we have not exchanged a single word since. Since ancient times, sane and righteous men have understood that there is a greater duty than mere loyalty to one's family. I have known this since I first learned to read it in the *Spring and Autumn Annals*. It was on my mind in [1646] when my father drove up to the capital. I made my decision then.
>
> Now, all of a sudden, you seek to lecture me on loyalty. You, who are a mouthpiece for the Manchus, talk of promoting me above the former ranks of earl and marquess. But since the Manchus have lied to you, what makes you think they do not lie to me? When Bolo marched into the Pass [of Misty Immortals], my father was already running. With flattery and sophistry, maybe ten groups of envoys sallied forth to win you over, offering to make you the viceroy of three whole provinces . . . That was several years ago. Where now is your princedom and your command? You cannot even travel through your home town. And you think they can be trusted?[9]

Coxinga had grown up watching Iquan humiliate people by mail; he had learned from the master. He ennumerated several incidents of Manchu treachery, including the cruel treatment of a Zheng family agent sent to enquire after Iquan's health, the earlier attack on Amoy that had led to the execution of Guan the Stork, and the fact that Iquan, formerly a duke under the Ming, had only recently been made a marquess under the Manchus. Pointedly, he made no mention of the death of Miss Tagawa – the magnitude of that particular incident was too great for words.

Coxinga counted through the difficulties of mounting campaigns in mountainous regions, and ridiculed the idea of horse-riding nomads taking on a seaborne fleet of warships. He hinted that reinforcements for his own armies were already *en route* from Japan and Indochina, and reminded the Manchus that his forces comprised several hundred thousand men.

He finished with a final flourish that must have irritated his father even more than a flat refusal. All these things considered, Coxinga wrote, settling his troops, returning them to civilian life, and keeping order in the province would take a lot more than the simple conferral of the dukedom of Haicheng. To ensure the right amount of *lebensraum* and resources, to make it clear to the local people that he was still in charge and not actually admitting defeat, to keep his navy from splitting up and reverting to piracy, he was going to need a lot more. He was going to need princely authority in, say, three provinces. He was going to need the exact title and territory that Iquan had coveted for himself.

It was a slap in the face for Iquan and the Manchus, and had been calculated as such. Even before he wrote the letter, Coxinga had laughed with his secretary that the Manchus were trying to trick him, but he would milk it for as long as he could, as a means of obtaining extra supplies for his men. Even when hinting to the Manchus that he might be prepared to deal with them, he remained loyal to the Ming.

But two could play that game. The Manchus ignored Coxinga's bolder demands, and instead notified him that two officials would be coming to Fujian to present him with the aforementioned dukedom. Coxinga refused the offer courteously but firmly. The accompanying edict from the Emperor of Unbroken Rule[10] was suspiciously similar in tone to the earlier letter from Iquan, reiterating a desire to see peace on the coast, and questioning how a son could treat his father in such a disloyal manner. Since Prince Dorgon was conveniently dead and fast falling out of favour, the edict placed the blame for the former impasse on him – it was one of many problems in the early 1650s that the Manchus attempted to write off as Dorgon's doing. The edict also made it abundantly clear that Coxinga and his followers were being offered a supreme pardon, and that there would be no hard feelings:

Even with the pacification of the coastal regions, We would still require the competent organisation of defences. Rather than search for another, would you not seem to be the ideal candidate? Your father remains confident in his family, and has recommended you highly . . . You may repel and destroy pirates at your discretion. You retain the responsibility for inspection and taxing of maritime cargo . . . You shall achieve the pacification of the seas. Such is Our inevitable command.[11]

Coxinga, however, continued to ignore the Manchus. He busied himself on a minor campaign in the Fuzhou region, tantalisingly under the nose of the governor with whom he was supposed to be negotiating. The aim of Coxinga's mission was to establish that the people of the surrounding region still supported him. Most appeared to do so, though a township to the south had foolhardily prevented the safe passage of Zheng family ships. Coxinga led a punitive assault on the town, making it clear to the alleged 'governor' of Fujian who was really in charge. The only place that Coxinga studiously avoided was the city of Quanzhou. In the dialect of the Amoy region, the city's name sounded very similar to the word for 'brick', and the superstitious Coxinga had not forgotten the warning of a fortune teller in his youth, that bad luck awaited him in such a place.

The governor, a Chinese turncoat, wrote to Coxinga himself in a note of desperation. He reminded the unswerving Ming loyalist that large Manchu forces were amassing outside Fujian. If Coxinga continued to make such a display of disobedience, the Manchu troops would enter the province and make life difficult for all concerned. The governor was not beneath adding some veiled threats of his own. After reminding Coxinga that life in the real world was always a compromise between principles and pragmatism, the governor added:

> Your father has been promoted in status above the highest minister, but your grandmother is frail in years. [The Manchu hold the territory] where can be found your ancestors' graves, though you of course do not require burial there yet. If your continued military actions were to cause harm to come to those tombs, it would cause unbearable stress to your honoured father. Even in his dreams, he would not get a moment's peace, nor would your grandmother have a quiet moment to sleep or eat.[12]

It was a threat designed to tug at the heartstrings of the most committed Confucian, but Coxinga ignored it. True to their word, the Manchus ordered their armies back into Fujian, and defiled the graves of the Zheng family. Manchu envoys arrived in the province

1. Coxinga with a soldier of the Black Guard. From *Gedenkwaerdig Bedryf der Nederlandsche Oost-Indische Maetshappye op de Kuste en in het Keizerrijk van Taising of Sina*, by Olfert Dapper, 1670. (*Courtesy of the Lilly Library, Indiana University, Bloomington, IN*)

2. A temple to Matsu, Goddess of the Sea.
(*Courtesy of SMC Publishing Inc., Taipei*)

3. The outskirts of Nanjing in the seventeenth century. From
L'Ambassadeur de la Compagnie Orientale des Provinces Unies,
by Johan Nieuhoff, 1665.
(*Courtesy of the Lilly Library, Indiana University, Bloomington, IN*)

4. Fort Zeelandia in its early days. This highly stylised picture still shows the basic fort at right, the town at left, and the gallows on the ground between them. From *The Start and Progress of the VOC*, Isaac Commelin, 1646. (*Courtesy of SMC Publishing Inc., Taipei*)

5. A Taiwanese aborigine, 1665. (*Courtesy of SMC Publishing Inc., Taipei*)

6. The Zheng stronghold on Amoy. From *L'Ambassadeur de la Compagnie Orientale des Provinces Unies*, by Johan Nieuhoff, 1665. (*Courtesy of the Lilly Library, Indiana University, Bloomington, IN*)

7. The Pieter Nuijts Incident. From *Oud en Niuew Oost-Indien*, by François Valentyn, 1724. (*Courtesy of National Museum of Taiwan History, Tainan*)

8. Coxinga orders Hambroek to deliver his message. (*Courtesy of National Museum of Taiwan History, Tainan*)

9. Hambroek's daughters beg him to stay in the castle. (*Courtesy of National Museum of Taiwan History, Tainan*)

10. Dutch troops fire on rioting Chinese. From *Oud en Niuew Oost-Indien*, by François Valentyn, 1724. (*Courtesy of National Museum of Taiwan History, Tainan*)

11. Shi Lang, admiral of the Manchu fleet.
(*Courtesy of SMC Publishing Inc., Taipei*)

12. The Treaty between Coxinga and Frederik Coyett. (*Courtesy of National Archief, Den Haag*)

13. Adam Schall in old age. From *China*, by Athanasius Kircher, 1667. (*Courtesy of Stanford University Libraries, Dept. of Special Collections*)

14. Coxinga expels the Dutch from Taiwan. Chinese propaganda print by Cheng Shifa, 1955. (*Private collection*)

with Lady Yan, Iquan's principal wife, accompanied by two of her sons, Shidu and Shiyin. They carried the title of duke of Haicheng, if only Coxinga would swear allegiance to the Manchu emperor, and shave the front of his head in the approved manner. The sarcasm of Coxinga's reply carries across the centuries:

> Who would have thought, so soon after the desecration of my ancestral tombs, that such grand embassies would arrive, heavy with silken, heartfelt sincerity? How could I refuse such offers? I'll be waiting for you. Maybe with a little present.[13]

His attitude was trying the envoys' patience, and they sent him a laconic reply that made it clear they had had enough of games. If Coxinga wanted the dukedom, he should come and get it, but he should arrive with his head already shaved in the Manchu manner. If he was not going to shave his head, they added, he might as well not turn up.

Realising that Coxinga was not treating the envoys with anything approaching the correct degree of respect, Nicholas Iquan wrote a desperate letter to his own younger brother Feng the Phoenix, now in retirement at White Sands near Amoy. In it, he begged Feng to convey to Coxinga the seriousness of the situation.

When Feng's reply came, it was in subtle support of Coxinga.[14] Feng had warned Iquan that defecting to the Manchus was a bad idea in 1646. Now, he pointedly recounted a chronicle of his ailments, particularly a ten-year-old foot injury that made it difficult for him to walk. Despite this, he wrote, he had somehow made it to Coxinga's island base, where he had pleaded with his nephew on behalf of Nicholas Iquan. With an exasperation that all but accuses the son of being exactly like his father, Feng wrote: 'He never listened to *you*, why would he listen to your little brother?'[15]

Feng's letter also gently rejected offers of Manchu noble titles for himself, claiming that he was happy with the quiet life. It was a good act, and almost convincing, except for its final section, when Feng's words betray a hint of his true feelings. 'I continue to enjoy my retirement here at White Sands,' he wrote, 'though if the Manchus return in force, I must remove myself by sail to somewhere beyond their reach. Even if it means danger on rough waves, I shall do so gladly.' Feng the Phoenix was staying put, and if the Manchus tried anything in Fujian, he would rather be carried onto one of Coxinga's evacuation ships than stay to greet the invaders. Nicholas Iquan was on his own.

It was not lost on any of the participants in this charade that 1654 was the tenth anniversary of the Manchus' arrival in Beijing, and the eighth since Nicholas Iquan's defection. For those members of the Zheng family who dwelt in Beijing with Iquan, the situation was turning frostier by the week. Coxinga's half-brother Shidu, the fourth of Iquan's children by his chief wife, cut through the protocol and went to see Coxinga in person, determined to impress upon him the mounting danger.

Weeping, Shidu threw himself at Coxinga's feet, begging him to preserve his family's safety by obeying the orders of the Manchus. Coxinga's reply shows a mixture of anger and doubt, and later repetition that implies high emotion:

> You children never understood the ways of the world. Since ancient times, nobody has bettered themselves by changing sides. Well, except under Emperor Guangwu in the Han dynasty. Should I enter a trap, merely because my father fell into it before me? For every day I reject their proposals, our father gets another day of glory at court. If I meekly shaved my head, don't think the safety would be assured of father *or* sons. Don't say any more. You think I'm inhuman, that I've forgotten my own father! A situation like this, it's not easy! It's not easy![16]

Nevertheless, Coxinga kept the emissaries guessing until early November, dispatching them home, and then sending contradictory messages as they were leaving, informing them that his astrologers had found a more auspicious day for the negotiations to begin. But after several months of prevarication, the emissaries were obliged to return to Beijing and report that they had failed. As they left, Shidu and Shiyin had a final tearful meeting with their rebellious half-brother, in which they begged him to reconsider: 'If these two ambassadors return empty-handed, then the mission is over,' they said. 'Once we report back, we will probably lose our lives.'[17]

Coxinga, however, was unmoved.

'No matter what you say or do,' he replied, 'I have made my decision. Speak of this no more.'

Despite his stern words, Coxinga was troubled by his half-brothers' situation. Nicholas Iquan had made his own decision, but the younger Zheng family members who had accompanied him to Beijing had had little choice. Coxinga tried to explain himself in a letter to his departing relatives.

When the panther roams the deep mountains, he is feared by all the other creatures. But once he is barred within a trap, he wags his tail and pleads for mercy, knowing he has lost mastery of his fate. But the phoenix can soar 8,000 ft above him, flying where it pleases in the firmament, free of the concerns of the common world. I am famous among the Chinese, and among the barbarians. I have experience in the command of troops. Do you think I would prefer to be a phoenix flying free, or a caged panther?[19]

Coxinga chose his animal analogies deliberately. His uncle, Bao the Panther, had recently defected to the Manchus, and now shared Nicholas Iquan's state of limbo in Beijing. But Feng the Phoenix remained loyal, and free. Though his leg wound made it difficult for him to walk unaided, Feng still flew high in the estimations of his idealistic nephew.

The envoys returned unhappily to Beijing, although they were not executed as they had feared. Conditions between the Zheng defectors and the Manchus did turn even less favourable, but for an unexpected reason. As Coxinga did not fail to remind his father, they had not communicated with each other for years. Iquan had only done so at the urging of the Manchus, and had failed to get the desired response from his son. But in 1655, Iquan wrote Coxinga a letter without the knowledge of his Manchu masters. Its contents were for Coxinga's eyes only, and it was to be smuggled out of Beijing by Zheng family sympathisers. Unluckily for Nicholas Iquan, it fell into the hands of Manchu agents, who denounced him at court. Whatever the letter contained, it was the final straw for the Manchus. Iquan, it was said, had written a message in secret support of his son's behaviour, urging him to continue his fight.[19]

The period of grace was over. Iquan was stripped of every noble rank the Manchus had given him, and imprisoned with the rest of his family, including Coxinga's half-brothers and the indignant Bao the Panther, who had only just arrived and had been hoping for a friendlier reception. The panther had truly been caged.

The Manchus returned to Fujian in force, with another army led by Prince Jidu. Jidu's men fought a succession of hard battles with Coxinga's forces, but although they gained some ground, their losses were immense. To outside observers, it was still unclear who was in charge in south China. Coxinga, however, made his allegiances clear. He accepted the title offered him by the distant Ming Emperor of Eternal Experiences. He now held an official rank usually translated as 'prince', although the word literally means 'king' – a rank dating from two millennia previously, when an ancient dynasty divided China into semi-autonomous satrapies. Coxinga was still subordinate to the emperor, but he was also now acknowledged as the ruler of his own domain in the emperor's name.[20]

Across the strait in Taiwan, the Dutch found all this activity to be extremely worrying. For ten years, they had relied upon Coxinga to provide their trade with the mainland, and supplemented the meagre trading permitted in Japan by using Chinese merchants flying a Zheng flag of convenience. Although the trade conditions and tariffs were not wholly in the Europeans' favour, it was better than nothing.

The Dutch had chased a Spanish settlement from the north of Taiwan, but were increasingly concerned about the Chinese population on the island. The year 1652 had seen an uprising among the island's Chinese population, which was eventually suppressed with much loss of life on the part of the Chinese.[21] All the evidence suggests that Coxinga had no direct involvement in the revolt[22] but the outgoing Dutch governor, Nicolas Verburg, still suspected that plans were afoot:

> [Verburg] advised Their Excellencies to be on their guard, since it was reported that the Chinese mandarin Coxinga – son of the pirate Iquan, and formerly tailor to Governor Putmans and interpreter to Governor de Witt – who was then fighting against the Tartars, intended, if driven from China, to go to Formosa and settle there.[23]

The Dutch took what measures they could, beginning with the construction of an additional small fort near the village of Sakkam on the shore of Tai Bay. Provintia was situated right on the shoreline of the bay, so close that the waters would lap against its red walls at high tide. It was not a particularly imposing presence, but nevertheless helped the Dutch feel a little more secure about being in the midst of so many potentially hostile tribesmen.

Rumours of a forthcoming assault on Taiwan continued throughout the 1650s. If more Chinese traders than usual arrived in Taiwan, the Dutch suspected it was an invasion fleet. If no traders arrived at all, the Dutch suspected that Coxinga was blockading the mainland ports to keep any spies from getting back to Taiwan with news of an approaching attack. If trade continued in a perfectly normal and unremarkable manner, with nothing untoward at all to report, the Dutch suspected that Coxinga was trying to lull them into a false sense of security.

Coxinga, meanwhile, was sending trading vessels further afield to fund his military operations. There is no proof that he ever had the Japanese or Indochinese reinforcements that he boasted of in his letter to his father, but his ships were a regular sight in the ports of those regions. The Dutch, who had hardly entered his thoughts for years, now began to annoy him, as his need for more funds brought him into increased contact with them. On Sumatra and the Malay peninsula, Coxinga's vessels came into direct competition with the Dutch, particularly over the trade in pepper, which had previously chiefly gone to China. With the Dutch spiriting it away to Europe by the sackful, the local price was going up. In 1654, Dutch East India Company representatives in Batavia received a letter from Coxinga demanding that the Dutch reimburse him for the cargo of a ship lost in nearby waters. The records of the company nervously reported:

> He demanded so large a sum of money that we could never have paid. Instead of payment, we offered him 100 piculs of pepper, two pieces of *perpetuan* and ten pieces of *mouris* as a present. We hope it will mollify him. He is now the man who can spit in our face in Eastern waters.[24]

The Zheng family had been useful to the Dutch during the days of détente under Jacques Specx and during the years of turmoil that accompanied the collapse of the Ming dynasty. But the last Ming imperial claimant was now far off in the landlocked interior, and the majority of China was under the heel of the Manchus. The Dutch decided that it was time to see if the Manchus were keener on trade with the outside world than their Ming predecessors. In particular, they still coveted a base on the coast of mainland China itself, such as the Portuguese still maintained in Macao.

The opportunity seemed to present itself when false rumours spread among the trading community that Canton was now a free port. The city had changed hands several times during the conquest of south China, and appears to have been kept alive through a long Manchu siege by seaborne supplies. European observers, unaware that Nicholas Iquan had switched sides, assumed that it was he who was sending aid to the town: 'That which most of all gave them a resolution to withstand the enemy was that they had one Iquon [sic] on their side, who had the command of a powerful fleet, wherewith he daily furnished the city with all necessary provisions.'[25]

When the city finally fell for good, it was placed under the command of Shang Kexi, a Chinese turncoat who had been made Prince Pacifier of the South by the Manchus. The Portuguese in Macao, fearing that the Chinese really would proclaim it a free port, began a smear campaign against the Dutch,[26] convincing local officials that non-Catholic Europeans were pirates and allies of Coxinga. The Dutch eventually sent a delegation to see the Emperor of Unbroken Rule, hoping to complain about the interference of the Portuguese and their Jesuit allies. Somewhat typically, they neglected to bring a suitable interpreter, but were told upon arrival that the court could arrange one for them. As they waited in an antechamber, they were joined by a pale old man, dressed in the robes of a palace minister, his white hair shaved at the front in the Manchu manner. He was like no Chinese they had ever seen before – imposingly tall, and, to the Dutchmen's disbelief, with what appeared to be blue eyes. When he opened his mouth to address them, he spoke in fluent German.

Much to the Dutch delegates' annoyance, the interpreter at their audience was to be one Adam Schall, who pointedly enquired after the health of several Catholic families he had known in Amsterdam. In private, he had already informed the Emperor that the Dutch were not to be trusted, having 'rebelled against God and against their king'.[27] He did, however, tell the ruler of China that he might find the visitors academically interesting.

Consequently, when the seventeen-year-old Emperor arrived for the audience, he simply sat on his throne in silence, peering at the strange hair and eyes of the new arrivals. While the Dutch knelt patiently thirty paces away, the Emperor stared for an agonising fifteen minutes, before getting to his feet and making for the exit. Just before he left, he turned for a final stare, and then he was gone. Adam Schall announced that the Dutch 'audience' was over, and escorted the visitors back outside, chatting amiably, secure in the knowledge that his Portuguese brethren a thousand miles to the south would not need to worry too much about Dutch incursions in the Canton region.[28]

Without the chance to say a word, the Dutch had missed the opportunity to offer the Emperor the one thing he did not possess: mastery of the seas. One delegate later argued with his colleagues that, since the Emperor was 'having wars with that Arch-Pyrate Coxinga, if we should but propose to assist his Imperial Majesty with our ships, I make no doubt but that he would quickly consent to give us free Trade in his Dominions'.[29] His suggestions, however, fell on deaf ears.

Quite possibly, the Dutch could not work out who they should support. If they carried out their plan to back the Manchus, Coxinga might be forced to retreat from the mainland and attack the Dutch in Taiwan. Much as the Dutch feared and hated Coxinga, if they really wanted him to leave them alone, their best option would probably be to *support* him on the mainland. But there was no way the Dutch were going to pour their resources into a resistance movement that seemed doomed to failure. For the moment, they preferred to do nothing.

Coxinga knew the Dutch were up to something, and sent another letter to the Company, making his position as clear as humanly possible. 'Such places as Batavia, Taiwan and Malacca are one inseparable market, and I am the master of this area,' he wrote. 'I will never allow you to usurp my position.'[30] If the Dutch wanted to sail the China seas, they would need to stay friendly with Coxinga, and not his Manchu enemies.

The Dutch stockpiled firewood at Fort Zeelandia sufficient for a siege. They improved their fortifications and increased the number of men in the garrison. However, in 1656, the sense of urgency seemed to fade away.

The island's new governor, Frederik Coyett, was a Swede in his mid-thirties who had lived on Taiwan throughout the upheavals of the previous decade. His appointment was a smart move on the part of his bosses in Batavia. In times of potential danger, it was far better to have someone experienced in charge, rather than incompetent predecessors such as Pieter Nuijts or Hans Putmans. As a witness to the revolt, the progress of the Manchu invasion, and of the fluctuations in trade over the previous ten years, Coyett was the perfect choice for Taiwan governor. He was in the ideal position to evaluate the situation, and well aware of the danger Coxinga presented. But Coyett's efforts to stay in control of the situation were thwarted by an enemy within.

At some point in the previous few years, Coyett had fallen out with the former governor, Nicolas Verburg, over an unspecified incident. Harsh words were exchanged between the two men, and Verburg, now installed at the Batavia headquarters in Java, was determined to get revenge. Even though Verburg himself had warned Batavia about Coxinga only two years earlier, he changed his tune now he was out of harm's way. Every time a message arrived from Coyett with details of new defences and intrigues, Verburg would ridicule him in the Batavia council. Verburg accused Coyett of being unnecessarily jumpy, and of wasting Dutch resources preparing for an attack that would never come.[31]

In fact, Coxinga *was* up to something, but it had nothing to do with the Dutch. He was planning a major counter-offensive out of Fujian, sailing up the coast with a huge fleet and thousands of men. His ships had been absent from Taiwan for a while simply because he was recalling all Zheng vessels to aid in his military exploits. Nor was he keeping quiet about it. In fact, he had even boasted of his plans in a long letter to the harassed governor of Fujian. Noting that the Manchus were troubled by new revolts and uprisings in the hinterland, Coxinga ridiculed their armies, calling them 'flocks of crows'. He noted that large areas of the Manchu domain were now cut off from their supposed ruler, and that, ironically, there were floods to the north of the Yellow river, and droughts to the south of it. With China wracked by earthquakes, floods and unspecified 'strange phenomena', Coxinga interpreted the upheavals as signs that Heaven was displeased with the Manchu invaders, and it was time for the loyal followers of the Ming dynasty to fight back.[32]

He still believed he was the spiritual child of the goddess of the sea. His enemy Prince Jidu led an assault on Quemoy that turned into a surprise victory for Coxinga. At vast expense and after great effort, Jidu managed to assemble a fleet, which sailed against the Zheng family headquarters on 9 May 1656.[33] As so often before in the naval ventures of the Zheng family, the elements themselves seemed to fight on Coxinga's side. The battle was interrupted by a fierce storm, forcing both sides to break off. Coxinga's experienced sailors ran ahead of the wind or put into friendly harbours near Quemoy. Jidu's invasion armada was not so lucky, and was all but wiped out by the elements.

The incident also led to another evacuation of Amoy. True to his word, the invalid Feng the Phoenix refused to stay at White Sands and surrender to the Manchus, but boarded a Zheng family vessel and sailed across the bay to the stronghold on Quemoy Island. The old soldier passed away in 1657, defiant to the last.

Since the early 1650s, Coxinga had been thinking over the ramifications of a major military operation. It had been a decade since the Manchus marched on Nanjing, a period throughout which Coxinga had carefully amassed funds for a counter-offensive. Though many of his men were happy simply to trade, Coxinga had always planned to take the war back to the Manchus, and now he decided that the time was right.

Coxinga's plan was to lead a giant fleet up the coast of Fujian, past the next province, and up to the mouth of the mighty River Yangtze itself. After years fighting small skirmishes along the edge of south-east China, he was going to lead his men towards the heart of the Celestial Empire.

The vanguard of the fleet was headed by Gan Hui, Coxinga's most trusted general, with 10,000 men, 20 large warships and 30 smaller supply and support vessels. The fleet's right wing was commanded by Maxin, another trusted general, with another 30 warships, another 30 support vessels, and another 20,000 men. The same numbers also comprised the left wing, which was led by the loyalist general Wanli. Coxinga himself brought up the rear with 120 warships and a further 40,000 men.[34] The fleet contained the very best of the Zheng organisation's fighting forces, including the loyal remnants of the Black Guard, and a mystery group known only as the Iron Men.

Coxinga had been progressively directing more of his forces towards the north of Fujian, seizing the offshore island of Zhoushan as way station for his invasion force. However, he was also obliged to pick people to leave behind and guard his holdings in south China. In what was to prove one of the biggest mistakes of his life, Coxinga chose Huang Wu to guard Haicheng. The town was the site of one of Huang Wu's earlier embarrassments – Coxinga had disciplined the general and forced him to pay an indemnity of 500 suits of armour during the last great Manchu offensive. Now Huang Wu was left in charge of the town while the landbased remnants of Prince Jidu's Manchu army continued to roam Fujian; the posting only served to bring back bad memories for him.

He was troubled chiefly by an incident several months earlier, in which Coxinga had ordered the execution of a general who had lost a battle with the Manchus. Huang Wu reasoned that if he remained at his post, he might die at the hands of the Manchus, whereas if he fought the Manchus but was forced to retreat from Haicheng, Coxinga would have him put to death. Faced with such a situation when a Manchu army appeared outside Haicheng, Huang Wu panicked. He murdered his fellow loyalist leader and ordered the gates of the town to be opened for Prince Jidu.

It was a bad year for Coxinga. Huang Wu's defection rattled him, and he must have suspected that the turncoat would spill some of the Zheng family secrets and fears to his new masters. In early June 1657, Coxinga's fleet took three towns in a row. The first was on the northern end of Fujian province. The next two were officially over the border in the next province up.

Coxinga's advance was slowed at the town of Wenzhou, whose garrison put up a particularly strong fight, safely behind the walls of a formidable castle. The seas grew increasingly rough, and Coxinga worried for the rest of his fleet. When two of his men were struck by lightning, he took the supernatural hint and moved on, leaving Wenzhou unconquered, and heading for the way station at Zhoushan.[35] There, he intended to join forces with Zhang Huang-yan, a local partisan who had been resisting the Manchus in the north for ten years. During the days when the Emperor of Intense Warring was still attempting to reconcile rival rebel bands under one unified Ming loyalist banner, Zhang had visited the court in Fuzhou, where he and Coxinga probably met for the first time.[36]

Zhang had spent the previous two years on the island of Zhoushan near the mouth of the Yangtze, training his men for a long-delayed assault on Nanjing. He had agreed to join forces with Coxinga, and was waiting for him there.

But after early successes, Coxinga flirted with disaster the following month. *En route* to the mouth of the Yangtze, his fleet put in at the small island of Yangshan ('Sheep Mountain'), where a secluded harbour offered anchorage for several hundred ships. Coxinga planned to wait out the day's unquiet sea, and to set sail the following morning for the last leg of the trip to Zhoushan.

The island supposedly took its name from the local animal life – supplicants could ask a favour of the gods by leaving a sheep there, and since the creatures were considered sacrosanct on the island, the population had grown to considerable numbers. To a fleet of hungry sailors eager for fresh meat, Sheep Mountain presented an irresistible temptation, particularly since the docile animals were not used to any form of predator, and were completely unprepared for humans armed with muskets. Soon, the beaches and shipboard galleys were alive with the smoke and crackle of roasting mutton, while a few superstitious crew members protested feebly that Sheep Mountain was emphatically not a supply station, but a sacred island. Others noted further superstitions: chiefly the fact it was considered impolite to stop at Sheep Mountain without making an offering to the local deity, a drowsy but irritable sea-dragon. Because the legendary dragon preferred peace and quiet, it was also considered the height of hubris to discharge muskets or cannon in Sheep Mountain Bay, but few crewmen paid the warnings much heed.[37]

Only a few hours out of the harbour on the following day, Coxinga's fleet was hit by the worst storm it had ever encountered. Waves broke over the decks, and driving rain made it impossible to steer properly. When certain helmsmen did manage to wrest control of their vessels from the wildly flailing rudders, they were still unable to see far enough ahead to properly navigate. Among the close-packed fleet, there were several collisions, while other ships were driven onto nearby reefs and smashed against the rocks.

Coxinga yelled at the heavens from the prow of his flagship, reminding the gods that he was humbly leading a mission to restore the Ming dynasty, and that if Heaven did not approve of the idea, it should sink every one of his ships and him with it.

The storm eventually died down, but only after considerable damage had already been done. The fleet had lost dozens of ships, with the death toll estimated at 8,000, including 231 members of Coxinga's household. A further 900 loyalists had survived shipwrecks, only to fall into Manchu hands on land. Among the drowned crew members and soldiers were members of Coxinga's own immediate family, when a support vessel sank with all hands. At least one of Coxinga's concubines, possibly as many as six, never made it back from the storm at Sheep Mountain. Three of Coxinga's very young sons also died that day, aged six, five and one.[38] Their bodies were recovered from the water, and Coxinga buried them on shore. His secretary reported that he did so with bitter laughter: a sign of a man on the edge.

The incident was enough to scare many of Coxinga's sailors, who worried that the goddess of the sea had finally withdrawn her support for the Zheng family. Coxinga assured his men that it was only a temporary setback, and authorised many weeks of repair and regrouping, in a series of loyalist enclaves along the coast. When the fleet reached the nearby port of Xiangshan, the people welcomed them with open arms, and the governor threw large banquets for Coxinga's men. The party atmosphere seemed deliberately designed to distract them from the recent misfortunes.

However, some in the fleet had already had enough. Coxinga was forced to contend with a number of defections or simple desertions, as loyalists decided that no reward, be it earthly or heavenly, was worth another storm like Sheep Mountain, particularly if all they had to look forward to in the north was a prolonged military campaign. Manchu agents and propaganda did everything they could to add to the loyalists' concerns, and made much of recent incidents in which former servants of the Manchus had returned to their invader masters. In some cases, this actually meant that former servants of the Ming, who had switched sides at least once before, were simply switching sides again, but it was enough to make Coxinga nervous. He dismissed all the leaders in his forces who had recently defected from the Manchus – he simply could not risk losing a squadron of ships at a crucial moment, and preferred lieutenants he could trust fully.

Paranoia began to reign in the fleet. One captain ordered for the oars on his ship to be painted red, supposedly to keep his sailors busy, and possibly to garner a little good fortune by brightening his vessel with China's lucky colour. Coxinga, however, sensed that something else was afoot, and accused the captain of preparing a secret signal for the Manchus. Coxinga believed that the red oars would be a covert signal to the Manchus not to attack a ship that planned to switch sides. He could not prove it, but had the captain replaced just in case.[39]

Coxinga's forces were now out of the home territory they had occupied for a decade. North of Fujian, they could not immediately count on the presence of local allies as spies and black marketeers, and were forced to proceed on the assumption that they had no friends in the area. Intelligence became more of a problem. Whereas in the south Coxinga could count on advance warnings of any Manchu activities, up in the Yangtze region he was plagued by insubstantial rumours. On several occasions, scouts brought news of approaching Manchu armies that turned out to be phantoms, but the sense of unease formed an enemy attack all of its own.

Disciplinary problems returned to haunt Coxinga, when he was forced to send one squadron in pursuit of another that had defected, and again when three of his generals allowed their men to pillage a newly captured town. Coxinga issued a warning to the men 'not to enjoy the victory too much', although it seems that his commanders saw it as an opportunity to encourage their men to forget the embarrassing setbacks of Sheep Mountain.

By the end of 1658, Coxinga had established a number of bases north of Fujian, suitable for keeping an expeditionary force supplied, and for guarding an exit route back to the sea if necessary.

In April 1659, he began his assault again, and brought his fleet to the mouth of the Yangtze itself. The Manchus, however, were ready for him. Although the Yangtze was miles wide, and one of the world's mightiest rivers, the Manchus had turned it into a fortress all of its own. Troops were stationed at key points all the way along the river, under the command of the general Luo Ming-sheng, who had been charged with keeping Coxinga away from Nanjing. The wide course of the Yangtze was barred by a series of obstacles: scuttled ships and chains designed to impede passage. Upstream nearer Nanjing itself was a notorious new defensive feature known as *Gunjiang Long*, the Boiling River Dragon. This was a ten-mile barrage linking natural river islands and floating platforms. It functioned like a fluvial Great Wall, with manned fortifications and cannon barges facing downriver. Each of the massive cedarwood platforms was large enough to hold 500 men, with artillery pieces and ammunition. Dwarfing Coxinga's largest vessel, these floating fortresses were loaded down with earth and rocks as ballast, and each had enough mass to crush a warship in its path if left to float downstream. However, for now, they were anchored in the river, and linked together by great chains designed to halt a warship at ramming speed.[40]

Coxinga believed that the Yangtze campaign would be the turning point of the loyalist struggle. The time was past for skirmish after small skirmish, far in the south where nobody could see him. He wanted to secure a propaganda coup by fighting a grand battle with the Manchus on supposedly pacified territory, hoping that news of the victory alone would lead to new loyalist uprisings further to the north. But first he would have to make it past the Boiling River Dragon.

Supernatural aid was called for to avoid another disaster like Sheep Mountain. Coxinga stopped at the midstream island of Jiaoshan ('Scorched Mountain'), and began three days of elaborate sacrifices, designed to ensure that Heaven remained on the side of the Ming loyalists.

The first day saw Coxinga and his closest followers attired in red, offering sacrifices to Heaven. The following day, dressed in black, they held a similar ceremony for the Earth. On the final day, dressed in white, the loyalists paid homage to the ancient founder of the Ming dynasty. The hundreds of ships in Coxinga's fleet all hoisted white flags aloft, and waved white banners from their decks, leading one chronicler to note that the river suddenly seemed to be awash with snow in the middle of summer.[41] The ritual ended with all the crews in the fleet chanting aloud the name of the great Ming ancestor three times. As thousands of voices united in praise of the Dynasty of Brightness, there were tears all round.

Coxinga was left in a maudlin state by the event. At least, that is the impression left by the poem he wrote on the day:

> An ancient prayer amid yellowing leaves
> A palace open to cold autumn winds
> Thicker and thicker grow the old oak trees
> Heedless, the birds return.

Stone monuments lie forgotten in the earth
Shrine steps covered with moss
To this place, where few visitors come
The sorrows of the world return.[42]

It was now August 1659, and Coxinga's fleet was ready for the next advance. The Yangtze region was unfamiliar to the coastal rebels, but the partisan leader Zhang Huang-yan took the lead, and proffered an elaborate multipronged assault to deal with the Boiling River Dragon.

Zhenjiang, the site of Feng the Phoenix's swift retreat during the Manchu invasion a decade earlier, was now a formidable fortress in enemy hands. Something would have to be done to keep its guns silent while the fleet dealt with other objectives. Coxinga himself, with Gan Hui and a number of his other closest associates, would lead a naval assault on the north-bank town of Guazhou. The capture of these two points would secure the end of the Grand Canal that led all the way to Beijing itself, and cut Nanjing off from any reinforcements sent from the north.

The fleet itself was also a crucial part of the assault, divided into a southern battle group (under the leadership of Zhang's people), and a northern one comprising Coxinga's own lieutenants. As the attack commenced, the fleet began a bombardment designed to keep the enemy gunners occupied and cut off from resupply. The Manchu cannon barges in midstream returned fire, but were unable to score any direct hits on the loyalist fleet. The constant barrage of heavy artillery went on for four thunderous days, until, just as Feng the Phoenix's had done a decade earlier, the Manchus eventually ran out of ammunition. Coxinga's ships then sailed straight past Zhenjiang towards the Boiling River Dragon. There, decoy ships blasted at the cannon barges, while fearless divers swam right under the floating platforms to hack at the chains.

On the south bank, Zhang Huang-yan's men bypassed the heavily defended Zhenjiang, riding upstream and inland with a small force carrying Coxinga's flag, hoping to encourage local support. Zhang was impressed by the response he received, as over thirty-two districts soon pledged their loyalty to Coxinga.

Meanwhile, the enemy leader Luo Ming-shen was cornered on a floating platform with 500 of his men. Their ammunition gone, they resorted to arrows, until they too were exhausted. The turncoats then fought to the death as wave after wave of Zheng family marines leapt onto the platform.

On the north shore, Coxinga's general Maxin volunteered to lead the final assault on Guazhou Castle, seemingly because he felt the campaign so far was going too easily. Maxin complained to Coxinga that he had been given high rank because he was a Zheng clan member, but had yet to see any real action, since much of the strategy in the campaign involved shelling the Manchus from a distance.

That was all very well for Maxin, but it was his marines who took the brunt of the damage, landing upriver behind the Guazhou fort. Their leader, Zhou Quanbin, ran from the river bank, up a steep ridge, and up the castle walls with scaling ladders, continuing to lead his men even after being wounded.[43] Shipboard observers saw fighting on the battlements, and then a group of their loyalists raising the Zheng family flag above the castle. Beneath the flag stood the victorious Zhou, with five enemy arrows still protruding from him.

The day was a stirring victory for Coxinga's forces, which also saw the capture of three cannon barges along with Yizuo, the surviving turncoat leader of the local defenders. When the man was brought to Coxinga, he begged for his life, hoping to appeal to Coxinga's well-known Confucian beliefs by announcing that he only wished to return to his home town to look after his aged parents.

Coxinga was aghast at Yizuo's willingness to twist the words of Confucius into a plea for mercy, and announced that he would not stain his sword with the blood of such a disloyal creature. Instead, perhaps in imitation of the Manchus during the invasion period and hoping to encourage other enemy soldiers to surrender, Coxinga gave the man 500 silver taels and sent him on his way. The moment he was out of Coxinga's sight, he immediately ran for Nanjing, where he helped organise the defence of the town against the Zheng forces.[44]

Maxin and Zhou Quanbin were decorated for their meritorious service, and the loyalist forces celebrated their victory. They had successfully captured a key point on the Yangtze river, cut off the Grand Canal and broken through the Boiling River Dragon barrage. The River Yangtze was now open to their fleet. They stood ready to advance on Nanjing itself.

THE WALL AROUND THE SEA

The news was not well received in Beijing. On hearing that Coxinga was only days from Nanjing, the 21-year-old Emperor of Unbroken Rule flew into a fit of insane rage. He yelled that he would personally lead a relief army to Nanjing – a rash promise that was sternly and swiftly quelled by his mother Borjigid. The irate Emperor snatched up a sword and attacked his own throne, hacking chunks off it until the intervention of Adam Schall finally calmed him down.[1]

The Emperor demanded revenge, and ordered his generals to do everything in their power to stop Coxinga. Post-riders rushed to carry the news to other parts of the Celestial Empire, and troops in the distant hinterland were ordered to mobilise and converge on the Yangtze region. It was inevitable that the news would get out among the general populace, and the Manchus prayed that they would not have to deal with any civil unrest. All over China, Manchus eyed the conquered Chinese with suspicion, wondering if they secretly plotted to join Coxinga's loyalist stand.

A Korean messenger arriving in Beijing noticed that the entire city was in a state of fear. Misinformed talk on the streets was that Coxinga had an army of *three hundred thousand* men, and that now Guazhou was in his hands, he intended to march north along the Grand Canal, on Beijing itself.[2]

Meanwhile, jubilation reigned among Coxinga's fleet. Those who had formerly been scared by the experience of Sheep Mountain were now convinced that it had been a divine test of their mettle, ensuring that those who advanced on Nanjing were pure in heart. News came from upstream and inland of the continued successes enjoyed by Zhang Huang-yan's advance party. All the indications were that Coxinga's arrival was inspiring the local populace to come out in support of him.

With Guazhou Castle captured, the north bank was secure. Opposite on the south bank stood Zhenjiang, the city that had once been abandoned by Feng the Phoenix. In 1645, Feng's departure had left Nanjing open to Manchu attack. Now, over a decade later, Zhenjiang was the next objective for the loyalist counter-offensive.

Zhenjiang was now held by Guan Xiaozhong, a turncoat general who had fought and won seventeen battles all over China. Although Zhenjiang was a good defensive position, Coxinga chose to land his forces on the western side, at the nearby slopes of Silver Hill, where the Manchu forces would have trouble deploying their cavalry.

Zhou Quanbin, the hero of the assault on Guazhou Castle, was on hand to spur on the troops. When a Manchu counter-assault arrived at midnight on the second day, it was Quanbin who roped off the escape route from his redoubt, in order to 'encourage' his men to hold their positions. However, although Zhou's presence was probably enough to strike fear into his own men, let alone the Manchus, it was not he who won the day. That honour went to Coxinga's elite division of specialist troops, the Iron Men.

The common soldiers called them *Shenbing*: 'the warriors of the gods'.[3] Five thousand in number, the Iron Men were specially selected for their incredible strength. They needed it, because each was clad in plate armour, dotted with distinctive metallic decorations that resembled a leopard's spots. Only a tiny slit in the helmet allowed them to see. Unlike the scales or links of traditional Chinese battledress, the Iron Men's armour was all but impervious to lances and swords. Reports from both sides certified it as bullet-proof. Their job was to stand at the very front of the troops like a metal wall, armed with long pikes designed for taking down horses – 'many wielded a formidable battle-sword fitted to a stick half the length of a man'.[4]

Considering the weight of their armour, the heavy horse-killing weapons, and the fact that it was the height of summer, the Iron Men must have been truly superhuman.[5]

The presence of the Iron Men was the undoing of the Manchus. As they marched ever forwards, Coxinga's other troops kept up a constant barrage of missiles. Yang Ying, who seems to have been present at the battle, wrote that 'gunfire, cannonfire, arrows and rocks, all rained down upon them'.[6]

The Manchu cavalry flung themselves in vain against the unstoppable wall of advancing armour. When the Manchu line broke and fled, the battle turned into a massacre. Coxinga's own cavalry charged past the Iron Men in pursuit of their enemies, chasing them for several miles along the banks of the Yangtze. Several thousand soldiers fled along narrow coastal roads surrounded by drainage ditches. Fleeing enemy soldiers pushed each other into the ditches and trampled on their fallen comrades. Footsoldiers were seen dragging cavalry from their mounts, and then fighting among themselves over who got to ride the captured horses to safety.

In the aftermath of the battle, the ditches near Zhenjiang were piled high with the bodies of Manchus and Chinese collaborators. The grisly remains of men and dismembered horses were strewn across the entire area, presumably owing to the activities of the Iron Men. The garrison commander, Guan Xiaozhong, was heard to say that it was the worst battle of his long career. He lost all but 140 of his 4,000 men, and other Manchu companies suffered similarly.

From the walls of Zhenjiang itself, the city defenders witnessed the carnage and decided to spare themselves a similar fate. Zhenjiang surrendered as Coxinga's victorious troops approached it, and the town became the latest loyalist prize.

Eager to continue the march upriver, Coxinga called his generals for a conference. Gan Hui advised caution, and a war of attrition. He pointed out that Coxinga's forces already held crucial points at the southern end of the Grand Canal, cutting off Manchu reinforcements from the north. Instead of advancing directly on Nanjing, Gan Hui advised going around it, seizing other towns inland, upriver and also to the south-west. Thereby, Gan Hui thought, Coxinga's forces would not only cut off reinforcements, but also the routes that kept Nanjing supplied with food. After that, it would be a mere matter of time before the city was forced to capitulate to its besiegers, without undue loss of life.

Many of the other generals agreed, pleased with Zhang Huang-yan's reports of popular support. Nanjing contained a million Chinese citizens, and only a small cadre of Manchu overseers. If the people of the surrounding countryside made their loyalty to the

Ming clear, Coxinga might even be able to count on an anti-Manchu uprising within the town while he besieged it.

Another point in favour of a siege was the sheer size of the region. Communications back to the coast were getting increasingly longer. Those generals with operational responsibilities were keen to establish local bases and supply lines. Although they had enjoyed early success, they were wary of advancing too far inland without strong defences and allies at their rear. All were only too aware that their nominal ruler, the Emperor of Eternal Experiences, was cut off from them far to the south-west. Coxinga had never even seen the Ming claimant he supposedly served, and nobody wanted to find themselves in a similar position, isolated from their coastal power base.

Coxinga, however, was keen to reach Nanjing. He fervently believed that the local people would waste no time in rededicating themselves to the Ming cause. But, he argued, that was part of the problem. Coxinga's men were bearing down on the notorious south capital, which had originally surrendered to the Manchus without much of a struggle. This was the place where Coxinga's own mentor, Qian Qianyi, had preferred surrender to armed struggle. Coxinga's chief concern was that the people of the region were only fair-weather friends and needed to see more loyalist victories. He believed that the support they currently enjoyed would only remain for as long as the army continued to advance. If they dallied too long outside Nanjing, the malleable minds of the local populace might swing back towards supporting the Manchus.

'We must conquer Nanjing,' Coxinga said. 'If we do not, our army will only grow older. Those soldiers who blew with the wind to join with us, will become disappointed and abandon us.'[7]

Coxinga's charisma had kept his people together for ten years. His passion and devotion to the Ming cause was one of the driving forces of the loyalist movement on the coast, and his power to inspire his followers is unquestionable. His generals were right to advise caution, but as the experience of the original Manchu invasion had shown, Coxinga was not wrong in his appraisal of the capricious nature of Chinese support. His words, however, were music to the ears of Zhou Quanbin, who still nursed his five arrow wounds from the assault on Guazhou Castle, and a few more scratches picked up during the landing at Silver Hill. The living embodiment of *gung-ho*, Quanbin agreed with Coxinga that their best hope was to run with the momentum they already had.

'We should capitalise on the current spirit,' he said. 'Swift attack is the key. This is no time for delay.' Once he had given Coxinga his vote of confidence, the other generals reluctantly came around. Coxinga spoke of their duty, and their 'mission' to restore the Ming. Among the generals, only Gan Hui continued to express his opposition to the plan, but he was outvoted. The decision was made to advance directly on Nanjing. The ever-eager Zhou Quanbin, however, was left in charge of the garrison at Zhenjiang while his many wounds healed.[8]

Events beyond Coxinga's control turned the upstream advance into an uneasy compromise. The wind changed on 10 August, making it impossible to sail upriver. Instead, the fleet had to be hauled against the current by teams of men on the river bank, a process which resulted in a two-week journey. Had Coxinga sent the bulk of his forces ahead of the fleet on land, he would have temporarily lost naval support, but would have reached the gates of Nanjing much earlier. The delay allowed a number of Manchu reinforcements to reach Nanjing from further upstream. Coxinga, however, was unperturbed by the news. Even with vast numbers of his soldiers holding key points downriver, he was still advancing on Nanjing with a force of 85,000 men.

Among the defenders was Yizuo, the cunning general who had managed to talk his way out of execution after the fall of Guazhou. Instead of lying low, he had run straight for Nanjing, where he offered its garrison the benefit of his experience. Yizuo reported that during his meeting with Coxinga, he determined the famous loyalist's one true Achilles heel. Not without justification, Yizuo claimed that Coxinga's fatal flaw was pride.

On Yizuo's advice, Viceroy Lang Tingzuo sent a message to Coxinga, heavy with flattery, announcing their intention to surrender. Lang advised Coxinga that he was only putting up a nominal resistance for the sake of appearances. The Manchu minority in the town, he said, were out of his control, but the Chinese were all ready to repledge their loyalty to the Ming dynasty. Their only concern was for their own family members, who were being held hostage in Beijing.

Under a pretence of utmost secrecy, Lang begged Coxinga to hold his troops from attacking for a limited period. Previous experience, he claimed, had taught Chinese collaborators that thirty days was the Manchu statute of limitations on loyalty. If Nanjing was seen to hold out for a month against Coxinga, the Manchus would regard its inhabitants as loyal servants overwhelmed by insurmountable odds, and not feel obliged to kill their hostages.[9]

Coxinga told his generals that he had Lang's word that Nanjing would fall after a month of inactivity. One of his advisers saw through the ruse immediately and berated Coxinga for his gullibility. It was, quite literally, a textbook case of deceit. Coxinga was reminded of Sun Zi's military classic, *The Art of War*, and its warning that 'The humble supplicant is false. One who asks for peace without guarantee is plotting.' Coxinga's staff pleaded with him to order an immediate attack, rightly suspecting that Nanjing was awaiting reinforcements, and that there would be no better time to seize it.

Whether he believed the garrison commander or not is debatable, but Coxinga seemed determined to take Nanjing without a fight, even if it meant a prolonged siege. The decision appeared to contradict all his earlier talk of rushing upstream, but made more sense when taken in the context of Coxinga's own life. He once lived in Nanjing, he had studied there, and he had fled the city as the Manchus invaded. The Nanjing that Coxinga knew was a Ming city, but one that had surrendered to the Manchus without a fight. Coxinga simply could not bring himself to attack Nanjing. If he had to do so, it would be a tacit admission that the city's populace were more loyal to the invaders than they had ever been to the Ming. The idea of fighting over Nanjing challenged the very foundations of Coxinga's devotion to the Dynasty of Brightness. And so he decided to wait thirty days, hoping that the city would capitulate.

The days stretched into two weeks, and Coxinga's army began to slacken in their discipline. With no resistance of any kind from Nanjing, they grew bored watching the walls for trouble that never came. Besiegers charged with guard duty would wander off and fish in a large pond that sat in front of the city walls. Others were found on guard duty with flasks of wine.

Some even deserted to the Manchus. As ever, Coxinga fought a constant battle to keep his men acting like soldiers, and not like unreformed criminals and armed peasants. As an example to his men, he paraded the supremely disciplined Tianbing, or 'Heaven's Soldiers': nine companies of fighting men with a spotless record for following orders.[10]

Not all of Coxinga's men were impressed by the display. Lin Mou was a long-term member of the Zheng family forces and a native of Fujian. Though he had fought long and hard in the loyalist resistance, he almost lost his life in the aftermath of Guazhou Castle, when he was caught raping a local girl. Coxinga's attitude towards the treatment of women was notoriously strict, and other men in his organisation had been executed for similar crimes. Perhaps because of his long service, Lin Mou was allowed to keep his life but forced to take a heavy pay cut. After two weeks at the gates of Nanjing, the brooding Lin Mou had had enough, and defected to the Manchus. In an audience with Viceroy Lang, he informed him of the growing unrest within Coxinga's army, of the weak points in army discipline, and of the coming preparations for Coxinga's birthday celebrations.[11] If the viceroy thought that the besiegers were lax in discipline now, said Lin Mou, the approaching night of Coxinga's birthday party would find them even more vulnerable.

It would appear that the 'siege' situation at Nanjing was quite easy-going. Lin Mou was able to walk into the town. Manchu reinforcements arrived by a rear gate, but this did not seem to trouble Coxinga. Officially, he announced that he hoped the Manchus brought as many reinforcements as they could, all the better to obtain their death or surrender in a single day, and save himself further battles elsewhere. His generals, however, began to wonder if Coxinga genuinely believed Viceroy Lang's unlikely promise to surrender in another fortnight.

Eventually Coxinga's old friend Gan Hui lost his patience. A division of Manchu soldiers had rushed out of the Gate of the Aspect of the Phoenix, which faced to the west, where the river curved around Nanjing. Had they run out of a northern exit, such as the Gate of Peace, they would have faced loyalist troops camped on the ground all around them for 180 degrees, but the west side of the city sat close to the river, and there was little room. It allowed the Manchus and their allies to keep the skirmish small, while the rest of Coxinga's army could do little more than crane their necks and watch from their tents. The attackers soon retreated back inside Nanjing, with little loss of life on either side, but Gan Hui could see that the Manchus were testing Coxinga's defences. This, he argued, was not the behaviour of people preparing to surrender.

Coxinga, however, was adamant that Nanjing should surrender to him without a fight. He told Gan Hui to calm down, reminding him the Manchus were not the only ones getting reinforcements, and that the size of the loyalist army still greatly outnumbered the troops in Nanjing. If they ever found themselves having to fight, he was confident they could still win. But it hurt his pride that Nanjing would resist him when it had been so swift to roll over for his enemies. 'We might attack them physically,' he said to Gan Hui, 'but that will not win us their minds.'[12]

Gan Hui stormed out of Coxinga's presence, saying: 'I will never speak of this again.'

Gan Hui was right – enemy agents were already among Coxinga's men. Viceroy Lang had sent spies disguised as local farmers into the besiegers' camp, offering food and wine for sale. Initially they were turned away, but as the siege wore on, the merchants came to be welcomed in the camp. While selling their wares, they also kept careful notes on the condition of Coxinga's army, and the location of key stores.[13]

On 8 September,[14] Coxinga's forces were reminded how vulnerable they really were. It seemed that the earlier confrontation outside the Gate of the Aspect of the Phoenix may have been a smokescreen to cover the completion of a secret operation. A large patch of bush clover (lespedeza) concealed a hole that had been tunnelled in the wall behind it. While Coxinga's men kept a watchful eye on the gate itself, they were unaware of the hidden exit from the town – presumably, the earlier attack had used the chaos to make a survey of the ground directly in front of it.

At midday, 500 Manchu soldiers came through the hole and hacked their way out of the lespedeza bushes, much to the surprise of the soldiers cooking their lunch in the camp. The attacking force was so small, and the loyalist camp so large, that it took some time before the outlying tents even knew they were under attack. The Manchus wiped out an entire division before retreating again. The commander of the division had not even had time to put on his armour. Naked flames were in plentiful supply from the numerous cooking fires, and helped magnify the damage caused by the 500 surprise attackers.

Safety had been compromised outside Nanjing, and Coxinga ordered a hasty withdrawal. The camp clustered at the north of Nanjing was too broad to defend, and lacked internal security measures. Coxinga's hasty night-time withdrawal placed a no-man's-land between his forces and the city, just in case there were any other hidden exits from the town that could surprise him.

However, although the withdrawal only moved Coxinga's camp a little way back, it put a large part of his soldiers on a north-facing slope that dropped into the Yangtze where the river curved back towards the east. Soldiers at the riverbank, or on the middle of the slope, could not see the city any more. Only Coxinga's vanguard, at the top, had a view of the walls.

The following day was Coxinga's official birthday. The Manchus chose that moment to strike in force, and charged out of the city gates. This time, they were not a mere company of a few hundred, but Banner-men numbering in the thousands. Down the slope, the men heard the sounds of fighting, and then the discharge of cannons. As they rose to their feet, Manchu artillery and fire-arrows began raining down from the other side of the slope.

The Manchu agents in Coxinga's camp also made their move. It is said that one of them had a bomb hidden in an empty wine pot, which he set off close to the camp's largest gunpowder store. The resulting explosion was powerful enough to take out not just the surrounding area, but also a nearby ship. At that moment, Coxinga's army thought themselves under attack from the city before them and the river behind them, and they panicked.

The Manchu soldiers reached the top of the ridge. They now held the high ground, while Coxinga's forces were trapped with their backs to the river. Seeing that they had the upper hand, the Manchus sent several thousand further reinforcements from Nanjing. Coxinga tried to arrange an orderly retreat, but it soon turned into a rout. His men began fleeing for their lives along the river to the east.

Several of his most skilful generals died in the fighting, including Gan Hui, who tried to cover the others' escape by leading a rearguard action. He was overwhelmed by charging enemies when his horse fell.

The retreating army limped back into Zhenjiang that evening, where they were met by Zhou Quanbin and the other soldiers left on guard. It took several days to take stock of exactly who had been killed, but it was clear that the battle had been a disaster. Back at the Nanjing river's edge, the Manchus pulled 4,500 bodies from the river alone – soldiers in heavy armour who had sunk to their deaths when trapped at the shore. Coxinga's ships sailed back upriver and managed to pick up a few stragglers who had been cut off by the retreat.

Coxinga searched for Gan Hui among the wounded, but eventually heard the story of his friend's last moments.

'This would not have happened,' he lamented, 'if I had listened to him.'[15]

Coxinga was not merely referring to Gan Hui's warnings before the attack. It was only now that he saw Gan Hui had been right all along. He should have consolidated his position in the previously conquered towns. That way, a defeat would only be a temporary setback – he might have been able to get reinforcements and support from the local people. Instead, he had marched on Nanjing, and now fell back on territory that was only being held by military personnel. In his desire to reach Nanjing and see it capitulate, he had not reached out to the local people.

Ten years of preparation had been ruined. The advance on Nanjing threatened to bankrupt the loyalists' funds, and Coxinga knew he would not be able to hold Zhenjiang for long. The Manchus were going to come after him, and he would have to run. After a heated debate with his generals, he ordered the fleet to head back for the coast, where he knew they would be safe.

His new-found associates in the Yangtze region were devastated. There are stories of allies falling weeping at his feet, begging him to stay. The partisan Zhang Huang-yan simply could not believe his ears. When he heard the news, he was miles upriver with a powerful fleet, and many messages of support from the surrounding countryside. He honestly believed that there was a chance to regroup at Zhenjiang and try again, and he urged Coxinga to reconsider. But Coxinga was already reassigning his men to new generals and preparing to abandon Zhenjiang.[16]

Coxinga informed his men that they were going to seize Chongming, a large island at the mouth of the Yangtze, and that Chongming would form the base for a new attack at an unspecified future date. As the defeated soldiers began the journey downriver, the insanely heroic Zhou Quanbin remained true to form, and volunteered to bring up the rear with his company – no doubt spoiling for one last fight on the way home, and hoping the Manchus would try something.

The army reached Chongming without incident, but failed to take it after two days of fighting. There was no time for a siege, and Coxinga saw that his surviving troops were tired and unwilling to put their all into what counted for little more than a holding action. When two generals were mortally wounded in the fighting, even Zhou Quanbin advised abandoning the campaign and returning another time.[17] Coxinga agreed that enough was enough. The fleet packed up and sailed for Amoy, and the Yangtze campaign was over.

Back in Amoy, the deflated Coxinga drafted a letter to the distant Ming Emperor of Eternal Experiences, resigning his princely status. He announced his hope that one day he would deserve to regain it, but until then, he desired to be known merely as the leader of the armies. He wrote a second letter, to the Manchu Emperor of Unbroken Rule in Beijing, in which he offered to begin negotiations for a truce.

In Beijing, the court's relief was palpable, but the time had passed for negotiation. Rumours spread in the city that Coxinga had been killed at the battle of Nanjing, and although they already had Coxinga's letter as proof of his survival, the Manchus did nothing to refute the stories. Liang Huafeng, the general who had led the devastating assault out of the gates of Nanjing, was rewarded with promotion to the rank of military administrator of the entire region immediately south of the lower Yangtze. Guan Xiaozhong, the general who had lost Zhenjiang so spectacularly, did not fare so well. He had all his property confiscated, was demoted and sold into slavery.[18]

The Emperor of Unbroken Rule appointed an imperial prince called Dasu to lead a counter-attack. As Coxinga struggled to prevent many of his own followers from deserting, Dasu gathered every ship he could find on the coast, and assembled that strangest of concepts: a Manchu fleet. Crewed chiefly by Chinese turncoats, the fleet sailed on Amoy, determined to oust the loyalists from their island stronghold. Enemy squadrons converged on the loyalists from three different directions, but Coxinga was still strongest on the sea. The Manchu fleet was almost totally destroyed, and Dasu was forced to retreat in shame.[19] Coxinga wrote of the incident:

The Tartars came down to these southern regions with a great army, to finish up the war in one battle; but as it happens, we on the tenth day of our fifth moon attacked them so furiously that over a hundred of their officers, besides numerous soldiers, were killed, and many taken prisoner, while the remainder had to fly precipitately for safer quarters, without daring to show themselves again.[20]

As he limped home, Dasu received a message from Coxinga, scrawled contemptuously on a woman's handkerchief. It said: 'If you do not wish to fight another battle, you may need this.'[21] But Coxinga's bravado hid his anxiety about the embarrassing retreat from Nanjing, and the fact that the Manchus had been able to take their counter-offensive all the way to the coast off Amoy itself. Coxinga knew he would see other Manchu fleets, and that next time he might not be so lucky.

Although Coxinga had been rattled by the experience, the court in Beijing saw only another loyalist victory. The Manchus were determined to crush Coxinga once and for all, and consequently were prepared to listen to any plan that might work. The Emperor of Unbroken Rule was reminded of a series of suggestions that had been made to him by a new recruit some years earlier.

Huang Wu had defected from Coxinga's side some years before. In gratitude, the Manchus had made him the Duke of Haicheng, the same noble title that Coxinga himself had once spurned. As a long-serving confidant of Coxinga, Huang Wu knew exactly how to hit him where it hurt. He wasted no time in writing a series of memorials to the Manchus, outlining how the loyalists might be defeated.[22] However, these reports had lain unheeded for several years. Now the time was right.

Huang Wu told the Manchus that they needed to cut off family support for Coxinga. Imprisoning Nicholas Iquan in Beijing was not enough – Huang Wu called for the Master of the Seas to be executed, so that he had no chance of collaborating with Coxinga or other Zheng family members. The Emperor of Unbroken Rule decided to give the idea some serious thought. For now, he simply ordered that Iquan be kept in chains, just in case Zheng agents attempted a rescue operation. He knew they wouldn't, but he also knew the shameful news would get back to Coxinga.

On the subject of the Zheng family ancestors, Huang Wu advised cutting off any support being provided to Coxinga from the afterlife, by ordering the complete destruction of the Zheng family tombs in occupied Fujian. The Emperor of Unbroken Rule thought it was a low blow, but it was one he was prepared to authorise.

That was only the first phase. Huang Wu had been richly rewarded for switching sides, and he advised that the Manchus should set up a fund to ensure that the incentive was there for others. Using cash confiscated from occupied Zheng holdings, the Manchus should offer high rewards to any Zheng defectors.

Of course, the Manchus had been doing this all along, but Huang Wu's suggestion was to institutionalise and streamline the process. He also strongly suggested that the Manchus make better use of the defectors they had already acquired. Most were posted far away from their home areas, in order to keep them from switching sides a second time. In the case of former loyalists from Coxinga's forces, this often meant that they were sent far inland as colonists, never to see the sea again. Huang Wu pointed out to them that many of these defectors could be better employed in a maritime capacity. Shi Lang, the greatest admiral of his age, had switched sides years earlier, but the Manchus had made no use of his naval knowledge. If anyone was going to defeat Coxinga at sea, it would be Shi Lang. The Emperor of Unbroken Rule found the idea intriguing, and decided to give it further thought.

That was not all. Huang Wu had other ideas that would have far-reaching consequences. The Manchus knew already that Coxinga's true power lay in the sea, but Huang Wu had details of its weak point. In his years in the Zheng organisation, he knew that the clan had always relied on supplies from secret allies on land. To really hurt the Zheng family, it would be necessary to make trading of *any* kind impossible.

There was no point in half-measures like edicts and proclamations – Huang Wu knew from personal experience that there would always be smugglers prepared to run the gauntlet and trade with the Zheng ships. Instead, the Manchus would have to fight fire with fire. Trade of any kind should be made completely illegal on the coast, and any offenders caught engaging in it would be summarily executed. Anyone reporting illegal traders would be entitled to all their confiscated property.[23] All ships found on the coast were to be burned. Huang Wu envisaged a situation where life on the coast entered such a parlous state that Coxinga's ships would have no resources for repairs, and his men would run so short of provisions that they would melt away in search of food.

In order to enforce such draconian measures, Huang Wu suggested setting up military camps all along the coastline, in order to stop the rebels landing. No ship of Coxinga's should be able to put ashore without facing a waiting company of Manchu soldiers ready to repel it. The Emperor liked the plan, but failed to see how such an arrangement would differ all that much from what the Manchus had been doing for years. They occupied parts of Fujian, and if they saw the Zhengs, they would fight them. So what was new?

Huang Wu's final suggestion was the clincher. It was an all-encompassing, grand scheme that would turn all his other suggestions from idle brainstorming into enforceable plans. It was an idea of such stunning magnitude that the Emperor of Unbroken Rule took a while to get used to it.

Huang Wu proposed a wall around the sea.

From Canton in the south to the northern coastal region near Beijing itself, the Emperor of Unbroken Rule ordered the evacuation of the shoreline. For a distance of thirty miles from the sea, no habitation was permitted, on pain of death. The farmers and fishermen, along with their families, were given mere days to evacuate. Manchu soldiers then arrived and destroyed everything within the designated no-man's-land. Houses and barns were burned, crops were razed and boats were sunk at their moorings.

People in some areas refused to take the edict seriously, convinced that it had somehow been garbled in its transmission. They stayed put, only to be surprised by the arrival of torch-bearing soldiers, who threw them out of their homes and burned down their villages. Hundreds of thousands of Chinese people became refugees, in a land stripped of food. Many died of starvation, or were hunted down by unsympathetic soldiers when the evacuation period expired.

The Manchus encouraged the conquered Chinese to share in their fear and ignorance of the sea. The former nomads preferred grassy steppes, mountains and lush forests – they had no wish to see a vast expanse of ocean, particularly when it harboured Coxinga and his followers. With their coastal prohibitions, they hoped not only to cut off Coxinga from his secret suppliers, but also to remove the sea from China's field of interest.

Nobody was safe, or immune from the lure of the rewards offered for turning in transgressors. One source reported a family who cooked dinner for a Buddhist nun, who looked into her soup bowl and discovered it contained seaweed. She sneaked some of the proscribed food away with her, and used it to blackmail her host. If he did not give her twenty gold pieces, she said, she would report him to the local magistrate as someone suspected of entering the zone of desolation.[24]

The depopulation was complete. One writer reported that 'the area is a wilderness, inhabited by foxes and badgers, tigers and wolves'. Supposedly, even the swallows' nests were empty.[25] The only humans left in the blackened no-man's-land were Manchu patrols, who remained ever watchful for Ming loyalist vessels.

Back in Beijing, the Emperor of Unbroken Rule had cause to celebrate. The implementation of Huang Wu's schemes had not defeated Coxinga, but it had effectively forced the Ming loyalists away from south China. There was still a climate of fear and violence in Fujian, but starving peasants and homeless refugees presented far weaker opponents than fanatical Zheng troops. With any luck, the Manchus hoped to starve the loyalists into submission, and thereby deal with one of the last obstacles to their conquest of China.

Celebration, however, was not on the agenda in Beijing. The Emperor of Unbroken Rule had other things on his mind. He had spent four years in a passionate relationship with his lover Xiao Xian. The attractive Manchu princess had become available to the Emperor after the sudden, unexpected and rather suspicious death of her husband, the Emperor's brother. She became an imperial concubine of the first rank less than a month after Bombogor died of 'grief', or possibly suicide.

As he reached his twenties, the young Emperor's health and behaviour grew increasingly erratic. He coughed blood, and was subject to extreme mood-swings and fits of rage, from which only his 'grandfather' Adam Schall seemed immune. There are reports of Schall arguing with the Emperor until his young ward was red-faced with embarrassment, but Schall remained untouchable at court.

The unstable Emperor of Unbroken Rule also developed a passionate interest in religion, not only the exotic Christianity of

Schall, but also the philosophies of Chan Buddhism (better known in the West by its Japanese pronunciation, Zen). For some years, he was locked in a power struggle with his mother Borjigid, who disapproved intensely of Xiao Xian. Borjigid was no stranger to gossip herself, having been accused in her youth of an affair with Dorgon, which only made her son's open disloyalty to Bombogor all the more painful. Though his reputation for sexual excess was legendary, the Emperor of Unbroken Rule had the gall to accuse his own principal wife of licentious and extravagant behaviour, using it as an excuse to exile her to a subordinate palace. If he had his way, Xiao Xian would have been made Empress in her stead, but Borjigid would not hear of it.

Inevitably, Xiao Xian became pregnant, but her young son died after three months. Breaking with tradition, the heartbroken Emperor ordered that the dead heir be known as the Beloved Prince of Glory – few deceased infants were given noble titles.[26] As befitting the customs of court lore and *feng shui*, the Manchu minister of rites sought a report from the Institute of Astronomy on the most auspicious time for the young child to be buried. Adam Schall's office duly informed him of the optimum moment, but for some reason, the minister ignored their advice.

To the superstitious Chinese, such incidents can have effects of their own. As time went on, Xiao Xian herself became ill, possibly with smallpox. When she died, the 22-year-old Emperor of Unbroken Rule was inconsolable. He reinstituted an unpopular Manchu custom, ordering that thirty of Xiao Xian's handmaidens should follow her into the afterlife. The nobles of the Empire were to mourn her for a month, while the common people should fast for three days. The funeral preparations were extravagant, but concealed high drama behind the scenes.

The Emperor of Unbroken Rule had tired of the world. In a series of heated debates with Adam Schall, he tried to find ways of leaving it. Schall was able to talk him out of suicide, but had greater trouble persuading him not to simply abdicate and become a Buddhist monk.

Within a few months, the fates supposedly granted the Emperor's fatalist wish, and struck him down with smallpox. The frail youth succumbed fast to the disease, and was soon beyond help. On his deathbed, he promised Adam Schall that he would become a

Christian if he survived, but not even the skills of the Master Who Comprehends the Celestial Mysteries were enough to save him.

The dying Emperor reputedly asked Adam Schall who should succeed him as the ruler of the world. The Emperor thought a cousin of his would be a good choice, but his mother Borjigid thought that one of the Emperor's sons by his other wives would be a better choice. Adam Schall sided with Borjigid, and persuaded the Emperor to name his six-year-old son Xuanye as his successor. Xuanye had already survived smallpox, and would guarantee the Celestial Empire the long reign it really required. Behind the scenes, older princes were also pleased that the Heir Apparent would be young and malleable for at least a decade. Lamenting that his sins made him unworthy to face God, the Emperor then passed away.

After the death of the Emperor of Unbroken Rule, four Manchu prince regents joined forces with Borjigid. Tearing up their late ruler's actual will, they issued a final proclamation in his name, in which the Emperor supposedly apologised for some of his bad decisions in government, wished that he had listened more to his mother, and lamented that he had been so extravagant in the arrangement of Xiao Xian's funeral.

Preparations were then made for the enthronement of Xuanye, who was to be given the reign title of *Kangxi* – Emperor of Hearty Prosperity.[27] The new child-Emperor was led through the streets in a ceremonial procession, before crowds of thousands bowing in respect. And, according to several contemporary sources, the former Emperor of Unbroken Rule was among them.

Before his 'death', he had made a cryptic comment to one of his ministers that he intended to join the crowds and kneel before his successor at his coronation. There are some stories that maintain he did just that, and that the story of his sudden affliction with smallpox was a fabrication designed to conceal the fact that he had merely gone into retirement. The Emperor, wrote one commentator, had 'thrown away the Empire as one who casts away a worn-out shoe . . . and, following the example of the Lord Buddha, preferred to seek the mystic solitudes'.[28]

Though there is no proof that his death was faked, there are certainly many bizarre stories about an abbot of the Tiandai Buddhist temple, some fourteen miles outside Beijing, whose gilt statue bears an uncanny resemblance to portraits of the deceased

Emperor. On three occasions in the decade that followed, the Emperor of Hearty Prosperity would visit the temple, where for some reason the abbot did not kneel before him in the manner of other commoners. When the abbot eventually died, at the strangely young age of thirty-five in 1670, the Emperor of Hearty Prosperity would donate a life-sized statue of him to the temple, and sent jewels to be buried in his tomb.[29]

Whether or not his father was really dead, the Emperor of Hearty Prosperity inherited a China that was growing increasingly peaceful. A generation had passed since the Manchus seized Beijing, and now there were only small pockets of resistance. From somewhere in the far south-west, reports reached him that the Ming claimant, the Emperor of Eternal Experiences, was actually no longer in China at all, but had crossed over the border into Burma. Meanwhile, on the coast, a zone of desolation cut China off from the sea, and forced the Ming loyalists to look elsewhere for their supplies.

The Manchu coastal prohibitions certainly made Coxinga take notice, but in the short term, they may even have helped him. His raiders raced to pick through whatever was left behind, and carried off what food and supplies they could from the abandoned villages before the Manchu demolition teams arrived.

The Manchus did not particularly care where the local population went; they merely wanted them to leave the coast. Leave they did, but many sought refuge with the Ming loyalists, who arrived to ship them across the straits to Taiwan.

Although the defeat in Nanjing might have finished Coxinga's reputation as an adversary of the Manchus, the ranks of his followers were swelled by thousands of disaffected coastal dwellers, who preferred to head east and out to sea, instead of west to an unknown fate on land. Zheng family ships took refugees in their thousands to colonies on Taiwan, swelling the Chinese population there.

As time passed, the effect of the coastal prohibitions began to make itself felt. Huang Wu had been right – the removal of any coastal dwellers seriously damaged Coxinga's ability to obtain supplies from allies inland. Communication with the distant Emperor of Eternal Experiences became more difficult, and the Zheng family clung only to a few coastal islands such as Amoy and Quemoy. However, Coxinga's fleet and followers remained supplied from a new source. Chinese refugees established in military colonies on Taiwan were able to clear land and farm new crops for the Zheng organisation. Mainland China might have been all but lost to Coxinga, but the Taiwan Strait continued to keep a Manchu counter-offensive at bay.

Protected from his enemies by the sea itself, Taiwan could be the perfect place from which Coxinga could plan his next move. It might take years to rebuild his forces to a level suitable for a repeat performance of the march on Nanjing, but Taiwan had the resources to make such a project possible. There was only one small problem.

The Dutch would have to go.

10

THE BLOOD FLAG

The subject of Taiwan had come up on numerous earlier occasions, but Coxinga and his followers had never seriously regarded it as a military objective. It was simply too far from the mainland to mount the kind of swift raid to which Coxinga's ships had become accustomed.

However, the Dutch remained concerned that Coxinga might try something, and eventually decided to send a messenger to Amoy to enquire after Coxinga's intentions. The man they sent, one Pincqua, was their most trusted interpreter – a position that only goes to show how desperate the Dutch situation must have become, as he was a long-term friend of the Zheng clan. Pincqua had once been an associate of Nicholas Iquan, but had remained behind on Taiwan in 1626 when Iquan had sailed against Xinsu to become the Master of the Seas.

Used by Governor Frederik Coyett as a messenger in the late 1650s, Pincqua had made several trips across the Taiwan Strait, and was able to assure the Dutch that Coxinga had no military intentions against Taiwan. At the time, that was actually true. Coxinga was preparing for the ill-fated assault on Nanjing, and had no interest in the island. Coxinga did, however, authorise Pincqua to collect the Zheng levy on incoming and outgoing ships. To smoothe the process, he authorised him to collect the levy in Taiwan itself, a challenge to Dutch authority on the island that caused Governor Coyett to hit the roof. A warrant was issued for Pincqua's arrest, and the old scoundrel fled the island to seek sanctuary with the Zheng clan on Amoy.

When he arrived, he reminded Coxinga and his followers about the weakness of the Dutch position on Taiwan. He told them about the recent revolt, which he had witnessed, and of the opportunity Taiwan presented as a distant base for the Ming restorationists. True enough, it was far from the mainland, but the Taiwan Strait was a natural moat that was guaranteed to keep out the Manchus. Coxinga would be able to prepare himself for a triumphant return to the mainland, without having to worry about the coastal prohibitions or skirmishes with his enemies.

Meanwhile on Taiwan, Governor Coyett suspected the worst. He repeatedly wrote to Batavia demanding better supplies and complaining about the poor defensive capabilities of his base. Fort Zeelandia was relatively safe on its isolated spit of land, but Coyett wanted funds to add small walls that would enclose the nearby civilian settlement. For just a small amount of money, Coyett argued he could extend Zeelandia's fortifications so that they protected the entire town.

Coyett also wanted to strengthen the nearby fort of Provintia in some way, since it sat in the middle of the village of Sakkam, and was not really large enough to resist any great assault.

The Council at Batavia was not completely deaf to Coyett's protestations, and had in fact sent a small fleet of 12 ships and 600 soldiers to Taiwan, under the command of one Jan van der Laan. However, the fleet arrived with a sternly worded missive from Coyett's superiors, advising him that the reinforcements were actually intended for another purpose. If Coxinga truly did appear in Taiwan then the soldiers would be there to defend it, 'but, in the event of calmness and tranquillity reigning there', the fleet had orders to sail for Macao. The city's status remained undefined in the midst of the Manchu coastal prohibitions, and the Portuguese were only avoiding the evacuation rules by paying substantial bribes to local officials.[1] Furthermore, the fortieth anniversary of the ill-fated Reijersen expedition was approaching, and the Dutch had decided that it was time to try another assault on the highly prized city.

Captain van der Laan's instructions were to remain in the vicinity of Taiwan until such time as it was proved that the rumours about Coxinga's forthcoming attack were false, 'on the distinct understanding that all danger is over and peace maintained'. Then, and only then, was he authorised to sail for home and attack Macao on the way. His instructions also stated that he was to consider himself a subordinate of Governor Coyett – it was Coyett who had the authority to release the fleet for the Macao expedition, and van der Laan was to obey him in all things, 'as far as these are not contrary to our instructions'.[2]

However, van der Laan was not the smartest of commanders. As far as he was concerned, the detour to Taiwan was an unwelcome waste of time, distracting him from his true purpose, which was filling his coffers with the spoils of an attack on Macao. It is likely that his hatred of the Portuguese, and his long record of plundering Portuguese possessions in India were contributing factors to his selection as leader of the expedition in the first place. On arrival at Fort Zeelandia, he announced that he had already been so bold as to put in at Macao for resupplies *en route*, thereby alerting the Portuguese to the presence of a potentially hostile fleet in local waters. When he finally reached Taiwan, the bulk of his men were too ill to stand, and their arrival only swelled numbers at the infirmary, not the barracks.

At least the garrison was now larger on paper. The soldiers' mere presence was enough to cheer up many of the Dutch, although their attitude soured when they got to know van der Laan better. He was rude, boastful and slapdash, leading some of the local Dutchmen to refer to him as Headstrong John, or John Against-All-Reason. Governor Coyett himself wrote that van der Laan was 'a man as clever in State affairs and police matters as a pig in the fables of Aesop'.[3]

With all the tact of his spiritual ancestor Pieter Nuijts, van der Laan wasted no time in telling the experienced Dutch on Taiwan that they were idiots. Eager to quit Taiwan and win a glorious victory in Macao, he poured scorn on the skittish behaviour of the Taiwan residents. He dismissed reports of Coxinga's military preparations as old wives' tales and laughed off the growing number of rumours spreading among the Chinese community. Besides, he added, even if the Chinese did attack, they were 'little better than poor specimens of effeminate men', and would present no danger to the Dutch.[4]

Van der Laan was getting ready to find fault in Coyett's judgement, thereby allowing himself to invoke the 'contrary to instruction' clause in his orders from Batavia. Coyett argued with him that his own ten years of experience in Taiwan were considerably longer than van der Laan's mere two weeks, and that the local Chinese were obviously preparing themselves for trouble ahead. He reminded van der Laan that the mere arrival of the reinforcements had probably been enough to stay Coxinga's hand for a while. Coyett suspected, rightly, that Coxinga was now waiting for van der Laan to sail for Macao, taking half Fort Zeelandia's military men with him, and leaving Taiwan defended by the infirm and the inexperienced. Few in the Dutch East India Company could forget the embarrassment of 1628, in which only a few hundred Japanese buccaneers had wrought such havoc on the island during the governorship of Pieter Nuijts. They were worried that a repeat performance was imminent.

In 1660, the Dutch sent another messenger to Taiwan with a number of questions and grievances for Coxinga's attention, and a reminder that he had yet to reply to several communiqués from Batavia. The messenger was also given secret instructions to spy on Zheng clan activities, and to see if the loyalists appeared to be up to anything. He arrived in Amoy to find the entire island on a war footing, with drilling troops, ships preparing for sail, and vast supplies being loaded ready for a large military campaign. He was taken to see Coxinga, who greeted him warmly and assured him that he had no ill intentions whatsoever towards the Dutch. The messenger timidly ventured to ask, if Coxinga was not planning on invading Taiwan, what exactly he might be intending to do with all the ships and soldiers outside. Sternly, Coxinga informed the messenger that he was 'not in the habit of publishing his designs', and sent him on his way with a letter.

The letter made sure to 'express our particular goodwill and affection for the Dutch nation', and chastised Governor Coyett for having believed 'many false reports'. Coxinga suggested that Coyett was merely investing too much credibility in the 'gossip of evil minded people', and assured him that, although there may have been rumours that the loyalists planned to attack Taiwan, these were of no consequence. Coxinga went on to reminisce about the first arrival of the Dutch on Taiwan, when 'the then ruling Prince, my father Iquan, opened, directed and continued successfully that mercantile trade'. After reminding the Dutch that he regarded the Dutch presence on Taiwan as an indulgence granted by his own father, Coxinga assured them in patronising tones that they had nothing to fear:

Certainly, I have for many years waged war for the recovery of my own territories, and have been so fully occupied in this way, that there was no opportunity for taking hostile action against such a small, grass-producing country [as Taiwan] . . . Moreover, when engaged in preparations for war, and arrangements have been quite concluded, my practice is to spread a report that I intend to make an exploit eastwards, while my own secret resolution will lead me towards the west.[5]

In other words, after reminding the Dutch that he regarded Taiwan as the property of the Zheng family, Coxinga told them that he always preferred to pretend to be doing the exact opposite of what he really intended. He then informed them, quite categorically, that he had absolutely no intention whatsoever of attacking Taiwan.

Meanwhile, a Chinese leather-worker arrived in Taiwan on one of the Dutch East India Company vessels, and reported that he had paid a courtesy call to his old friend Pincqua while in Amoy. Pincqua not only told him that Taiwan was doomed, he also revealed that Coxinga had recently hired 300 pilots with knowledge of the treacherous waters in the area around Fort Zeelandia. Such a number would be enough to land a fleet bearing soldiers that numbered in their *thousands*. He added that a date had already been set for the invasion, but that it was likely to be postponed for perhaps a month while Coxinga obtained greater supplies of ammunition. As if the loyalist intentions weren't obvious enough, Pincqua also produced a wooden scale-model of Fort Provintia, and talked his friend through a series of scenarios for its capture.

The Dutch panicked. Coyett was now convinced that Coxinga was planning a naval assault on the island, and begged van der Laan to listen to reason. Soldiers in Taiwan had their tours of duty compulsorily extended, and Fort Zeelandia began stocking up in case of a siege.

Meanwhile, Coyett's men reported strange phenomena that only spooked the puritanical Dutch even further. The island was struck by several earthquakes, with aftershocks that continued for fourteen days, and watchmen filed reports that they had seen a mermaid frolicking in the channel between Tai Bay and the sea. For reasons nobody could explain, sounds came from the Company armoury at Fort Zeelandia of a great battle, with clashing swords and firing guns, although when the room was unlocked and checked, nothing appeared to have been disturbed.

Coyett himself wrote off many of these tales as idle fancy, but was himself unnerved when one of the fort's towers seemed to become wreathed in ghostly fire. A similar phenomenon was seen on the waters of the channel that led out to sea, as if 'changing into fire and flames'. Coyett also appears to have experienced for himself a supernatural event on the execution ground between Fort Zeelandia and the Dutch settlement, reporting 'a woeful groaning was heard, as of dying people, the voices of the Hollanders being distinguishable from those of the Chinese'.[6]

Such superstitious talk only made van der Laan all the angrier. Relations between him and Coyett became increasingly antagonistic, until they erupted in a blazing row. As if Coyett did not have enough on his mind, van der Laan complained that he had felt insulted on the day of his arrival, when the governor had not gone out to meet him at the harbourside, and when a guard of honour had not awaited him at Government House. Van der Laan became so irate that he eventually ended up threatening Governor Coyett, swearing that he would avenge himself on the fearful Dutch in Taiwan, who persisted in delaying the seizure of Macao that was the true nature of his mission, and, he believed, his destiny.

Eventually, in February 1661, van der Laan left for Batavia, determined to secure Coyett's dismissal, and thereby to free his soldiers for the Macao expedition. Van der Laan remained convinced that Coxinga presented no danger at all. Coxinga, on the other hand, sprung into action the moment van der Laan set sail.

He called a council of war with his generals, and told them officially what they had known for months: that the Manchus were still a threat, and that eventually, the loyalists would have to mount new campaigns to defeat them. Coxinga added:

The year before last, Pincqua told us of the bounty of Taiwan, that it possessed ten thousand hectares of fields and gardens, a thousand *li* of undeveloped arable land, and revenues of several hundred thousand [taels]. Our artisans would have ample opportunity there for shipbuilding and arms manufacture. Of late, it has been occupied by the red-haired barbarians, but they number barely a thousand. We need but lift our hands to capture it. I wish to secure Taiwan as a base, so we can move you generals' families there, then to punish the east and condemn the west, without concern for the home front.[7]

Coxinga's generals were uneasy at the idea. Some felt that an attack on Taiwan would only take the loyalists further away from their true objectives. Others, lacking the maritime heritage of the Zheng clan, were intensely nervous about the idea of sailing out of sight of the coast of China. Some tried to point out that the Dutch possessed powerful guns, that could outperform anything in Chinese hands. But Coxinga was not in the mood for arguments. When one of the lesser generals expressed his concern that Taiwan was a land rife with disease, poor soil and unlucky *feng shui*, Coxinga all but accused him of mutiny. The generals got the message, they were going to Taiwan whether they liked it or not.

Preparations began in earnest. Coxinga's adopted brother Zheng Tai, now the chief revenue officer for the Zheng family, was left in charge on Quemoy, with orders to maintain supply lines across the Taiwan Strait. But Zheng Tai was forced to recognise the authority of Coxinga's twenty-year-old son Jing, who was left in charge of the base on nearby Amoy. It is unlikely that Zheng Tai, an adopted son of Nicholas Iquan and long-serving clan member, was too happy about taking orders from a mere boy, but at least he got to avoid the malarial swamps of Taiwan. Such sentiments were expressed by numerous other members of the staff left behind at Amoy and Quemoy – the idea of a Taiwan campaign was not popular with Zheng clan members who had grown used to their own family castles and fortresses.

Coxinga's fleet comprised about 900 warships, with a total complement of 25,000 troops. The leaders of the ground forces were two of his most trusted generals from the Nanjing campaign, Maxin and the ever-enthusiastic Zhou Quanbin. The fleet was under the overall command of Coxinga himself, and gathered on 21 April 1661 in Liao-luo Bay, the site of Nicholas Iquan's legendary victory over Hans Putmans's Dutch ships almost thirty years earlier.

The first leg of the journey went smoothly, with the vast fleet putting into the deep anchorage of the Pescadores the next day. But there it remained, while a storm blew up and made the final crossing to Taiwan too dangerous.

The delay was troublesome, as the invasion force had brought little in the way of food or supplies. With Taiwan less than two days away, and populated by thousands of sympathetic Chinese, Coxinga was not expecting to require substantial supplies for the journey. By 26 April, Coxinga had 25,000 hungry mouths to feed, and was forced to send parties ashore for resupply. But the Pescadores had never been a bountiful source of food, and the sailors returned with very little – only what they could scavenge from the local populace.[8]

Coxinga ordered his ships to set sail regardless, even though the sea was still rough. The northern monsoon, of which the storm was merely a powerful manifestation, was a vital means of getting across the Taiwan Strait, and Coxinga feared that if he waited too long the wind would die completely. The lack of food was another consideration, as was the unpleasant memory of Sheep Mountain – once again, Coxinga's followers were riding out bad weather with a growing sense of impending doom.

Some of Coxinga's men, remembering the great loss of life at Sheep Mountain, petitioned him to wait just a little longer, but the invasion of Taiwan had become an obsession. After the disappointment of Nanjing, Coxinga seemed willing to push himself, his men, and their supposed divine protectors to the limit. Some stories claim that Coxinga ordered his cannons to open fire on the sea itself, others simply report his steely and somewhat foolhardy resolve.

'Can we walk on ice?' he said. 'Yes, if Heaven wills it. If Heaven decrees that we should conquer Taiwan, then after we set out tonight, the wind and waves will suddenly quieten. The soldiers cannot sit here and starve among these scattered islands.'[9]

Fearing for their very lives, the ships of the invasion fleet sailed into the night storm – the rain was less of a problem than the incredible swell, which threatened to swamp them. But after a few hours' sailing, the storm dissipated completely.

The following day, the vanguard ships spied land on the horizon – they were nearing Taiwan.

'This,' Coxinga told his men as he looked at the coast, 'is proof that compassionate Heaven has not forsaken me. Heaven takes pity on its orphaned subject, and grants me this haven.'[10] He also wrote a poem, 'On Restoring Taiwan', that likened him to ancient heroes who fled across the sea rather than submit to the First Emperor. It included the words: 'Amid trials and suffering, I cannot bear to leave', suggesting that Coxinga may have been planning to stay in Taiwan for the long haul.[11] It was precisely the kind of thing that the mainland-oriented generals like Zhang Huang-yan did not want to hear.

But Coxinga's obsession with an immediate attack was not mere religious fervour. He had another reason for the apparently foolhardy rush to reach Taiwan – secret intelligence from Pincqua. The Dutch had filled several old boats with rocks and sunk them in the channel that ran into Tai Bay. The scuttled ships were designed to keep any of Coxinga's warships from sailing into sheltered waters, but Pincqua had a plan. For the first three days of each lunar month, the water of the Deer's Ear Channel into Tai Bay was at least 2ft higher at high tide – it was a small increase, but enough to allow Coxinga's ships to sail through, and into a safe harbour out of the open sea.

Later accounts put a more supernatural spin on events, claiming that Coxinga prayed to his patron Matsu, the goddess of the seas, and that she obliged her favourite by raising the level of the waters just enough to permit the ships access to Tai Bay.[12]

From the battlements of Fort Zeelandia, Governor Coyett watched helplessly as the Chinese fleet arrived. His diary of the event recounted the operational panic in his head, as he went over his supplies. He had about 30,000lb of gunpowder, and perhaps enough food to last 6 months, but he was responsible for 1,100 Dutch people at Zeelandia, and had barely 40 fighting men with any real experience. As for vessels, the departure of van der Laan had left Coyett with just two warships, the *Hector* and *'s Gravenlande*, and two smaller craft, the *Vink* and the *Maria*.

Over by the village of Sakkam, the smaller Fort Provintia was now cut off across the bay. Coyett's lieutenant Jacob Valentyn, seeing himself trapped from the main body of the Dutch, ordered his own guns to open fire on the Chinese ships, but did little damage.

Coyett's army captain, Thomas Pedel, volunteered to lead a force of 240 to the Chinese landing ground in an attempt to dislodge them. Meanwhile, Coyett ordered his pitiful complement of ships to try to hold off the Chinese advance.[13] The largest ship, the *Hector*, sailed straight for the Chinese fleet, and Coxinga ordered sixty of his own vessels to peel off and hold it at bay. Each of the Chinese ships was comparatively small, armed with just two guns, but the sheer number of sails must have presented a daunting sight. Faced with a huge armada of oncoming enemies, the *Hector* opened up with her large guns, sinking several of the smaller boats.

On the battlements, Coyett watched in dismay as the *Hector* was surrounded by six of the bolder Chinese ships, the guns on both sides firing with such rapidity that they were soon obscured by a thick shroud of smoke. The Dutch in the fort waited nervously as the sounds of combat continued, the *Hector*'s distinctive cannon booming repeatedly, at a speed that could only mean the crew were forced to discharge armaments simultaneously at targets on all sides. Suddenly, the waters of the bay erupted in an explosion so fierce that the windows of Fort Zeelandia itself shook, and the bay was silent for several minutes.

When the smoke cleared, there was no sign either of the *Hector* or of her attackers. The Dutch ship's powder store had exploded, taking everything in the surrounding area with it. It was a calamitous loss of life for both sides, but it was worse for the Dutch, who now faced Coxinga's armada with just three ships. Realising the momentous impact of the loss of the *Hector*, dozens of the smaller Chinese boats began swarming towards the remaining defenders.

The Dutch vessels fought on — they still had superior guns, but the sheer weight of Chinese numbers presented too many targets to fire upon. Two Chinese ships managed to get behind the *'s Gravenlande* and the *Vink*, attaching themselves with grappling hooks. The smaller *Maria* fled for open water, hoping to evade her attackers with speed where power would not do.

The men on the two Dutch vessels rushed to repel boarders, kicking Chinese marines away, and hurling hand grenades into the attached boats. But soon two more junks had successfully attached themselves to the *'s Gravenlande*, followed by several more. Wave after wave of Chinese marines stormed the ship, until the Dutch sailors were pressed back, and Chinese saboteurs began hacking at the rigging in an attempt to leave the ship dead in the water. The sight of this drove the Dutch crew into such a panic that they began throwing their grenades and firing their own forecastle guns at the deck of their own ship. The remedy was extreme but successful, wiping out the Chinese vanguard and allowing the Dutch to regain control of the battered *'s Gravenlande*.

After prolonged fighting, the crew of the *'s Gravenlande* successfully hacked away the chains that attached all but one of the boats. But if the Chinese were unable to capture the *'s Gravenlande* by boarding her, they were ready to resort to tactics that had been used in the past by Coxinga's father. The last Chinese boat was packed with explosives and inflammable items, which the Chinese duly lit. The flames leapt up its ropes and sail, and crossed over to the *'s Gravenlande* herself, while the Dutch crew rushed frantically to put out the flames before the explosives could ignite. Miraculously, they managed to do so, leaving the *'s Gravenlande* damaged but still afloat. The remainder of the Chinese fleet kept at a respectful distance, leaving the *'s Gravenlande* and the *Vink* free to flee. They ran for the open sea, and none of the ships were seen again.[14]

Meanwhile, Captain Thomas Pedel marched out with his 240 soldiers to fight off Coxinga's landing party on the Baxemboy sandbank north of Fort Zeelandia's peninsula. At the other end of the square mile of sand, the Dutch faced an invasion force in the thousands.

As far as Captain Pedel was concerned, the Chinese were still at a disadvantage. As his men nervously stood their ground at the southern end of the sandbank, he reminded them of the failed Chinese revolt of 1652, in which only three hundred or so Dutch soldiers had successfully suppressed an uprising of thousands of locals. He assured them that 'the Chinese had no liking for the smell of powder, or the noise of muskets; and that after the first charge, in which only a few of them might be shot, they would immediately take flight and become disorganised'.[15]

Captain Pedel was unwisely prepared to equate Coxinga's hardened veterans of the Manchu resistance to the timorous, untrained peasants who had been massacred by their hundreds in the 1652 riots. He regarded a single Dutch soldier as the equal of twenty-five Chinese, and confidently led his men in rows of twelve towards the newly landed Chinese.

With military precision, the column of Dutch soldiers marched within range of the Chinese, and fired three timed volleys of musket balls at the Chinese ranks. Pedel waited expectantly for the Chinese to break ranks and run screaming for the water. But the Chinese front line comprised the infamous Iron Men, who simply shrugged off the musket-fire and held their ground. Then, Coxinga's archers responded in kind, with 'so great a storm of arrows that they seemed to darken the sky'.[16]

The hail of arrows decimated the Dutch musketeers, who looked up to see that the Chinese had sent a detachment of soldiers to sneak along their flanks. Captain Pedel bravely got to his feet and began issuing orders to hold their ground. But even as he spoke, some of his company were throwing down their guns and running in fear.

The Chinese, seeing the Dutch disarray, charged *en masse*, falling upon the little Dutch detachment in overwhelming numbers. Those Dutch who had stood their ground were crushed by Coxinga's shield-men: groups of fantastically strong brawlers trained to face down Manchu cavalry. In his journal, Governor Coyett wrote in disbelief:

> With bent heads and their bodies hidden behind the shields, they try to break through the opposing ranks with such fury and dauntless courage, as if each one still had a spare body at home. They continually press onwards, notwithstanding many are shot down; not stopping to consider, but ever rushing forward like mad dogs, not even looking round to see whether they are followed by their comrades or not.[17]

Although some of the Dutch soldiers managed to wade to safety, 118 of the company were killed in the fighting, including Captain Pedel himself.

A similarly disastrous attempt was made by the Dutch to send reinforcements to Fort Provintia on the opposite shore. By the end of the day, Governor Coyett was forced to admit that the Chinese had control of the harbour, and that the two forts were now both under siege and unable to offer assistance to each other.

Coyett sent some men in a small boat to the Pescadores, hoping to obtain some firewood and additional supplies. It was, with 20/20 hindsight, not a wise move considering the number of Chinese vessels in the vicinity. Thirteen men were captured by the Chinese, and put on a ship heading back towards Taiwan, there to be interrogated by Coxinga. Fearing, quite rightly, that they faced torture, the Dutchmen hatched a plan to escape. Although the Dutch were watched by armed guards, there were only thirty Chinese on the boat, of which half would be below decks asleep at any given time. The Dutch agreed to wait until Fort Zeelandia was in sight, and then overpower their captors and seize control of the vessel. It was a risky plan, and likely to cost many of them their lives, but anything was preferable to falling into Coxinga's hands. Unfortunately for the twelve Dutchmen, the thirteenth member of their group was a French mercenary by the name of Etienne, who thought the idea sounded too dangerous. Preferring to take his chances with the Chinese, Etienne informed his captors of the plan.

Back in Taiwan, the Dutch were brought in chains before an indignant Coxinga, who took it as a personal insult that his captives had not shown him more gratitude for being allowed to keep their lives. Intent on showing the occupants of Fort Zeelandia that he meant business, Coxinga ordered that the noses, ears and hands be hacked off the prisoners. Their amputated extremities dangling from pieces of twine around their necks, the mutilated Dutchmen were then permitted to run from the town back to Fort Zeelandia, where the fort physicians were able to save their lives.[18]

Fort Zeelandia, surrounded on several sides by sea, and with ample supplies of food, would be able to hold out for some time. However, the smaller Fort Provintia stood less of a chance. Packed with men, women and children from the nearby village of Sakkam who had come there in search of safety, Provintia's supplies were extremely limited. Furthermore, the well inside the fort had collapsed, and the soldiers on its battlements were deprived of sleep through the need to be constantly on watch. Matters were not helped by a conspicuously low supply of gunpowder, such that Provintia barely had enough ammunition to fight off a single prolonged assault. The blame fell on the fort's commissar, one Cornelis Rosewinckel, who appeared to have scammed several tonnes of gunpowder ten weeks earlier, and sold it to the captain of a ship headed for Siam. Nobody except Rosewinckel knew where the missing gunpowder really was, and Rosewinckel was unable to settle the matter either way, as he had been killed during the initial assault.[19]

In Fort Zeelandia, Governor Coyett called a meeting of the council. It was agreed that Fort Provintia could not be saved, a fact that led the assembled leaders to appoint two ambassadors to begin negotiations with Coxinga. They were instructed to broach the subject of handing over Fort Provintia, and somehow to do so in

Coxinga's presence without giving any indication of how afraid the Dutch were. The Fort Zeelandia journal also records that, in dealing with Coxinga, the ambassadors were instructed 'to greet His Highness, and show in a gentle way our dissatisfaction at his arrival in our country with such a large army etc.'[20]

The Dutch believed that they still might be able to retain Zeelandia. The council had resigned themselves to the idea of acknowledging Coxinga as the ruler of the island, and even ruefully speculated that their Christian missionary work was done for. But they still clung to the notion that Taiwan's new master might permit Fort Zeelandia to remain in Dutch hands as a trading post.

The ambassadors, accompanied by several assistants and bearers, walked out of Fort Zeelandia, and down the long tail of land that stretched to the south. A mile later, they were able to wade across the shallow water that cut Zeelandia's island off from the mainland, and then back around the bay towards the little village of Sakkam, and its attendant fortress. Coxinga was besieging Provintia in a desultory fashion – he was so confident of the fort's imminent surrender, that he had simply not bothered to dig entrenchments or defences. Instead, 12,000 men camped all around the fort – the other soldiers having been sent off in detachments to subdue other areas. As the Dutch rightly suspected, the sight of Coxinga's banner was enough in most places to convince the Taiwanese natives that their former Dutch masters had abandoned them. All over the island's eastern seaboard, tribes were pledging their allegiance to Coxinga, and the era of Dutch rule was falling apart.

The envoys nervously made their way through Coxinga's men, observing the numerous unorthodox troops under his command.[21] Some were simply humble swordsmen, others highly trained archers. The envoys tried to hide their fear of the Iron Men, with their strange armour and their outsized swords, but it was the sight of the Black Guard that really irritated them. Coxinga had two companies of Black Guard among his army, hardened by a decade of fighting on the mainland, and granted special privileges in the Chinese forces. It irked the Dutch greatly that Coxinga's elite musketeers were Africans and Indians, particularly since some of the Black Guard's newer recruits appeared to be former slaves of the Dutch. In his diary of the event, Coyett wrote bitterly that the 'Black-boys' had caused much harm to him in the course of Coxinga's invasion.[22]

The ambassadors were shown to a tent, where they were asked to wait for Coxinga. The leader of the Chinese, they were told, would be with them as soon as his hair was done. Time dragged on, and Coxinga did not appear. Hundreds of soldiers in full battledress marched past with impressive discipline, and the ambassadors' minder commented that they were just 'a few men going to relieve the watch'.[23]

One of Coxinga's lieutenants arrived to convey the ambassadors to another tent. Once again, they were left there for a long while, with nothing to observe but the sight of more heavily armed troops marching past outside the tent's entrance. Their minder informed them that the second detachment of troops were being sent out to outlying villages to establish a Chinese presence there. However, the ambassadors were convinced that they recognised some of the soldiers from the earlier march-past – Coxinga was merely trying to scare them into believing his army was even more powerful than it was.

After enduring this charade, the ambassadors finally got to meet Coxinga. Their adversary sat behind a square table, his hair now suitably brushed and adorned, his advisers and lieutenants standing at his side in long robes. The Dutch doffed their hats and presented Coxinga with a letter from Coyett, which had been translated into Chinese by the son of the late Captain Pedel. Addressing Coxinga as 'serene and renowned prince', Coyett's letter lamented that the two men had not met under different circumstances. Specifically, Coyett suggested that a better time to become friends would be when Coxinga had not landed in Taiwan with an invasion fleet. Coyett also attempted to remind Coxinga of the Zheng family's long-standing alliance with the Dutch (at least some of the time); to help him in his argument, he even dredged up the old comradeship between Nicholas Iquan and Jacques Specx:

His Excellency [Coyett] looked for nothing save neighbourly friendship from Your Highness, out of respect for the memory of Your Highness's highly esteemed Father, who often showed his gratitude for the Honourable Company's numerous acts of kindness, for which he was much indebted to the Lord-governor personally, who always manifested good feeling and acted in a friendly way.[24]

Coyett's letter went on like this for some time, but Coxinga had heard it all before. When the ambassadors finished reading, Coxinga curtly informed them the Dutch cared no more for him than they did for any other 'Indian', and that he knew from personal experience that their promises would last for only as long as it suited them. Contrary to the assertions of the ambassadors, Coxinga added, the Dutch had no right to demand any explanation from him at all. However, since it pleased him to do so, he would remind them that he was in the middle of a war with the Manchus, and that he deemed it necessary to take repossession of Taiwan.

Coxinga assured the Dutch that, in spite of their numerous swindles in the past, he still held them no ill will. However, he did require them to leave – the Chinese now had need of the island. Finally, Coxinga spoke the words he had been waiting to say since his childhood at Anhai:

> You Hollanders are conceited and senseless people; you will make yourselves unworthy of the mercy which I now offer; you will subject yourselves to the highest punishment by proudly opposing the great force I have brought with a mere handful of men which I am told you have in your Castle; you will obstinately persevere in this. Do you not wish to be wiser? Let your losses at least teach you, that your power here cannot be compared to a thousandth part of mine.
>
> You have by this time surely seen with your own eyes what your iron ships, with which you think you can accomplish wonders and on which you boast so much, can do against my junks; how one of them [the *Hector*] has been burned . . . and has disappeared in smoke; how the others would have met with the same doom had they not taken to flight and gone out to sea.
>
> On land you saw how the pride of Captain Pedel was so much humbled that he with his men, who are as foolish as himself, could not even bear the look of my men; and how, on the mere sight of my warriors, they threw down their arms and willingly awaited their well-deserved punishment with outstretched necks. Are these not sufficient proofs of your incompetency and inability to resist my forces?
>
> I will give you more and stronger ones. But if you still persist in refusing to listen to reason, and decline to do my bidding, and if

you wish deliberately to rush to your ruin, then I will shortly, in your presence, order your Castle to be stormed. My smart boys will attack [Fort Provintia], conquer it and demolish it in such a way that not one stone will remain standing. If I wish to set my forces to work, then I am able to move Heaven and Earth; wherever I go, I am destined to win. Therefore take warning, and think the matter well over.[25]

The ambassadors protested that Taiwan had been granted to the Dutch in 1622, by decree of the very same Ming dynasty that Coxinga claimed to serve. But Coxinga was not in the mood for legal debates. He gave them until eight o'clock the following morning. If the Dutch were prepared to accept his terms, then the next day they should hoist the flag of Prince William of Orange, and make preparations for leaving Taiwan. If, however, the Dutch did not wish to cooperate, they should raise the blood-red flag of battle above Fort Zeelandia, and prepare for war.

The ambassadors pleaded with Coxinga to listen to reason. They were hoping to cling in some way onto their trading post at Fort Zeelandia, and might have even been persuaded to acknowledge Coxinga's suzerainty and pay rent on the land.[26] But they knew that Coyett would never give up the Dutch claim on Taiwan itself – the island was a vital component of the trade-route to Japan. With heavy hearts, they returned to Fort Zeelandia to pass on the message to their superiors. Before they left, they were permitted to communicate with the inhabitants of the besieged Fort Provintia, who confirmed that they were low on gunpowder, and had barely enough water to last another eight days. Fort Provintia was going to fall sooner rather than later.

Back at Fort Zeelandia, the Dutch were stunned at the latest announcements. Governor Coyett was unsurprised by the news, but irritated by the behaviour of some of his fellow council-members. Only a few weeks before, they had sided with Jan van der Laan, and chastised Coyett for wasting money on building fortifications and gathering stores to resist an enemy invasion that would never come. Now, with the enemy camped right outside their door, they were trapped in a small fort on a sandbank thousands of miles from home. 'There they sat, innocent,' Coyett wrote bitterly, 'and with their hands through their hair.'[27]

The Dutch decided to hold out for a miracle. The following day, they unfurled the blood-red flag, and raised it defiantly above the battlements of Fort Zeelandia. Despite their fear, some regarded the mere fact they were prepared to defy Coxinga as some kind of moral victory. To others, it was a gesture of futility. Even as the red flag rose over Zeelandia, Coxinga's negotiators were standing at the doors of its little sister fort. They informed Jacob Valentyn, the commander of Fort Provintia, that his choice was simple – he could surrender immediately and keep his life, or be prepared to have every living creature within the walls massacred. He went for the safer option, and gave up the castle to Coxinga.

While the inhabitants of Fort Zeelandia watched helplessly from across the bay, the Dutch at Provintia became prisoners of war, and Provintia passed into enemy hands. Coyett expected that Coxinga would immediately move on Fort Zeelandia, and observed several thousand of Coxinga's troops seemingly preparing for battle. Coyett planned an ambush among the sandbanks, hoping to use his paltry twelve horsemen to lead a Chinese party into a cross-fire. However, his musketeers merely wasted a day waiting for the opportunity. Though Coyett could not have known it, the Chinese had no intention of attacking that day because they still lacked supplies. Although Coxinga had laid on a rich banquet for the Dutch envoys, this was another case of bravado and deception. In fact, the Chinese army was still suffering from a supply problem – Zheng Tai's promised provisions had yet to arrive from the mainland. Accordingly, while the Dutch waited nervously for an assault on Zeelandia, Coxinga was preoccupied in the north part of the bay, meeting local Taiwanese chieftains.

Once again, he bluffed by ordering a lavish feast to be prepared from the invaders' dwindling food supplies. His plan worked, and the local chieftains proclaimed their allegiance to Coxinga – whether out of fear or amity remains a hotly debated topic to this day. Coxinga was welcomed as a conquering hero, enjoying several days of glad-handing and greeting, as he attempted to establish local contacts for supplies. Meanwhile, his assistant Yang Ying was fiendishly combing nearby villages and captured Dutch supply dumps, in search of any food that might have been set aside for troop consumption. He struck gold, or rather, grain, in one of the nearby villages, and thus alleviated Coxinga's supply problem, albeit temporarily.[28]

Back at the castle, Governor Coyett had a new headache. Fort Zeelandia stood between Coxinga's army and the small settlement of Dutch merchants at the very end of the little spit of land. Those men, women and children now demanded entrance to the fort, rightly fearing that the Chinese were planning to simply walk past Fort Zeelandia and take possession of the small town it supposedly protected. Coyett had kept them out for a while, but now faced a crowd of increasingly panicked citizenry, made all the more jumpy by the sight of a row of Chinese warships, anchored out of the range of Zeelandia's guns.

Coyett would not have had this problem if he had been allowed to fortify the town as he had requested. Reluctantly, he allowed the other Dutch into the fortress, further eating into his limited supplies. In order to keep the Chinese from requisitioning anything to use against him, he also ordered his men to set fire to the settlement, but Coxinga's forces occupied it swiftly and put out the flames.

The two sides eyed each other uneasily across the battle-lines, and each waited for the other's next move.

On 24 May, Coxinga tried another letter. Realising that he might be placing too much faith in the abilities of Zeelandia's occupants to read Chinese, he combed the captured occupants of Provintia for a translator. Deciding that Valentyn would do, he made him render his latest letter into Dutch, and then searched for a suitable messenger. He found the ideal candidate in the form of Anthonius Hambroek, an aging Dutch missionary who had made Taiwan his home since 1648. Hambroek, his wife and two of his children had been captured at Provintia, but their two other daughters were still in Zeelandia. Coxinga reasoned that Hambroek would prove to be an ardent negotiator on his behalf, eager to see his sundered family reunited by peaceful means.

The letter Coxinga gave to Hambroek made his mood abundantly clear:

> You Dutch, scarcely a hundred in number, how can you war against us, who are so mighty? Surely you must be wandering out of your senses and deprived of reason.[29]

Coxinga taunted the Dutch for their Christianity, reminding them that their God encouraged them to seek life instead of death –

possibly the result of an earlier conversation with the Reverend Hambroek. He reminded the Dutch that Provintia had supplied the Chinese with a number of hostages, and advised immediate surrender. His letter betrayed some annoyance that the population of Zeelandia were not as willing to capitulate as their associates in Provintia, and petulantly remarked that as a result, he would not give them as long to gather their belongings when they left.

Despite this, Coxinga's letter offered the Dutch reasonable terms. Fort Zeelandia was forfeit, but he saw 'no guilt or misdeed' in a continued Dutch presence on Taiwan for trading purposes. He merely wanted the island restored to Chinese hands.

'When I say something,' he wrote, 'the whole world has confidence in me, and knows that I shall keep my word. I am inclined neither to lie nor deceive', he lied [30]

The Reverend Hambroek, however, was anything but the ideal choice of messenger. He delivered Coxinga's letter to the Dutch in Zeelandia, and calmly informed them that it was his duty to return to Coxinga with their answer. If they refused to surrender, Hambroek suspected that he, his wife, son and daughter would be killed along with the rest of the Provintia hostages.

Hambroek added that he had every intention of returning to Coxinga and telling him that the Dutch would never bow before a tyrant. He urged the dumbstruck inhabitants of Zeelandia that they should not give up hope of rescue, and that Coxinga's army already showed signs of dissent. Coxinga had lost many of his best men already, ships were deserting and the Formosans could still be encouraged to rise up against the Chinese. Hambroek readily admitted that he would be signing his own death warrant by returning to Coxinga, but advised his fellow Dutchmen that Coxinga was a bloodthirsty devil-worshipper who planned to massacre all the Dutch as soon as they surrendered. Coxinga's letter, he said, was a trap set by a 'heathen of whom no faith or loyalty could be expected'.[31]

Coyett and the other Dutchmen urged Hambroek to stay in the castle. If he truly believed that the hostages would all die, there seemed little point in sacrificing himself, too. But Hambroek insisted, saying that there remained a thin chance that his return might save the lives of his wife, son and daughter, who would otherwise be tortured to death if he stayed.

Hambroek only wavered once, when he had to bid farewell to his two other daughters, who were now sure that their father was walking to his death. They begged him through their tears to stay, but he stood his ground. One fainted, but the other flung her arms around his neck and refused to let go. Extricating himself before his resolve collapsed, Hambroek said some final words to the weeping Dutch:

> Men, I am now going to my certain death in the hope of doing a service to you and my captured comrades . . . May the Lord preserve you. I do not doubt that He shall give you a final solution according to your wishes, keep up good courage, and patiently bear the labours of war.[32]

The Dutch watched the priest as he walked calmly from the castle, and back to the waiting Chinese in the township. In the far distance, they saw Hambroek bow before someone, and then their view of him was obscured by a fluttering banner. They never saw him again.

True to his word, Hambroek returned to Coxinga and told him the Dutch would never surrender. The irate Coxinga ordered his death, and that of all the male Dutch in his custody. The Dutch captives had been divided into groups of thirty or forty and scattered among the outlying villages. There, they were dragged outside, killed, and thrown into mass graves. Valentyn, his wife and children, and a number of other infant Europeans, were transported to China as hostages. Most of the remaining womenfolk were divided among Coxinga's commanders as slaves. Coxinga even picked out one of the Dutch girls as a concubine for himself – a 'sweet and pleasing maiden' who turned out to be Hambroek's other daughter.[33]

On the morning of the 26 May, Frederik Coyett was awoken by what he first assumed to be a thunderstorm. In fact, it was a Chinese artillery barrage. Coxinga's men had set up a series of guns around the newly captured area by the castle, and were relentlessly bombarding the walls of Fort Zeelandia. Coyett peered gingerly over the battlements, and noticed that none of the Chinese guns were in decent cover. Their operators, loaders and spotters were all fully exposed, along with hundreds of onlookers cheering on the assault.

As the thunderous barrage continued, Coyett shouted for his men to bring up every gun they had, and to load them all out of sight. With so many soft targets in full view, the Dutch did not even bother to use many cannonballs, but stuffed their artillery with large quantities of small-bore musket balls and iron nails.

The Chinese cannon continued to pound the walls of Fort Zeelandia, as the Dutch carefully wheeled their own cannons to the battlements. Coyett ordered each to be placed at an angle, in order to ensure a field of fire that covered every inch of the terrain outside.

Then, at a predetermined moment, Coyett gave the order for every one of his guns to fire simultaneously. The hidden cannons were wheeled into their final positions, and discharged in one mighty roar. The Chinese guns were immediately silenced. The giant hail of Dutch shrapnel killed hundreds of enemies in mere seconds, and wounded many more. The attackers fled back into cover into the streets and lanes of the former Dutch community, abandoning their artillery pieces half-loaded for the next firing, surrounded by the dead and the dying.[34]

The Dutch congratulated themselves on a job well done, laughing that the late Captain Pedel had not been completely mistaken when he had ridiculed the Chinese experience in real war. But then, to Coyett's utter disbelief, a group of Chinese gunners ran back to the abandoned cannons, and began loading them up again. 'Their commander, who seemed very obstinate,' wrote the incredulous Coyett, 'was said to have promised Coxinga, on the forfeit of his head, that he would storm the castle in this first attack.' With such a description, Coyett could only have been watching an assault led by the excitable Zhou Quanbin.

The new Chinese gunners began firing once more, leading Coyett to order his men to load up and let them have it. The Dutch guns wiped out several waves of artillerymen, with estimates of the total enemy casualties climbing into four figures. Only then, presumably with no gunners left in the vicinity, did the Chinese attack cease. The Chinese melted back into the alleys of the former Dutch settlement, allowing the Dutch to turn their guns on a detachment of several thousand Chinese soldiers, who had been making their way across the sandbank in the hope of clambering through a breach in the walls. With no breach forthcoming, due to the silenced guns, the soldiers were exposed and vulnerable, and

Coyett wrote wryly in his diary that his men gave them a 'hearty welcome' with their guns.

The attack successfully beaten back, the Dutch seized the chance to consolidate their position. The Chinese guns now stood exposed and undefended – several had been destroyed by direct hits from the Dutch artillery, but the remainder were still operational.

Before the Chinese could return, a party of Dutch soldiers ran out from Fort Zeelandia and over to the unattended artillery-pieces. They climbed up onto them and hammered iron spikes into the barrels, rendering them useless. The Chinese realised what they were doing and rushed to intervene, leading to an exchange of gunfire and arrows, as Dutch musketeers picked off enemy archers while the spikers did their work. The Dutch spiking party also tore down thirty-two Chinese banners that had been erected around the gun-site, and stole several pack-animals. They began to head back across the open ground towards the castle with these trophies, but could not resist stopping to snipe at a couple of Chinese stragglers. They taunted their enemies, and shot at a few more of the hidden archers, until Coyett impatiently rang the Fort Zeelandia bell, to remind them that their mission was over and they were to return to the castle.

Back inside, the Dutch took stock. They had successfully neutralised the threat of the Chinese artillery, and lost only two or three men in the dangerous spiking operation. The men were also rather emboldened by their victory, since they had returned with a couple of flags and managed to liberate several donkeys from Coxinga's army. They argued with Coyett that the Chinese were cowards, and that if a handful of musketeers could do such damage in a simple raid, the Dutch should seriously consider fielding larger numbers in other raiding parties.

Coyett, however, was not prepared to take the risk. He did not think the Chinese were cowards at all – the death of Captain Pedel had shown exactly how good the Chinese could be against European musketeers. These foes were not peasants like the participants in the 1652 uprising. They were soldiers hardened by years of battle on the mainland. And, frankly, even if the Dutch continued to regard all the Chinese as a pushover, Coxinga's army also contained the Black Guard and the Iron Men. True, the gunnery attack had been badly managed (presumably by Zhou Quanbin), but when the Chinese artillerymen had retreated, they had done so in an orderly fashion. They had not fled screaming from the Dutch bombardment, and in fact, they were so disciplined that they had soon returned to recommence their own firing, despite obvious danger from Fort Zeelandia's own guns. The Chinese were a force to be reckoned with, and Coyett was not prepared to risk any more of his men, particularly when placing musketeers in the field reduced the numbers of men available to provide cover from the battlements.[35]

The guarded respect was mutual. Coxinga was equally impressed with the Dutch heroism, and ordered for a change in plans. Chinese accounts try to put a gloss on the incident. Coxinga's assistant Yang Ying made no mention of the disastrous loss of life, but simply wrote that Coxinga decided to play a waiting game. Fort Zeelandia was isolated at the end of a spit of land, blockaded by Chinese troops, and had little hope of resupply or rescue. Without a shred of irony, Yang commented that it seemed smarter to starve the Dutch out, rather than risking any human life in a dangerous assault.[36]

The waiting began in earnest, and two whole months passed without further incident. Within the walls of Fort Zeelandia, the Dutch community eked out their food supply and prayed that their water supply would not run out. Outside in Tai Bay, Coxinga was fêted by the local Chinese, while his men stood their ground and held out for the sight of a Dutch flag of surrender.

Although Coyett did not know it, his enemies had troubles of their own. Coxinga had ordered two divisions of his mainland troops to join his forces in Taiwan, but found his generals unwilling to make the trip. Instead, witnesses to the full effect of the coastal prohibitions which were only now taking hold, they prevaricated for as long as possible, and then defected to the Manchus.[37] As time wore on, Coxinga's army began to run out of food once more. Back on the mainland, troubled with the coastal evacuations, Zheng Tai had neglected his responsibilities and not sent any of the required rice ships.

Coxinga's men were forced to requisition further supplies from the natives, and many were sent further afield on 'campaigns' to both ensure local support and spread the drain on local resources. The lack of adequate supplies, combined with the height of the Taiwanese summer, caused many of Coxinga's soldiers to succumb to disease. The news of such afflictions reached the Zheng clan forces stationed on the mainland, and only strengthened their resolve to avoid Taiwan at all costs.

But Coxinga kept this news from his enemies. Instead, he wrote them a series of letters, advising them that resistance was futile, and that the Dutch had no hope of holding out all summer for the arrival of a relief fleet. Coyett refused to negotiate with Coxinga, and continued to wait for a miracle.

On 30 July 1661, after three months of siege, the Dutch looked out from the battlements of Fort Zeelandia, and saw something unexpected in the west. There were sails on the horizon. They were Dutch ships, and they were heading straight for Taiwan.

11

THE CITY OF BRICKS

Far off in Batavia, the council of the Dutch East India Company had finally made a decision. After months of complaints and reports about Coyett's supposed paranoia, the council had decided to relieve him of his command.

The Dutch craft arriving off the coast of Taiwan were not relief ships or messengers bringing news of reinforcements. They were the *Hoogelande* and the *Loenen*, Company vessels under the command of Herman Clenk, an accountant who had been appointed as the new governor of Taiwan. Clenk had been specially selected for his sense of realism – unlike the disgraced Coyett, he was unlikely to believe tall stories about Chinese invasions and local unrest. Clenk, it was hoped, would be able to take control of Fort Zeelandia and turn round the island's fading trade fortunes.

In his hands Clenk clutched a letter for Coyett, in which the council officially demanded his resignation. The reasons included his refusal to cooperate in the planned assault on Macao, and his willingness to believe rumours about an impending Chinese assault. One of its choicest paragraphs read:

> Surely if Coxinga cherished any intention at all to come, he would have done so long ago . . . The statement that Coxinga, hearing of Your Honour's great preparations to resist him, had postponed his intended attack to a better opportunity, is entirely unacceptable, as was shown afterwards. He never appeared on our shores with evil intentions, although he had ample opportunity of doing so, and we should never be able to hold our possessions there in peace if we allowed ourselves to be kept in continual alarm by such idle threats.[1]

Clenk planned to arrive in Taiwan and get down to the serious business of trading with the Chinese. He was expecting no resistance whatsoever, except perhaps a few harsh words from the outgoing governor. It was thus with some surprise that he found Fort Provintia surrounded by tens of thousands of invading troops, and the bay crawling with warships. The blood-red battle-flag flying atop Fort Zeelandia was also an unexpected sight.

Paralysed by the situation, Clenk remained aboard his vessel, but unwisely sent a party ashore to deliver the letter to Coyett. Its claims that Coyett was a fool, that the Chinese would never attack, and that Taiwan was completely safe from invasion 'caused great dissatisfaction to the officials, soldiers and people'.[2] Clenk's presumption and Batavia's delusions were not the greatest annoyance. The arrival of a single pair of ships, bedecked with banners and bunting in celebration of Clenk's appointment and Coyett's dismissal, was a sure sign that no other reinforcements were on their way.

Though Coyett's problems were anything but over, he welcomed the opportunity to rub his masters' noses in it. He repeatedly invited Clenk to come ashore and take office, but Taiwan's new governor-designate had developed a strong desire to remain aboard ship. When a storm blew up a few days later, Clenk saw his chance, and announced that he would sail in search of safer anchorage, possibly in Japan.

He did not return to Taiwan but set out to sea, where he took out his frustrations and embarrassment on a passing Chinese vessel. Seeing a single merchantman in the distance, Clenk suddenly regained his boldness and ordered his men to storm the ship. With superior forces and numbers, they swiftly seized it and all its cargo, much to the annoyance of its captain, who brandished a trading certificate from the council at Batavia. Realising that he had just committed piracy against one of his own vessels, Clenk now tried to cover his tracks by tearing up the certificate, scuttling the captured ship and marooning its crew on a deserted island.[3] With little to be proud of, Clenk took his time returning home, and tried to work out how he was going to explain the situation to the council.

The council, however, were already aware of Coxinga's invasion. Shortly after Clenk had left for Taiwan, a tiny, battered Dutch ship put into Batavia after sailing through a thousand miles of storms.

After the destruction of the *Hector* in Tai Bay, the sloop *Maria* had fled for open water, never to return to Taiwan. Instead, her captain Cornelis Claes Bennis[4] had sailed against the prevailing winds, across open sea and then through the Philippines. His heroic 53-day voyage eventually brought him to Batavia, where he informed the red-faced council of the extent of their mistakes.

The council took immediate action, not to save Coyett but to hide their own incompetence. A yacht was dispatched to chase after Clenk and retrieve the letter before he made a fool of everyone by delivering it to Coyett. It was not successful in its mission, and returned empty-handed to Batavia a few days later.

Eventually, the council grudgingly agreed that they ought to help the countrymen they had abandoned to a Chinese invasion. Nobody voiced the thought on everyone's minds — that the arrival of Clenk on Taiwan might cause the Dutch to lose hope of reinforcements and surrender before a relief-fleet could now arrive. Ten ships were stocked with supplies and gunpowder, and seven hundred soldiers were put onboard in addition to the normal crews. However, the council had great trouble in finding someone prepared to lead an expedition. The merchants and council members who had been so willing to ridicule Coyett were now reluctant to go to his aid. Everyone agreed that 700 soldiers would be ample to defeat a force of cowardly Chinamen, but despite such self-assurance, no volunteers could be found.

The best the council could do was Jacob Caeuw, a lawyer with no military experience, described by Coyett as 'a person so defective in the power of speech, that one almost required an interpreter to understand his words – which were all spoken through his nose'.[5] Caeuw was sent to Taiwan with a sheepish about-face from the council, announcing that Coyett would be permitted to retain his post for the time being, as 'it would be inopportune now to alter the policy of the government'.[6]

Caeuw's fleet arrived shortly after Clenk had abandoned the Dutch in Fort Zeelandia to their fate. The sight of his approaching ships restored the resolve of the besieged Dutch, and brought a new will to resist.

Caeuw, however, was unable to approach too close to Tai Bay. The weather was still unsettled, and while it kept the Chinese huddled in the bay, the rough waters also prevented Caeuw from sailing his ships into the channel beside Fort Zeelandia to unload any of his cargo or men.

The weather showed no sign of easing up on the following day, but Caeuw risked a landing anyway. His ships rocking dangerously in the choppy channel by Fort Provintia, he managed to unload 2,200lb of gunpowder, and a large number of his troops. However, he was forced to sail into open waters when the weather took a further turn for the worse.[7]

The arrival of Caeuw's ships caused Coxinga some consternation. Neither he nor his generals could understand how the Dutch in Batavia could have heard so swiftly of his invasion. Even hardened sailors of the Zheng clan could not believe that the missing *Maria* could have gone all the way to Batavia against the monsoon winds. The arrival of ten ships, bearing (as the Chinese incorrectly estimated) perhaps 2,000 reinforcements might not be a relief-fleet at all, but merely an arrival that the Dutch had long been planning. If that were truly the case, then the Chinese feared that still more reinforcements would arrive when the news of the invasion did eventually reach Batavia.

Coxinga sent 40 of his own vessels across the bay to harrass Caeuw's fleet, while a company of 150 soldiers approached Fort Zeelandia in an attempt to sabotage the unloading. They returned claiming limited success, although it was clearly the weather that had beaten Caeuw back, and not the Chinese.

Not all the Chinese attackers returned. Some took the opportunity to give themselves up to the Dutch, fearing that Caeuw's arrival was the beginning of the end for Coxinga. The defectors reported to the Dutch that Coxinga continued to be dogged by supply problems, and that the Chinese troops were growing restless.[8] By this time, Coxinga had given up waiting for Zheng Tai to carry out his duties, and sent ships north to Japan to buy up emergency rations.[9] The fact he did not send vessels directly across the Taiwan Strait to China implies that he feared a second Dutch fleet was somewhere between him and the mainland, preying upon his supply ships.

In fact, the situation was worse than that. Rival divisions of Coxinga's army were forced to compete with each other over supplies, creating additional unrest in a stand-off that also involved several mutually antagonistic tribes of local aborigines. Coxinga was forced to send one of his elite units to break up a fight in the outlying village of Datu. The men of Coxinga's rear assault and rear auxiliary had joined forces with disgruntled local tribespeople and declared open war on the left vanguard, whom they believed to be getting better supplies and resources. Coxinga's general Yang Zu, leader of the Marvellous Troops division sent to intercede, was fatally wounded in the ensuing battle.[10]

Datu village was not the only place where there was unrest. A Dutch soldier, Hendrick Robbertz, somehow evaded his captors at Fort Provintia and swam over to Fort Zeelandia. He reported that two Dutchmen had recently been executed in front of the Provintia residence, their alleged crime one of inciting local tribespeople to revolt against the Chinese. The Dutchmen, a schoolmaster and an interpreter, never ceased protesting their innocence, but were nailed to crucifixes by their hands, calves and torsos. They took several days to die, during which they were mystifyingly guarded by Dutch soldiers – presumably the surrendered Valentyn had been forced to acquiesce to Chinese demands for retribution.[11]

However, despite the growing sense of unease about the Taiwan campaign, Coxinga soon stumbled on some extra intelligence that allayed at least some of his men's fears. While Caeuw's fleet remained at large for several weeks, one of its smaller support vessels strayed disastrously close to Taiwan. The *Urk* was wrecked on the coast to the north of Tai Bay, and her crew captured by Coxinga's men. Under torture and interrogation, the prisoners revealed that they were the sum total of the Dutch reinforcements, and that Coxinga could expect no further arrivals for months to come. He had until the end of winter to defeat Coyett and the besieged Dutch, assuming that his disaffected men would be able to survive that long on their meagre rations and scrapings of tree bark. He also put up a sign outside his own tent, announcing to his troops that he had another enemy. It read: 'The first to be punished will be the Revenue Minister'.[12] When Coxinga got home, *if* Coxinga got home, there would be hell to pay for the unreliable Zheng Tai.

The stormy weather finally died down in the second week of September, and Caeuw's fleet was able to enter Tai Bay and unload the rest of its supplies. Repeating errors so often made by the Dutch in their dealings with the Chinese, the new arrivals refused to believe that Coxinga posed much of a threat. Coyett protested that

Coxinga was no ordinary enemy, but was outvoted by a war council swelled with Caeuw's eager men. It was decided to mount a counter-assault on the former Dutch township beside Zeelandia, in the hope of regaining control of the headland, and forcing the Chinese away from the immediate vicinity of the fort. The Dutch decided to do this by hatching a supposedly cunning plan of subterfuge, which was all but a carbon copy of Cornelis Reijersen's assault on Macao in 1622.

The Dutch planned to send the ships *Koukerken* and *Anckeveen* around the headland as decoys, with orders to commence bombarding the Chinese gun positions. While the Chinese were occupied, Dutch troops would head out from Fort Zeelandia itself, hoping to surprise the Chinese in the town area. A further force, comprising three larger ships and fifteen small boats, would head towards the dozen vessels that Coxinga kept close to Zeelandia. If they were successful in taking those ships, they had the option of heading further afield to attack a second squadron.[13]

On 16 September, Coyett watched from the battlements of Fort Zeelandia as the force set out. The new arrivals, of course, had no experience of dealing with Coxinga's supernatural luck, and had paid little heed to some of their countrymen's claims that the weather itself fought on the side of Coxinga.

Mere moments after the boats put into the water from Fort Zeelandia, the wind suddenly dropped. Considering the blustery, unpleasant weather of the last month, the Dutch patiently waited for the wind to come up again. It eventually did so, but was now blowing in the opposite direction, *away* from the Chinese ships. The large Dutch ships were now unable to sail towards Coxinga's squadrons, which effectively removed any chance of artillery cover for the smaller boats. Any sensible commander (such as Coyett who saw disaster looming), would have pulled the boats back and waited for a more favourable opportunity.

Instead, the skipper of the *Cortenhoef*, determined to show Coyett how easy it was to take on the Chinese, ordered the small boats to approach Coxinga's ships without cover from the larger vessels. Coyett would record the battle for posterity in his memoirs:

Suffice it to say that the leaders were so foolhardy as to row towards the enemy in all the available small boats manned with warriors, and engage in battle, rather unsuccessfully, for about an hour; the Chinese being well covered, while our own men were exposed on every side. At length, three of our boats were seized, and the remainder retreated in confusion to their ships. These, however, did not fare much better; for two of them were stranded by the tide which followed the great calm, one was blown to pieces by means of the enemy's heavy firing, and the other was set on fire by one of the Chinese fireboats.[14]

The Dutch lost 128 men in the fighting compared to 150 Chinese – a negligible price for Coxinga, but a disastrous one for his enemies. Caeuw angrily ordered an enquiry into the blunder, but soon gave up when the skipper of the *Cortenhoef* died in another skirmish. The survivors blamed several officers for the decision to proceed with the attack, but all of the accused were now dead.

Pointing out that the garrison at Zeelandia was 'daily diminishing', Coyett finally persuaded the war-council to make better use of their resources, chiefly the remaining warships at their disposal. Three were sent to the north of the island, where a few healthy Dutch soldiers occupied an old fort that the Dutch had taken from the Spanish some years earlier. They were instructed to bring the fresh soldiers back to Zeelandia, along with fresh provisions.[15]

The Dutch also finally began what Coxinga had been afraid they had been doing for weeks – sending two ships to patrol the waters between Taiwan and the Pescadores, with instructions to waylay any approaching Chinese supply vessels.

Now the besiegers themselves were besieged. Malaria decimated the forces on both sides, but the Chinese were also low on food. On 3 October, Coyett sent two more warships out with the simple mission of sailing beyond the zone of Chinese control and foraging for fresh food, and possibly firewood. Yang Ying, Coxinga's supply officer, kept meticulous records of the available Chinese provisions – by October, his diary is a continuous account of hungry men, and stop-gap measures. He found grain enough to supply one company for a few days, and made trips to outlying camps to dole out meagre rations to men pleading for food. In his tent, Coxinga seethed about the failure of his mainland generals to keep him supplied, and watched angrily as the Dutch topped up their supplies with the cargoes of returning warships.

'Just about this time,' wrote Coyett, 'our people were informed by several deserters from the enemy that Coxinga's affairs in Formosa were faring as badly as they had done in China; that during this siege he had lost more than 8,000 of his ablest soldiers; that his junks and vessels cleared away whenever a suitable opportunity offered; that the loyalty of his soldiers and other Chinese in Formosa had somewhat diminished.'[16] Coyett may have been economical with the truth about the means in which the information was received. Caeuw's journal reported that two escaped slaves reached Fort Zeelandia from the occupied township.[17] They passed on an amount of valuable intelligence about events outside the fort, and confirmed the occupants' worst fears about the fate of some of their fellow Europeans. However, Caeuw also reports that the Dutch suspected the slaves had been sent to spy on them, and tortured them just to be sure.

The two hapless 'black boys' were not the only victims of Dutch paranoia. In November, a Dutch surgeon dissected a live Chinese prisoner in front of a crowd of onlookers at Zeelandia – the desire for venegance was rising, even among the puritanical Dutch.[18]

In addition to the problems of food, disease and morale, Coyett faced increasing opposition from some of the mercenaries at Fort Zeelandia. The 'Dutch' forces in the Far East were not limited to men from the Netherlands, but included soldiers from other European countries.[19] Those whose tour of duty had been compulsorily extended were increasingly annoyed that they were being held prisoner by the East India Company, which forced them to fight a hostile army of Chinese, and had little to pay them except IOUs. A French mercenary, Abraham Dupuis, indignantly asked Coyett for permission to leave, and Coyett snapped. He shouted at Dupuis that his time would come when the 'fortress sailed out to sea'.[20]

New hope arrived from an unexpected source, when Coyett somehow received an offer of an alliance with the governor of Fujian province, Li Shuaitai. The Dutch ships he had sent to north Taiwan had been blown off course in the storm, and put ashore at Yung-ning, near Amoy. Much to their surprise, the crews received a warm welcome, and representatives were taken to Fuzhou where they were handed letters for Coyett from the governor and from his princely superior Geng Zhimao. Anyone remembering the epistolary deceptions of Nicholas Iquan would be rightly suspicious, but the offer was genuine – with the full authority of his Manchu superiors, Li was prepared to offer assistance to the Dutch. He even invited them to come to Amoy and attack Zheng family shipping in the area.[21] The Manchus' willingness to cooperate with the Dutch was well-known to the Zheng family, who had done their best to maintain a coastal blockade to keep the news from reaching Taiwan. Coxinga and his son had desperately tried to stop the letters reaching Coyett, and sent ships to sweep the Taiwan Strait. However, the mail ship somehow got through – Coyett was elated, and rushed to the war-council with news of the proposal.

Li Shuaitai's proposal was a little confusing – although he offered to cooperate with the Dutch in the fight against Coxinga, his main interest seemed to be in getting the Dutch to send some ships to the mainland to fight Coxinga's men there. However, the Dutch saw that this might still work to their advantage. If the Dutch fleet sailed away from the besieged Fort Zeelandia, and provided naval support to a Manchu army attacking Coxinga's son on the mainland, Coxinga might evacuate at least some of his troops from Taiwan in order to aid in the defence. If the assault were successful, Coxinga would have his supply lines completely cut. If it were not, it might still alleviate some of the pressure on Fort Zeelandia, if only for a while.

The idea appealed very strongly to the Dutch war-council, and they started making fresh plans. They now saw that there was still hope in their battle against Coxinga, but that they needed to make some difficult economies. There were simply too many mouths to feed within the walls of Fort Zeelandia – if they were going to continue their war footing for any further amount of time, they should make plans to evacuate the women and children. There was ample space on the Dutch ships to transport non-combatants to Batavia, but not their possessions. Accordingly, the council drew up company cheques as insurance against the valuables they would force the civilians to leave behind. If Fort Zeelandia fell, the company was unlikely to honour them, but they served a propaganda purpose if nothing else.

Jacob Caeuw bravely volunteered to lead the civilian evacuation. He announced that he felt he could better serve the Dutch East India Company by making a detailed report to Batavia in person. The other Dutch present greeted this offer with some suspicion:

Every member of Council was much surprised at this, and they pointed out to Caeuw how little such a request would accord with his mission, his own honour, and his reputation. He had been sent as a general to save Formosa from Coxinga's grip; and yet, he now wished to return simply as a letter-bearer, leaving behind the troops under his command, without either having drawn his sword against the enemy, or performing any act of importance in vindication of the trust imposed upon him.[22]

Caeuw bristled at the rebuke, and claimed that he had received 'secret instructions' which overrode the council's own decisions. When asked to produce these orders, he refused, announcing that he was not at liberty to do so. If Caeuw genuinely had such orders, he would not have needed the council's approval to leave anyway, and the irritated Dutchmen threw him out of the meeting.

It was eventually decided that evacuating the civilians would have to take second place to the attack on Coxinga's mainland operations. Instead, the council resolved to send five vessels to Li Shuaitai in order to commence the counter-assault.

Caeuw immediately volunteered to lead the mission, pleading with the council that they had been right, and that he 'had not yet had any opportunity for manifesting his anxiety and zeal for the interests of the Company'.[23] The council relented, and issued Caeuw with new instructions. He was to sail directly for the mainland, unless weather proved adverse. If such conditions arose, he was to put in to the Pescadores to ride out the storm, and then proceed with all haste to rendezvous with Li Shuaitai. Caeuw agreed.

The Dutch were extremely excited at the alliance. If it worked, they hoped it would not only turn round their fortunes in Taiwan, but increase the chances of a more permanent treaty with the Manchus. If everything went according to plan, they would finally be able to wipe out the Zheng clan that had plagued them for forty years, and finally gain the mainland foothold they had desired for so long.

That, of course, would require everything to go according to plan. On 3 December, Caeuw set sail under clear skies, taking the hopes of the Dutch with him. The moment he was out of Tai Bay, he ordered his befuddled commanders to make a course for the Pescadores. His captains protested that there had never been a better day for sailing, and that Caeuw was only supposed to head for the Pescadores if there were a storm, but Caeuw overruled them.

Something was on Caeuw's mind, and he ordered his ships to drop anchor once they reached the Pescadores. The captains protested that they were in 35 fathoms of water, but once again Caeuw insisted. It was almost as if Caeuw was praying for a storm, so he had an excuse to stay away from the mainland. The five Dutch ships were buffeted by the choppy waters in their deep, ill-chosen anchorage, until three of them lost their anchors, and were obliged to return to Taiwan.

They found Fort Zeelandia as they had left it, with Chinese attackers camped outside, beleaguered Dutch defenders within, and an increasingly irate council demanding to know why they were not shelling Amoy at that very moment. The ships were given new anchors and sent back to the Pescadores, with crystal clear instructions for Caeuw that he should get on with his mission, and lead the vital counter-attack designed to distract Coxinga.

However, when the ships got back to the Pescadores, Caeuw was nowhere to be seen. He had fled for Siam, taking the other vessel with him. They ran for the open sea and neither of the ships was seen again.[24] The three remaining ships returned to Taiwan in utter dismay, and reported to the council that the mission to the mainland had failed before it had even started. Some of Fort Zeelandia's best men, best guns, and much-needed supplies were now halfway to Batavia, along with two vital warships.

As if to add insult to injury, the goddess of the sea chose this moment to flood the castle. The dejected Dutch sloshed around a Fort Zeelandia ankle-deep in water, with ever dwindling supplies, and barely 400 fatigued men left able to fight. For some, it was the final straw.

The mercenary Abraham Dupuis regarded the floodwaters with a Gallic shrug, and decided that they were a message from God. The fortress had indeed, in a way 'sailed out to sea', giving Dupuis the excuse for which he had been waiting. With a handful of other disaffected mercenaries, he sneaked out of the castle, and headed for enemy lines, where, he hoped, he would be welcomed like his countryman Etienne. Coyett sent their German sergeant, Hans Jurgen Radis, to order them back to the castle, but Radis also decided that it was time to abandon the Dutch.[25]

The defecting mercenaries were greeted with great interest by Coxinga, who listened eagerly to their stories of life inside the castle. He was extremely pleased to hear of the utter failure of Caeuw's planned counter-assault, which would have placed his campaign in serious jeopardy had it gone ahead. However, he was less happy to hear that the Dutch still had enough supplies to last until the spring.

Hans Jurgen Radis, however, had a solution. A veteran of many wars in Europe, he had only recently been promoted to sergeant.[26] But he knew a poor defensive position when he saw one, and told Coxinga that he had defected because he knew there was little hope of the Dutch holding out for much longer. We will probably never know exactly how the conversation proceeded – the chief source for Radis's treachery is Coyett's *Neglected Formosa*, written by a man who was not present at the meeting. Yang's *Veritable Record*, the only source that might tell us what was said, makes no mention of him.[27] Possibly, Radis only inadvertently revealed the weaknesses in the Dutch defences, but his later actions imply that Coyett's accusations were correct, and that he became an active ally to Coxinga.

After the defection of Radis, the Chinese went back on the offensive. Early in January 1662, the Dutch of Fort Zeelandia witnessed a sudden burst of activity on the part of their besiegers. The Chinese began constructing three new artillery batteries, each at points within range of Utrecht, the small tower that provided cover from the high ground. The Chinese could also be seen digging an extensive network of trenches, sufficient to keep thousands of troops in cover, both to defend the artillery positions, and for the potential mounting of an assault on the tower. They also piled up large quantities of *gabions*: baskets of earth and rocks used in a similar fashion to contemporary sandbags.

Coyett ordered his own gunners to fire at will on the Chinese, hoping to dissuade them from their construction. But although Dutch bombardment caved in several trenches, the Chinese refused to give up. Coyett called an emergency meeting of the council. Somehow, Coxinga had found out about Fort Zeelandia's weakest point. He was clearly planning to direct the full force of his assault on Utrecht. If Utrecht fell, the Chinese would have a vantage point from which they could shoot at anything in the lower grounds of Zeelandia itself. In effect, the Dutch would be besieged from within their own castle, much as Pieter Nuijts had been so many years earlier.

If Utrecht fell, Fort Zeelandia would be untenable. Coyett called for desperate measures, and asked the council to approve an assault on the Chinese positions. However, the Dutch now had only a few hundred fighting men; even if that were enough to assure victory against the three positions, there would be nobody left behind in the castle to provide artillery support, or to defend the castle from a Chinese counter-attack. Accordingly, the Dutch decided to hold out for one last miracle. They assigned three months of provisions to the men in Utrecht, and told them to hold out for as long as humanly possible.[28] For all Coyett knew, reinforcements might already be preparing to leave Batavia for Taiwan, and Fort Zeelandia could still be rescued.

On the morning of 25 January, Coxinga's twenty-eight guns opened up. The Dutch counted around 2,500 cannonballs pounding into the tiny tower. Twice the bombardment ceased, only to allow a force of Chinese soldiers to charge up the hill at the tower. Each time the concussed Dutch inside managed to repulse the assault, the Chinese retreated, and the guns started up once more. By the end of the day, Utrecht's battlements were a jagged ruin, and there was little cover within its walls for the men.

Realising that there was little hope of defending against a third assault, the Dutch in Utrecht cut their losses and ran. They spiked the guns in the tower to prevent them from falling into enemy hands, and fled from the tower, across the courtyard that would shortly be within gunnery range of their enemies, and into Fort Zeelandia itself.

The Chinese rushed forward to occupy the tower, fully aware of the implications for the siege. Amid all the elation, Coxinga himself began to walk towards Utrecht, determined to look down into Fort Zeelandia for himself. However, his new-found military adviser Hans Jurgen Radis told him to wait, suggesting that no enemy would quit such a vital position without leaving some form of final surprise.[29]

Sure enough, the Utrecht tower suddenly exploded in a fireball. Coyett's men had left four giant barrels of gunpowder in the basement, attached to a slow-burning fuse. The Chinese occupying the tower were blown to pieces along with it, souring the initial celebration. The Dutch permitted themselves a wry smile as the remains of Utrecht rained down over the castle and township, but it was a bitter victory. The tower might have gone, but the high ground still belonged to the Chinese.

During that night, the Chinese began to sneak towards the castle, using gabions as cover, and then running out from behind them to stack further baskets of earth closer to their objective. The Dutch knew (as probably did the Chinese, thanks to Radis) that a time would come when the attackers would get close enough to the Fort that the Dutch guns would be unable to tilt at a steep enough angle to fire down upon them – another design fault in the castle that had been inherited from its builders.

Desperate to hold off the final assault at any cost, Coyett ordered the Dutch gunners to fire throughout the night, lighting up the winter darkness in a constant barrage, firing blindly in the direction of the nearing Chinese. Other Dutch soldiers, hoping to strengthen the battlements against possible breaches, ejected the occupants from the houses that stood against the inner wall and began filling the dwellings with sand.

Coyett argued that the time had come for a final assault against the Chinese, and told the council so. Considering the relentless bombardment of Utrecht, the council was convinced that Coyett had taken leave of his senses. But the governor argued that there remained a chance, however small, that Coxinga had expended most of his gunpowder in the assault on the tower. Over two thousand gunshots used up an impressive amount of powder, and the Dutch knew that Coxinga's supplies were still low. Could it be that now was the ideal time to strike, since, although Coxinga appeared to have the upper hand, he might be lacking the ammunition to repulse a counter-assault?

Of the twenty-nine men present, only four voted in favour of Coyett's plan. They were asked to provide their reasons. Two changed their minds when put on the spot. Of the two merchants remaining, Daniel Sicx said that he believed the Dutch had nothing left to lose, and might as well go out with a fight. The other, Paul de Vick, said that he knew little of war, but remembered reading in the Bible that God had watched over Gideon when he had fought seemingly insurmountable odds, and that if the Dutch believed they were fighting with God's grace, then a miracle would surely happen.[30] With such 'support', Coyett's plan was soundly rejected. That left the

Dutch with just two options – to fight to the bitter end and expect no quarter, or to surrender now and hope for better terms.

The Dutch sent a message to Coxinga, announcing that they were prepared to talk, and after almost a week of deliberation, the two opposing sides drew up an eighteen-point contract of surrender.[31] Much of the negotiations appear to have revolved around the preservation of Dutch honour. The Europeans were permitted to 'come forth with flying banners, burning fuses, loaded rifles, and beating drums, marching thus for embarkation under Command of the Governor'. As if the victory belonged to them, and not the Chinese, the Dutch marched proudly from Zeelandia, and crammed themselves on a handful of ships, with enough supplies to get them to Batavia.

Article Nine of the surrender document granted the return of 'every servant of the company now imprisoned by the Chinese in Formosa'. Since most of the menfolk had been massacred after Hambroek's last stand, this list chiefly comprised the women who had been divided among Coxinga's generals. When these women were returned to Dutch care, some of them were found to be pregnant. Some reported that they had been 'considerably caressed' by masters fascinated with the exotic and erotic appeal of European women, and that they had been well-treated. Coyett wrote that they 'did not complain too loudly . . . having not suffered although they had half a Chinese in their belly'. Such was the experience of the women whose masters were previously unwed – those Dutch girls who fell into the hands of married Chinese reported an altogether different experience, 'as the Chinese wives are beset by the jealous devil'. These European women had spent months of hard labour as slaves or kitchen workers and were vocal in their hatred of the Chinese, who had forced them to chop wood, tramp rice and carry water in the Taiwanese heat.

Coyett also reported a third category among the returning Dutch women, since it would appear that not all of them had suffered the same fate. 'Those who had been kept honest by the ugliness of their faces, those were the women who were the loudest of all and who accused their companions of whoring and merry-making with the Chinese.'[32]

Not all the Europeans left with the fleet. Defectors like Etienne, Radis and Dupuis would never be allowed back into European society, and had sentenced themselves to life among the Zheng clan, who mainly despised them for betraying their former allies. Valentyn and twenty or so others were still held hostage, and, although the treaty supposedly guaranteed their return, many of them would never see home again. An estimated 900 Europeans sailed away from Taiwan, leaving around 1,600 dead behind.

As the Dutch vessels left the harbour on 1 February 1662, Coxinga's men took possession of Fort Zeelandia, raising the Zheng family banner where once the blood-red flag had flown. The Dutch had taken everything they could carry, but still left behind quantities of gold and amber and valuable corals. There was also food, which many in Coxinga's army were still lacking – the besiegers were still hungrier than the besieged, and fell eagerly upon the castle food supply before the Dutch sails were over the horizon.

Coxinga announced that henceforth the town would be known as the eastern capital of the glorious Ming dynasty. He reclaimed Taiwan in the name of the Emperor of Eternal Experiences, that distant ruler in exile whose face he had never seen, and from whom no communication had been heard in months. He sent word to his forces back on the mainland that victory was his, and decided that while Fort Zeelandia would need to be occupied by military personnel, the smaller Fort Provintia in the village of Sakkam would make an excellent private residence for the Imperial Namekeeper.

Sakkam, however, was not a Chinese name. It was a mispronunciation of Zhikan, or Red Cliffs, thought to have been the name of a tribe who once lived in the area. At some point, somebody told Coxinga this and chattily added that the locals called it by still another name. With all its bizarre alien stonework and the foreign building materials used in Fort Provintia, the area was also popularly known as *Zhuanzi Cheng* – the City of Bricks.

'How difficult it is,' commented Coxinga ruefully, 'to escape fate.'[33]

12

THE SLICES OF DEATH

As far as the Dutch were concerned, Taiwan 'relapsed into its original condition of heathenism and Chinese idolatry'. The Chinese colonists took a different view, and welcomed Coxinga as a hero. The Taiwanese natives were less pleased, since their island was merely swapping one set of conquerors for another. As news spread beyond the environs of Tai Bay, however, Coxinga's prowess and nobility grew with the telling.

Stories soon sprang up among the tribes about a Sage King from a distant land, who was the favourite of the sea goddess. Coxinga, it was said, had power over the ocean itself, thanks to a magic jade bracelet that he had been given by an immortal. He had come to Taiwan in search of three supernatural artefacts, which he required to restore the power of the Emperor of Brightness. The jade bracelet would make him a master of the seas, a black flag would make the savage mountain tribes swear allegiance to him, and a magical bottomless pot of grain would feed his army forever.[1] It was generally agreed that the magical pot of grain was still at large – many of Coxinga's soldiers had been assigned to outlying locations and told to farm their own food. Back on Quemoy, Zheng Tai was keeping very quiet and refusing to answer any messages.

Supposedly, the victorious Coxinga toured the entire island, giving rise to numerous tall tales about local geographical features. In fact, he only made a brief inspection of the villages near Fort Zeelandia, accompanied by 900 troops, but many contemporary legends retain a vestigial memory of Coxinga's lieutenants and their desperate search for supplies. Several wells and springs dotted across Taiwan are said to have been created when a thirsty Coxinga arrived and thrust his sword into the rock. One is supposedly haunted by the spirits of his soldiers, who gather there in the form of birds. Another manifests phantom images of Coxinga's sword, still another a sword that transforms into a dragon at times of crisis.[2]

Coxinga, it is said, once raised a magical cannon from the waters near Amoy, which only he could use. He gave it a rank in his army, and called it the Mouthless General – perhaps a garbled reference to the use of artillery in the siege of Fort Zeelandia, and the fact that of all commodities required by the army, gunpowder does not appear to have run out. The Mouthless General, it is said, was also Coxinga's magical means of defeating the fumes from a sulfurous spring near modern Taipei. The conqueror of the Dutch also supposedly killed a giant tortoise which breathed noxious fumes at his army. The slain monster was transformed into an island off Taiwan's east coast – as with most of these fanciful tales, even the location is apocryphal, as neither Coxinga nor his army travelled far from Taiwan's south-west corner.

Other legends of Coxinga have roots in his desire to use Taiwan as a base for supplying a counter-attack on China. Folk traditions remember that he came to Taiwan looking for *something*, but disagree on exactly what it may have been, since the local tribes were unlikely to comprehend the complex demands placed upon their new ruler. In search of a piece of jade to use as his seal, Coxinga supposedly climbed Taiwan's highest mountain to enter a sacred grotto guarded by giant leeches. He obtained the precious stone and had it engraved with the words: 'The Seal of the Imperial Namekeeper, Zheng Chenggong.' However, when he tried to use it, the characters magically transformed into a phrase in praise of the goddess of mercy – only an emperor could use jade in a seal, and Coxinga had pushed too far.[3]

The story may contain elements of truth, not in Coxinga's desire to become Emperor, but in its depiction of his motives and attitude once he reached Taiwan. The Zheng clansmen back at Amoy and Quemoy remained suspicious that he would forget all about mainland China, and that he would force them all to relocate to disease-ridden swamps. Others reported increasingly bizarre behaviour from their leader, whose eternal insistence on his divine mission seemed to take on a new tone. Coxinga's pride and vanity, which had proved to be so disastrous during the Nanjing campaign, threatened to ruin him a second time.

Coxinga certainly wanted to stay in Taiwan for a while, but he still intended to prepare another attack on the Manchus. In a meeting in late February 1662, he informed his generals that their first priority was the establishment of self-sufficiency in provisions. Coxinga's generals were assigned patches of land on the coast and immediate hinterland, and instructed to put their soldiers to work on land reclamation and farming. It was Coxinga's plan that the men would farm for half the year, and then resume military training in each off-season – the only exception being two brigades retained at full military alertness in case of a Dutch or Manchu counter-attack.[4]

The numbers of troops on Taiwan were also swelled by civilians. Coxinga took advantage of Manchu coastal prohibitions by sending his fleet to transport refugees from the mainland to Taiwan. He offered dispossessed peasants a new life if they agreed to work as farmers in the military colonies, and many took him at his word.

Coxinga maintained his severe insistence on absolute discipline, even though the immediate military danger had passed. He ordered the executions of two local officials accused of taking bribes, much to the annoyance of Maxin, who pleaded with him to grant his new found subjects a little leeway. Coxinga, however, would not relent, and regaled Maxin with historical precedents until his associate gave up arguing.[5]

Coxinga was troubled by a number of problems. The Zheng generals on the mainland were still surly and uncooperative, fearful that they and their families would be forced to leave their luxurious homes and move to a wild frontier with a high mortality rate. The soldiers were annoyed that their hard-won victory had directly led to their new occupations as glorified peasants in a foreign land, and it is likely that Coxinga himself was fretting over his long-term goals. Turning Taiwan into a suitable base for attacking the Manchus would take years, perhaps even an entire generation. By the time the Ming loyalists returned to the mainland, they would encounter Chinese people who had known nothing but the rule of the Manchus. The Chinese thought nothing now of shaving their heads in the Manchu fashion, and knew little but government propaganda about the fall of the previous Dynasty of Brightness. Coxinga's army would have a harder time winning over the hearts and minds of the people on the mainland – particularly with still no sign of any word from the distant Emperor of Eternal Experiences. Such concerns made Coxinga increasingly irritable, particularly since he received several reminders of his own mortality.

The first was old news, but had been kept quiet for many weeks by the Manchus. On 1 February 1662, even as Coxinga was signing the treaty of surrender with Coyett, a herald in Fuzhou made an official announcement on behalf of the Manchu Emperor of Hearty Prosperity. He reported that it had become clear that Nicholas Iquan held little sway over his son Coxinga. There seemed little point in relying upon Coxinga's atrophied sense of filial piety to come to a peaceful resolution between the Manchus and the Ming loyalists. With that in mind, it seemed prudent to follow the earlier advice of the defector Huang Wu, and to end the charade of Nicholas Iquan's house arrest.

After the failed negotiations of 1657, Nicholas Iquan had been kept in chains by Manchu authorities afraid that he would somehow escape and rejoin his son in the south. His funds increasingly low, he found that his only friends were now occasional Jesuit visitors, who could not ignore the plight of a fellow Catholic, and slipped him money – presumably to use for bribes to his jailers to obtain small comforts. Iquan reportedly promised to reform his heathen ways, pleading in his prayers, 'if it is granted to me to be restored to my former fortunes, I shall not be ungrateful'.[6]

In November 1661, the regents for the Emperor of Hearty Prosperity had ordered that it was time to enact the death sentence that had hung over Iquan's head for four years. Knowing that the news would reach Coxinga on Taiwan, the February edict was careful to specify the exact details. Nicholas Iquan had been tortured to death by the 'slow-slicing method', starting with mutilation to his extremities, and working inwards in a veritable death of a thousand cuts. Each time the scalpel cut his flesh, the wound was immediately cauterised with a red-hot iron, stemming the bleeding but adding to his suffering. His last moments were made all the more unbearable by his fellow victims – Iquan was first obliged to watch as two of his sons suffered the same fate. The boys, who had once begged Coxinga to surrender to the Manchus and save their lives, finally met with agonising death in a Beijing jail cell.

Even though his own banner had once called for Iquan's death, a distraught Coxinga ordered public mourning. But Iquan's execution was by no means the last of the spring surprises of 1662. Iquan's generation may have finally breathed its last, but there was a new member to the Zheng clan. At thirty-nine years of age, Coxinga was now a grandfather.[7]

The news was doubly unexpected, because few had expected to see Coxinga's son Jing provide an heir so soon. Raised by the fierce Cuiying, the boy had led a pampered life at the Zheng palace in Anhai until 1650, when he had relocated to Amoy. Jing had been betrothed as a child to the granddaughter of a clan ally, but the couple had yet to produce any children. Dominated by his mother, the 21-year-old Jing displayed little interest in girls of his own age, but had a string of affairs with middle-aged women. Eventually, the truth came out in pieces, wrecking Coxinga's elation in slow slices of its own.

For nine months, Coxinga had heard perilously little from Amoy and Quemoy – Zheng Tai was an embittered and resentful adopted clan-brother who thought little of Coxinga, so his behaviour was understandable if not advisable. But Jing had remained quiet for a similar period, and kept many of the facts of the pregnancy quiet from his father. When pressed for details of the mother, Jing revealed that it was not his principal wife, but 'a concubine'. It was only after the child was born that Jing's grandfather-in-law angrily broke the full story to Coxinga. The mother of the Zheng heir was not a sanctioned concubine at all, but the Lady Chen, a wet-nurse at Amoy. She was retained at the palace as a source of nourishment for one of Coxinga's infant children, a position which under the strict terms of Chinese family tradition made her an honorary wife of Coxinga, and Jing's stepmother.[8]

Coxinga was furious, accusing the Zheng clan at Amoy of conspiring to keep the news from him. Jing had committed an act of statutory incest, and instead of dealing with the matter, Cuiying had helped her son cover up the incident. Now it was presented to Coxinga as a *fait accompli*, with the errant family members presumably hoping that Coxinga would be overcome with grandfatherly joy and shrug the incident off.

But Coxinga had proved his obsession for severe discipline on several occasions. He ordered the mandatory punishment – death, and not just for the child, but also for Lady Chen, Jing and Cuiying. A messenger was dispatched to the mainland with the sentence, which led to heated discussions between Zheng Tai and his advisers.

Tai had had enough of Coxinga's attitude, and ignored the order.[9]

Meanwhile, Coxinga heard a rumour that one of his admirals off the coast of Amoy was planning on defecting to the Manchus. He immediately dispatched Zhou Quanbin (ever ready for a fight), with instructions to kill him. Soon after, Coxinga sent another messenger after Zhou with additional orders – before returning to Taiwan, he was to put in at Amoy and see that Zheng Tai, the other rebellious generals, and Jing and Cuiying were all put to the sword. The message never reached Zhou, but it did reach Zheng Tai, who threw Zhou into prison before he could receive it.

As the folk tales with their stories of hubris imply, Coxinga was growing increasingly unstable. He had won a 'victory' against the Dutch and conquered an entire island, but the reluctance of his lieutenants to accompany him was a source of great annoyance. Deep down, he may have appreciated the bitter truth, that like his father before him he belonged to the sea. For as long as Coxinga kept to the oceans and the coastlines, he was assured of some success, but on land he had little talent for warfare. The defeat at Nanjing still stung him, as did the long wait he would have to endure before he stood the remotest chance of trying again. In the meantime, he decided to fight even further afield.

On 21 April 1662, Coxinga sent a letter to the Spanish governor of the Philippines, demanding reparation for alleged Spanish crimes against him, and the establishment of the regular payment of tribute. His letter addressed Governor Don Sabiniano Manrique de Lara in the name of the Emperor of Eternal Experiences, suggesting that Coxinga felt suitably absolved of the Nanjing defeat to at least speak once more on behalf of the Ming dynasty. Flushed with his success against the Dutch, and determined to expand the Ming dynasty in a new direction beyond the sea, Coxinga's letter implies that he intended to play to his strengths and keep to the seas. Notably, he also referred to himself as a prince – reclaiming the title that he had resigned after the Nanjing débâcle:

It is a well-known fact, in both ancient and modern times, that enlightened princes chosen by Heaven should be recognised with tribute from foreign nations. The stupid Dutch, unaware and uncomprehending of the mandate of Heaven, conducted themselves without fear and without shame . . . Had they come to me earlier in humility, understanding and recognising their sins, they would perhaps not be suffering so much travail as they do today. Your small kingdom has harrassed and attacked my trading vessels in like manner as the Hollanders did, thus giving rise to clashes and discord . . . At first, I thought of leading personally the armada to punish your evil ways, but then I remembered that your small kingdom, although it has given me reason for displeasure, has lately shown signs of repentance . . . I have therefore decided, in contrast with my action towards the Dutch. . . to give you an amicable advice that your small kingdom, if it recognises its own faults and the wishes of Heaven, should bow down and come to my throne every year to offer tribute.[10]

Considering that the Philippines, while 'small', certainly covered a larger area than that held by Ming loyalists in 1662, the arrogant letter is puzzling. Either Coxinga truly was suffering from delusions of grandeur, or the letter was a deliberate bluff, hoping to capitalise on the news of the Dutch defeat as it spread throughout Asia.

In a way, it worked. Within days of the arrival of Coxinga's letter in Manila, Governor Manrique de Lara had taken action. He recalled Spanish troops from outlying forts, ready to defend Manila. He called upon the assistance of the priesthood, ordering the saying of Masses in defence of Spanish territory. He also convened a council of war. Coxinga, the Spaniards suspected, was either bluffing or overconfident. What worried them more was the effect that Coxinga's threat would have on the large population of Chinese in Manila.

Desperate times called for desperate measures, and the presence of so many Chinese in their midst was likened to 'an unwholesome humour' that needed to be bled from the body of the state.[11] The Spaniards were concerned that the local Chinese might 'dangerously divide our attention and our forces' in the event of an attack by the Zheng clan, a reasonable fear considering the progress of events on Taiwan.

Reluctantly, the Spaniards agreed that the only available course of action was to expel all Chinese who were not Christians. They resolved to do it peacefully, and to allow all of the 'hibernating' Chinese merchants in Manila to take their property with them. However, they also realised that news of their decision might cause a panic, and agreed to keep it quiet until soldiers were in place to conduct the evacuation under sufficiently strict martial law.

The mere news of secret council meetings, followed by the recall of troops from all over the Philippines, led the Chinese population to suspect the worst. Some made preparations to flee, creating a momentum of rumour and counter-rumour leading others to believe that their lives were in danger. Even if the local Chinese had not originally been supporters of Coxinga, the misunderstanding transformed them into the very thing that Manrique de Lara had feared: a mob in revolt. Soldiers sent into the Chinese quarter to keep the peace were met with armed resistance.

Several Catholic priests entered the Chinese quarter to assure the occupants of their safety, but two soldiers had already died in the fighting, and the crowd also killed a Dominican friar who tried to reason with them.[12] An uneasy stand-off ensued, but the priestly negotiators were eventually able to reach a truce. The mutinous Chinese, who by now had barricaded themselves in in several townships, were persuaded of the Spaniards' desire for a peaceful solution, and escorted to evacuation ships. In the areas of Cavite and Tondo, the Chinese were rounded up and decapitated by over-eager cavalry, and some others fled into the mountains, but the majority were packed into ships for Taiwan. One junk reportedly left port loaded with 1,300 Chinese, packed so tightly that they could barely sit down, each paying ten pesos to flee with his life.

Meanwhile, Governor Manrique de Lara wrote a stinging rebuke in which he mocked Coxinga's self-assurance, sternly suggested that amicable relations were in the interests of both nations, and delivered an ultimatum of his own. He also addressed his letter 'to the Kuesing, who rules and governs the seacoasts of the Kingdom of China', making it abundantly clear that he did not regard Coxinga as a rightful representative of any emperor. Manrique de Lara informed Coxinga that he had expelled the Chinese from his islands, but had not bothered to have them killed. 'Rather,' he wrote archly, 'I wish to double and redouble your power which you brag so much about, tempering my impulses with my duties.' He further added that Philippine ports would be closed to all Chinese shipping until Coxinga apologised, unless, of course, Coxinga insisted on pursuing his campaign against the Philippines. Just to rub salt into the wound, Manrique de Lara pointed out how unsafe Coxinga's current position truly was:

> [We] Spaniards will meet you anywhere on being advised, although in this you will have to reckon with the Tartars, those of your own followers who hate you, and the Dutch who are looking for an opportunity to strike back at you . . . You cannot thus be sure of having the upper hand.[13]

The Spanish were ready to fight, and if the war of words were any indication, Coxinga might have finally met his match. But the high point of Manrique de Lara's letter is his personal attack on Coxinga, a straight-talking stream of open abuse which, inadvertently or otherwise, would have insulted Coxinga to the very core:

> It is therefore my answer that large and small kingdoms are not made by your will alone, because your life and intellect are short and limited. You were born yesterday and you shall die tomorrow without leaving on earth even a memory of your name.

Coxinga's ambassador began the short journey back to Taiwan, hoping for dear life that his master would not shoot the bearer of impressively bad tidings. Luckily for the messenger, Coxinga never got to read the letter.

Back in Taiwan, Coxinga was still waiting anxiously for news of Zhou Quanbin's mission to the mainland, and still mourning his father. He had also developed a fever – possibly the malaria that had struck so many of his soldiers – or pneumonia. Whatever it was, the same disease seemed to also afflict Maxin, the last of his most trusted generals. Despite his fragile condition, Coxinga insisted on stepping out onto the battlements of Fort Provintia each day and looking out across Tai Bay for a sign of any ships bearing news from abroad.

As May turned to June, there was a storm on the coast of Taiwan, which left the carcass of a huge whale beached on the shoreline. The superstitious Chinese regarded it as a bad omen, particularly those in the Zheng clan who knew that the whale was Coxinga's totem animal, and the symbol of his affinity with the sea.[14]

In late June, a junk arrived from the Philippines.[15] Its captain, Nachiu, had sailed for Taiwan at the first sign of trouble with the

Spanish, and had successfully evacuated a number of refugees. Weeping before Coxinga, Nachiu informed him that the Spanish had executed all of the Chinese in the Philippines. This was not strictly true – Nachiu merely *assumed* that he had fled ahead of a massacre.

Coxinga flew into the greatest rage of a notably irate life, swearing to 'reduce the Spaniards to ashes', and proclaiming that he would personally visit a 'war of blood and fire' upon the Philippines. His fever preying on his sanity, he even announced that he would declare a truce with the Manchus, and invite them to accompany him on the mission. That night, as he raved and shivered in his bed, his servants were only able to calm him by assuring him that his orders had been carried out, and that 'the world [had been] killed, in particular the Spaniards'.[16]

Now so weak that he could not walk without support, Coxinga still insisted on watching the ocean. One account reported him standing on the battlements of Fort Provintia, shouting at something his servants could not see. Covering his eyes in fear, and then pointing at nothing, he ordered his servants to remove the decapitated bodies piled before him, claiming that they were looking for him (*sic*), and accusing him of causing their undeserved deaths.[17]

In an altered mental state, believing himself abandoned by the goddess of the sea, possibly suffering from tropical disease, and certainly weakened by ten years of warfare, Coxinga was dying. Fate dealt him a final twist of the knife when further news arrived from China. The Emperor of Eternal Experiences was dead.

Crowned in 1647, the last of the Ming Emperors had spent fifteen years on the run. Pushed away from the coastal regions, his court and supporters had been forced further inland and to the west. During the early 1650s he had enjoyed the protection of a warlord in Yunnan, China's south-westernmost province, before his guardians quarrelled and fought among themselves.

The situation had become so desperate, that the last Ming loyalists were prepared to try anything. Some of their most fervent supporters were members of the Christian religion – the Jesuit order, unafraid to hedge its bets by having an agent on both sides, had left a Father Xavier Koffler with the imperial party. Just as Adam Schall had once done in Beijing, Koffler worked his alien charms on the women of the imperial household, and eventually persuaded the

Emperor's mother, stepmother and wife to convert to Christianity. When they did so, they also took with them the Emperor's newborn son and heir, who was baptised with the suitably imperial name of Constantine.

The Emperor's stepmother, the Grand Empress Dowager, then wrote a letter to Pope Innocent X in distant Rome. In it she asked him for absolution, should death come to the imperial family at the hands of the Manchus. She expressed her regrets that she could not kneel personally before the Pope's throne to learn more about Christianity. And, as subtly as possible, she mused that in the event of a crusade to restore the Ming dynasty, China would have a Christian emperor.[18]

The Grand Empress Dowager's letter was placed in the hand of Koffler's assistant, a Polish Jesuit called Michael Boym, who made the arduous journey back to the other side of the world. It took him some time to convince the Vatican of the authenticity of his letter, and by the time he received a papal audience, Innocent X was dead and had been succeeded by Alexander VII. The new Pope eventually drafted a non-committal reply, which Boym carried with him back to the Far East. Prevented from entering China through the Canton region, he eventually crossed the Chinese border through northern Annam, but died soon afterwards.

The Pope's letter never reached the Grand Empress Dowager, who had herself died in the meantime. Meanwhile, her stepson, fearing for his life, had stepped out of China entirely, crossing the border a month ahead of the luckless Boym. The palace women had long since sold their jewellery, and the Emperor was reduced to making empty promises to be honoured on his restoration. Writing in his own blood on a strip of silk torn from his robe, he even promised half of China to his most loyal general, assuming that half of China would one day be his to grant.

The Emperor of Eternal Experiences and his entourage left the Celestial Empire, heading further south-west into a barbarian land. They spent a further two years in the Burmese town of Sagaing, as guests of King Bintale, who regarded the Chinese arrivals as visitors inviting unwelcome attention.

Bintale suspected that the Manchus themselves would come looking for the Ming loyalists, and kept them under a state of house arrest while he deliberated on the best course of action. In June

1661, the decision was made for him by his brother Pyè Min, the Prince of Prome, who murdered Bintale and usurped his throne. Pyè Min was even less welcoming to the Chinese, and ordered that the Ming officials should attend a ceremony at a local temple to 'drink talisman water' with him.

The request was not welcomed by the Emperor's chief guardian, the Captain of the Brocade Guard. The post had once been held by Coxinga's uncle Bao the Panther, but was now the responsibility of the south-western noble Duke Mu. The duke saw through Pyè Min's ruse, and refused to allow his charges to leave the relative safety of the mansion where they were staying. Pyè Min took matters into his own hands and sent 100 war-elephants and a battalion of soldiers the following day.

In the ensuing attack on the imperial compound, Duke Mu and several thousand other Ming supporters were massacred. It would appear that Pyè Min had given orders for all to be killed, but a messenger arrived at the last minute, bearing a change in the plan. The Emperor of Eternal Experiences was spared, along with his mother, wife, concubine, son and eunuch servant.[19] With them were a handful of seriously wounded soldiers, one already in a coma – this was the last of the Ming army.

The imperial family were mystified. They could not understand why Pyè Min had not allowed them to die with their followers. Then the Emperor heard that the Burmese king had received a letter that had caused the sudden reversal of his orders. The imperial family assumed that it had been a message from a loyalist general, announcing that a Ming army was waiting outside the town, and that they had come to retrieve their Emperor.

The imperial family were left in their blood-stained mansion for forty days without further word, until a messenger arrived from Pyè Min, announcing that it was time for the Emperor to leave. Troops were indeed arriving to collect him.

At sunrise the next day, 5,000 horsemen arrived on the opposite river bank. They had no banners or insignia, and their allegiance was difficult to determine at such a distance in the half-light.

A party of troops, conspicuously unarmed, approached the compound and announced that they were loyalists, come to transport the Emperor back to China. They were led by a soldier who was last seen four years earlier among the Ming troops, but the

Emperor was still suspicious. He had come to believe that the letter which had so scared Pyè Min was not from a Ming loyalist at all, but from the general who had infamously betrayed them in 1644.

'Have you been sent by Wu Sangui?' asked the Emperor, only to be met with uneasy silence.

It was the only answer he needed, and he berated the turncoats for trying to deceive him. They relented, admitting that they were in the service of the Manchus, but assuring him that they had been ordered to ensure that no harm came to his imperial person.

The last of the Ming had little choice. They left Burma with the turncoat soldiers, and began the three-month journey back into China. Their captors treated them with the greatest respect, but the Emperor was sorely troubled, refused most meals and began to develop increasingly bad asthma.

The Emperor and the pitiful remains of his entourage eventually reached the capital of Yunnan province. The entire region was now under the rule of Wu Sangui, the general who had first invited the Manchus into China, now a fifty-year old honorary prince of China's new ruling dynasty. Wu had spent the 1640s hounding the last remnants of Li Zicheng's rebel army across China, before arriving in the far south-west and wiping out the last remnants of the Ming loyalists. Now he was the master of the entire region, almost a king in his own right, ruling on behalf of the Manchus. Chen Yuanyuan, the woman for whom he had sacrificed his country, was at his side. As a symbol of his integration into the Manchu imperial lineage, his son Yingxiong was married to a Manchu princess. As a reminder of his enforced allegiance, Yingxiong was kept in Beijing as a hostage.

The presence of the Emperor of Eternal Experiences caused stirrings among the troops. As with all other armies of the period, only a handful of officers were actual Manchus – the rest were Chinese, and some felt stirrings of long-forgotten patriotism at the sight of a Ming ruler, albeit one in such a sorry state.

Wu Sangui sent word to Beijing that he had the last of the Ming held captive. Now that four hard-line regents were ruling in the name of the Manchu Emperor of Hearty Prosperity, the news was greeted with the same brutality that had removed Nicholas Iquan. Beijing replied with new orders.

On 19 May 1662, the Emperor of Eternal Experiences and his son

Zixuan Constantine were ordered into Wu Sangui's presence. Ruefully announcing that he believed his time had come, the Emperor did as he was told. Wu Sangui personally read out the edict from Beijing, ordering the deaths of the Ming claimant and his fourteen-year-old heir. Even as Wu Sangui was reading the last words of the letter, lieutenants stepped forward and grabbed the Emperor and his son. Then and there, they strangled them with bowstrings.[20] On hearing the news, the Emperor's wife smashed a porcelain bowl and successfully slit her own throat with a fragment before guards could stop her.

Heaven itself seemed angry. Soon afterwards, the sky became dark with clouds. Thunder and lightning followed, and a summer hailstorm pounded the city. Many inhabitants went into mourning for the last of the Ming, causing a nervous Wu Sangui to execute many of his own troops, afraid they might revolt in remorse. But as the days passed, the rains lifted, the guilt-ridden mourning abated, and China was finally under Manchu rule.

The news travelled fast. Post-riders carried it to Beijing immediately, and the regents knew within days that their rule was now uncontested. From Beijing it reached other urban centres with relative speed, while slower, civilian gossip spread it at a more leisurely pace eastwards from Yunnan. Within a couple of weeks, the death of the last Ming Emperor was common knowledge in Fuzhou on the coast.

In far Taiwan, Coxinga watched the sea from Fort Provintia, mourning the father he still hated, cursing the son and wife who had betrayed him, loathing the Spaniards who had defied him. He fretted, too, about the likelihood of a Dutch counter-assault, and whether he would ever be able to set foot on the Chinese mainland again, at the head of a conquering army.

Even in his waking hours, he was haunted by visions of the dead and the dying; his disease had taken hold. But despite his advanced illness, he insisted on pacing the battlements with a captured Dutch telescope in his hands, even as the waves grew choppy, and another summer storm began to spit rain.[21]

A ship arrived bearing news from the mainland, but it was news of the death of the Emperor of Eternal Experiences, Coxinga's unseen lord for fifteen years. A broken man, Coxinga shakily donned his ceremonial robes, and fought off the attempts of his servants to help him. In slow, agonised steps, he struggled to make his way through the dark corridors, past shutters clamped down against the storm outside. Deep in his personal chambers, he staggered to his family shrine, where the ancestral tablets of his mother and father took second place to a memorial written by the founding emperor of the Ming dynasty.

His hands trembling, he took the Ming testament and lifted it reverently, bowing his head before it. The effort was too much, and Coxinga crumpled to the ground, cradling the memorial in his arms, sobbing openly. His courtiers stood at a distance, unwilling to leave, but knowing he wanted no one near him. The grief-stricken warrior looked up at his followers. 'How can I meet my Emperor in Heaven with my mission unfulfilled?' he cried.[22] Coxinga bowed forward, covering his face with his hands, his chest heaving as he wept. And with that, the last defender of Brightness stopped breathing. His followers were unable to resuscitate him, and he died as he had lived, clutching the spirit of the Ming dynasty to his heart.

13

A THOUSAND AUTUMNS

The storm grew more violent. According to legends of Coxinga's life, it was a tempest equalled only by that which had witnessed his birth thirty-nine years earlier. Up in the mountains, it dislodged a giant 'iron bark tree' which tumbled into the river and floated downstream towards Tai Bay.[1]

When Coxinga's death was announced the following morning, those who had known him the longest read their own significance into the fall of a 'Big Tree'. They fashioned the tree into a coffin for their lord.

The Zheng family was immediately split by Coxinga's death. Within a week, Zheng Jing had proclaimed himself Coxinga's rightful heir on Amoy. Jing released Zhou Quanbin from his imprisonment, appointing the man sent to kill him as the supreme leader of the Zheng armies.

On the other side of the Taiwan Strait, Coxinga's soldiers found themselves with no high-ranking officers. Their leader had perished, Zhou Quanbin was absent, and Maxin had also succumbed to disease. Believing, or perhaps hoping that the sentence of death against Jing had been carried out, two commanders proclaimed Coxinga's younger brother Shixi the new leader of the Zheng family forces. They did so with the supposed authority of Coxinga's last will and testament, a highly suspect document that mystifyingly favoured their own chosen candidate, instead of any of Coxinga's surviving sons. Even if Coxinga had seriously intended to put Jing to death, he had five other sons who stood ahead of their uncle in the succession.[2] Before long, the rebellious officers realised that there would be trouble, and began to make preparations for an assault by Jing's supporters.

In Amoy, Jing began his rule by imitating the Ming loyalty of his father. He passed details of his administration and plans to a minor Ming noble, Zhu Shugui, the Prince of Peace, who then reported Jing's deeds to an empty throne. Concerned about more pressing matters, Jing delayed the process of selecting a replacement for the executed Emperor of Eternal Experiences. In fact, he seemed confused by the nature of his inheritance, unsure whether he was a prince loyal to the Ming dynasty, the independent ruler of a coastal nation, or a local warlord ready to make peace with the Manchus.

Ambassadors soon arrived from the Manchus. As they had done with Jing's father and grandfather, they offered him a pardon and high office in the Celestial Empire, if he only agreed to submit to the Emperor of Hearty Prosperity and hand over his Ming dynasty seals. The ambassadors added that, of course, Jing would also be expected to shave the front of his head in the prescribed Manchu manner.

It is unlikely that Jing found the proposal attractive, but he was already making preparations for attacking his uncle's forces on Taiwan, and needed to keep the Manchus from launching an attack at his rear. He sent a reply asking to be considered as the king of an independent island nation, and offering to attach Taiwan to China as a tributary state in the manner of Korea. The Manchus would never agree to it. Ever since the initial invasion led by Dorgon, the adoption of the Manchu hairstyle had been a fundamental part of their assimilation of the Chinese. If Jing were to agree to the shaving of his head, then the Manchus might be able to do a deal, since he would not be the first local warlord to submit to the Manchus but retain kingly powers in his own region. China's southernmost regions had already been divided up between three turncoat generals, who ruled as princes: Wu Sangui in Yunnan in the south-west; Shang Kexi in Canton in the south; and Geng Zhimao in Fujian on the south-east coast. The Manchus offered Jing a similar position as the ruler of Taiwan, but Jing held out for a more independent status – Taiwan was not part of China proper, but a separate land like Korea or Burma. Jing hoped that wrangles about his exact status would keep the Manchus busy while he dealt with his uncle.

On 16 November 1662, Jing set sail for Taiwan with an invasion fleet commanded by Zhou Quanbin. He sent word ahead to Tai Bay that Coxinga's loyal son was coming to attend his father's funeral, hoping thereby to give local commanders a chance to proclaim their allegiance to him without bloodshed. Most of them took him at his word, and waited in their barracks for news of his arrival.

That left only the two generals who had falsified the will and put Shixi in charge. They met with Jing's landing force on the shores of Tai Bay on the morning of 27 November. Fighting in thick fog, the rebels seemed to be winning until Zhou Quanbin personally entered the fray, dragging back his retreating soldiers and leading them in a charge that resulted in the death of one of the rebel generals. Jing came ashore to see the remaining rebels for himself.

'The commander of your forces lies dead,' his herald proclaimed. 'Let us all join the standard of the true son of our late beloved king.'[3]

The other troops eventually surrendered, and Jing pardoned his uncle, telling him that they had both been led astray by their underlings. Other members of the clan were not so fortunate. In the camp of the rebel generals, Jing found letters not only revealing that Zheng Tai in Amoy had been the instigator of Shixi's rival claim to power, but that Tai was already in secret negotiations with the Manchus. On Jing's return to Amoy, the feckless Tai was arrested at a banquet, and soon died in prison under suspicious circumstances.[4] On hearing of his father's death, Tai's son went over to the Manchus, taking a quarter of the Zheng clan forces with him.

Jing ruled in Taiwan for nineteen years, but although he used the Ming calendar, he soon gave up most pretences of loyalty to the dead dynasty. Zhu Shugui, the Prince of Peace in Jing's own entourage, was an ideal candidate as a new Ming imperial claimant, but Jing never bothered to install him as such. Instead, he called upon the prince's advice with decreasing frequency, and eventually ignored him completely, leaving him to brood on his lost inheritance with several concubines in a Taiwanese mansion.

In his later dealings with the Manchus, Jing proclaimed that he was not a Ming loyalist, but a king, and demanded recognition of his independent status. He called his Taiwanese kingdom *Dongning*, or Eastern Peace, and hoped the Manchus would leave him alone.

The Manchus, however, wanted all potentially hostile inhabitants removed from Taiwan. Unwilling to do it themselves, they instead sought the help of unlikely allies: the Dutch.

Following the disastrous loss of Taiwan, the Dutch in Batavia wanted revenge. Clenk and Caeuw, the two feckless individuals who had contributed most greatly to the Dutch defeat, managed to somehow escape punishment, and got off with minor reprimands. In search of a scapegoat, the Dutch dumped all of the blame on poor Frederik Coyett, the man who had fought for so long to warn his superiors of Coxinga's plans for Taiwan. Coyett was marched out to the execution ground and forced to kneel before the headsman's axe in a symbolic death sentence, later commuted to life imprisonment on a remote island. Coyett eventually made it home in 1674 after a prolonged campaign by friends and relatives back in Holland.[5]

The Dutch East India Company in Batavia could not allow their reputation to suffer, and dispatched a new fleet, setting sail the day after Coxinga died. While Jing was preoccupied with the succession crisis, the Dutch revenge fleet raided several Zheng settlements along the Chinese coasts. The ships held many veterans of the siege of Fort Zeelandia, and showed no mercy to the followers of their deceased arch-enemy, slaying men, women and children.[6] The Dutch raids were conducted with the open assent of the governor of Fujian, who had promised them trade privileges if they would only rid him of the Zheng clan. He was lying, of course.

Over several seasons, a number of Dutch fleets raided along the coast of China, preying upon any ship they found on the principle that the Manchus had made ocean travel illegal, and that any vessel they found must therefore belong to the enemy. Meanwhile, a curious three-way negotiation began as each of the opponents in the conflict tried to get what they wanted. Ambassadors from the Manchus continued to visit Zheng Tai (until his arrest and death) and Jing, offering them pardons and noble rank if they submitted to the Emperor of Hearty Prosperity. Meanwhile, Dutch negotiators tried to pin down the exact nature of the Manchus' promises to them, earnestly presenting the Manchus with charts and maps, and suggesting a number of places where they might build their permanent base. The Manchus, it seemed, were happy for the Dutch to attack Zheng shipping, but less keen to allow the foreign barbarians to trade with them on a regular basis. What the Manchus really wanted was for someone to wipe the Zheng clan off the face of the earth, whereas the Dutch would have dearly loved some Manchu assistance in retaking Taiwan. From Beijing, the aged Adam Schall wrote to Jesuit colleagues and informed them that the Manchus had no intention whatsoever of trading with the Dutch.

They planned on treating them with courtesy while they had a common enemy, and then cutting them off with a series of delays and prevarications once the Dutch had served their purpose.[7]

The Dutch, however, already suspected this. A third line of communication had opened between them and Zheng Jing himself, who openly told them of the Manchu deception. Jing urged the Dutch to forget past enmities and return to Taiwan as friends.

This strange three-way contest continued for many months, and had its fair share of defections. Some members of the Manchu forces went over to the Zhengs – presumably as the last resort for wrongdoers facing the death penalty. Meanwhile, many more of the Zheng clan defected to the Manchus, including Zheng Tai's son, and Coxinga's pardoned brother Shixi.

In November 1663, negotiations were broken off when a joint Dutch–Manchu fleet attacked Amoy and Quemoy. The last communications received were from Jing's fleet commander, Zhou Quanbin, advising the Dutch that their new allies could not be trusted.[8] Zhou was resorting to desperate measures because he knew that this time his 'Manchu' opponents were not the seasick former horsemen of yesteryear. Finally giving in to overwhelming evidence, the Manchus had done the sensible thing and put former Zheng clansmen in charge of their fleet. The squadron of Manchu ships that fell on Amoy and Quemoy was commanded by Huang Wu and Shi Lang, the two defectors whose departure had done so much to damage Coxinga in the 1650s.

Although the Zheng clan bravely resisted, Amoy and Quemoy soon fell. The Dutch smashed the heathen idols in the local temples, and celebrated what they hoped would be the first stage of their campaign to retake Taiwan. They were expecting immediate help in the reconquest of Taiwan, but Manchu assistance suddenly faded after the acquisition of the Zheng clan's two largest coastal strongholds.

Eventually the Dutch fleet sailed for Taiwan on its own, where its commander, Balthasar Bort, squabbled for a while with Zheng clan representatives, and then sailed away for Batavia, without either retrieving the hostages left from the fall of Zeelandia, or initiating an attack. The Chinese told themselves that it had been sunk *en route* by the goddess of the sea:

Suddenly, heaven and earth grew pitch-black, bolts of lightning flickered and shone, a typhoon brought storms and rains, the billows roared and out of the sea iron lotuses burst forth that pierced and drowned all the ships of the Dutch – they died to the very last man.[9]

The Dutch, who remained quite unmolested by any iron lotuses in real life, fully intended to return after they had mopped up the Zheng presence on the mainland – two coastal strongholds still remained. Jing, however, pulled the last of his troops away from the coast, abandoning all pretence of a mainland presence.

For some, it was a sign that the end was nigh. A number of Zheng clan commanders defected to the Manchus, including the long-serving Zhou Quanbin. When he submitted to his new masters, he was accompanied by an anonymous European, presumably one of the defectors who had quit Coyett's service at Fort Zeelandia. Whoever this man was, he will have enjoyed the unique position of having fought on all three sides of the prolonged conflict.[10] True to their mercantile origins, many of the Zheng clan members brought large cargoes of goods, realising that once they were Manchu subjects, they would no longer be able to import goods from abroad, but could sell off anything they happened to bring with them.

However, the Dutch became bogged down in further negotiations with the Manchus. Realising that Jing's warnings might have been right, they held off further attacks on Taiwan until they were sure that they were not better off swallowing their pride and trading with the Zhengs. The ensuing uneasy truce lasted over a decade, and the Dutch trade with the Manchus was irregular at best.

The Dutch were defeated by Coxinga's invasion, by Manchu obfuscation, and, to some extent, by enemies in high places. Paramount among them was the Jesuit Adam Schall, determined to oppose any anti-Catholic presence in Asia. Schall, however, had problems of his own. On 20 April 1664, at the venerable age of seventy-two, the Jesuit father suffered a stroke that left him unable to walk unaided, and with considerable difficulty in speaking and writing. His long-term enemies at the court decided it was time to strike, preparing a list of accusations. Schall and his Jesuit colleagues, it was alleged, had treasonably preached a false religion and destroyed the ancient traditions of Chinese astrology with their alien science.

More seriously, Schall was accused of deliberately employing his arcane Catholic sorcery in cursing the Manchu imperial family. As the man ultimately responsible for the place and time of the burial of the infant son of the late Emperor of Unbroken Rule, Schall had wilfully employed negative *feng shui* to his own ends. The inauspicious funeral arrangements, it was said, had directly contributed to the death of the child's mother, and later his father, the Emperor himself.[11]

By this time, the disabled Schall was unable to speak in his own defence, and had to mumble phrases to be conveyed through an intermediary. His answers at his trial display some small vestige of his former wit, but are clearly the words of a man in pain. The trial wore on for several months, and each stage ended with a guilty verdict for Schall and his fellow priests. Piece by piece, Schall was stripped of his honours and noble titles, and then consigned to prison in chains.

However, the regents of the Emperor of Hearty Prosperity were reluctant to sign off on the final verdict, not because they did not want Schall dead, but because he had friends in high places. The Emperor's grandmother Borjigid remembered Schall fondly, not only for his medical help in her time of need, but for his long and enduring friendship with her son. Although Borjigid enjoyed little actual power, she could still make her influence felt – the regents were obliged to prolong the trial and throw the final judgment to a Grand Council of Manchu princes.

The deliberations continued for several more months, with the accused Schall now so infirm that he collapsed in court. At the end of the long process, the council reached their verdict – Schall was found guilty of treason and sorcery, and sentenced to be beheaded. With the responsibility for the verdict safely spread among a large number of nobles, Schall's enemies took the opportunity to add a final twist, altering the punishment from a simple beheading to death by slow slicing.

Before the sentence could be carried out, it required the approval of the Emperor of Hearty Prosperity. The eleven-year-old boy was expected to read his regents' recommendations, and then apply his seal to make the document law. However, on 13 April, a comet appeared in the sky above Beijing – the irony was not lost on opponents of the former head of the Institute of Astronomy. Three days later, the city was struck by an earthquake that not only levelled many houses, but also destroyed one of the walls of Schall's prison. The superstitious in the court interpreted it as the intense disapproval of both Heaven and Earth. Added to the continued protests of Borjigid, it was enough to save Schall's life. Although Schall continued to be hounded by his enemies in Beijing, he was freed and eventually died peacefully in his sleep the following year.[12]

As time wore on, the Celestial Empire finally appeared to be at peace. All of mainland China was now united under the rule of the Manchus, and the generation that remembered life under the Ming dynasty was all but gone. Zheng Jing ruled Taiwan as a king, but the land had never been part of China proper, and did not present too much of a danger. He pointedly did not install the Prince of Peace as the new 'Ming Emperor', but insisted on dealing with the Manchus as the king of an independent state. Ambassadors argued with each other about exact definitions on a semi-regular basis, but neither side possessed the wherewithal to take military action. For some years, at least, the Zheng clan was safe on Taiwan. Coxinga's dream of restoring the Ming dynasty died with him.

Jing had lost his holdings on the mainland after all, but, like his grandfather Nicholas Iquan, persisted in occasional smuggling operations. One of the strangest commodities in the new criminal operations turned out to be women, who were supposedly kidnapped by the dozen on the coast of Fujian and shipped to be the brides and concubines of the remnants of the Zheng clan on Taiwan.[13] More traditional trade became more widespread after 1668, when the coastal prohibitions began to relax, and the Zheng clan found it easier to trade with their Chinese countrymen under the noses of bribable officials. Although the Dutch temporarily gave up on the idea of trading with China or Taiwan, Europeans of another sort returned to Taiwan in the form of the English East India Company, which signed a trading deal with Jing in 1670.[14]

The final flourish of the Zheng clan came in the form of an unexpected alliance with the Ming dynasty's bitterest enemies. As China settled into a time of peace under the Emperor of Hearty Prosperity, its most distant regions were ruled by the most powerful of the turncoat generals – princes who realised that their usefulness was at an end if China was truly pacified. Wu Sangui, for example, had only been made the warlord of Yunnan in the far south-west because of its proximity to the Ming Emperor in exile in Burma.

Now that the last of the Ming claimants was dead, strangled before Wu's own eyes, there was no need for him to have such powers and a standing army. Now nearing his sixties, the man who had let the Manchus into the country in the first place was now an old soldier facing retirement. In order to keep up the pretence of the need for his satrapy in the south-west, Wu began a series of unnecessary military campaigns against 'rebellious' aborigines, hoping to be left to his own devices, and not recalled to a life of inactivity at the capital, or to live out his dotage in the harsh winters of his native Liaodong. His gamble paid off in 1667, when he demonstrated superficial willingness to retire, officially requesting to be relieved of his duties on account of failing eyesight. Beijing took the bait and requested Wu stay on in his post – reasoning that there might still be the threat of rebellion among the aborigines.[15]

At Fujian, in the south-east, of course Prince Geng Zhimao could always argue that Taiwan remained a threat, however distant. Similarly, in Canton in the far south, his turncoat colleague Shang Kexi tried a similar tactic. Falsifying reports of troublesome raids from the *tanka* boat people of the region, he allowed Beijing to believe that he was involved in a protracted war on piracy in his region, thereby hoping to cling on to his powers for a while longer. Beijing approved the continued maintenance of armies in the southern regions for some time, but the expense was extreme. The armies of the 'Three Feudatories' in the south cost the state over 11 million taels a year – almost half of the entire tax revenue of the Celestial Empire. Eventually, someone was going to ask questions about the need to keep so many soldiers at full alert in what was supposed to be a time of peace.[16] There was also the obvious danger to consider, of leaving half the country under the control of three generals who had so willingly betrayed their former master, each with an army large enough to wage a significant war on the Manchus. This fact did not escape Coxinga's son Jing in 1670, when he sent an emissary through Manchu territory to Wu Sangui in Yunnan. The message was a tempting one – if Wu was prepared to rise up against the Manchus, the Zheng clan on Taiwan were ready with 10,000 ships and an army of 100,000 men.[17]

The tension below the surface finally manifested itself in 1673, when Shang Kexi genuinely tired of the military life. Deciding that he really did want to return to Liaodong and retire, he tendered his resignation to Beijing and asked that his son Zhixin take over his duties. Beijing accepted his resignation, but added that there was no need for Zhixin to assume command, as there were no longer any pacification duties to be carried out.

The decision sent shockwaves throughout China. The Manchus had stated, however obliquely, that the Celestial Empire was officially at peace. Etiquette now demanded that Wu Sangui and Geng Zhimao should also tender their resignations, and with extreme reluctance, they did.

Everyone knew the implications and the subtexts. The Emperor of Hearty Prosperity, still only nineteen years old, held emergency meetings in Beijing. Overruling his councillors' advice to let sleeping dogs lie, he sent a message to Wu accepting his resignation. It was a risk he had to take, but it backfired.

On 28 December 1673, Wu Sangui murdered the governor of Yunnan, imprisoned the Emperor's messengers, and proclaimed that the Ming dynasty still lived. The word spread out from Yunnan that Wu Sangui had finally woken up to his true loyalties, and decided to support the cause of the 'Prince of Zhou' against the Manchus. Few knew exactly who this mysterious Prince of Zhou was, although many rightly suspected that it was Wu himself. In some parts of China, Wu's revolt was regarded as the resurgence of the Ming dynasty, while in others it was seen as Wu's attempt to establish an all-new, but demonstrably Chinese alternative to the Manchus. In either case, after being a bystander at the deaths of the Emperor of Lofty Omens in 1644 and the Emperor of Eternal Experiences in 1662, Wu now wanted the throne for himself.

The Beijing government dragged Adam Schall's cannons out of mothballs and sent an army of 10,000 men to put down Wu's rebellion.[18] But as winter turned to spring, it became clear that such a small number was nowhere near enough. By April 1674, Wu and his allies claimed to have regained a full third of Chinese territory in the name of the lost Ming dynasty (or the new Zhou dynasty, depending on who you asked). The southern and western provinces of Yunnan, Guizhou, Hunan, Sichuan and Guangxi were in Chinese hands. On 21 April 1674, the ruler of Fujian officially joined the revolt. Geng Jing-zhong, son and heir of the man who had warred with Coxinga for two decades, now proclaimed that the Manchus were his enemies. Since the enemy of his enemy could now become his friend, he sent an ambassador to Taiwan with an offer for the Zheng clan.

Geng offered Jing two prefectures in Fujian, and the official return of Amoy and Quemoy, if the Zheng clan agreed to mount naval operations in south China. Envoys from both sides also hastily agreed to an ultimate goal: a joint attack on Nanjing itself, and the chance to avenge Coxinga's defeat a generation earlier.

However, relations soon soured between the two unlikely allies. Reporting to Geng after their visit to Taiwan, the Chinese envoys said that the Zheng clan was not all it claimed to be. Contrary to Jing's assertions, Geng's ambassador reported that Taiwan had little more than 100 ships and maybe 10,000 men. Though it is likely that Jing may have talked up his forces somewhat, the ambassador's report was highly suspect. The Zheng forces were, of course, scattered in military farms all along the coast, and the fleet would not be assembled in one place purely for the ambassador's entertainment.[19]

Jing, meanwhile, began to have doubts of his own, supposedly about the true allegiances of the rebels. He announced that the Zhengs fought for the Ming dynasty, not some new empire that Wu Sangui had concocted. Whether this was bluster or genuine patriotism it is difficult to tell – Jing had done little for the Ming cause for a decade, though it remains possible that he had merely been lying low while he built up his father's forces once more. When he heard that Geng had officially reneged on his promise to give parts of Fujian to the Zheng clan, he decided to take them for himself. The Zheng fleet, long absent from coastal waters, reappeared off Amoy and captured several Chinese towns. The Zhengs were well armed with foreign guns, supplied to them by the English traders in Taiwan, who did a brisk business in powder, shot, artillery and mortars.

Although Wu Sangui sent mediators to try and resolve the dispute, Geng and Jing seemed unable to get along. Zheng forces successfully conquered a large part of Fujian, and two prefectures in Canton. In 1676, as the resurgence of the Zheng clan reached its height, the damage caused by the rivalry between the rebels took its toll. Geng surrendered to the Manchus who had attacked him from the north, while at the coast his sometime ally Jing waited with military forces numbering 200,000 – hardly the pitiful number that

Geng's ambassadors had claimed. The greatest loss in the rebellion was not one of men or materials, but of opportunity, since Jing demonstrated that he had ample forces to make an assault on Nanjing. If only Geng had been prepared to cooperate with him, things could have been very different.

The defeat of Geng allowed the Manchus in the east to concentrate their attacks on Jing. The Manchus began to force the Zheng clan back, not merely on land, but on sea, where a Manchu fleet surprisingly won several victories.

Meanwhile, Jing's unlikely ally Wu Sangui finally made his true intentions clear. Suffering similar setbacks in the hinterland, he proclaimed himself the ruler of a new dynasty in 1678. Henceforth, Wu Sangui desired to be known as *Zhaowu*, the Emperor of Shining War. Five-and-a-half months later, Wu Sangui was finally dead, defeated not by the Manchus, but by dysentery. His son had been killed in Beijing by his Manchu captors, but Wu's grandson tried to keep the dynasty going, using the optimistic name *Honghua* – Emperor of Increasing. But his powers dwindled, and he committed suicide to evade capture in 1681. Wu's concubine Chen Yuanyuan, for whom he had infamously sacrificed his country, survived her lover and became a Buddhist nun.

In Beijing, the Emperor of Hearty Prosperity decided that the time had come to deal with Taiwan once and for all. He summoned a likely candidate to Beijing, holding an audience with Coxinga's former naval commander Shi Lang, now an old man in his sixties. The Emperor of Hearty Prosperity commissioned him to build and train a fleet of warships with one express aim: the conquest of Taiwan.

On Taiwan, Jing had given up. He had pulled his forces back from the mainland, and occupied himself with concubines and wine. Taiwan continued to be ruled by the regent who had administered it during Jing's long absence on the mainland: his eldest son Kecang.

Family resemblances in the Zheng clan seemed to skip a generation. If Jing's licentious behaviour was the image of his grandfather Nicholas Iquan, the intense, serious Kecang was Coxinga reborn.[20] Jing had doted on the boy in his younger days, and had every confidence in leaving him in charge of Taiwan while he was away. Other members of the Zheng clan were not so appreciative of Kecang, particularly once Jing's health took a turn for the worst. Coxinga's widow Cuiying despised her eldest grandson for the low birth of his mother, his illegitimate origins, and perhaps his very resemblance to her pious late husband.

On 17 March 1681, Jing called his leading generals Feng Xifan and Liu Guoxuan to his chambers. The king of Taiwan was dying, aged just thirty-nine like his father Coxinga before him. Jing was concerned about the succession, particularly since the recent death of Kecang's powerful father-in-law. He demanded that the generals swear allegiance to him, and promise to faithfully serve Kecang as the new ruler of Taiwan. Earnestly, the generals assured their leader that they would do so.

Before Jing's body was even cold, Feng Xifan was planning a coup. He won over the support of four of Coxinga's other surviving sons, and the plotters then went to see Cuiying herself. Cuiying agreed to support their claims that Kecang was not the son of Jing at all, but the clandestine offspring of an unknown father, who had somehow been passed off as Jing's own.[21]

On 19 March, Kecang was summoned to his grandmother's quarters, where he was surprised to see his four uncles waiting for him. There, Kecang was 'by the black slaves barbarously strangled', and a more suitable heir found to replace him.[22] Jing's next eldest son was an eleven-year-old boy called Keshuang, and it was agreed that he would be ideal. Since he was so young and inexperienced, it was deemed necessary to find a regent to rule in his stead, and a handy candidate presented himself in the form of the child's eldest uncle, Zheng Cong. Cong became the nominal ruler of Taiwan, although the true power rested in the hands of his mother Cuiying, and in Keshuang's father-in-law, who happened to be Feng Xifan.

Several further deaths, coincidental or otherwise, helped Feng Xifan secure his hold on power. Regent Zheng Cong was dead by the end of the month, and the widow Cuiying supposedly died of natural causes that August.[23] With Keshuang still a minor, Feng Xifan was the ruler of Taiwan in all but name, but the supposed reign of the young Keshuang went from bad to worse. His father-in-law regent ordered several executions in the palace after discovering a plot to unseat him in December 1681.[24] Aborigines in the north revolted against Zheng family conscription policies in 1682, forcing Feng to cancel the unpopular scheme. Early in 1683, Taiwan was struck by a famine.

All the while, Shi Lang was assembling his fleet on the other side of the strait. He battled with local politics, and insisted on full control of all military operations. The arrogance that had brought him into conflict with Coxinga in the past also caused friction with Fujianese officials, but eventually he got what he wanted: the imperial stamp of approval. In the Emperor's name, Shi Lang assumed control of the entire operation, and by the summer of 1683, he had a fighting force of 20,000 men, and a fleet of 300 warships.

Like both Coxinga and the Dutch before him, Shi Lang's first stop was the Pescadores. There, the Zheng were waiting for him, with heavy fortifications, gun emplacements and 20,000 troops of their own. A Zheng squadron chased Shi Lang's reconnaissance ships out of nearby waters, and when the admiral returned with the main body of his fleet, he faced fierce resistance. Placing too much faith in his superior numbers, Shi Lang led his ships straight towards the main line of Zheng defenders, into a chaotic free-for-all. Shi Lang's inexperienced sailors proved to be reluctant warriors, and many shied away from combat. The Zheng clansmen fought to the death and took many of the attackers with them. Twenty-two Zheng vessels turned out to be suicide ships loaded with gunpowder, exploding for maximum effect when surrounded by unsuspecting Manchu vessels.

Shi Lang himself was injured in the battle, losing his right eye to shrapnel. He returned six days later for a rematch, following the advice of a former Zheng clansmen to use his superior numbers more effectively. Several Manchu ships clustered around single Zheng vessels, cutting off all means of escape and fighting until the crews surrendered. Few actually did – Shi Lang's account of the battle lists barely 5,000 prisoners. It also reports a bizarre incident in which his newly blind eye supposedly 'saw' a woman standing by his side for an instant, her robes soaked from the waist down. When he looked, she was gone.

With the Zheng forces defeated, Shi Lang came ashore at the Pescadores to offer thanks in a local temple. Upon seeing the statue of Matsu, goddess of the sea, he announced to his men that he had already met her, and that the Manchu fleet had a new and unexpected ally. As a later imperial memorial put it: 'the seas make manifest Her divine justice'.[25] The goddess of the sea had abandoned the Zheng clan.

On shore in Taiwan, the last of the Zheng argued over their next course of action. Some wanted to take to the ships and run for the Philippines, hoping to seize a new base there. But it was a last-ditch measure that nobody took seriously – such an expedition required long-term planning, not a sudden dash into battle. Besides, with the Pescadores now under enemy control, Shi Lang's fleet could easily blockade Taiwan and prevent any Zheng ships from escaping.

Emissaries of the boy-king Keshuang arrived at the Pescadores to speak with Shi Lang. With them, they bore a letter of unconditional surrender. Shi Lang deliberated for a few weeks, keen to establish that Keshuang was not surrendering alone in the style of Nicholas Iquan, but on behalf of his regents, his soldiers and his people. Shi Lang made it brutally clear that this was no time for half-measures. Taiwan would not be recognised as an independent state, and the Zheng were unlikely to be permitted to remain in close proximity to the sea. All subjects were to swear allegiance to the Emperor of Hearty Prosperity, to disavow the departed Ming dynasty, and to shave their heads in the prescribed Manchu manner.

Not all the Zheng clan were ready to agree. In his house on the outskirts of the town, the Ming Prince of Peace committed suicide, preceded by his five concubines. Seventeen other minor Ming nobles kept their lives, but lost their hair. When it was established that the Zheng were indeed ready to capitulate, Shi Lang made the final trip to Tai Bay in early September 1683.[26]

He came ashore to meet young Keshuang and his regent, who had shaved the front of their heads and adopted the hated Manchu queue. Then, Shi Lang went to the house where the Prince of Peace had died, there to offer thanks to his new found patron. The former mansion is now a temple to the goddess of the sea.[27] Keshuang was taken to Beijing for an audience with the Emperor of Hearty Prosperity himself. There, the last of the Zheng clan, abandoned by his patron goddess, said:

When kneeling at the feet of Your Majesty, I look upon China's greatness which has existed in unbroken brilliance for ages, I cannot do otherwise than acknowledge it is the will of Heaven which has vested you with the supreme power.[28]

The Zheng were defeated, and the dream of restoring the Ming was officially over. For bringing an end to the resistance by surrendering, Keshuang was named as the Duke Who Quells the Seas. He became a minor noble in the Manchu aristocracy, and remained in north China, where he was classified as a member of the Bordered Yellow Banner. Shi Lang, the man who defeated him, received even greater honours, and some years after his own death, was officially deemed a name worthy of worship in the Temple of Eminent Statesmen.[29]

On Shi Lang's recommendation, Taiwan was incorporated into the Celestial Empire, to prevent any other foreign powers from using it as a base in the Dutch manner. The surviving soldiers of the Zheng clan, still numbering some 40,000, were relocated far from the sea to prevent any changes of heart. Many found themselves serving on the northern borders in China's later conflicts with Russia and some of the peoples of the steppes. Some, however, escaped back to the sea, and their distant descendants would return to plague the south China coasts more than a century later.[30] The last vestiges of the Ming were preserved in the south by Chinese loyalist Duong Ngan Dich, who escaped with a small refugee fleet several months ahead of Shi Lang's assault, and eventually settled in south-east Asia, in the Mekong delta region.[31]

There, the story of the Zheng clan should end, except that Chinese biographies often extend into the afterlife. Coxinga, the Zhengs' most famous son, was no exception.

The desecrated graves of the Zheng clan were restored in 1700, as the first of several steps in which the Manchu conquerors paid their respect to the enemy who had caused them so much trouble. Coxinga remained a hero to the Chinese, and even to the Manchus, who could not help but admire his dogged refusal to betray his beloved Dynasty of Brightness. The Manchu state, founded to a large extent on the willingness of Chinese defectors to switch sides, eventually recognised Coxinga as a Paragon of Loyalty in 1787. He was held up to successive generations as a hero to be emulated.

Coxinga's crowning glory came in 1875, over two centuries after his death, in a China threatened by foreign powers. In recognition of the first Chinese warrior to inflict a resounding defeat upon barbarians from beyond the sea, Coxinga was elevated to divine status with the dedication of a temple to him. In fact, statues and pictures of Coxinga had long been found on altars all around Taiwan, where local people were found to be seeking his aid from beyond the grave. To the Chinese on Taiwan, he was the 'loyal and pure' Prince of Yanping, or the Sage King Who Opened Our Mountains.

In 1898, when Taiwan was handed over to the Japanese as a spoil of war, the new Japanese governor immediately paid his respects to Coxinga, the 'Japanese' conqueror who had originally wrested the island from foreign invaders. Coxinga was honoured by the island's new masters with incorporation into the pantheon of Japan's native Shinto religion, thereby achieving the rare distinction of becoming a god twice.[32]

Coxinga's sometime ally, the partisan Zhang Huang-yan once wrote that 'for a thousand autumns, men will tell of this'. Barely a third of that number has passed since Coxinga's death, and yet the hero remains a popular subject in plays, novels and films.[33]

In the twentieth century, his memory became a rallying point for Republican Chinese determined to oust foreign aggressors. Coxinga was regarded as a saintly predecessor by Chiang Kai-shek's government-in-exile on Taiwan, but also became a hero for the Communists – he was both the man who banished the Western imperialists, and also the conqueror who helped make Taiwan part of China. None can agree if he was a pirate or a king, a loyalist or a madman. But in parts of Taiwan, people still pray to him for rain.

APPENDIX I

NOTES ON NAMES

A perennial problem with popular accounts of Chinese history lies in the confusion of the characters' names. Chinese has a very low count of syllables, differentiated by a tonal system that is difficult to convey with English notation, and of little use to the lay reader. Matters are further confused by the Chinese habit of using public and private names, many of the seafarers' habits of using *noms de guerre*, and inconsistency of romanisations employed by European writers. In many cases I have simply chosen one readily recognisable appellation for each character, and stuck with it throughout the book, even where occasionally anachronistic – Coxinga, for example, did not receive that name until he reached his twenties. Some characters are identified by the name they used with foreigners, others by their surname, and still more by their first-name. With Iquan's animal menagerie of brothers, I have added an English semi-translation for ease of recognition. This works in a populist account, but falls down if a reader attempts to do further research, and swiftly discovers that other sources have different names for the same historical figures. This appendix lists the variant names of the principal figures appearing in this book.

Some might complain that I use the Pinyin romanisation system for Chinese names, since it was only invented in the 1950s, but there seemed to be little point in clinging to the confusing Wade-Giles system, which precedes it by less than a century. Pinyin is free of the scatty apostrophes of Wade-Giles, and presents a more realistic sense of the sound of Chinese words on the page – the Wade-Giles *Peking* is still supposed to be pronounced 'Beijing', and I see no reason why I should not use the more sensible spelling in Pinyin, which is of course, Beijing.

Another problem is the modern-day split that separates the last redoubt of the Republic of China (i.e. Taiwan) from the *People's* Republic of China. Many sources on the history of Taiwan cling to the Wade-Giles romanisation system, as it would be politically inappropriate to adopt the Pinyin system invented by their Communist rivals. An English researcher is thus presented with the daunting proposition of just having to *know*, for example, that the *Fujian*, *Fukien* and *Hokkien* of different authors' accounts refer to the same place. In many cases, it is less trouble simply to learn Chinese.

Aberhai – Also Abahai. Without any proof of his actual Manchu name, modern Manchu scholars often prefer to call him Hung Taiji, which was how he was known in China. This seems to be a corruption of *qung-tayiji* (also *khungtaiji* and *kontaisha* in some sources), a Manchurian title for a war-leader.

Augustin – His true name was Li Da-she; he adopted Augustin as his Christian name upon baptism. As the Captain's eldest son, he was often referred to as 'Iquan' (see Nicholas Iquan, below, for further details), leading to many occasions in which foreign sources confused him with his bitterest rival.

Bao the Panther – Zheng Zhibao (Cheng Chi-pao). Also Zheng Mang'er.

Borjigid – Strictly speaking, Borjigid-shi, or 'Miss Borjigid', since Borjigid was her clan-name, not her given name. She was later known as Xiaozhuang Wen once her family became the rulers of China.

Captain China – His Chinese name was Li Dan (Li Tan). The Dutch and English in Hirado also referred to him as Andrea(s) Dittis – presumably a 'Christian name' adopted as easier for foreign barbarians to remember.

Coxinga – His mother called him Fukumatsu, combining the characters for the *Fu* of Fujian, with *Matsu*, which means pine tree, and is also the *Matsu* of Matsuura, the ruling family of the Hirado area. His father called him Sen, meaning Forest, and he gained the public name Da Mu (Ta Mu), or Big Tree. As an adult, he received the name Zheng Chenggong (Cheng Ch'eng-Kung; Japanese: Tei Seikö). The Emperor also bestowed upon him the right to use the Ming imperial surname of Zhu (Chu), leading to the appellation Guo Xing Ye (Kuo Hsing Ye), Imperial Namekeeper or Knight of the National Name. In the local Amoy dialect, this was corrupted to Kok Seng Ya, and was picked up by the Dutch, Portuguese and English variously as Koxinga, Cocksinja and Coxinga, or Kokusenya in Japanese. The name was Latinised in Jesuit documents as Quaesingus. Other variants include Cogseng, Con-seng, Kuesim, Quoesing, Coxiny, Quesim, Quesin and Cocxima. He was also referred to as Maroto (presumably 'The Marauder'), and Pompoan or Pun Poin, both likely European corruptions of *Benfan* ('Our Leader'), by which Coxinga is known in his secretary's accounts. He also received a number of honours from the Southern Ming, which had little more than words to reward its subjects: Count of Loyalty and Filial Piety (1646), Marquess of Weiyuan (1646), Duke of Zhangguo (1647), Prince of Yanping (1653), Prince of Chao (1655). 'Prince' translates the spirit rather than the letter of the Chinese *Wang*, which literally means king. The Manchu invaders briefly made him Duke of Haicheng *in absentia*, but Coxinga scorned this attempt to buy him off with a title.

Coyett, Frederik – His name is given as Prince Kuiyi in Chinese sources.

Cuiying (Ts'ui-ying) – Her full name was Deng Guotai (Tung Kuo-t'ai); Cuiying was the personal name she used with family members. Letters of the English East India Company, written during the period of Jing's rule in Taiwan, refer to her as the Queen Mother.

Feng the Phoenix – Zheng Zhifeng (Cheng Chi-feng), also sometimes referred to simply as 'Third Uncle'.

Fujian (Fukien) – In the local dialect, it is pronounced Hokkien, by which name the dialect itself is known outside China.

Geng Zhimao (Keng Chi-mao) – Referred to in Dutch sources as Simlagong or Simtagong.

Hongguang Emperor (The Hung-Kuang Emperor) – His given name was Zhu Yousong (Chu Yu-sung), also known as the Prince of Dechang (Te-chang), and the Prince of Fu after his father's death at the hands of Li Zicheng.

Hu the Tiger – Zheng Zhihu, called Sisia in Dutch sources.

Iquan – His name was Zheng Zhilong (Cheng Chih-lung, Japanese: Tei Shiryû). Nicholas was widely understood to be the name he assumed on his baptism in Macao, and thought to be the name of a wealthy European patron. Iquan was a Portuguese corruption of Yi-Guan, meaning 'First Son'. Contemporary European accounts call him Nicholas Iquan, Nicolas Icoan, or sometimes Gaspard or Jaspar. He was created the Earl of Nan'an by the Emperor of Grand Radiance (1645). Strictly speaking, using the translation policy followed for his brothers in this book, we might also call him Long the Dragon.

Jing – As a fair indication of the family's high hopes for the next generation, his childhood name was Jin-She – 'Bright Prospect for the House'; his given name Zheng Shifan – 'Model for the World'. In much the same way as the family name Caesar became confused with the term for the Roman emperor, some sources mistakenly referred to Jing as Coxinga, and also Pompoan (see Coxinga, above). He is also referred to as Kimpsia or Sepoan in Dutch accounts.

Kangxi Emperor (the K'ang-hsi Emperor) – His birth name was Xuanye (Hsuan-ye).

Kecang (K'o-tsang) – Referred to in letters of the English East India Company as Camcock.

Lady Ren (Lady Jen).

Li Kuiqi (Lee Kuei-chi) – Called Quitsick in Dutch sources.

Li Shuaitai (Li Shuai-t'ai) – Referred to as Taising Lipovi in Dutch sources.

Appendix I

Longwu Emperor (the Lung-wu Emperor) – His given name was Zhu Yujian (Chu Yü-chien), also known as the Prince of Tang (T'ang).

Matsu, goddess of the sea – A-Ma-Gong, more properly Mazu.

Maxin (Ma-Hsin) – Coyett's *Neglected Formosa* mentions that Coxinga's 'chief officer was Bepontok, a deserted Tartar'. This has confused later historians, since Coxinga is not known to have had any Manchus in his forces. There are some stories, however, that claim Maxin was a Chinese originally loyal to the Manchus, who defected to Coxinga in the 1650s after the ill-treatment of his wife at the hands of a Manchu official. As the joint leader with Zhou Quanbin of Coxinga's ground-attack forces in Taiwan, Maxin seems to be the likely candidate for the mysterious Bepontok.

Nurgaci – Also known as Nurhachi. Later Chinese documents refer to him as *Qing Taizu* (the Qing Ancestor) or by his posthumous name *Wu Huangdi* (Warring Emperor).

Pincqua – This name is used in Dutch sources. Chinese sources call him He Ting-bin, or He Bin (Ho Pin).

Suetsugu Heizo – He appears in Dutch accounts as Fesodonno or Phosodonne.

Sakkam – Also Saccam and Sakam, and thought to be a local dialect form of *Zhikan* (Chi-k'an) or 'Red Cliffs'.

Shi Lang (Shih Lang) – Also called Sego in letters of the English East India Company.

Taiwan – Called *Ilha Formosa*, the Beauteous Isle, by the Portuguese and the Dutch when they first arrived, it was also known as Dai Liuqiu ('Great Ryukyu Island'), as distinguished from the Lesser Ryukyu Islands that extend up to Japan. Confusingly, some Chinese maps also referred to it as *Little* Ryukyu Kingdom (Xiao Liuqiu Guo). These latter appellations have fallen out of favour, as they imply a Japanese right to the island. During the period of Zheng

Jing's rule, even Manchu documents referred to it by his chosen rebranding of Dongning, or 'Eastern Peace'.

Immigrants in the fifteenth century may have referred to their swampy, malarial isle of exile as Maiyuan – the 'Place of Unjust Burial', which was pronounced Daiwan in the Fujian dialect. Strictly speaking, the original 'Tayouan' was the name of the small sandbank where the Dutch built their base. After the construction of Fort Zeelandia, both Chinese and Dutch sailors began to refer to the island by the name of its best known port – Dawan (the Big Bay), Tywan or Taiwan (the Curved/Terraced Bay). After the Manchu conquest, the entire island was referred to as Taiwan thereafter. One, or some, or all of these explanations contribute to the name we give the island today.

Theyma – She is listed only as Lady Huang (her surname) in Chinese sources. Theyma appears in Dutch documents, and is likely to be a corruption of *Zheng Ma*, or Mother Zheng.

Xinsu – His full name was Xu Xinsu (Hsu Hsinsu), so strictly speaking, he should be referred to as Xu in a historical narrative that uses people's surnames. I kept with Xinsu, to avoid confusion between Xu (Xinsu) and Hu (Iquan's brother). Dutch accounts of the period called him Simsou.

Yizuo – His full name was Zhu Yizuo (Chu I-tso), but I have used his given name rather than his surname to avoid confusion in the text.

Yongli Emperor (the Yung-le Emperor) – His given name was Zhu Youlang (Chu Yu-lang), also known as the Prince of Yong-Ming.

Zeelandia – Fort Zeelandia was originally called Fort Orange, but was renamed in 1634.

Zheng Tai – He is also referred to as Zheng Gongchuan in Yang's *Veritable Record* (p. 151).

Zhou Quanbin (Chou Chüan-pin).

APPENDIX II

OFFICES AND APPOINTMENTS

Emperors of China

1567 Ming no. 14 Wanli, Emperor of Ten Thousand Experiences
1620 Ming no. 15 Taichang, Emperor of Tranquil Prosperity
1621 Ming no. 16 Tianqi, Emperor of Heavenly Enlightenment
1628 Ming no. 17 Chongzhen, Emperor of Lofty Omens
1644 Qing (Manchu) no. 1 Shunzhi, Emperor of Unbroken Rule
1661 Qing no. 2 Kangxi, Emperor of Hearty Prosperity (d. 1722)

The 'Southern Ming' Claimants

1644 Ming no. 18 Hongguang, Emperor of Grand Radiance
1646 Ming no. 19 Longwu, Emperor of Intense Warring
1647 Ming no. 20 Shaowu, Emperor of Bringing Belligerence
1647 Ming no. 21 Yongli, Emperor of Eternal Experiences (d. 1662)

The Zhou Pretenders

1678 Zhou no. 1 Zhaowu, Emperor of Shining War
1679 Zhou no. 2 Honghua, Emperor of Increasing

Governors-General of the Dutch East India Company (in Batavia from 1622)

1619 Laurens Reael
1619 Jan Pieterszoon Coen
1623 Pieter de Carpentier
1627 Jan Pieterszoon Coen
1629 Jacques Specx
1632 Hendrick Brouwer

1636 Anthony van Diemen
1645 Cornelis van der Lijn
1650 Carel Reynierszoon
1653 Johan Maetsuyker
1678 Rijklof van Goens
1681 Cornelis Speelman
1684 Joannes Camphuys

Governors of the Dutch Colony on Formosa

(1622)Cornelis Reijersen (Expedition Leader)
1624 Martinus Sonk
1625 Gerrit de Witt
1627 Pieter Nuijts
1629 Hans Putmans
1636 Johan van der Burg
1641 Paulus Traudenius
1643 Maximilian le Maire
1644 Francois Caron
1646 Pieter Antoniszoon Over't Water
1650 Nicolas Verburg
1653 Cornelis Caesar
1656 Frederik Coyett

Emperors of Japan

1611 Go-Mi-no-O Emperor
1629 Meisho Empress
1633 Go-Komyo Emperor
1656 Go-Sai Emperor
1663 Reigen Emperor
1687 Higashiyama Emperor

Shogun of Japan

1603 Ieyasu (d. 1616)
1605 Hidetada (d. 1632)
1623 Iemitsu (d. 1651)
1651 Ietsuna
1680 Tsunayoshi

APPENDIX III

THE RISE OF THE MANCHUS

The Chinese governor of the Liaodong strip in the later sixteenth century was Li Chengliang, thought to be a sinified Korean.[1] Manchu folklore claims that Li accepted the post of Liaodong governor, along with a secret mission to hunt down and kill the last prince of the Manchu tribes. He adopted a local orphan boy called Nurgaci and raised him as his own son. Supposedly, the boy noticed two birthmarks on Li's feet when the two were bathing, and asked him what they were. Li answered that such blemishes marked their owner out as a ruler in the making, at which the boy raised his own feet and proudly showed his stepfather that he had not two, but seven.

Li realised that the future Manchu leader was actually living under his roof, and plotted to murder the boy, but Nurgaci was warned by his stepmother, and fled Li's house in the company of a dog and a black horse. The wrathful Li Chengliang killed his wife for her insubordination, and burned down the forest where he thought Nurgaci was hiding. The boy's dog died in the flames, but Nurgaci fled on horseback, concealed from the eyes of searching soldiers by a swirling flock of magpies. The horse bore him to safety before it perished from exhaustion, and the boy swore revenge – honouring his stepmother in the afterlife, and repaying his animal allies. The magpie he adopted as his guardian spirit, the dog was for ever excluded from Manchu sacrifices, and the Chinese word for the clear black coat of the horse lent its name to the name of the dynasty that would eventually conquer China – Qing.[2] Or so the story went.

The historical reality is hardly less incredible. Li Chengliang was never Nurgaci's stepfather, but instead an occasional trading partner with the Manchus. Demonstrating a bipolar and occasionally hostile attitude strangely familiar to that which the Dutch would adopt a generation later in south-east China, Li Chengliang alternately traded peacefully with the Manchus, before warring against them in a series of disputes over territory and jurisdiction. Nurgaci reached manhood during a period of peaceful commerce with Li Chengliang, when the Manchus gained considerable riches, particularly over their supplies of the magical root *ginseng*, which was literally worth its weight in silver.

Records are vague as to how the break between the Manchus and Chinese came about. It is known that Nurgaci's father and grandfathers perished in a battle at the remote stronghold of Mount Gure, but it is less clear on which side they fought. Later Manchu records would claim that the feckless Chinese attacked Nurgaci's grandfather Atai, and that the other relatives perished when they rushed to his aid with reinforcements. However, it is also possible that Atai had fallen out of favour with the other Manchus, and that Nurgaci's other grandfather, Giocangga, had formed an alliance with Li Chengliang in order to do away with him. Whatever the truth, something went wrong at Mount Gure, and both grandfathers perished in the fighting, along with Nurgaci's father Taksi.

Now the leader of the tribe, the 23-year-old Nurgaci demanded that his former ally somehow make amends for the disaster, but the Chinese governor refused to either pay reparations or return Taksi's body to his people. Nurgaci reputedly left the matter unresolved, but began a series of campaigns in the interior against other tribes, uniting many of the tough warriors of Manchuria in a new confederacy. In the early years of the seventeenth century, it was the Manchus who began to encroach on the land of the Chinese, crossing the 'uncrossable' borders they had earlier agreed by treaty with Li Chengliang, and seizing a number of Chinese towns. In 1616, on the first day of the Chinese New Year, Nurgaci proclaimed himself to be more than a mere lord among other tribal leaders. He proclaimed himself to be a *khan*, the ruler of the area and the supreme commander of the other clan leaders. At an elaborate ceremony at his capital, he received pledges of fealty from ambassadors from other tribes, from Mongolia, from Tibet and from Korea. It was a direct challenge to the Ming dynasty that ruled China, and a sign that Nurgaci regarded himself as a rival to the ruler of the Celestial Empire itself. He was encouraged in this by many of his new recruits – Chinese turncoats who had tired of the corruption of the Ming regime, and astrologers who pointed at the terrifying conjunctions and aspects that awaited the Ming dynasty over the next few years. As part of the climactic changes that were bringing harsh droughts and cold winters, the period also saw magnificent and striking outbursts of the *aurora borealis* – Nurgaci believed that the lights in the sky were messages to him.[3]

For some years, as he consolidated his power north of the Great Wall, Nurgaci dealt with a peculiar state of affairs. The Manchu political system was forced to deal with a situation wherein the ruling class was greatly outnumbered by its Chinese vassals. The people of the Liaodong peninsula were included in the Manchu government itself, and turncoat generals and officials were co-opted into the Manchu state, by marriage and appointment. Nurgaci sat at the head of a nation that was, in the eyes of the Chinese, little more than a barbarian upstart, but was already setting up a system of conquest and inclusion that his descendants would put into effect on China itself. He also established the military system that would eventually conquer the Celestial Empire, dividing his people into legions or 'Banners', each led by a Prince. The initial Yellow, White, Blue and Red Banners, were later augmented with Bordered Yellow, Bordered White, Bordered Blue and Bordered Red Banners. Initially, foreign allies fought under their own Black Banner. Later, Nurgaci incorporated them into the main legions. The headmen of conquered villages were appointed as captains in specific Banners, thereby involving both them, their menfolk and the rest of their village directly in further conquests. By the time the Manchus invaded China, the 'Eight Banners' actually comprised twenty-four separate armies, the original eight now augmented by further legions of Mongols and Chinese. The Banner system, which cunningly swept aside former clan allegiances in favour of loyalty to a military unit, itself part of a greater whole, became so important to Manchu identity that it even entered the Chinese language – the descendants of Manchus can still be heard referring to themselves as *qiren*, Banner People.

The growth of Nurgaci's power throws some light on the situation in distant Fujian. In 1626, as Chinese officials prepared to buy off criminals like Nicholas Iquan, their counterparts in the north of the Empire faced a terrifying sight. The Manchus were marching ever closer to the Great Wall, and one of the last cities in their way was the strongly fortified town of Ningyuan. Nurgaci suffered one of the only setbacks of his campaign when he failed to take the town, but it was also to be his last battle. Wounded in the fighting, he died of medical complications that September.

The military official in charge of Ningyuan proudly reported to Beijing that he had halted the Manchu expansion – a claim that would return to haunt him a mere two months later, when Nurgaci's son Aberhai led a second assault. Aberhai was also beaten away, but not for long.

The continued military advance of the Manchus hid a power struggle behind the scenes, as the sons of Nurgaci debated the succession. Nurgaci had three wives and many concubines, creating rivalry among their male children. At his death, the government was in the hands of four senior princes. Daisan was the son of his first wife, Manggultai the son of his second, Amin was his nephew, and Aberhai was the son of a concubine. Some believed that Nurgaci intended the monthly rotation of ruler to continue after his death, while others argued that Nurgaci had merely set up that system in order to observe how each brother handled the task. As Nurgaci lay dying, he ordered that the junior princes Ajige, Dorgon, and Dodo, his three sons by his third wife, should each receive command of an entire Manchu legion. Although they were among his youngest children, command of such forces would give them considerable power among the other princes, and the fact they shared a single mother could unite them even more. According to a report from a Korean observer,[4] it was Nurgaci's wish that Dorgon would eventually become the leader, with Daisan as regent until the teenager reached manhood.

Daisan was having none of it. A stern man in his fifties, he ensured that only two legions were handed over to the three brothers. The eldest, Ajige, had to make do with a few companies borrowed from the other two. Daisan also convinced his relatives that the best choice as overall ruler would be Aberhai, the youngest of the senior princes, and hence the easiest to control.

Aberhai, however, was fiercely ambitious, such that the belligerent Nurgaci himself had rebuked him on several occasions for his attitude. Before long, he had managed to talk the other senior princes out of sharing the throne dais with him – all the better, he claimed, to emulate the Chinese system they were preparing to conquer. In 1630, cousin Amin was accused of cowardice after retreating ahead of a Ming counter-offensive. He died in prison, and his Bordered Blue legion was handed over to a supporter of Aberhai.

Aberhai's next victim was Manggultai, a prince whose bloodline had been gradually falling from favour. He had been obliged to kill his own mother in 1620, when she was accused of hoarding jewellery and flirting with Daisan.[5] In 1631, Manggultai drew his sword in a quarrel with Aberhai during an argument at the siege of a Chinese town.[6] Though he was restrained by other relatives, he was later censured by a council of the princes, and suffered a loss in rank. Manggultai and his brother were dead by 1635, but the campaign against them continued long after. In 1636, it was discovered that Manggultai had been preparing seals proclaiming himself as Emperor. It was the excuse that Aberhai needed to execute Manggultai's children, and expunge him from the family records.[7]

Within months of the removal of his last serious rival, Aberhai proclaimed himself the imperial ruler of the Manchus. He left the Ming Chinese alone for a while, creating a period of relative peace for a couple of years – notably, the lessening of Manchu pressure on the north led to prosperity elsewhere, and this was the period when Coxinga was brought from Japan to Anhai. Instead, Aberhai sent armies against the Chakhar Mongols, the last descendants of Khublai Khan, who had once ruled all China. After a prolonged campaign, Aberhai's generals obtained the surrender of the Chakhar, and also possession of the great seal of the Mongol khan. As its owner, he could now claim to be the successor of Genghis Khan, and his power on the steppes of Asia increased. It was just one of several incidents which showed the Manchus were practising for the conquest of China itself. The period also saw Aberhai adopt a number of policies, laws and practices of Ming China – the barbarians north of the Great Wall were now aping and shadowing the Ming system, rehearsing for a time when they would seize it for themselves.

However, although he proclaimed himself the Emperor of the forthcoming Qing dynasty, and prepared to attack China himself, Aberhai would never see Beijing. The aging warrior, now in his sixties, died in 1643, even as his armies amassed for the march on China.

The Manchus needed to select a new ruler from among his brothers or sons. There were a large number of candidates, though the chief prospects seemed to be Aberhai's eldest son Haoge, and Aberhai's younger brother Dorgon.

Fully understanding the crippling responsibilities of the emperorship, Haoge turned down the offer. It is possible that he also refused to involve himself in family power politics. Although Haoge was an obvious choice as Aberhai's heir, he was the master of only a single legion. Dorgon, Dodo and Ajige were still close as brothers, and were no longer the children they had been at the death of Nurgaci.

Dorgon, however, also refused to accept the emperorship, claiming it would be disrespectful to the man who had all but raised him since the death of his father. In the years since Aberhai's succession, Dorgon and his brothers had been loyal servants of the usurper. From the age of fourteen, Dorgon had led his legion in almost every military campaign the Manchus undertook for a decade. At sixteen, he had earned the sobriquet 'wise warrior' during the campaign against the Chakhar Mongols, and was the leader of one of two Manchu armies that made a brief incursion into China itself in 1638. Aberhai may have hoped that his half-brother would meet with an untimely end on one of a hundred battlefields, but Dorgon returned from every campaign. By the time of Aberhai's death, the 31-year-old Dorgon was one of the greatest and most respected generals among the Manchus, and a prince of the first rank. He was the perfect choice as a figure to unite the Manchus ready for their attack on China. But Dorgon was not called the 'wise warrior' for nothing – he instead suggested another candidate. Dorgon recommended Aberhai's youngest son Fulin who was barely five years old.

Before the time of Aberhai, wives and concubines of a dead ruler had been obliged to commit ritual suicide on their master's death. Aberhai had reformed this practice, which now called merely for *principal* wives to follow their lord into the afterlife. In fact, he ensured that one of the last noblewomen to take her own life in such a way was Dorgon's mother, in a failed attempt to reduce the unity and connections between Dorgon and his two full brothers. On Aberhai's own death, two of his main spouses had killed themselves, thereby removing themselves from any debates over the succession, and possibly reducing the support for their sons. However, Aberhai's youngest wife Borjigid was not called upon to commit suicide on account of her junior status. She was a formidable woman of thirty, a descendant of the famous Genghis Khan himself, and the mother of the young Fulin. At various points in years to come, palace rumour-mongers would also suggest that the young princess was a secret lover of Dorgon – her imperial husband was an old man, but the handsome young general was only a year her senior. Some even whispered that Fulin might not be Aberhai's son at all, but Dorgon's.

The choice of Fulin pleased all parties, or at least displeased almost everyone equally. Dorgon became co-regent with his cousin Jirgalang, although there were still some members of the royal family who would have preferred Dorgon to be the absolute ruler. Discussing such thoughts *after* the accession of a new leader was tantamount to treason – when Prince Daisan discovered that his own son and grandson were plotting to put Dorgon on the throne, he reported the incident immediately, and the two minor royals were also executed.

The descendants of Nurgaci were finally back in control of their domain. A mere six months after they had crowned their child-Emperor, news reached them of trouble in China. Their long-term enemies, the Ming dynasty, whom the Manchus had always intended to overthrow, had just been overthrown by someone else. The Manchu nobles listened in disbelief as messengers described the madness of the Emperor of Lofty Omens, his assault on his own family members, and his suicide. Now Beijing was under the control of Li Zicheng, the 'dashing general', who had proclaimed himself the ruler of a new dynasty. The time was right for the Manchus to strike.

The Zheng Family in the Seventeenth Century
(Highly simplified)

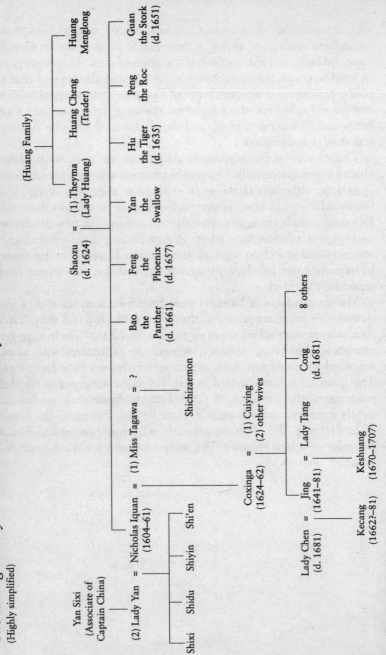

Huang Family

Shaozu (d. 1624) = (1) Theyma (Lady Huang)

Hu the Tiger (d. 1635)

Yan the Swallow

Huang Cheng (Trader)

Peng the Roc

Huang Menglong

Guan the Stork (d. 1651)

Feng the Phoenix (d. 1657)

Bao the Panther (d. 1661)

Yan Sixi (Associate of Captain China)

(2) Lady Yan = Nicholas Iquan (1604–61) = (1) Miss Tagawa = ? Shichizaemon

Shixi   Shidu   Shiyin   Shi'en

Coxinga (1624–62) = (1) Cuiying (2) other wives

Cong (d. 1681)   8 others

Lady Chen (d. 1681) = Jing (1641–81) = Lady Tang

Kecang (1662–81)   Keshuang (1670–1707)

The Ming Dynasty and Southern Ming
(Highly simplified)

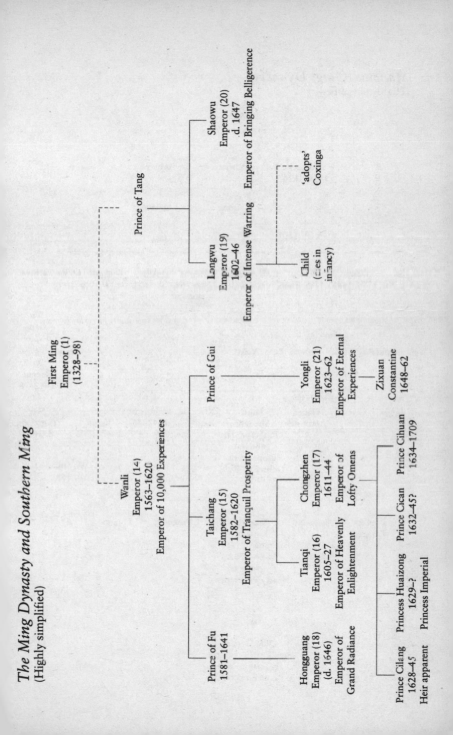

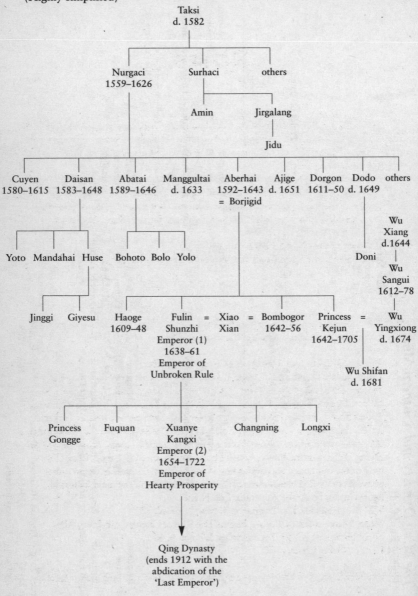

Manchu (Qing) Dynasty
(Highly simplified)

Taksi
d. 1582

Nurgaci   Surhaci   others
1559–1626

                 Amin   Jirgalang

                               Jidu

Cuyen   Daisan   Abatai   Manggultai   Aberhai   Ajige   Dorgon   Dodo   others
1580–1615 1583–1648 1589–1646   d. 1633   1592–1643   d. 1651   1611–50   d. 1649
                                                 = Borjigid

                                                                                   Wu
                                                                                   Xiang
                                                                                   d.1644
                                                                         Doni
Yoto Mandahai Huse   Bohoto Bolo Yolo   Wu
                                                                                   Sangui
                                                                                   1612–78

Jinggi   Giyesu   Haoge   Fulin   = Xiao = Bombogor   Princess   =   Wu
                    1609–48   Shunzhi   Xian   1642–56   Kejun   Yingxiong
                               Emperor (1)   1642–1705   d. 1674
                               1638–61
                               Emperor of
                               Unbroken Rule   Wu Shifan
                                                                             d. 1681

Princess   Fuquan   Xuanye   Changning   Longxi
Gongge   Kangxi
                         Emperor (2)
                         1654–1722
                         Emperor of
                         Hearty Prosperity

                         Qing Dynasty
                         (ends 1912 with the
                         abdication of the
                         'Last Emperor')

NOTES

Prologue

1. Struve, *Voices from the Ming-Qing Cataclysm*, Yale University Press, 1993, pp. 7–8.
2. Wakeman, 'The Shun Interregnum of 1644', in Wills and Spence, *From Ming to Ch'ing: Conquest Region & Continuity in Seventeenth-Century China*, Yale University Press, 1979, p. 44.
3. Parsons, *Peasant Rebellions of the Late Ming Dynasty*, p. 81; Wakeman, *The Great Enterprise*, p. 339; Backhouse and Bland, *Annals and Memoirs* (Taiwan edn), pp. 89–90. Li was by no means unique. His chief lieutenant, a Chinese Muslim, famously killed and ate a wife who had displeased him, saying: 'The former favourite is the dish of the day.'
4. Wakeman, *The Great Enterprise*, p. 266.
5. Backhouse and Bland, *Annals and Memoirs* (Taiwan edn), p. 88.

Chapter One

N.B. – Campbell's *Formosa Under the Dutch* is appreviated as *FUD* throughout the notes. Jiang's *Taiwan Waizhi* is abbreviated as *TW*.

1. *TW*, pp. 2–3; Croizier, *Koxinga and Chinese Nationalism*, p. 39.
2. Dutch accounts called her Theyma, thought to be a corruption of *Zheng Ma*, or Mother Zheng. See Blussé, 'The VOC as Sorcerer's Apprentice', p. 101.
3. In fact, Iquan is simply a Portuguese misspelling of Yi-Guan, which simply means 'Eldest Son'. Like other pirate leaders, Iquan had many names, and seemed to have a different one for each race he dealt with. Matters were further confused by the numerous ways foreign observers romanised his given name, which would be Zheng Zhilong in the Pinyin system I have used throughout, and Cheng Chih-lung in the outmoded and misleading Wade-Giles system still in use in some places. For detailed breakdowns of the names used for all the main historical figures in this book, see Appendix 1 on Names.
4. *TW*, p. 3; Foccardi, *Last Warrior*, p. 3; Iwao, 'Li Tan', 72.
5. Blussé 'Minnan-Jen or Cosmopolitan? The Rise of Cheng Chih-Lung Alias Nicholas Iquan', p. 253; Foccardi, *Last Warrior*, p. 4.
6. Keliher, *Out of China*, p. 50.
7. *TW*, p. 3.
8. Lin Renchuan, 'Fukien's Private Sea Trade in the 16th and 17th Centuries', p. 172.

279

9. Sung, *Chinese Technology in the Seventeenth Century*, p. 177.

10. *Ibid.*

11. Keliher, *Out of China*, p. 39.

12. Ye Mengzhu, quoted in Lin Renchuan, 'Fukien's Private Sea Trade in the 16th and 17th Centuries', p. 206.

13. See Lin Renchuan, p. 207.

14. Boxer, 'Rise and Fall of Nicholas Iquan', p. 411n.

15. Palafox, *History of the Conquest of China*, pp. 81–2.

16. *TW*, p. 3.

17. To be fair, the 'Japanese' pirates that supposedly threatened the Chinese were not always Japanese. Many hailed from the Ryukyus or Taiwan, others from Korea and China itself. The fact that the Chinese authorities paid a bounty on the head of every Japanese pirate caught guaranteed that the Japanese were, more often than not, blamed for the attacks of local bandits. One famous incident of a supposedly 'Japanese pirate' assault involved the sacking of a Chinese city some thirty miles inland by a squadron of heavy cavalry – hardly the seaborne raiders of popular legend.

18. In 1616, Europeans were restricted to the ports of Hirado and Nagasaki, and found it almost impossible to obtain permits to travel further inland. Starting in 1624, Japan severed all ties with the Catholic nations of Spain, Mexico and the Philippines, and their citizens were banned from entering Japan. In 1633, even ships with trading permission had to renegotiate their licences, and any Japanese living abroad were forbidden from returning on pain of death. 1636 saw the official *Sakoku* Edict, which closed the country's borders and even restricted the trading activities of the Chinese. After the expulsion of the Portuguese in 1639, Japan's foreign dealings were limited to the tiny Dutch community huddled on the ghetto island of Deshima in Nagasaki harbour for the next two centuries. See Boxer, *The Christian Century in Japan*, p. 439.

19. For some of the deeds of the Matsuura in the Korean war, see Turnbull, *Samurai Invasion*.

20. Will Adams (1564–1620) was an English sailor serving as a pilot on the Dutch vessel *Liefde*. Ship-wrecked in Japan in 1600, he was refused permission to leave the country, and instead stayed and took a Japanese wife. He became the confidant of the shogun, and was instrumental in securing the English with permission to trade in the country. He helped set up the East India Company's Japanese operation, and undoubtedly met Captain China, though he had probably died by the time Iquan arrived in Japan. Adams remains famous to this day, as the *anjin* (pilot) after whom the Tokyo district of Anjin-cho is named, and also as the historical inspiration for the character of John Blackthorne, the hero of James Clavell's novel *Shogun*.

21. Cocks, *Diary*, vol. 3, p. 34. The captain's selection came after the unexpected death of his brother Hau in Nagasaki.

22. Cocks reports the incident in his *Diary*, vol. 2, p. 414. He seems to have been genuinely fond of Elizabeth, and as she grew older, she of him.

23. E.M. Satow, *The Voyage of Captain John Saris to Japan, 1613*, p. 88, in Iwao, *Li Tan*, p. 28.

24. William Foster, *Letters Received by the East India Company from its Servants in the East*, vol. 2, p. 99.
25. Blussé, 'The VOC as Sorcerer's Apprentice: Stereotypes and Social Engineering on the South China Coast', in *Leyden Studies in Sinology*, pp. 87–105.
26. There is some debate over her first name, and no trustworthy authority has ever supplied evidence of what it was. She has been called *Weng* or *Wen* in Chinese sources, while another repeats characters that could be read in Japanese as *Fuku* or perhaps Lady *Aya*, or Lady *Fumi*. Not even Japanese authorities are prepared to decide. A romantic might suggest that a clue lies in the name she gave her first-born son, while his father Iquan was away at sea. *Fukumatsu* is a homonym for 'Fuku Waits'. See Ponsonby-Fane, 279–80, but cf. Lin, *Zheng Chenggong*, p. 14. For reasons known only to himself, Terao is convinced her name was Asa, *Tei Seikô*, p. 14.
27. Liu Xianting's *Guangyang Zazhi*, as quoted in *Fujian Wenhua* by Yang Shufang, itself quoted in Keene, *Battles of Coxinga*, p. 168.
28. There is some speculation that Yan Sixi and Captain China are one and the same, but Li Dan is described as a man in his seventies by contemporary Dutch accounts, while Yan Sixi is clearly placed at thirty-six years of age in the *TW* (p. 4), which claims Iquan began working for him while still in his teens.

Chapter Two

1. Letter from Jan Pieterzoon Coen to the Directors of the Dutch East India Company, 21 January 1622, quoted in Charles Boxer, 'The 24th of June 1622 – A Portuguese Feat of Arms', p. 46.
2. *Ibid.*
3. Campbell, *FUD*, p. 28.
4. Goddard, *Makers of Taiwan*, p. 4.
5. *Ibid.*
6. Campbell, *FUD*, p. 33.
7. *Ibid.*
8. Iwao, 'Li Tan', pp. 54–5.
9. *Ibid.*, p. 57.
10. Considering later developments, it is likely that the soldiers and sailors who liberated the Pescadores would return later as the component parts of some of the pirate organisations Iquan would fight in the 1630s.
11. Campbell, *FUD*, p. 35.
12. Letter of rural district officer Chen Tie to Nan Juyi, from the *Chao-an Xianzhi* [*Prefectural History of Chao-an*], quoted in Iwao, 'Li Tan', p. 62.
13. *Liangchao Cong Xinlu*, quoted in Iwao, 'Li Tan', pp. 60–1.
14. Iwao, 'Li Tan', p. 45.
15. Lin, 'Fukien's Private Sea Trade', p. 187.

Chapter Three

1. TW, p. 8.
2. Croizier, Koxinga and Chinese Nationalism, p. 38.
3. The exact site, of course, is as much open to conjecture as the rest of the story. During the nineteenth century, there were four different spots marked as 'Coxinga's birthplace'. The modern monument marks the end of a long argument.
4. Presumably, many of them died in the massacre at Tongshan (see below). TW, p. 17. The doubling of E the Osprey may have been caused by the use of simplified Chinese characters by its twentieth-century mainland publisher, and may have originally referred to another brother with an avian name.
5. Mulder, Hollanders in Hirado, p. 210.
6. Iwao, 'Li Tan', pp. 65–6.
7. The proximity of their reported deaths has led some scholars (e.g. Terao, Tei Seikô, p. 16) to suggest that Yan Sixi and Captain China were one and the same, but contemporary Chinese accounts distinctly separate them.
8. Palafox, History of the Conquest of China, pp. 68–9.
9. Ibid., p. 68.
10. Letter from Gerrit de Witt to Pieter de Carpentier, 29 October 1625, in Iwao, 'Li Tan', p. 78.
11. Palafox, History of the Conquest of China, pp. 69–70.
12. Ponsonby-Fane, Sovereign and Subject, p. 282.
13. TW, p. 20, recounts an argument between Iquan and Hu, with Bao the Panther trying to intercede.
14. Palafox, History of the Conquest of China, p. 72.
15. Ibid., p. 68.
16. He Qiaoyuan to Nicholas Iquan, translated from a Japanese version in Blussé, 'Minnan-Jen or Cosmopolitan? The Rise of Cheng Chih-Lung Alias Nicolas Iquan'. p. 257.
17. Ibid.
18. Foccardi, The Last Warrior, p. 16.
19. Parsons, Peasant Rebellions of the Late Ming Dynasty, p. 11.
20. Mulder, Hollanders in Hirado, p. 211. In years to come, the English had a similar appellation for unsavoury characters in their own East Asian possession – the acronym FILTH, for 'Failed In London, Try Hong Kong'.
21. Valentyn, Oud en Nieuw Oost-Indien, in FUD, pp. 36–7.
22. There is a brief biography of Suetsugu in Miyamoto's Vikings of the Far East, pp. 149–51. His family remained prominent in the region's trade for several generations, but his son bizarrely became a good friend of the Dutch, to the point that his credibility with his own countrymen was compromised. His descendants were wiped out during Japan's Sakoku era when, unsurprisingly, they were found to be secretly trading with the Chinese.
23. Mulder, Hollanders in Hirado, p. 169.
24. Valentyn, Oud en Nieuw Oost-Indien, in FUD, p. 38.
25. Letter from Jan Pieterszoon Coen to the Directors of the East India Company, 6 January 1628, quoted in Iwao, 'Li Tan', p. 78.

26. Letter from Pieter Nuijts to Cornelis van Nijenroode, 16 June 1628, *FUD*, p. 38.
27. *Ibid.*
28. *Ibid.*, p. 39.
29. Letter from Pieter Nuijts to Cornelis van Nijenroode, 16 June 1628, *FUD*, p. 40. A 'soap-knife' is the Dutch term for a pole-arm such as a halberd or the Japanese *naginata*.
30. *Ibid.*, p. 39.
31. *Ibid.*, p. 40.
32. *Ibid.*
33. Letter of Pieter Nuijts to the Council at Fort Zeelandia, 4 July 1628, *FUD*, p. 47. It was only with hindsight that Nuijts realised he had pushed the Japanese too far.
34. Anonymous account of Hamada Yahei's kidnap of Pieter Nuijts, *FUD*, pp. 41–8.
35. The other hostages were Pieter Muyert, Joannes van der Hagen, Jan Hartman and Abraham de Mourcourt.
36. Mulder, *Hollanders in Hirado*, p. 170.
37. Letter from Nicholas Iquan to Jacques Specx, quoted in Blussé, 'Minnan-Jen or Cosmopolitan?' p. 258n.
38. Letter from Pieter Nuijts to the Gentlemen XVII, 30 September 1631, quoted in Blussé, 'Minnan-Jen or Cosmopolitan?' p. 258n.
39. Blussé, 'Minnan-Jen or Cosmopolitan?' pp. 258–9.
40. The former Governor General, Jan Pieterszoon Coen, had a notorious temper and had perished of a heart attack on the day that Specx's fleet appeared on the horizon. For Coen it was a small mercy, as there was no telling what Specx would have done to him if he had still been alive when he arrived. While Specx had been away, his daughter Sara had remained behind in Batavia – she was half-Japanese, and consequently not permitted to go to Europe. Lodging with Coen as a handmaid to his wife, the twelve-year-old Sara had reputedly sneaked her fifteen-year old lover into her room in the governor's apartments, leading the irascible Coen to have the boy executed, and Sara flogged in front of the town hall. The handling of the incident caused an a vengeful Specx to exclude three councillors from receiving the sacrament. Though reports showed that Sara's lover Pieter had bribed slaves to get *himself* into Sara's apartment, it was Sara who got the blame, and she appears to have been shunned by Batavian society. Left behind like nearly all other Eurasian children when her father returned to the Netherlands for good, she would eventually find a way to escape. See Chapter IV. Also Taylor, *The Social World of Batavia*, p. 21; Dash, *Batavia's Graveyard*, p. 174; Blussé, in *Strange Company*, p. 161, reports the boy's age as seventeen.
41. Specx was not wholly supportive of Iquan, but preferred the devil he knew. If he had stayed in Batavia, he might well have turned on his old friend himself, as Iquan's 'uncertain position, continuity and maintenance, as well as the unsteadiness of such a robber's mind put everything again in confusion'. Letter of Jacques Specx to Hans Putmans, quoted in Blussé, 'The VOC as Sorcerer's Apprentice', p. 101. See also Blussé, *Strange Company*, pp. 60–1.

42. Surviving letters from a prominent government official outline his annoyance that only Iquan's family can be trusted to carry out military operations. See Blussé, 'Minnan-Jen or Cosmopolitan?', p. 261.
43. *Ibid.*, p. 260.

Chapter Four

1. Mulder, *Hollanders in Hirado*, p. 214n.
2. Some Japanese sources claim that Shichizaemon was Iquan's son, including one that appears to have been written with the cooperation of his modern descendants. See Terao, *Tei Seikô*, p. 269. Compare to the readiness of Chinese sources to believe that Miss Tagawa was of Chinese descent; both countries are keen to claim Coxinga as their own.
3. *TW*, pp. 38–9.
4. See Ming and Zheng, *Zheng Chenggong Gushi Chuanshuo*, [*Stories Told About Zheng Chenggong*], pp. 16–19; Foccardi, *Last Warrior*, p. 16.
5. *TW*, p. 39.
6. *Ibid.* Hummel, *Eminent Chinese of the Ch'ing Period (1644–1912)*, p. 108 claims that Big Tree was a pen-name conferred upon Coxinga by his tutor Qian Qianyi in Nanjing (see Chapter V), but I see no reason why it cannot be both.
7. Kessler, *The Maritime Laws and Their Effect on Sino-Western Relations During the Early Ch'ing Period: 1656–1684*, p. 14.
8. Palafox, *History of the Conquest of China*, p. 73.
9. Blussé, 'The VOC as Sorcerer's Apprentice', p. 102. Also Goddard, *Makers of Taiwan*, p. 13.
10. Letter from Nicholas Iquan to Hans Putmans, 19 October 1633. Quoted in Blussé, 'The VOC as Sorcerer's Apprentice', p. 102.
11. Letter from Augustin Li Da-she to Hans Putmans, 14 September 1633. Quoted in Iwao, 'Li Tan', p. 81.
12. *TW*, p. 42. Terao, *Tei Seikô*, p. 200 disagrees, claiming that Hu the Tiger and Zheng Tai are the same person.
13. Lin, *Zheng Chenggong*, pp. 21–5. Terao's *Tei Seikô*, presumably using Japanese sources, relates a similar tale and similarly names the tutor as one Hanafusa, adding that he was a teacher of the Nito-ryû 'Two-Sword' technique popularised by local resident Miyamoto Musashi, and that the six-year-old Coxinga had been his youngest pupil, pp. 15–16.
14. Foccardi, *Last Warrior*, p. 23.
15. Ming and Zheng, *Zheng Chenggong Gushi Chuanshuo*, pp. 214–15. Palafox, *History of the Conquest of China*, p. 148, claims that 200 of them joined the Manchus after Iquan's defection.
16. Palafox, *History of the Conquest of China*, p. 148.
17. Michener and Day, *Rascals in Paradise*, p. 74.
18. Letter of Revd Robertus Junius to Hans Putmans, 24 January 1636, in Blussé and Everts, *The Formosan Encounter – Notes on Formosa's Aboriginal Society: A Selection of Documents from Dutch Archival Sources*, vol.II: *1636–1645*, p. 29.

19. Letter of Rev. Robertus Junius to the Amsterdam Chamber of Commerce of the East India Company, 5 September 1636. *FUD*, p. 116.
20. From the Day-Journal of the Taiyouan Council, 29–31 March 1636. *FUD*, p. 113.
21. Letter of Hans Putmans to Jacques Specx, 5 October 1630, *FUD*, p. 102.
22. Letter of Jacques Specx to Hans Putmans, 31 July 1631, *FUD*, p. 104.
23. See Boxer, *The Christian Century in Japan*, p. 439.
24. These edicts may answer another historical mystery: why Miss Tagawa would be so prepared not only to leave Japan, but also to leave her son Shichizaemon behind. If she were genuinely of mixed Chinese ancestry as some sources have claimed, her position in Japan might have become dangerous. Shichizaemon, however, may have qualified as a 'true' Japanese through having three Japanese grandparents.
25. Mulder, *Hollanders in Hirado*, p. 185.
26. Variant translations can be found in Paske-Smith, *Japanese Traditions of Christianity*, p. 57, and Boxer, *Japan's Christian Century*, p. 378.
27. Mulder, *Hollanders in Hirado*, pp. 189–96.
28. Boxer, 'Notes on Early European Military Influence in Japan (1543–1853)', p. 76.
29. Palafox, *History of the Conquest of China*, p. 80.
30. *Ibid.*, pp. 80–1.
31. Goddard, *Makers of Taiwan*, pp. 7–8. Goddard relies heavily on the unreliable Palafox but implies with the phrase 'by all accounts' that other sources mention Iquan's mystery daughter. If they do, I have not found them. Goddard also claims that this daughter and her Portuguese husband remained with the Zheng family on Taiwan for a considerable time, throughout the reign of Coxinga's son, Jing.
32. Iwao, 'Li Tan', p. 76.

Chapter Five

1. Ponsonby-Fane, *Sovereign and Subject*, p. 286.
2. Croizier, *Koxinga and Chinese Nationalism*, p. 39.
3. Hummel, *Eminent Chinese*, pp. 148–50.
4. Confucius, *Analects*, VIII, v. 13.
5. Ponsonby-Fane, *Sovereign and Subject*, p. 286.
6. Ming and Zheng, *Zheng Chenggong Gushi Chuanshuo*, p. 32.
7. Lin, *Zheng Chenggong*, p. 47.
8. Attwater, *Adam Schall: A Jesuit at the Court of China 1592–1666*, p. 54. Although his writings seem to have tipped the balance, Schall was not Beijing's first choice. He was a replacement for a more senior Jesuit who died in 1630.
9. Spence, *The China Helpers: Western Advisers in China 1620–1960*, pp. 13–16.
10. Attwater, *Adam Schall*, p. 60.
11. Dunne, *Generation of Giants*, p. 318.
12. *Ibid.*
13. Attwater, *Adam Schall*, p. 61.
14. This was later improved by the Manchus themselves in the 1650s and 1670s, and was variously known as the Willow Stockade, the Willow Palisade or, simply, the Pale. See Melikhov, 'The Northern Border of the Patrimonial Estates of Manchu

(Ch'ing) Feudal Lords During the Conquest of China (1640s to 1680s)', pp. 14–23.

15. See 'K'ung Yu-tê', in Hummel, *Eminent Chinese*, pp. 435–6.
16. For a detailed breakdown, not only of Wu's acts, but of the misleading tales that have grown up about them, see Wakeman, *The Great Enterprise: The Manchu Reconstruction of Imperial Order in Seventeenth-Century China*, pp. 290–7.
17. Shang, *Tales of Empresses and Imperial Consorts in China*, pp. 357–8.
18. Backhouse and Bland, *Annals and Memoirs* (Taiwan edn), p. 103.
19. *Ibid*.
20. Backhouse and Bland, *Annals and Memoirs* (Taiwan edn), p. 104.
21. *Ibid*., pp. 113–14.
22. Attwater, *Adam Schall*, p. 75.
23. Wakeman, *Great Enterprise*, p. 283.
24. Attwater, *Adam Schall*, p. 79.
25. Tsao, *Rebellion of the Three Feudatories*, p. 24.
26. The story of the arrival of the Manchus and the battle of the Sha river can be found in Wakeman, *Great Enterprise*, pp. 309–11.
27. Attwater, *Adam Schall*, p. 80.
28. Wakeman, *Great Enterprise*, p. 315.
29. *Ibid*., p. 317.

Chapter Six

1. It was not until 1695 that Li Zicheng's likeness was found on the tomb of an anonymous one-eyed man, who had supposedly arrived at a remote Buddhist temple in 1646. The stranger had become a monk under the name Jewel of Heaven's Grace, eventually dying of advanced old age in 1674, and delivering a strange deathbed speech in which he described himself as 'an Emperor who had renounced the pomps and vanities of this world'. See Backhouse and Bland, *Annals and Memoirs*, p. 117. (Taiwan edn).
2. Hummel, *Eminent Chinese*, pp. 195–6.
3. Wakeman, *Great Enterprise*, p. 339.
4. *Ibid*., pp. 528–35.
5. Backhouse and Bland, *Annals and Memoirs*, p. 172 (Taiwan edn).
6. *Ibid*., p. 173.
7. Wakeman, *Great Enterprise*, p. 562n.
8. Peers, *Late Imperial Chinese Armies, 1520–1840*, pp. 42–3; Ross, *The Manchus*, pp. 261–2.
9. Martini, *De Bello Tartarico Historia*, p. 115.
10. Hummel, *Eminent Chinese*, pp. 529–30. Liu Shi had also once been Coxinga's calligraphy teacher.
11. Wakeman, *Great Enterprise*, p. 580.
12. *Ibid*., p. 581.
13. Dodo was probably telling the truth. The Jin Dynasty (1115–1254), whom the Manchus claimed as their ancestors, had only ever ruled China north of the

Yangtze. It is likely that the Manchus would have been content with the same territory, and left south China in the hands of the Chinese.

14. According to Ponsonby-Fane's *Sovereign and Subject*, p. 288, Iquan actually resisted the selection of *any* emperor at this point, but was outvoted by a faction led by Feng the Phoenix. The honours heaped on him, and the implied consideration of Coxinga for the imperial succession, may have all been intended to buy off his opposition.

15. The Emperor of Intense Warring had to deal with the embarrassing discovery of a rival 'regent', who had independently proclaimed himself the last defender of the Ming further inland. However, their squabbles over who was really in charge are beyond the scope of this book. See Struve, *Southern Ming*, pp. 75–94.

16. *TW*, p. 70.

17. *TW*, p. 74.

18. *TW*, chapter V, quoted in Cheng, 'Cheng Ch'eng-Kung's Maritime Expansion and Early Ch'ing Coastal Prohibition', p. 232.

19. Ponsonby-Fane, *Sovereign and Subject*, p. 191.

Chapter Seven

1. Struve, *Southern Ming*, p. 95.

2. Foccardi, *The Last Warrior*, p. 32.

3. Ponsonby-Fane, *Sovereign and Subject*, p. 293.

4. Foccardi, *The Last Warrior*, p. 33.

5. Palafox, *History of the Conquest of China*, p. 96.

6. *TW*, p. 98; Foccardi, *The Last Warrior*, pp. 37–8. Terao's *Tei Seikô*, p. 36, reports that both Bao the Panther and Feng the Phoenix were at the castle with Miss Tagawa, but that she volunteered to cover their escape, 'sick at heart that her lord Iquan had betrayed her'. He also agrees with a Chinese source, cited by Keene in *Battles of Coxinga*, p. 169, that claims Miss Tagawa hanged herself after being raped by Manchu soldiers. Ponsonby-Fane's *Sovereign and Subject*, p. 295, quotes a letter from Shichizaemon, Tagawa's other son, which simply reports: 'my mother, fleeing towards Amoy, was captured, but thinking that to pass into the hands of the enemy and be killed by them was shameful, she killed herself'. Many sources have Coxinga hearing the news of his mother's death third-hand, but Terao, p. 37, has him and his soldiers arriving at the castle of Anping in time to chase off the Manchus, but too late to save his mother. This would, at least, explain how the castle could still remain in Zheng hands after the events described.

7. Terao, *Tei Seikô*, p. 37–9 reports that the news of the death of Miss Tagawa also caused Iquan to fly into a rage, and ended any trust he may have had in the Manchus. Terao's ordering of events suggests that it was this sudden change of heart on Iquan's part that caused the fracas between his men and Bolo's, and led to his subsequent incarceration in Beijing.

8. Foccardi, *The Last Warrior*, p. 39. Most historians agree that the burning of the Confucian robes is a later embellishment, though both Ponsonby-Fane's *Sovereign*

and Subject, p. 297, Terao's *Tei Seikô*, p. 40, and Ming and Zheng's *Zheng Chenggong Gushi Chuanshuo*, p. 48, not only report it, but identify the location.

9. Foccardi, *The Last Warrior*, p. 43.

10. Terao, *Tei Seikô*, p. 42. Struve, *Southern Ming*, p. 232, notes that 'the number of Chinese ships that went to trade in Japan increased markedly from 1639–1646'. Perhaps 'Chinese' should be itself in inverted commas, as the Japanese trade restrictions on foreigners suddenly put the Zheng organisation at an advantage as middlemen for surplus Dutch products. In 1647, a group of Zheng sailors were marooned in Korea after 'an explosion on their ship'. They told their rescuers that they were running trade from Cambodia to Japan, using the funds from the Emperor of Intense Warring, with the authority of Nicholas Iquan. See Cheng, 'Cheng Ch'eng-Kung's Maritime Expansion'. pp. 231–2.

11. For the brief and tragic tale of the Shaowu Emperor, see Struve, *Southern Ming*, pp. 101–3, and Wakeman, *Great Enterprise*, pp. 737–8.

12. Palafox, *History of the Conquest of China*, p. 99, puts the number of soldiers at a mere twenty. Wakeman, *Great Enterprise*, p. 738, has a more realistic estimate of 'no more than a thousand'.

13. Palafox, *History of the Conquest of China*, p. 101. Wakeman, *Great Enterprise*, p. 738, has the horsemen executing the Emperor instead of finding him dead.

14. Struve, *Southern Ming*, pp. 157–8.

15. Terao, *Tei Seikô*, p. 47.

16. Foccardi, *Last Warrior*, pp. 41–2.

17. Struve, *Southern Ming*, p. 120; Wills, 'Maritime China', p. 224.

18. *TW*, pp. 110–11; Hummel, *Eminent Chinese*, p. 653; Foccardi, *Last Warrior*, p. 46; Terao, *Tei Seikô*, p. 60–1.

19. Terao's *Tei Seikô*, p. 60, goes so far as to say that Shi Lang 'shaved his head' and later announced that he wanted to be a monk. We can only speculate as to if the original head-shaving was in the Manchu style, later widened to include the whole head in order to disguise his original intention to defect.

20. Foccardi, *Last Warrior*, p. 47.

21. Letter from Coxinga to Nicholas Iquan, dated September 1653. The text of Coxinga's letter implies that he left Amoy in 1649, but was gone for many months. He would need to have been in the south for at least a year for his activities to tally with other records of the assault on Amoy, which happened in 1651. The letter appears on p. 63 of the *Xian Wang Shilu Jiaozhu*, or *Veritable Records of the Former Prince*, a tattered document found in 1927 hidden away in a former Zheng family dwelling. It proved to be the work of Coxinga's secretary Yang Ying, and is an invaluable source on Coxinga's last decade. See also Struve, *Voices from the Ming-Qing Cataclysm*, p. 186.

22. Hummel, *Eminent Chinese*, p. 112.

23. Terao, *Tei Seikô*, pp. 59–60; also Chang, *English Factory*, p. 741. Or so the story goes. In 1661, however, Coxinga preferred the company of another wife during the invasion of Taiwan, although leaving Cuiying behind in Amoy may have been an act of kindess considering the deprivations of the siege. Cuiying's later behaviour, however, was not that of a dutiful wife – see Chapter XII.

24. Cheng, 'Cheng Ch'eng-kung's Maritime Expansion', p. 235, claims this fine took place in 1656.

25. Ross, *The Manchus, or, the Reigning Dynasty of China*, pp. 392–3. The same page has Coxinga retreating to Haicheng, 'immediately, closely and vigorously besieged. Over a hundred feet of the city wall were knocked down, but [Coxinga] obstinately held out, himself constantly surrounded by showers of shot, stones and arrows. One day, hearing a blank cannon shot fired, [Coxinga] said: "That is a signal cannon. They are about to storm the walls." He therefore ordered every man to provide himself with a hatchet, and on the wall and in the breaches, await the attack. In a little time, Hwang's men were swarming up all sides of the wall like ants.' Ross is less forthcoming about how Coxinga could have escaped from such a dire situation, simply later saying 'the siege was immediately raised' without providing much reason.

26. Letter from the Batavia Council to Governor Verburg in Taiwan, 26 May 1653, *FUD*, p. 160.

27. Foccardi, *Last Warrior*, p. 50.

Chapter Eight

1. There is no documented meeting between Schall and Iquan, but it is extremely unlikely that their paths did not cross during the decade Iquan spent in Beijing.

2. Attwater, *Adam Schall*, p. 87.

3. Hummel, *Eminent Chinese*, p. 256. Attwater, *Adam Schall*, p. 104, claims that it was not Borjigid who was ill, but Fulin's betrothed, Berjijit. In Attwater's account, however, Borjigid is still the woman who sent for Schall and asked him to cure her would-be daughter-in-law, and subsequently addressed him as 'foster-father'.

4. Not all the contenders were actually alive at the time. Some, such as Dorgon, continued to exert influence from beyond the grave as their activities in their lifetimes were interpreted and reinterpreted by successive generations. Dorgon's biography in Hummel's *Eminent Chinese of the Ch'ing Period*, pp. 215–19, actually continues for two whole pages after his death, as his supporters and descendants are buffeted by factional infighting. He was only finally confirmed as a great prince, and cleared of all posthumous charges in 1773, over a century after his death.

5. She was a Manchu of the Donggo clan, daughter of Osi, and sister to Fiyanggu, who would later become a famous general of the late seventeenth century. Chinese sources and most other history books use her Chinese name Xiao Xian. Shang's *Tales of Empresses and Imperial Consorts in China*, pp. 368–72, repeats a later garbling of her biography, confusing the twenty-year-old consort with a forty-year-old Chinese concubine with a similar name.

6. It would seem that Fulin learned such behaviour from the late Dorgon, who had famously conducted a relationship with the widow of Fulin's brother Haoge.

7. Attwater, *Adam Schall*, pp. 98–100.

8. Yang, *Veritable Record*, p. 62. He is summarising a letter from Nicholas Iquan to Coxinga, dated September/ October 1653.

9. Letter from Coxinga to Nicholas Iquan, dated September/October 1653, quoted in Yang, *Veritable Record*, p. 62. Icily polite, the original does not use direct personal

pronouns, but I have used them in the translation to give a better impression of the effect the letter would have had on its recipient. For a fuller translation of the same letter, see Struve, *Voices from the Ming-Qing Cataclysm*, pp. 184–9.

10. Yang, *Veritable Record*, pp. 69–70.

11. Edict of the Emperor of Unbroken Rule, *c.* June 1654, quoted in Yang, *Veritable Record*, p. 70.

12. Letter from Liu Qingtai, governor of Fujian, to Coxinga, *c.* July 1654, quoted in Yang, *Veritable Record*, p. 77.

13. Letter from Coxinga to the Manchu ambassadors, quoted in Yang, *Veritable Record*, p. 80.

14. Letter from Feng the Phoenix to Nicholas Iquan, in Yang, *Veritable Record*, pp. 89–91. Yang files the letter *after* the minutes of Coxinga's final meeting with his half-brothers, but its tone implies that it was sent while the negotiations were still proceeding.

15. Letter from Feng the Phoenix to Nicholas Iquan, in Yang, *Veritable Record*, p. 91. A 'ten-year-old wound' would have to have been inflicted during the Manchu invasion – a subtle way of reminding Iquan whose side he used to be on.

16. Yang, *Veritable Record*, p. 85. The term 'you children' is used here for Coxinga's actual term of *fanzi*, which could mean either 'you kids', as in a disparaging term for the younger Zheng family members, or possibly 'you ordinaries' or 'you mortals', implying that Coxinga thought of himself as a superior breed of Zheng. The Emperor Guangwu, to whom Coxinga refers, was a ruler of the Eastern Han dynasty in the first century AD. It is typical of Coxinga to append a scholarly footnote to a statement, even in the middle of a family argument.

17. Yang, *Veritable Record*, p. 87.

18. Letter from Coxinga to Shidu, November 1654, quoted in Yang, *Veritable Record*, p. 89. The actual altitude of the phoenix is measured in the original as a thousand *ren*. A *ren* is a Chinese fathom, of roughly eight feet.

19. Strangely, although Huang Wu (see Chapter IX) would later allege that Iquan and Coxinga had been in *secret* contact for some time, there is no mention of any such correspondence in Yang Ying's *Veritable Record*.

20. Hung, *Taiwan Under the Cheng Family 1662–1683*, p. 86. Coxinga was able to call himself a king, although the Chinese fully understood that his actual authority was that of a high-ranking feudal lord. Such linguistic fine points were not appreciated by some foreign observers, who began referring to him as a king in the European sense.

21. More than 4,000 Chinese died in the uprising. The Dutch only lost two men.

22. See Huber, 'Chinese Settlers Against the Dutch East India Company', p. 268.

23. Valentyn, *Oud en Nieuw Oost-Indien*, quoted in FUD, p. 64. Although Valentyn knows the relationship between the two men, he still seems to confuse Iquan's former career with Coxinga's. Hung, in 'Taiwan Under the Cheng Family', p. 72, suggests that the rebel leader Guo Huaiyi was a former acquaintance of Nicholas Iquan, but this is still merely circumstantial evidence for Coxinga's involvement in the uprising.

24. Correspondence of the Dutch East India Company, 1654, quoted in Yamawaki,

'The Great Trading Merchants, Cocksinja [sic] and His Son', p. 108. *Perpetuan* is a durable woollen fabric, *mouris* is plain white cotton from the Coromandel coast.

25. Bowra, 'Manchu Conquest of Canton', p. 92. 'Iquon' seems to be a garbled reference to Iquan's son.
26. Kessler, 'Maritime Laws and Their Effect on Sino-Western Relations', pp. 91–2.
27. Attwater, *Adam Schall*, p. 118.
28. Dunne, *Generation of Giants*, pp. 347–8.
29. Nieuhoff, *An Embassy from the East-India Company of the United Provinces*, p. 97.
30. Letter of Coxinga to the Governor General of the East India Company, 1655, quoted in Yamawaki, 'The Great Trading Merchants', p. 108.
31. See, for example, Coyett's catalogue of Verburg's treachery, in Campbell, *FUD*, p. 387.
32. Letter of Coxinga to Liu Qingtai, winter 1655–6, quoted in Struve, *Southern Ming*, pp. 179–80.
33. Yang, *Veritable Record*, p. 134.
34. Terao, *Tei Seikô*, p. 109.
35. *Ibid.*, p. 110.
36. Hummel, *Eminent Chinese*, p. 41.
37. Yang, *Veritable Record*, p. 176; Ross, *The Manchus*, pp. 396–7. Terao, *Tei Seikô*, p. 111, notes that Coxinga had taken a great risk by setting sail at the beginning of the typhoon season. No supernatural explanation is really required!
38. Ponsonby-Fane, *Sovereign and Subject*, p. 309, reports that Coxinga eventually built memorials to the three drowned children on Taiwan – empty graves which were rediscovered in the early twentieth century. See also Struve, *Southern Ming*, p. 183.
39. Terao, *Tei Seikô*, p. 112.
40. Yang, *Veritable Record*, p. 197.
41. Terao, *Tei Seikô*, p. 116.
42. *Ibid.*
43. *Ibid.*, p. 119. The same battle is described with considerably less derring-do in Yang, *Veritable Record*, p. 198.
44. Terao, *Tei Seikô*, p. 119.

Chapter Nine

1. Hummel, *Eminent Chinese*, p. 257.
2. Terao, *Tei Seikô*, p. 139. The messenger had arrived in Beijing to report the death of the King of Korea. The Manchus kept him in town until they had better news to send back with him.
3. Terao, *Tei Seikô*, p. 121.
4. Coyett, *Neglected Formosa*, in *FUD*, p. 420.
5. Terao, *Tei Seikô*, p. 110, suggests that the Iron Men were Japanese mercenaries. Masterless samurai were a growing problem in Japan, and were even responsible for a failed coup attempt in 1651. It is not inconceivable that some may have made it to China by jumping ship from the Ryukyu Islands, but Terao can offer no real evidence of the Iron Men's origins, except their prowess in battle and the awe

they inspired in the Chinese. Though if I ever had to guess who would volunteer to wear full-body plate armour in the middle of June and throw themselves at charging Manchu cavalry, the Japanese would be at the top of the list. Croizier, in *Koxinga and Chinese Nationalism*, p. 61, reports that Terao is not alone among Japanese historians in holding this view.

6. Yang, *Veritable Record*, p. 201.
7. Terao, *Tei Seikô*, p. 123.
8. Yang, *Veritable Record*, p. 202.
9. Terao, *Tei Seikô*, p. 127.
10. Yang, *Veritable Record*, pp. 202–3. Terao, *Tei Seikô*, p. 122, uses the term 'Heaven's Soldiers'. They were not, however, a special battalion like the Iron Men, merely the nine best-disciplined companies among Coxinga's forces. Their name could imply the presence of Christians, perhaps even the remnants of the Black Guard who did not defect with Nicholas Iquan.
11. Adjustments in calendars and contemporary guesswork make Coxinga's exact birthdate unclear. Matters are not helped by contradictory biographical information in China and Japan. His birthday is generally accepted to be 28 August, which means the actual celebrations should have taken place four days after the army reached Nanjing.
12. Terao, *Tei Seikô*, p. 129.
13. *Ibid.*, p. 133.
14. Yang, *Veritable Record*, p. 214, gives the date as the 22nd of the eighth lunar month. I have followed Struve's *Southern Ming*, p. 188, which converts the dates to Western reckoning.
15. Terao, *Tei Seikô*, p. 132.
16. Zhang Huang-yan continued to fight in China, hoping for the Zheng clan's swift return. He finally gave up and retired in 1664, only to be betrayed by a former lieutenant and executed a month later. Collections of his poetry survive along with his *Failure of the Northern Expedition*, an account of his long march back to the coast. See Hummel, *Eminent Chinese*, pp. 41–2.
17. Terao, *Tei Seikô*, p. 138.
18. Struve, *Southern Ming*, p. 253n.
19. Yang, *Veritable Record*, pp. 229–31; Struve, *Southern Ming*, p. 189.
20. Letter from Coxinga to the Dutch, November 1660, quoted in Campbell, *FUD*, p. 405. The letter therein is an English translation of a seventeenth-century Dutch translation of Coxinga's original Chinese – hence the long sentences in the style of the day.
21. Terao, *Tei Seikô*, p. 148.
22. See Kessler, 'Maritime Laws', pp. 33–6. The full text of Huang Wu's memorials is on pp. 124–8.
23. Edict of the Emperor of Unbroken Rule, quoted in Cheng, 'Cheng Ch'eng-Kung's Maritime Expansion and Early Ch'ing Coastal Prohibition', p. 239.
24. Cheng, 'Cheng Ch'eng-Kung's Maritime Expansion', p. 240.
25. *Ibid.*
26. Hummel, *Eminent Chinese*, p. 301.

27. The name seems deliberately calculated to imply wholesome health in opposition to his father.
28. Backhouse and Bland, *Annals and Memoirs*, p. 236.
29. *Ibid.*, p. 237.

Chapter Ten

1. In fact, the Portuguese position in Macao was saved in part through the efforts at court of Adam Schall, and partly because the Emperor liked lions. See Kessler, 'Maritime Laws', pp. 70ff. In 1667, a Portuguese diplomatic mission was sent to Beijing to negotiate with the Emperor of Hearty Prosperity. The thirteen-year-old ruler of the world let it be known that he would very much like to own a lion, and the Portuguese duly shipped two at great expense from Mozambique. The male died *en route*, but the lioness reached Beijing in time to give birth to a litter of cubs. When she also died, a mere fifteen days after the diplomats left Beijing, the Emperor, by now in his late teens, commanded that she be buried with full honours. See Kessler, 'Maritime Laws', p. 84n.
2. Coyett, *Neglected Formosa*, *FUD*, p. 400.
3. *Ibid.*, p. 402.
4. *Ibid.*
5. Letter of Coxinga to Frederik Coyett, November 1660, *FUD*, p. 405.
6. Coyett, *Neglected Formosa*, *FUD*, p. 407.
7. Yang, *Veritable Record*, p. 244.
8. *Ibid.*, p. 245.
9. *Ibid.*, pp. 245–6.
10. Croizier, *Koxinga and Chinese Nationalism*, p. 22.
11. Qin, *Zheng Chenggong*, p. 379.
    I cannot improve on the translation in Croizier, *Koxinga and Chinese Nationalism*, p. 23.
12. Croizier, *Koxinga and Chinese Nationalism*, p. 37.
13. Though most sources rely on *Neglected Formosa* for this, the same battle is described in Yang, *Veritable Record*, pp. 249–51.
14. The *'s Gravenlande* and the *Vink* sailed for a Dutch outpost in the north of Taiwan, where they informed the inhabitants of Coxinga's invasion, and offered to take them off Taiwan before Coxinga's army could reach them. From there, they sailed for Nagasaki. It is thought that some of the evacuees were the first European women to set foot in Japan. See Boxer, 'The Siege of Fort Zeelandia and the Capture of Formosa from the Dutch 1661–1662', pp. 28, 33 and 36–7.
15. Coyett, *Neglected Formosa*, *FUD*, p. 416. Pedel was particularly keen on attacking the Chinese, as his son William had lost an arm in an earlier skirmish.
16. Coyett, *Neglected Formosa*, *FUD*, p. 416.
17. *Ibid.*, p. 420.
18. *FUD* omits Coyett's appendix on 'Considerable Facts touching the true cause of the Chinese Cruelties and Tyranny', from which this account was taken. An

English translation by Leonard Blussé can be found in the Beauclair edition of
Neglected Formosa, p. 89. References to a 'Beauclair' version hereafter denote this
edition.

19. Coyett, *Neglected Formosa*, in *FUD*, p. 425.
20. *Ibid.*, p. 484.
21. Coyett's *Neglected Formosa* chooses this moment to break the narrative and
    describe the nature of Coxinga's troops. This implies that details of such units as
    the Iron Men and the Black Guard only reached Coyett after the ambassadors'
    return. See *FUD*, p. 420.
22. *Ibid.*, p. 421.
23. *Ibid.*
24. Coyett, *Neglected Formosa*, in *FUD*, p. 422.
25. *Ibid.*, pp. 423–4. His use of the term 'iron ships' is poetic licence – the Dutch
    vessels were made out of wood, of course.
26. Coyett does not mention it in his own account, but Yang's *Veritable Record*,
    p. 250, records that Dutch negotiators offered to pay rent of a million taels a year,
    a trade levy on all docking vessels, and an indemnity to Coxinga's army of a
    further 100,000 taels.
27. Coyett, *Neglected Formosa*, in *FUD*, p. 426.
28. Yang, *Veritable Record*, p. 252.
29. Letter from Coxinga to Frederik Coyett, 24 May 1661, in Keene, *Battles of
    Coxinga*, p. 57. Coxinga's use of the term 'hundred' is a mystery. Although he
    was not above belittling his enemies in the past, the letter could also suggest
    that he had vastly underestimated the size of the garrison remaining at
    Zeelandia. Was Valentyn sending a coded message to Coyett in his
    translation, or was this the same innate hyperbole that led Coxinga to
    ridicule the Dutch 'iron' ships?
30. *Ibid.*, p. 58.
31. Beauclair, *Neglected Formosa*, p. 91.
32. *Ibid.*, p. 92.
33. From Jacob Caeuw's diary, 21 October 1661, quoted in *FUD*, p. 326. Of the Dutch
    sent to China as hostages, eleven survivors were eventually returned to Batavia by
    the Manchus in 1684. See also Boxer, *Dutch Merchants and Mariners in Asia*, IV, p.
    183n, and Vixseboxe, 'A XVIIth Century Record', Campbell, *FUD*, p. 85, names
    seventeen survivors of the 22-year ordeal, ten of whom were children at the time
    of their abduction, although some of them were probably *born* in captivity. The
    discrepancy between the numbers is due to the fact that two mothers were
    Taiwanese natives who elected not to 'return' to a place they had never seen, and
    stayed in Sakkam with their half-Dutch offspring. However, see also *FUD*, p. 85,
    which reports a claim made in 1663 by Coxinga's son Jing that he held Dutch
    'men, women, and children to the number of nearly a hundred' at Sakkam.
34. Coyett, *Neglected Formosa*, in *FUD*
    p. 429. Coyett's estimate of the dead is based on the reports of later captured
    Chinese.
35. Coyett, *Neglected Formosa*, in *FUD*, pp. 431–2. The council at Batavia would
    eventually accuse Coyett of dereliction of duty for not ordering an assault out of

Fort Zeelandia. Concerning their armchair generalship, he wryly noted that 'the best navigators are sometimes found on land'.

36. Yang, *Veritable Record*, p. 253.
37. *Ibid.*, p. 254.

Chapter Eleven

1. Coyett, *Neglected Formosa*, in *FUD*, p. 436.
2. *Ibid.*, p. 440.
3. Clenk then went to Japan, where he forgot all about his refusal to accept his new post, and claimed to be the new governor of Taiwan. The crew of the vessel he attacked were eventually rescued by a passing Chinese ship, and returned to Batavia where they lodged an official complaint against Clenk. By that time, however, he was already preparing to leave for the Netherlands. See Boxer, 'The Siege of Fort Zeelandia and the Capture of Formosa from the Dutch 1661–1662', p. 37, and Coyett, *Neglected Formosa*, in *FUD*, p. 441.
4. Despite the heroic acts of Bennis, he is not named in Coyett's account of events. This may have something to do with the company he kept, since he appears to have been a friend of Hans Jurgen Radis. Radis was aboard the *Maria* for its epic voyage and returned to Taiwan as one of the soldiers in Clenk's relief fleet. See Keene, *Battles of Coxinga*, p. 172n.
5. Coyett, *Neglected Formosa*, in *FUD*, p. 439.
6. Letter from the Batavia Council to Frederik Coyett, 5 July 1661, quoted in *Neglected Formosa* as Authentic Proof no. 27, *FUD*, p. 485.
7. Coyett, *Neglected Formosa*, in *FUD* p. 442. As part of the scapegoating of Coyett, he was later accused of *ordering* Cacuw to stay out at sea. His enemies went so far as to argue that the increased power of the storm was God's own wrath at Coyett.
8. Coyett, *Neglected Formosa*, in *FUD*, p. 443.
9. Foccardi, *The Last Warrior*, p. 90.
10. Yang, *Veritable Record*, p. 257.
11. Beauclair, *Neglected Formosa*, p. 90.
12. Yang, *Veritable Record*, p. 257.
13. Coyett, *Neglected Formosa*, in *FUD*, p. 487. (Authentic Proof no. 29). Coyett's records make it clear that the attack was led by one Ruth Tawheroon Buys. Skipper Isbrant Bomur was Buys's second-in-command, and the likely instigator of the disastrously unsupported assault.
14. Coyett, *Neglected Formosa*, in *FUD* p. 444. The same battle is described by an equally dumbfounded observer in Yang, *Veritable Record*, p. 257.
15. In fact, the northern forts had already been reached by the *'s Gravenlande* and the *Vink*, and the occupants evacuated to Japan.
16. Coyett, *Neglected Formosa*, in *FUD*, p. 445.
17. Caeuw, journal entry for 21 October 1661, *FUD*, p. 327.
18. Wills, *Pepper, Guns and Parleys*, p. 34.
19. The playwright Chikamatsu implies that there were also Europeans among the Chinese forces – a list of Coxinga's followers includes references to what appears to

be a Spaniard and an Englishman. This is, however, highly unlikely. See Keene, *Battles of Coxinga*, p. 127.

20. Keene, *Battles of Coxinga*, p. 60. Keene's main source for this story is a 1679 account by another Frenchman, Tavernier's *Recueil de plusieurs Relations et Traitez*.

21. Wills, *Pepper, Guns and Parleys*, p. 26.

22. Coyett, *Neglected Formosa*, in FUD, p. 447.

23. *Ibid.*, FUD, p. 448.

24. Caeuw had further adventures on his way home. He was initially welcomed in Siam by Company representatives who assumed that he had defeated Coxinga. He certainly acted as if he did, firing a hundred salutes to himself with his ship's cannon, and insisting on being accompanied at all times by half-a-dozen men in full battledress as a guard of honour. When he was eventually asked to leave Siam by suspicious Company representatives, he returned to Batavia, where he gave numerous false depositions about events in Taiwan. Found guilty of negligence, he was suspended from duty for six months – as if anyone would notice the change in results.

25. Keene, *Battles of Coxinga*, p. 60. Keene's account, *pace* Tavernier, lists two deserters: Dupuis and the 'sergeant sent after him'. Coyett, however, implies a larger number, saying that 'some soldiers tried to save their lives by walking over to the enemy. Among these . . . was a certain sergeant called Hans Jurgen Radis.' See Coyett, *Neglected Formosa*, in FUD, p. 450.

26. When he arrived in Batavia on the *Maria*, his rank was given as corporal. He must have been promoted on his return to Taiwan. See Keene, *Battles of Coxinga*, p. 172.

27. Chinese sources, unwilling to credit Coxinga's greatest victory with foreign assistance, are silent on the involvement of Radis. See Foccardi, *The Last Warrior*, p. 91.

28. Coyett, *Neglected Formosa*, in FUD, p. 489. (Authentic Proof no. 31).

29. *Ibid.*, p. 452.

30. *Ibid.*, p. 453.

31. Coyett includes the surrender document in *Neglected Formosa*, in FUD, pp. 455–6. Its sixteenth article deals with the exchange of hostages until such time as arrangements were made, noting that one of the men placed with the Dutch from Coxinga's forces was 'Captain Moor Ongkun', presumably an officer in the Black Guard.

32. Beauclair, *Neglected Formosa*, p. 93.

33. Croizier, *Koxinga and Chinese Nationalism*, p. 39.

Chapter Twelve

1. Croizier, *Koxinga and Chinese Nationalism*, p. 37.

2. A Taiwanese tourist website laments that Coxinga's sword has not appeared in the 'Kuo-Xin' well since it was defiled by a child urinating in it in the late twentieth century – a handy excuse.

3. Croizier, *Koxinga and Chinese Nationalism*, p. 39. See also Lin, *Zheng Chenggong*, pp. 214–18, for actual locations of the legendary sites mentioned.

4. Hung, 'Taiwan Under the Cheng Family 1662–1683: Sinicization After Dutch Rule', p. 129.
5. *Ibid.*, p. 133.
6. Keene, *Battles of Coxinga*, p. 64. Keene's source is Rougemont's *Historia Tartaro-Sinica*, from 1673. See also *TW*, p. 202.
7. Hung, 'Taiwan Under the Cheng Family', p. 141.
8. *TW*, pp. 204–5.
9. Hung, 'Taiwan Under the Cheng Family', p. 142, and Wills, *Pepper, Guns and Parleys*, p. 28, both agree that the wet-nurse and the baby were executed at this point, and that their heads were sent to Coxinga in the hope that his rage would pass. Other sources assume that both mother and baby survived. This would certainly explain Cuiying's later attitude towards the unwelcome heir Kecang, and how the favoured Keshuang could have an elder sibling. It is not impossible that Jing fathered another child between the birth of the wet-nurse's baby and Keshuang, but surely more likely that the wet-nurse's baby *was* Kecang.
10. Letter of Coxinga to Sabiniano Manrique de Lara, 21 April 1662, in Zaide, *Documentary Sources of Philippine History* (Document no. 194), vol. 4, pp. 453–7. I have made a couple of minor refinements to the translation. The letter was delivered by Vittorio Ricci, an Italian Dominican friar who had befriended Coxinga in Amoy during the 1650s.
11. The reports of the Chinese revolt of 1662 are taken from an anonymous Jesuit account, found in Zaide, *Documentary Sources*, (Document no. 196), pp. 461–84.
12. One of the friars sent to reassure the Chinese was Vittorio Ricci himself, Coxinga's own ambassador, which suggests that he was an extremely reluctant warmonger. Zaide, *Documentary Sources*, p. 466.
13. Letter of Sabiniano Manrique de Lara to Coxinga, 10 July 1662, in *ibid.*, Document no. 195, pp. 457–60.
14. Croizier, *Koxinga and Chinese Nationalism*, p. 38.
15. See Keene, *Battles of Coxinga*, pp. 69–73, for a detailed analysis of differing accounts of Coxinga's last days. No source can agree on the order in which news arrived of Jing, the Philippines and the Emperor of Eternal Experiences – my interpretation here is open to debate. The original can be found in Zaide, *Documentary Sources*, p. 483, though the editor dismisses it as 'nothing but a Spanish gossip'.
16. Keene, *Battles of Coxinga*, p. 69. For this scene, Keene uses a Spanish account, based on news of Coxinga's death recounted in the Philippines when Vittorio Ricci arrived in 1663 with a placating letter from Jing.
17. Keene, *Battles of Coxinga*, p. 71.
18. Struve, *Voices from the Ming-Qing Cataclysm*, pp. 237–8.
19. *Ibid.*, p. 252. The 'eunuch servant' was Yang Deze, who had led an incredible life. Orphaned as an infant by rebels in Jingzhou province, he had been adopted by the bandit who killed his parents. In 1656, when the Emperor of Eternal Experiences required new servants, Yang's foster-father reluctantly handed his son over to be neutered, and the boy eventually became the personal aide to the Empress, and, it seems, a playmate for Prince Constantine,

who was about the same age. Yang would survive to write a memoir of his time
with the imperial family, which gives an eyewitness account of the last
moments of the Ming imperial line.

20. *Ibid.*, p. 259. The Emperor's mother and daughter died of natural causes in Beijing
    some years later.
21. *TW*, p. 206.
22. *Ibid.*, Davidson, *The Island of Formosa*, p. 52; It is possible that Coxinga went to his
    grave ignorant of the death of the Emperor of Eternal Experiences, since the news
    was not *widely* known until the following year. However, I have kept to the
    traditional version of events. Keene, *Battles of Coxinga*, pp. 69–73, examines
    several contradicting accounts of Coxinga's final moments. I have chosen to
    follow the *TW* account, since it is, for once, the least untrustworthy of the
    available sources.

Chapter Thirteen

1. Croizier, *Koxinga and Chinese Nationalism*, p. 40.
2. Hung, 'Taiwan Under the Cheng Family', pp. 143–4.
3. Davidson, *Island of Formosa*, p. 51.
4. Wills, *Pepper, Guns and Parleys*, p. 52. In fact, it took six months for the final
   drama of Zheng Tai to play out, but I lack the space for it here. The loss of Zheng
   Tai also led to a long legal battle in Japan, where most of the Zheng family silver
   was kept. Jing was obliged to go through the Japanese courts to establish his right
   to the silver, which was opposed by Tai's turncoat son. The case was not resolved
   in Jing's favour until 1675. See Hung, 'Taiwan Under the Cheng Family',
   pp. 198–203.
5. Coyett died in 1689.
6. So it is reported in Dutch records, quoted in Wills, *Pepper, Guns and Parleys*, p. 46.
7. Wills, *Pepper, Guns and Parleys*, p. 85.
8. *Ibid.*, p. 72. See also Kessler, *Maritime Laws*, pp. 100–5.
9. Idema, 'Cannons, Clocks and Clever Monkeys: Europeana, Europeans and Europe
   in Some Early Ch'ing Novels', p. 473 (quoting Jiang, *Taiwan Waizhi*).
10. Wills, *Pepper, Guns and Parleys*, p. 97
11. Attwater, *Adam Schall*, p. 146.
12. *Ibid.*, p. 155.
13. Davidson, *Island of Formosa*, p. 58.
14. *FUD*, pp. 501–2.
15. Tsao, 'The Rebellion of the Three Feudatories', p. 63.
16. *Ibid.*, p. 67.
17. Hung, 'Taiwan Under the Cheng Family', p. 242.
18. Tsao, 'The Rebellion of the Three Feudatories', p. 86.
19. Hung, 'Taiwan Under the Cheng Family', p. 244.
20. Davidson, *Island of Formosa*, p. 60.
21. *TW*, p. 371; Hung, 'Taiwan Under the Cheng Family', p. 265; Davidson, *Island of
    Formosa*, p. 60. The four uncles were Coxinga's second son Cong, fifth son Zhi,

seventh son Yu, and eighth son Wen. See Chang, *The English Factory in Taiwan*, p. 726.

22. *Ibid.*, p. 457. Presumably, the murder of Kecang was the last notable act in the long career of the Black Guard.

23. *TW*, p. 377.

24. Chang, *The English Factory in Taiwan*, p. 459.

25. Keliher, *Out of China*, p. 50; Chen *et al.*, *Historical Sites of the First Rank in Taiwan and Kinmen*, p. 180.

26. Huang, 'Taiwan Under the Cheng Clan', p. 273.

27. Chang *et al.*, *Historical Sites of the First Rank in Taiwan and Kinmen*, p. 180.

28. Davidson, *Isle of Formosa*, p. 61.

29. Hummel, *Eminent Chinese*, p. 653.

30. Paramount among them were Zheng Yi, a descendant of one of Coxinga's soldiers, and his wife Xianggu Zheng Yisao, the 'Pirate Queen', who flourished in the early years of the nineteenth century.

31. Chang, *English Factory in Taiwan*, p. 467. There was one last burst of Ming support in 1707, when an old man in Jiangsu province was discovered to be Prince Cihuan, the last surviving son of the Emperor of Lofty Omens. A series of brief restorationist uprisings ensued, but Cihuan was executed by the Manchus. Thereafter, anti-Manchu opposition was the preserve of secret societies and criminal organisations, and had little to do with the Ming. See Struve, *Southern Ming*, p. 256.

32. For an in-depth appraisal of Coxinga's posthumous honours and uses, see Croizier, *Koxinga and Chinese Nationalism*, pp. 50–62.

33. See Keene, *Battles of Coxinga*, chapters III and IV; Croizier, *Koxinga and Chinese Nationalism*, chapter V, and the extensive list of Japanese stories in Terao, *Tei Seikô*, pp. 241–4. Some of the high points of Coxinga's apocryphal adventures include the incredible derring-do of the Japanese playwright Chikamatsu's *Battles of Coxinga* (1715), the oriental despot of Johannes Nomsz's Dutch play, *Anthonius Hambroek* (1775), and the Japanese colonialist propaganda of Kashima Oto's *The Last Days of Coxinga* (1915). More recent accounts of his life seem determined to inject even more adventure into an already incredible life. The Taiwanese TV series *Recapturing Zhikan* (1965) inserted a romance between Coxinga and Frederik Coyett's previously unmentioned half-Chinese daughter to add extra drama. The movie *Sino-Dutch War 1661* (2001) insists on giving Coxinga yet another new female love-interest, in the form of his step-sister Xueliang, a beautiful musician and sometime martial artist, who is found by Miss Tagawa clutching driftwood from a wrecked ship in the Taiwan Strait. The most recent incarnation to date, the Chinese TV series *Great Hero Zheng Chenggong* (2002) introduces the entertainingly unlikely character of Frederik Coyett's wayward sister Linda, a red-haired minx in a shocking-pink ballgown, who is almost ravished by the lusty Feng the Phoenix, falls in love with Coxinga, disguises herself as a boy to spring a rebel aborigine chieftess from jail, and eventually dies in tragic circumstances.

Appendix III

1. Crossley, *The Manchus*, p. 48ff.
2. Not that any evidence is required to disprove a clearly apocryphal story, but Nurgaci never used the word *Qing* to describe his dynasty. He preferred *Jin*, or 'Golden', in an attempt to establish a line of continuity with an earlier Jin Dynasty that had ruled China in the twelfth century. The *Qing* dynasty was proclaimed by his son, Aberhai.
3. Wakeman, *Great Enterprise*, p. 57.
4. Hummel, *Eminent Chinese*, p. 303.
5. *Ibid.*, p. 598.
6. This was Dalinghe, defended by Wu Sangui's uncle by marriage, Zu Dashou.
7. Hummel, *Eminent Chinese*, p. 562.

SOURCES AND FURTHER READING

Antony, R. (2003) *Like Froth Floating on the Sea: The World of Pirates and Seafarers in Late Imperial South China*. Berkeley, CA: University of California Center for Chinese Studies, China Research Monograph 56.

Attwater, R. (1963) *Adam Schall: A Jesuit at the Court of China 1592–1666*. Milwaukee: Bruce Publishing.

Backhouse, E. and Bland, J. (1914) *Annals and Memoirs of the Court of Peking (From the 16th to the 20th Century)*. London: William Heinemann. Edition consulted is Taiwanese reprint, Ch'eng Wen Publishing.

Beauclair, I. (ed.) (1975) *Neglected Formosa: A Translation from the Dutch of Frederic Coyett's 't Verwaerloosde Formosa*. San Francisco: Chinese Materials Center.

Blussé, L. (1981) 'The VOC as Sorcerer's Apprentice: Stereotypes and Social Engineering on the South China Coast', in W. Idema (ed.), *Leyden Studies in Sinology*. Leiden: E.J. Brill, pp. 87–105.

—— (1986) *Strange Company: Chinese Settlers, Mestizo Women and the Dutch in VOC Batavia*. Dordrecht: Foris Publications.

—— (1990) 'Minnan-Jen or Cosmopolitan? The Rise of Cheng Chih-Lung Alias Nicolas Iquan', in Vermeer, Development and Decline of Fukien Province pp. 245–64.

—— and Natalie Everts (1997–2000) *The Formosan Encounter – Notes on Formosa's Aboriginal Society: A Selection of Documents from Dutch Archival Sources*. 2 vols. Taipei: Shung Ye Museum of Formosan Aborigines.

Bowra, E.C. (1872) 'The Manchu Conquest of Canton', in *China Review* I, 86–96.

Boxer, C.R. (1974) *The Christian Century in Japan 1549–1650*. London: University of California Press.

—— (1965) *The Dutch Seaborne Empire 1600–1800*. Harmondsworth: Penguin, 1990 repr.

—— (1931) 'Notes on Early European Military Influence in Japan (1543–1853)', in *Transactions of the Asiatic Society of Japan*, second series, VIII, 67–93.

—— (1941) 'The Rise and Fall of Nicholas Iquan', *T'ien-Hsia Monthly*, XI 401–439.

—— (1926) 'The Siege of Fort Zeelandia and the Capture of Formosa from the Dutch 1661–1662', in *Transactions and Proceedings of the Japan Society, London* XXIV (1926–7), 16–47.

—— (1988) *Dutch Merchants and Mariners in Asia, 1602–1795*. London: Variorum Reprints.

—— (1991a) 'Capitães Gerais e Governadores de Macau', in *Estudos Para A História de Macau: Séculos XVI a XVIII (Obra Completa I)*. Lisbon: Fundaçao Oriente, pp. 193–282.

—— (1991b) 'Portuguese Military Expeditions in Aid of the Mings Against the Manchus, 1621–1647', in *Estudos Para A História de Macau: Séculos XVI a XVIII (Obra Completa I)*. Lisbon: Fundaçao Oriente, pp. 105–11.

—— (1991c) 'The 24th of June 1622 – A Portuguese Feat of Arms', in *Estudos Para A História de Macau: Séculos XVI a XVIII (Obra Completa I)*. Lisbon: Fundaçao Oriente, pp. 43–102.

Campbell, W. (1903) *Formosa Under the Dutch: Described from Contemporary Records*. Taipei: Ch'eng-Wen Publishing (1967 repr.).

Carioti, P. (1996) 'The Zhengs' Maritime Power in the International Context of the Seventeenth-Century Far East Seas: The Rise of a "Centralised Piratical Organization" and its Gradual Development into an Informal "state"', in *Ming-Qing Yanjiu*, pp. 29–69.

Castro, P. (1954) *Misioneros agustinos en el Extremo Oriente*. Madrid: Instituto Santo Toribo de Mogrovejo.

Chang, H. et al. (eds) (1995) *The English Factory in Taiwan 1670–1685*. Taipei: National Taiwan University.

Chang, T. (1973) *Sino-Portuguese Trade from 1514 to 1644: A Synthesis of Portugese and Chinese Sources*. New York: AMS Press.

Chen, C. et al. (eds) (1987) *Historical Sites of the First Rank in Taiwan and Kinmen*. Taipei: Council for Cultural Planning and Development.

Chen, M. (1971) 'Three Contemporary Western Sources on the History of Late Ming and the Manchu Conquest of China'. Doctoral dissertation, University of Chicago.

Chen, S. (ed.) (1979) *Zheng Chenggong Quanzhuan [The Compendium of Coxinga]*. Taipei: Taiwan Shiji Yanjiu Zhongxin.

Cheng, K. (1990) 'Cheng Ch'eng-Kung's Maritime Expansion and Early Ch'ing Coastal Prohibition', in Vermeer, Development and Decline of Fukien Province in the 17th and 18th Centuries, pp. 217–44.

Chikamatsu, Monzaemon (1922). *Chikamatsu Monzaemon Zenshu [Complete Works of Chikamatsu]*, ed. Tatsuyuki Takano and Kanzo Kuroki. Tokyo: Shunyodo.

Chin, S. (1999) *Tei Seikô: Hayate ni Hirogeyo [Zheng Chenggong: Speak to the Whirlwind]*. Tokyo: Chuo Koron.

Cocks, R. (1615–1623) *Diary Kept by the Head of the English Factory in Japan*. Tokyo: Tokyo University Press. 3 vols (1978 repr.).

Collis, M. (1941) *The Great Within*. London: Faber and Faber.

Coyett, F. (1675) *Neglected Formosa* (a partial translation of the text also published in book form as Beauclair [ed.], above), in Campbell, *Formosa Under the Dutch*, pp. 383–492.

Crozier, R. (1977) *Koxinga and Chinese Nationalism: History, Myth and the Hero*. Cambridge, MA: Harvard East Asian Monographs.

Crossley, P. (1997) *The Manchus*. Oxford: Basil Blackwell.

Dardess, J. (2002) *Blood and History in China: The Donglin Faction and Its Repression 1620–1627*. Honolulu: University of Hawai'i Press.

Dash, M. (2002) *Batavia's Graveyard: The True Story of the Mad Heretic Who Led History's Bloodiest Mutiny*. London: Weidenfeld and Nicolson.

Davidson, J. (1903) *The Island of Formosa*. Yokohama: [The publisher's name is not given in the SOAS library copy, which is, aptly, a Taiwanese pirate edition].

Sources and Further Reading

Dunne, G. (1962) *Generation of Giants: The Story of the Jesuits in China in the Last Days of the Ming dynasty.* Notre Dame, IN: Notre Dame University Press.

Farrington, A. (1991) *The English Factory in Japan 1613–1623.* London: British Library. 2 vols.

Foccardi, G. (1986) *The Last Warrior: The Life of Cheng Ch'eng-kung, the Lord of the 'Terrace Bay': A study on the T'ai-wan wai-chih by Chiang Jih-sheng (1704).* Wiesbaden: O. Harrassowitz.

Foster, W. (1900) *Letters Received by the East India Company from Its Servants in the East.* Vol. 2, p. 99. London : Sampson, Low, Marston & Co.

Gernet, J. (1982) *A History of Chinese Civilization.* Cambridge: Cambridge University Press.

Goddard, W. (1964) *The Makers of Taiwan.* Taipei: China Publishing.

Huang, R. (1981) *1587: A Year of No Significance: The Ming dynasty in Decline.* New Haven, CT: Yale University Press.

Huber, J. (1990) 'Chinese Settlers Against the Dutch East India Company: The Rebellion Led by Kuo Huai-I on Taiwan in 1652', in Vermeer, *Development and Decline of Fukien Province*, pp. 265–96.

Hung, C. (1981) 'Taiwan Under the Cheng Family 1662–1683: Sinicization After Dutch Rule'. Doctoral dissertation, Georgetown University.

Hummel, A. (ed.) (1943) *Eminent Chinese of the Ch'ing Period (1644–1912).* Washington: US Government Printing Office.

Idema, W. (1990) 'Cannons, Clocks and Clever Monkeys: Europeana, Europeans and Europe in Some Early Ch'ing Novels,' in Vermeer, *Development and Decline of Fukien Province*, pp. 459–88.

Iwao, S. (1958) ''Li Tan, Chief of the Chinese Residents at Hirado, Japan, in the Last Days of the Ming dynasty', in *Memoirs of the Research Department of the Toyo Bunko 17*, pp. 27–83.

Jiang, R. (c. 1692) *Taiwan Waizhi [The Historical Novel of Taiwan].* Shanghai Guji Chubanshe, (1986 repr.).

Keay, J. (1991) *The Honourable Company: A History of the English East India Company.* London: Harper Collins.

Keene, D. (1951) *The Battles of Coxinga: Chikamatsu's Puppet Play, Its Background and Importance.* London: Taylor's Foreign Press.

Keliher, M. (2003) *Out of China, or Yu Yonghe's Tales of Formosa.* Taipei: SMC Publishing.

Kessler, L. (1962) 'The Maritime Laws and Their Effect on Sino-Western Relations During the Early Ch'ing Period: 1656–1684', Masters dissertation, University of Chicago.

Ledyard, G. (1971) *The Dutch Come to Korea.* Seoul: Royal Asiatic Society, Korea Branch in conjunction with Taewon Publishing.

Lin, R. (1990) 'Fukien's Private Sea Trade in the 16th and 17th Centuries,' in Vermeer, *Development and Decline of Fukien Province*, pp. 163–216.

Lin, S. (ND) *Zhongguo Mingren Zhuanji: Zheng Chenggong [Biographies of Famous Chinese: Zheng Chenggong].* Taipei: Guangtian Publishing.

Lui, A. (1989) *Two Rulers in One Reign: Dorgon and Shun-chih 1644–1660.* Canberra: Australian National University, Faculty of Asian Studies Monographs no. 13.

Martini, M. (1654) *De Bello Tartarico Historia* [Concerning the Tartaric War]. London: John Crook.

Matsuura, A. (1995) *Chûgoku no Kaizoku* [Pirates of China]. Tokyo: Tôhô (Oriental Press).

Melikhov, G. (1982) 'The Northern Border of the Patrimonial Estates of Manchu (Ch'ing) Feudal Lords During the Conquest of China (1640s to 1680s)', in S.L. Tikhvinsky (ed.), *Chapters from the History of Russo-Chinese Relations: 17th–19th Centuries*, Moscow: Progress Publishers, pp. 13–47.

Michener, J. and Grove Day, A. (1957) *Rascals in Paradise*. London: Mandarin (1993 repr.).

Milton, G. (2002) *Samurai William: The Adventurer Who Unlocked Japan*. London: Hodder & Stoughton.

Ming, H. and Zheng, Y. (1996) *Zheng Chenggong Gushi Chuanshuo* [Stories Told About Zheng Chenggong]. Taipei: Nanxin Cultural Publications.

Miyamoto, K. (1975) *Vikings of the Far East*. New York: Vantage.

Molewijk, G. (ed.) (1991) *'t Verwaerloosde Formosa*. Zutphen: Walburg Pers.

Mulder, W. (ND) *Hollanders in Hirado 1597–1641*. Haarlem: Fibula.

Nieuhoff, J. (1673) *An Embassy from the East-India Company of the United Provinces, to the Grand Tartar Cham Emperor of China, Deliver'd by the Excellencies Peter de Goyer and Jacob de Keyzer, at His Imperial City of Peking*. Trans. [from the Dutch] John Ogilby. London: John Crook.

Oxnam, R. (1975) *Ruling From Horseback: Manchu Politics in the Oboi Regency 1661–1669*. Chicago: University of Chicago Press.

Palafox, J. (1649) *History of the Conquest of China*. [Historia de la Conquista de la China por el Tartaro]. New Delhi: Deep & Deep Publications (1978 repr.).

Paludan, A. (1998) *Chronicle of the Chinese Emperors: The Reign-by-Reign Record of the Rulers of Imperial China*. London: Thames & Hudson.

Parsons, J. (1970) *Peasant Rebellions of the Late Ming Dynasty*. Ann Arbor, MI: Association for Asian Studies (1993 repr.).

Paske-Smith, M. (1930) *Japanese Traditions of Christianity: Being Some Old Translations from the Japanese with British Consular Reports of the Persecutions of 1868–1872*. Kobe: J.L. Thompson.

Peers, C. (1997) *Late Imperial Chinese Armies 1520–1840*. London: Osprey.

Ponsonby-Fane, R. (1937) 'Koxinga: Chronicles of the Tei Family, Loyal Servants of the Ming', in *Sovereign and Subject*. Kyoto: The Ponsonby-Fane Memorial Society (1962 repr.), pp. 269–330.

Qin, J. (2002) *Zheng Chenggong: Taiwan zhi Fu* [Zheng Chenggong: Father of Taiwan]. Taipei: Shixue.

Ross, J. (1891) *The Manchus, or, The Reigning Dynasty of China: Their Rise and Progress*. London: Elliot Stock.

Shang, X. (1994) *Tales of Empresses and Imperial Consorts in China*. Hong Kong: Hai Feng.

So, K. (1975) *Japanese Piracy in Ming China during the Sixteenth Century*. East Lansing: Michigan State University Press.

Soullière, E. (1987) 'Palace Women in the Ming dynasty: 1368–1644'. Doctoral dissertation, Princeton University.

Sources and Further Reading

Spence, J. (1969) *The China Helpers: Western Advisers in China 1620–1960*. London: Bodley Head. pp. 13–16.

Spence, J. and Wills, John E. (eds) (1979) *From Ming to Ch'ing: Conquest, Region and Continuity in Seventeenth-Century China*. New Haven, CT: Yale University Press.

Struve, L. (1984) *The Southern Ming: 1644–1662*. New Haven, CT: Yale University Press.

—— (1993) *Voices from the Ming-Qing Cataclysm: China in Tiger's Jaws*. New Haven, CT: Yale University Press.

Sung, Y. (1637) *Chinese Technology in the Seventeenth Century: T'ien Kung K'ai Wu*. New York: Dover (1997 reprint).

Takahashi, W. (1999) *Shûhan: Tei Seikô Seiun-roku* [*Vermilion Sails: The Determination of Zheng Chenggong*]. Tokyo: Shogakukan.

—— (1999) *Dohan: Tei Seikô Byôfû-roku* [*Sails of Wrath: The Madness of Zheng Chenggong*]. Tokyo: Shogakukan.

Taylor, J. (1983) *The Social World of Batavia: European and Eurasian in Dutch Asia*. Madison: University of Wisconsin Press.

Terao, Y. (1986) *Meimatsu no Fû'unkyo: Tei Seikô* [*Zheng Chenggong: Hero of the Fall of the Ming*] Tokyo: Tôhô (Oriental Press).

Tsao, K. (1965) 'The Rebellion of the Three Feudatories Against the Manchu Throne in China 1673–1681: Its Setting and Significance'. Doctoral dissertation, Columbia University.

Turnbull, S. (2002) *Samurai Invasion: Japan's Korean War 1592–98*. London: Cassell.

Vermeer, E. (ed.) (1990) *Development and Decline of Fukien Province in the 17th and 18th Centuries*. Leiden: E.J. Brill.

Vixseboxe, J. (1981) 'A XVIIth Century Record of a Dutch Family in Taiwan', in W. Idema (ed.), *Leyden Studies in Sinology*. Leiden: E.J. Brill, pp. 106–7.

Wakeman, F. (1979) 'The Shun Interregnum of 1644', in Wills and Spence, *From Ming to Ch'ing*, pp. 41–87.

—— (1985) *The Great Enterprise: The Manchu Reconstruction of Imperial Order in Seventeenth-Century China*. Berkeley: University of California Press.

Wills, J. (1974) *Pepper, Guns and Parleys: The Dutch East India Company and China 1662–1681*. Cambridge, MA: Harvard University Press.

Wills, J. (1979) 'Maritime China from Wang Chih to Shi Lang: Themes in Peripheral History,' in Spence and Wills, *From Ming to Ch'ing*.

—— and Spence, Jonathan (eds) (1979) *From Ming to Ch'ing: Conquest, Region and Continuity in Seventeenth-Century China*. New Haven, CT: Yale University Press.

Yamawaki, T. (1976) 'The Great Trading Merchants, Cocksinja and His Son', in *Acta Asiatica* 30, 106–16.

Yang, Y. (c. 1661) *Xian Wang Shilu Jiaozhu* [*Veritable Record of the Former Prince*]. Fujian: Fujian Renmin Chubanshe [1981 repr.].

Zaide, G. (ed.) (1990) *Documentary Sources of Philippine History*, vol. 4. Manila: National Book Store.

INDEX

Index